MW00823640

Waiting for the new subway to come.

the *Subway*
and the *City*
celebrating a century

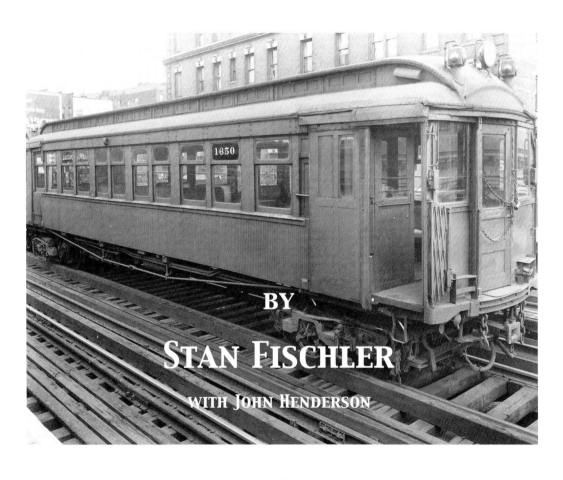

BY
STAN FISCHLER
WITH JOHN HENDERSON

Frank Merriwell Incorporated
New York

Front cover: Workmen digging for the new subway under Times Square in August 1915 rub shoulders with the theatre crowd, not to mention passing trolleys.

Back cover: In the years prior to World War I, elevated lines criss-crossed Manhattan. Both the Third Avenue el (foreground) and the Second Avenue line (background) are visible in this May 1912 scene.

The Subway and the City
celebrating a century

Copyright © 2004 by STAN FISCHLER

LIBRARY OF CONGRESS CONTROL # 2004105210

ISBN 0-8373-9251-9 (Paperbound)
ISBN 0-8373-9551-8 (Clothbound)

FRANK MERRIWELL INCORPORATED
212 Michael Drive, Syosset, New York 11791
(516) 921-8888 • (800) 632-8888

All rights reserved, including the right of reproduction in whole or in part, in any form or by any means, electronic or mechanical, including photocopying, recording, or by any information storage and retrieval system, without permission in writing from the Publisher.

Publisher and Editor-in-Chief: Michael P. Rudman
Editor and Graphic Designer: Bonnie Freid
Research Editor: Anthony Affrunti

Photographs in the "Now: Gallery of Contemporary Subway Photos" and "Transit Museum" sections were taken by David Perlmutter.
All other photos in this book are courtesy of the Robert Presbrey collection, unless otherwise indicated.

Printed in Canada

Contents

Acknowledgments

On a visit to the Transit Authority's vast Coney Island Overhaul facility during the late 1990s, I was awed by the number of workers involved in the maintenance and repair of our subway fleet.

There were electricians working on the car lighting fixtures, motor experts tending to the trucks and painters ensuring that the revitalized products look as good as new, among many other specialists at the Overhaul center.

Without their expertise, our enormous and complicated rapid transit system could not function.

The same holds—albeit in a smaller sense—when it comes to producing a book of this scope. Writing is possible only after vast research, editing, photo selection, captioning and good, old-fashioned advice, to name just a few vital elements.

For starters, there had to be *someone* who believed in the book. Michael Rudman, publisher, friend and *confidante*, was the motorman. He, more than anyone, made the project go and for that, I offer a low bow of gratitude.

Another good friend, John Henderson, endorsed the 100th anniversary book idea many years ago and maintained his interest until we coupled our train to Rudman's.

Without Henderson's perspicacious commentary, the manuscript might have been detoured to the Coney Island Overhaul facility instead of Rudman's publishing house.

We were ably abetted in the photography department by a pair of worthies one normally is not so lucky to find on one project in a lifetime.

Robert (Bob) Presbrey's knowledge of—not to mention affection for—subway history is as unmatched as his photo collection. To call it voluminous would be an understatement.

Fortunately, Bob opened his archives to us and we remain grateful for his generosity and guidance.

David Perlmutter, friend for a half-century, became a professional ally on this project. He agreed to provide a collection of contemporary pictures and outdid himself in the process. Whenever I mentioned that a photo would help embellish a chapter, Dave unhesitatingly grabbed his camera and made a bee line for the subject, whether it was shooting the A train in Rockaway, the Times Square Shuttle or the last stop on the Dyre Avenue line.

Perlmutter's perserverance and determination in pursuing the superior picture have helped make this a much better book than it would have been without him.

Likewise, train buffs William J. Brennan and Eric Oszustowicz provided priceless photos of their own. Their help enabled us to provide the comprehensive scope of illustrations that marks this book special. We thank them for their support along with Williamsburg pal, Harvey Bien, as dependable a clutch-hitter as we could find when help was needed.

From the Transit Authority, Neil Neches was a Grade-A answer man.

As well, good transit friends Joe Cunningham, Bernie Ente and Don Harold provided priceless information.

Thanks also to John Rotundo and Antonio Spotorno.

We want to thank Harvey Bien for his excellent photography and research work. Also, kudos to Junnko Tozaki for her help at the Transit Museum.

A special thanks goes out to my good friend John Landers. John's efforts in this project and many others have been invaluable, and I truly appreciate his contributions. Not to be overlooked was the inspirational—not to mention editorial—help of Jane and Merle Perlmutter.

New York City Transit Authority Press Office spokesperson Charles Seaton gets a standing ovation from me for all his help, and his assistant, James Anyansi, has my heartfelt thanks.

On the research side, Anthony Affrunti proved to be a literary ferret on the spur of good information. His patience and fortitude are appreciated. Ditto for office staff members Seth Cantor, Howie Falkenstein, Ben Joelson, Dan Rice, Linda Knox, and Ulises Gonzales Garcia.

A book of such scope requires someone to pull it all together; roughly equivalent to the subway stationmaster, studying an assortment of different trains on different tracks and adjusting the switches accordingly.

Bonnie Freid—indispensable, indefatigable, insightful—orchestrated the project with a deft hand and a disposition that accentuated the positive. We were deeply indebted to Bonnie for being a part of our subway history.

There are many more kudos to deliver—and for those we have inadvertently overlooked, we'll make sure you are mentioned the second time around. Remember, there's always another train on the way!

Foreword

The New York City Subway System Celebrates 100 Years

No other city in the world is as defined by its subway as is New York. Boston's rapid transit system is older and London's is marginally larger, but neither the T nor the Underground characterize so completely the cities they serve.

Over the past 100 years, the New York City subway has evolved and grown from a nine-mile line to a four-borough system consisting of 26 lines and 468 stations. Carried on upwards of 600 trains, more than 4.5 million people depend on it each business day to reach destinations near and far.

Composed of a staggering sum of superlative statistics, the subway has managed to capture the imaginations of generations of New Yorkers, commuters, tourists and even moviemakers. The longest subway line, the "A" Eighth Avenue Express, stretches more than 32 miles from a point near the northern tip of Manhattan to the extreme southeast section of the borough of Queens. The deepest station is located 180 feet beneath the bedrock of 191st Street in the Washington Heights section of Manhattan on the No. 1/9 Lines. The highest, perched 88 feet above street level, serves the F Line at Smith and Ninth Street in the Gowanus section of Brooklyn. But

the system is about far more than sheer numbers. Without the subway, New York would hardly be the economic powerhouse it is.

As a city, New York is a full 240 years older than the oldest segment of its subway system. In many ways, though, it did not begin to form its true and modern identity until the first subway train rolled north out of the old City Hall Station on

October 27, 1904, guided by no less a public official than the mayor himself. With his hands firmly set on the controls, Mayor George McClellan blazed the trail for a greater New York at the head end of a subway train filled with dignitaries and first-time subway riders.

Prior to the subway's opening there were no skyscrapers, simply because there was no efficient way to fill them with workers. Northern Manhattan, the Bronx and Queens were sparsely populated—rural, in fact, with residents bound for the job center of lower Manhattan forced to endure long travel times on elevated trains, trolley cars or ferries.

The idea of building a subway system in New York City dates back at least 20 years before construction actually began, but concrete plans needed the technology that would allow electric propulsion and multiple-unit operation. Politically, solid plans for an underground transit system awaited only the will of Tammany Hall to sweep aside the financial concerns of the operators of the city's antiquated elevated train and trolley systems.

Once the first line was open, New Yorkers swarmed the new railroad and the city's appetite for underground rapid transit only grew. Extensions to the Bronx and Brooklyn soon followed, and in 1915, the Interborough dipped beneath the East River and roared into Queens through the Steinway Tube, which had been originally constructed for streetcars.

There was an explosion of subway construction in the first third of the 20th century. Ground was broken for the IRT in 1900, and the major segments of the state-of-the-art IND lines were carrying passengers by 1936.

The 722 miles that make up the New York City subway are actually a combination of three separate subway endeavors — the privately owned IRT and BMT Lines and the city-owned and operated IND or Independent. Since 1940, the three systems have been joined as a common operation, though they have managed to retain much of their individual personalities.

Even now, one hundred years later, the desire for new subway routes is not fully satisfied. In fact, planning for the construction of the Second Avenue subway line is well underway, and when it is completed, riders along Manhattan's east side will benefit from a high-tech 21st century subway line, that ironically will relieve much of the pressure on century-old east side IRT.

Though it is indeed called the subway, New York City's rapid transit system runs in tunnels beneath the streets but also rises to travel atop elevated structures, along grade level right-of-ways and in open cut service. Subway design and construction was varied to match the conditions and topography of a city that is incredibly diverse geographically.

The subway's designers, for the most part, planned the railroad in such a way as to not just meet the demands of the time, but also future requirements of a city bursting at the seams with promise and new development. One of the most important elements of the New York City subway system is the four-track design that allows local and express service and also provides the flexibility required to operate around service problems.

Today, we are standing on the shoulders of giants—August Belmont, John B. McDonald and William Barclay Parsons—the men responsible for the construction of the first subway. Add to that esteemed list the name of Granville T. Woods, whose invention of the electrified third rail made the subway possible.

The design, financing and construction were all enormous hurdles to overcome, but overcome them they did. Today's challenges are no less daunting, but now as was the case 100 years ago, the team of people entrusted with running the finest rapid transit system in the world look forward to it each day.

Lawrence G. Reuter
NYC Transit President

Dedication

To Shirley, who worked tirelessly on the manuscript,
and to my children, Ben and Simon,
who so often accompanied me on my subway travels.

Also, to David Perlmutter, a dear friend
whose enthusiasm in photographing train people grew by the month,
thereby providing considerable artistry and inspiration for our book.

And to another pal, Harvey Bien,
who, like the U.S. Coast Guard,
has lived the motto Semper Paratus—always ready—
whenever help is needed.

Plus, to Jack Goldstein,
who helped bring the project together along with Michael Rudman.

Last, but not least, to the workers—
from operators to conductors; maintenance experts and car cleaners—
everyone who makes our subway the greatest in the world!

Introduction

If it is possible for a book to be an expression of one man's love affair with the New York subways as well as a history of our wonderful rapid transit system, then this *is* it.

For seven decades, I have been an avid subway rider, first in my parents' arms—neither of them ever drove a car—and then on my own.

My fascination with our vast underground railroad began in earnest when I was three years old.

Walking out of our house at 582 Marcy Avenue in Brooklyn's *Williamsburg* neighborhood with my mother one day, I noticed a corps of laborers digging up the street just a few yards in front of us.

"Mama," I said, "what are those men doing?"

She gazed at the trenches which were forming on a street that once had boasted the Marcy Avenue trolley line to Brighton Beach and said, "Stanley, they are building a subway right under our noses."

And so they did.

From 1935 to 1937, the city-owned Independent Subway's Brooklyn-Queens Crosstown Line was constructed before my very eyes.

When it was finished—Opening Day was July 1, 1937—a brand-new Myrtle-Willoughby Avenue station was situated directly below my front window.

Only a half-block away—at the corner of Myrtle and Marcy—was the entrance to trains that could take me to Aunt Lucie and Uncle Ben in Forest Hills, Queens, or to Aunt Sadie and Uncle Max in Washington Heights, Manhattan.

Our very own *GG* Line boasted magnificent—at least *I* thought so—sixty-foot long cars with four sets of double doors that looked distinctly different from those on the then private IRT or BMT lines.

In a word, they were classy. As a matter of fact *everything* about my home *GG* train seemed *de luxe* to me. The cars featured a big front window, out of which even a little kid like me could gaze without being lifted by either momma or poppa.

What's more, the doors at each end of the car—transit people call them *storm doors*—could be opened while the train was moving. Which meant that nervy lads like me could walk from one car to another, something that could not be done on the BMT, which had its storm doors locked at all times.

Not that I disliked the BMT; actually I loved the system because the BMT operated the Myrtle Avenue elevated line, which could be seen from our backyard as well as from the front of our house.

With its ancient, open-ended gate cars, the el provided a slow but delectable ride from Downtown Brooklyn all the way out to Metropolitan Avenue in Middle Village, Queens.

But my favorite BMT ride—by far—was on the Brighton line's 67-foot Standard

The Myrtle-Willoughby (IND) subway station was located just to the right of the oncoming Myrtle Avenue trolley. My house, on Marcy Avenue, is just to the left of the trolley. The Myrtle Avenue el is above. The photo was taken on April 10, 1946. I was 14 years old at the time.

cars, because they had a little jump seat next to the front window which allowed even the smallest youth to put his feet on the *rattan* and peer out of a window that actually opened!

I was five years old when the big trains came to Marcy Avenue in 1937 and the little electric trains—Lionel O27 model—were given to me by Uncle Ben and Aunt Lucie. My Lionel Pennsy *Torpedo* were my toy trains in our living room while I regarded the GG as my *other* toy trains, however large they might be.

This infatuation with the subway never abated. Whether I was attending Brooklyn College or, later, as a reporter for the New York *Journal-American* newspaper, I took rapid transit everywhere and invariably made my way to the front window as any certified subway buff would.

My passion intensified as a professional journalist. Assigned by chance one day to cover a subway story in Queens, I wrote the piece, then told my editor, John W. Newton of my interest in mass transit. He obliged by putting me on the beat and I soon became a regular at the weekly Transit Authority meetings at 360 Jay Street.

Handling the subway beat enabled me not only to write hard news but also to do features about the TA art club—I wound up paying $250 for a Gil Reiter painting called *Brighton Local* which still hangs on our country house living room wall—and other offbeat aspects of the system.

I met wonderful folks on that tour of duty including some fine p.r. people—Joe Spaulding, Kass Pollock, Joe Harrington, Leo Casey and Syl Pointkowski—as well as good-guy reporters like Ed Silberfarb of the *Herald-Tribune*.

Each experience whet my literary apetite to write a history of the New York subway and, finally, I fulfilled that ambition in 1976 with publication of *Uptown, Downtown—A Trip Through Time On New York's Subway.*

Happily, I can report that it went into seven printings and led me to other transit projects and a chance meeting with train publisher–hockey fan, John Henderson, at the *New York Bound* book store in Rockefeller Center.

A kindred spirit if ever there was one, Henderson encouraged me to write *Confessions of a Trolley Dodger From*

Stan's first year as a subway buff. It's 1935; he's three-and-a-half years old. Digging for the GG subway has begun on Marcy Avenue (behind shrubbery). Fischler obviously is pleased with the results.

Brooklyn and backed up his confidence by publishing it as well as *The Subway*, an updated and enlarged version of *Uptown, Downtown.*

But none of my transit tomes enabled me to convey the powerful *personal* feeling I have long experienced *vis-à-vis* the subway until publisher Michael Rudman entered my life.

I had known Rudman as a passionate hockey fan who operated a publishing company primarily dedicated to educational books. As a result, I considered it a longshot when I suggested that we commemorate the New York subway's 100th birthday with a *unique* personal history of the system.

To my delight, Michael agreed, and—along with John Henderson's absolutely indispensable guidance and assistance—the project was underway.

As the reader will see, each of the first ten *Going To* chapters includes my personal recollections of riding each subway line and why the IRT Flushing Express or the BMT's Sea Beach Local means so much to me.

Intermingled with the personal, I included as much history as possible, covering a wide variety of subjects, from baseball's *Subway Series* to the *Transit Museum.*

No less significant are the photos from Bob Presbrey's comprehensive collection to the original, contemporary pictures taken expressly for this book by David Perlmutter.

Like the A train, running from Rockaway Beach to Washington Heights, I have tried to cover the subway map—with words and pictures.

Hopefully, I have reached my destination.

Stan Fischler, New York City,
March 2004

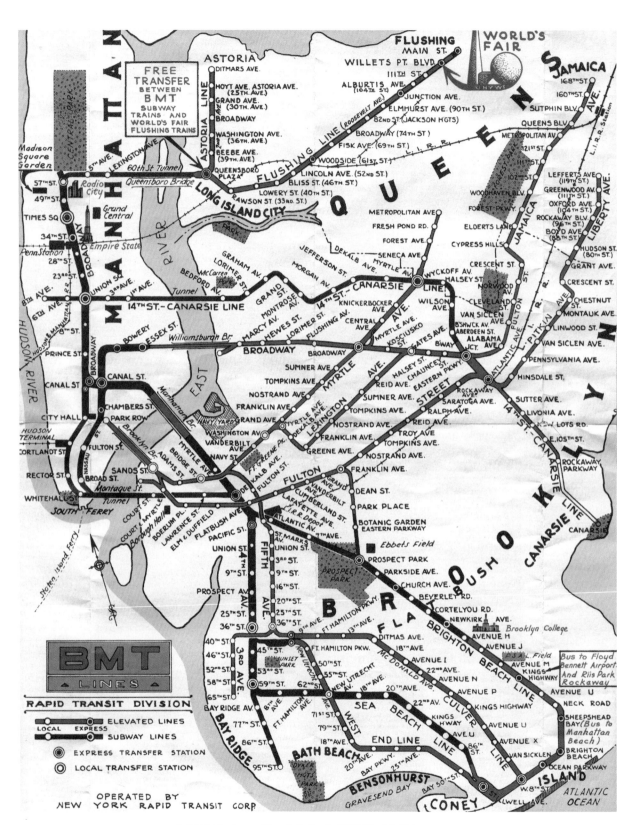

A 1929 Manhattan Transit Authority BMT World's Fair map.

PART I

TAKING THE TRAIN

Ticket window at City Hall Station awaits its first customers.

Before South Brooklyn Had Els

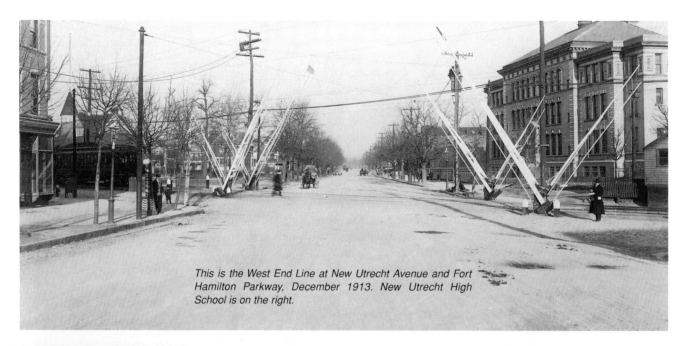

This is the West End Line at New Utrecht Avenue and Fort Hamilton Parkway, December 1913. New Utrecht High School is on the right.

A West End six-car train passes 48th Street on New Utrecht Avenue early in 1914.

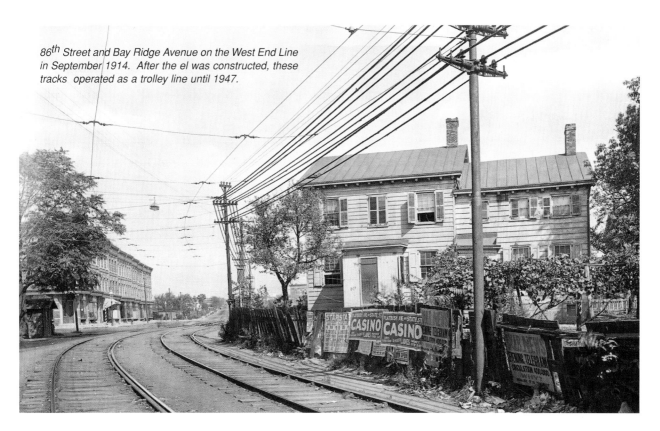

86th Street and Bay Ridge Avenue on the West End Line in September 1914. After the el was constructed, these tracks operated as a trolley line until 1947.

The junction at Ninth Avenue and the Culver cut in Brooklyn where the Culver and West End Lines merge. The photo was taken in March 1914.

13th Avenue crossing of the Culver Line. The station is a remnant from the Prospect Park and Coney Island Railroad steam days.

Looking north on Shell Road from Coney Island Creek in 1918. The two-car train on the right is on the original Culver Line route. When elevated, the line proceeded down Shell Road. In the 1930s, Shell Road was renamed McDonald Avenue. The old right-of-way on the right became a trolley line until it was removed by construction of the Belt Parkway in 1940.

4 THE SUBWAY AND THE CITY

CHAPTER ONE

GOING TO

Coney Island

By The Sea, By The Sea,
By The Beautiful Sea;
You And Me, You And Me;
Oh, How Happy We'll Be!

Good-bye My Coney Island Baby;
Good-bye My Own True Love.

They sang many a sweet song about Coney Island—and well they might have!

To almost every Brooklynite—and many, many other New Yorkers as well—it was *the* beach resort of choice as far back as anyone can remember.

And that goes back a good 400 years; well before it was nicknamed The Nickel Empire.

The Canarsee Indians loved it long before Peter Stuyvesant and his Dutch pals landed at the tip of Manhattan. And the immigrants from Holland who began settling in the Southern part of Brooklyn liked it as well. So did the legion of hares.

If the Indians didn't have a name for the appealing spit of land, the Dutch did.

Jacques Cortelyou, a surveyor, and many fellow Dutchmen, who frequented the land along the Atlantic Ocean, couldn't get over a phenomenon peculiar to that beachfront in the 1600s.

It was over-run by wild rabbits; otherwise known as *konijn* in Dutch. In time *konijn* became "Coney" and, since it still was an island, Coney Island it was, by the early 1800s when hares and their heirs no longer were the attraction.

So, Coney Island has come a long way over four centuries. But how it was transformed from a desolate appendage of New Netherlands to the world's most famous amusement area is a tale of speculators and subways.

The speculation began honestly enough.

By the start of the 19th Century, Brooklyn was being eyed by some intrepid immigrants as a most reasonable place to live; an alternative to burgeoning, bustling

"By the Beautiful Sea," words Harold R. Atteridge, music Harry Carroll,
Shapiro, Bernstein & Co., Inc., © 1914
"Good-bye My Coney Island Baby," words and music Les Applegate,
SPEBSQSA, © 1911

Manhattan. But it wasn't until Robert Fulton's steam ferry began crossing the East River in 1814, linking Lower Manhattan with Brooklyn Heights, that Kings County began evolving into one of the world's first commuter suburbs.

And what could be a better destination as a Summer resort than a five-mile long, virtually uninhabited sand beach fronting on the Atlantic Ocean!

Of course, none of the prevailing entrepreneurs viewed Coney Island as a haven for the masses. For one thing, the masses weren't really massed yet. For another, even if there were masses, there was no mass transit to bring them there.

Ah, but Coney could be viewed—as the *Cote d'Azur* was seen by the European elite in the 19th Century—as an ideal hostlery for the wealthy or semi-wealthy; not to mention those who could fake it in one way or another.

With that in mind, the Terhune brothers obtained acreage near what is now the Transit Authority's mammoth Coney Island repair shops at Shell Road. The Terhunes premiered their Coney Island House in 1824 and soon were drawing a crowd that could not be confused with the *hoi polloi*.

Such golden names of the era as Daniel Webster and P.T. Barnum became patrons of the Coney Island House and, slowly but inexorably, the shore's attractiveness soon brought more investors.

Most of the development would be bounded by Coney Island Creek to the north, to the South by the Atlantic Ocean, to the West by Norton's Point, the farthest tip of the island, and to the east by Sheepshead Bay. The inlet—now fronting Bedford, Nostrand and other main avenues—was particularly hospitable for

small fishing boats. By the early 1800s, the inlet soon was transformed by construction of wooden shacks for the fishermen.

In due time, the catches of the day inspired the opening of sea food restaurants, and by the end of the Civil War, both Coney Island and Sheepshead Bay had become legitimate, if not overly crowded, summer resorts.

Unfortunately, travel was limited to horse-drawn coach or boat, neither of which was particularly rapid nor relaxing. And, although Brooklyn was not yet a full-blown city—rather, it was a group of self-contained villages such as New Utrecht, Flatbush, Williamsburg, et. al.—the community was growing almost as fast as New York on the other side of the river.

The need for a faster form of transport was essential. When it arrived—in the form of the steam locomotive—Coney Island was ready for the metamorphosis of its life.

Just as the iron horse opened the West to Americans, so did it open Coney Island to the masses. But the first group to invade Coney—which included Brighton Beach, Oriental Beach and Sheepshead Bay—were those with large bank accounts and cash to spend.

The Coney Island House spawned such splendiferous hotels as the Brighton Beach, Oriental, Manhattan Beach, the Prospect and the Ravenhall *only* because trains would be available to take the resort-seekers to the shore.

Planned before the Civil War, the first railroad to reach the Atlantic Ocean at Coney Island—an earlier one linked East New York with Canarsie—was the Brooklyn, Bath and Coney Island line. When, in later years, its terminal was built at the western sector of Coney Island, the line was renamed the Brooklyn, Bath and West

End. The term "West End Line" still is in use today for the "B" train.

The first spike was hammered home in 1862 at a terminal near 26th Street and Fifth Avenue adjoining Greenwood Cemetery. Today it is known as the Sunset Park community. Extensions were built along 39th Street, followed by New Utrecht Avenue, in what now is Bensonhurst and Bath Avenue.

Although it still was short of Coney Island, the BB&CI began operation in 1864, while a further extension was spiked home to the still-nascent beach resort in 1867.

Surprisingly, the original rolling stock consisted of horse-drawn railway carriages, which remained in play until steam locomotives took over in 1875.

The virgin beaches, stretching east from Norton's Point—in what now is Sea Gate—to Sheepshead Bay, would give way to playgrounds for the society crowd. Bluebloods would camp at such lavish resorts as the Manhattan Beach Hotel, swim in the ocean, gamble at amusement areas which were blossoming by the year and, eventually, have the luxury of gambling at nearby race tracks.

The hotels followed the railroads. In 1877, no less a figure than President Ulysses S. Grant, ceremonially opened the Manhattan Beach Hotel. The Brighton Beach Hotel was as ornate as any resort in Newport, while the Prospect Hotel would become the first to show motion pictures in Coney Island.

To accommodate the surging urge for the seaside, a second railroad was built.

The sugar-daddy behind this one was one Andrew Culver, whose name would remain part of Brooklyn subway lore to this day.

Culver's line was formally called The Prospect Park and Coney Island Railroad. To Brooklynites it was more intimately known as "The Culver Line."

It began rolling in 1875 from a terminal just south of Prospect Park at Ninth Avenue (Prospect Park West) and 20th Street in a neighborhood now known as Windsor Terrace. It terminated at Gravesend Neck Road, just north of the present Transit Authority repair facility and, shortly thereafter, was extended to Coney Island in the Summer of 1875 along with a spur to Norton's Point.

The southern depot, which would become *the* terminus for many lines in due time, was appropriately called Culver Depot. It opened on June 27, 1875. To a certain extent, the run followed by contemporary trains traces that of the original Culver Line.

Thus, the sleepy Gravesend community suddenly was transformed from farmland to a coveted area of development.

Previously, Gravesend—named for a city at the mouth of the Thames River in England—was known as one of the six original towns of Kings County. A group of religious dissenters, whose leader was Lady Moody, originally settled there in 1643.

Ah, but Lady Moody would not have approved what would change Gravesend two centuries later. Not one, but three race tracks—including the Gravesend course—rose in the environs.

The famed Preakness Stakes were run at Gravesend while the Futurity and Suburban Stakes were held at Sheepshead Bay's new track, just a short gallop from the Brighton Beach Race Track at the Brighton Beach Fairgrounds.

Luminaries were sprinkled throughout the Coney landscape. Big moneymen such as Harry Payne Whitney, William Kissam Vanderbilt and Leonard W. Jerome indulged in *all* of Coney's pleasures.

As Brooklyn historian Elliott Willensky noted in *When Brooklyn Was The World,* "They would drive their trotters to elaborate seaside hostelries to treat their ladies to grouse and champagne at fifty dollars a dinner, quite a sum in those days."[1]

The intertwining of hotel and railroad interests was never made more vivid than with the Brooklyn, Flatbush and Coney Island Railroad.

Beginning on July 2, 1878, the first BFCIRR train left its Prospect Park terminal and rolled all the way to the very *steps* of the almost mythical Brighton Beach Hotel. In its original conception, the hotel was erected perilously close to the incoming ocean tides. Rather than raze and rebuild the hotel, it was decided to move it 200 yards away from the original site. To do so, six Brighton line locomotives were required to do the pulling while the structure was mounted upon rollers. A year later, service at the northern end of the BFCIRR was extended to a new depot near the Long Island Rail Road's downtown Brooklyn terminal.

As the railroads grew, so, too, did Brooklyn. The first lines began servicing communities en route to Coney Island and at the heyday of steam operations, the BFCIRR boasted headways of 20 minutes to a half-hour during the height of the Summer resort rush.

Of the quartet of ocean-reaching railroads, none had a more romantic—nor practical—name than the last to be built. The New York and Sea Beach Railroad— eventually to be known as "The Sea Beach Line"—linked a ferry at the northern tip of Bay Ridge (61st Street and First Avenue) via

ABOUT OPEN CUTS AND ELS

Although the common perception is that el lines are obsolete and mostly history, this is far from the case. There remain four route miles of els in Manhattan, 28 route miles of elevated lines in Brooklyn, 20 in Queens and 18 in the Bronx. The grand total of el route miles is 70. Apart from that, the Transit Authority has 23 more route miles of outdoor track, which embraces open cut—as in the Brighton and Sea Beach lines—embankment and surface trackage.

train to a Coney amusement area known as the Sea Beach Palace. The N train in part follows the original Sea Beach run.

When the trans-Brooklyn railroad-building boom had finally ended late in the 19th Century, no less than five lines were in place, more than at any other resort. Granted, the ride was less than luxurious— engines were smoky and the rolling stock was mostly made of wood—but to most passengers, the end justified the means.

What's more, the "end" was becoming more and more of an attraction. In addition to the race tracks and hotels, amusement areas soon were sprinkled across Coney. In the early 1870s, an immigrant named Charles Feltman opened an establishment called Feltman's Ocean Pavilion Hotel, which featured the world's first hot dog.

Perhaps the most outlandish hotel that Coney was ever to see was erected in 1882. Designed in the shape of a gigantic elephant—two huge, white tusks included—the Elephant Hotel was made of wood but covered with tin. According to one description, spiral staircases were enclosed inside the pachyderm's legs. A gazebo sat atop the elephant's back and served as an observatory from where one could view not only the ocean but Lower New York Bay as well as the railway tracks leading to the island.

It also had a cigar store and a diorama; not to mention a handful of rooms for tourists. Because of its uniqueness, the Elephant Hotel drew more sightseers than actual guests.

LaMarcus A. Thompson, who had invented seamless hosiery, saw another bonanza in Coney Island. On June 16, 1884, he opened the world's first roller coaster on West 10th Street, within shouting distance of the steam trains at the Culver Depot.

As the western end of Coney took on more and more of a cheaper amusement image, the swankier hotels of Manhattan and Brighton Beach kept themselves at arm's distance from their more rowdy neighbors. And they were able to maintain this distance from the more boisterous elements as long as not too many Average Joes came to the beach.

But that hope would dramatically disappear like the smoke from the steam engines as soon as electricity was adapted by New York's transit barons as a more practical energy source than coal and wood.

The historic transformation would take place on November 10, 1893 when the West End Line went electric, followed by the Sea Beach four years later and, finally, the Culver and Brighton lines a year before the turn of the century.

Coney Island would never be the same after that because getting there never would be the same.

Soon, it would be easier, cheaper and

faster. What's more, beginning in 1898, the Brooklyn Bridge began carrying through electrified elevated service from Park Row (City Hall) in Manhattan to Downtown Brooklyn and beyond. Any Manhattanite could take an el from as far north as the Upper West Side, connect with the Brooklyn Bridge els and, eventually, ride all the way to Coney Island.

And it was only a *nickel* to ride the electric trains!

Where once the rabbits roamed, Coney Island's turf now was filled with all manner of amusements and sporting facilities.

In addition to the race tracks, an arena was constructed on Surf Avenue and West 8th Street (precisely where the current West 8th Street elevated station stands). Boxing matches were its primary source of revenue and in 1899, the Coney ring made headlines around the world when Jim Jeffries and Tom Sharkey battled for the heavyweight championship. Jim Jeffries was declared the champ when he connected with a knockout punch in the 25th round.

But, by far, the biggest lures for the "nickel-subway-crowd" were the gigantic amusement parks which began sprouting in the late 1890s.

The first—and most famous—was the creation of George C. Tilyou. It was called Steeplechase Park, bounded by the Boardwalk, Surf Avenue, West 16th Street and West 19th Street.

In 1897, while steam locomotives still were plying the rails to Coney Island, Tilyou foresaw the millions who would stream to the island once all the trains were electrified and the proletariat could reach his turnstiles for a nickel—and in a hurry!

What's more, the numbers were guar-

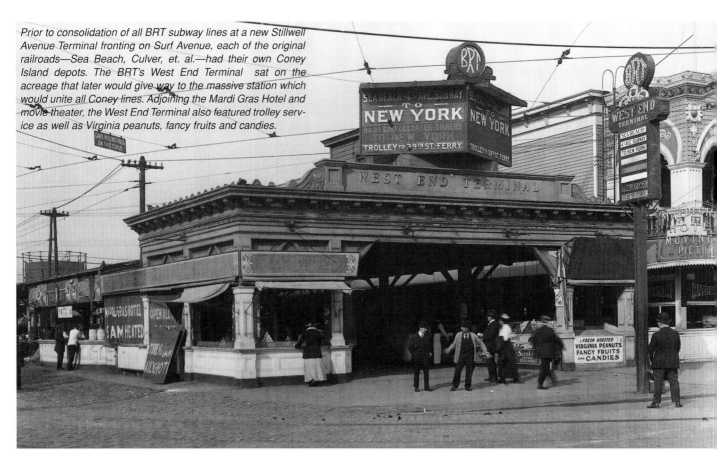

Prior to consolidation of all BRT subway lines at a new Stillwell Avenue Terminal fronting on Surf Avenue, each of the original railroads—Sea Beach, Culver, et. al.—had their own Coney Island depots. The BRT's West End Terminal sat on the acreage that later would give way to the massive station which would unite all Coney lines. Adjoining the Mardi Gras Hotel and movie theater, the West End Terminal also featured trolley service as well as Virginia peanuts, fancy fruits and candies.

The first luxurious rapid transit rolling stock to reach Coney Island were the BRT "Standards," which measured 67 feet long and featured such amenities as commodious rattan seats and powerful motors. Tested on the new Sea Beach Line in 1914, the cars were an immediate hit and eventually would be placed on all BRT routes to the shore. Shown at the old Sea Beach station at Coney, these Standards would later be modified with improved ventilation and a front window that actually opened!

In the years immediately preceding World War I, it had become apparent that Coney Island's rail links required major upgrading. It would all begin by moving the surface tracks to an elevated level with a consolidated terminal at the intersection of Surf Avenue and Stillwell Avenue. The BRT's Culver Line, which had its own depot dating back to founder Andrew Culver's late-19th Century days, still was using the old, wooden street level platforms while the steel superstructure in the background was being completed in 1917. The elevated portion would link Brighton Beach with Coney Island. The elevated structure being completed here in the background connects the Brighton and Culver lines to the new Stillwell Avenue terminal. The box girder steel below it, used to build the lower Culver el, was made from the razing of the two-track Fulton Street el. Structural steel was hard to come by in a war-strapped 1917. The center ramp connects the old terminal with the new West 8th Street station.

anteed to multiply, because, in 1898, the city of Brooklyn consolidated with the City of New York—the five boroughs encompassed Kings County, Richmond County, Manhattan, Bronx County and Queens County—thus assuring its even more rapid growth.

Just a dime's throw from the Culver terminal, Steeplechase was true to its name; and then some. It featured a mechanical race horse that dashed around the amusement park's perimeter on monorail-type tracks.

The ride itself began in an attractive, glass-paneled Pavilion of Fun, and terminated—about four, fun-packed minutes later—in the same attractive white-covered shed. Known to Coney denizens simply as "The Horses," this Steeplechase favorite was scarier than the name implied. In certain spots the iron rails climbed as high as 35 feet and, often, couples joined arms thinking—even though they were well-strapped-in—that a false move could deposit them, heaven-knows-where.

Perhaps the scariest aspect of the ride—for the women, only—occurred at the end where ventilators hid huge underground fans which blew directly up the females' skirts, causing no end of embarrassment. Adding insult to the injury, clowns also "goosed" the gals with electric rods as they fled the scene.

White was a primary color at Steeplechase which featured no less than 31 different rides and novelties including a full-fledged roller coaster, Ferris wheel, and gigantic slides that landed terrified patrons on a series of speeding circular disks. They were guaranteed to make you dizzy or bruised—or both, as the circumstances would have it.

That Tilyou hit the jackpot was evident in several ways. For starters, he had several imitators and for finishers, his Steeplechase outlasted all of his competitors, although a 1907 fire compelled Tilyou to rebuild with considerably more glass than wood. Adding such notable rides—directly from the 1939-40 World's Fair in Flushing Meadow, Queens—as the Parachute Jump, Steeplechase remained a Coney staple through the 1960s.

By the time all shore-bound trains were electrified, Frederick Thompson and Elmer Dundy blueprinted Steeplechase's first significant rival, Luna Park at West 10th Street and Surf Avenue (across the street from the contemporary Cyclone Roller Coaster). Looking nothing like Steeplechase, Luna Park accented its moon theme to the hilt.

Thompson and Dundy went so far as Buffalo where they transferred the hit attraction, "Trip To The Moon," from the Niagara Peninsula to Coney Island. With electricity now a household word, Luna Park was adorned with no less than a million light bulbs which rimmed every one of its attractions, among them a classic roller coaster with an equally classic name, "The Mile Sky Chaser." Opened in 1903, Luna Park proved a worthy challenger to Steeplechase, battling it for customers for over four decades before a calamitous fire in 1944 also ignited its eventual demise—after two more blazes—in 1947.

Not to be outdone, William H. Reynolds invested $3.5 million of his developing fortune into a third amusement park, Dreamland, which had an *ambience* all its own. Reynolds already had demonstrated his investment acumen by turning seemingly useless land in Borough Park, Brooklyn and Long Beach, Long Island into real estate bonanzas. This time he chose a site which, today, is occupied by the Coney Island

Before the actual subway arrived in Coney Island, the resort was accessible first by steam railroads and then elevated-type trains using overhead trolley wires. This 1916 view of the "station" at Ocean Parkway reveals its proximity to one of the area's famed bathhouses, Parkway Baths. When the Brooklyn Rapid Transit later completed its subway-el to Coney Island, Ocean Parkway station would be one of the precious few art-deco terminals on the system.

When it came to linking with Coney Island's fun palaces, the Brooklyn Rapid Transit (BRT) got up-close and personal. BRT tracks head directly toward Surf Avenue, the resort's main drag, and Norton's Point. But to get there, the BRT Culver Line ran directly under the huge Luna (amusement) Park signage. One of Coney's foremost attractions, Luna Park would remain a fixture through the World War II years. Kister's Theater and Hotel, in the background, didn't last that long.

Aquarium, shoulder-to-shoulder with the Cyclone.

Now a sandy beach fronted by the ubiquitous Boardwalk, Dreamland's turf featured a tower near Surf Avenue, a Rialto-type bridge over an ocean-inlet and a massive pier at which paddle-wheel steamboats from Manhattan would deposit their passengers.

If the five-cents subway fare revolutionized Coney Island, the Big Three amusement parks proved a radical departure from any previous huckstering the island had known.

As historian Kenneth T. Jackson noted in his *Encyclopedia of New York City*, "The new parks had several features that transformed the amusement industry; they charged admission, banned alcohol, and offered mechanical rides that awed the public by combining speed with a hint of danger.

"On an average weekend in 1907 visitors mailed about 250,000 postcards from the area, spreading the reputation of the parks nationwide."[2]

During its heyday in the early 1900s Luna Park, for one, would average more than 85,000 daily patrons.

A nickel subway ride also delivered straphangers to some of the best ocean-facing eateries with sea-food, of course, being the magnet item. At Feltman's Pavilion, it was possible to stop at one of two bars and an array of nine restaurants—live orchestras included—adorned with such lyrical names as Wisteria Pergola and the Garden Club.

Comparing Dreamland to Steeplechase and Luna Park was roughly equivalent to equating a jump tune and a fox trot, respectively, to a waltz. Dreamland was relatively slow-paced, tastefully laid out. It announced "Avenues wide and imposing—

no crowding"—and even had an extremely popular song composed after it opened to rave notices, "Meet Me Tonight In Dreamland—Under a Starlit Sky."

Unfortunately, the popularity of its namesake song far outlasted the amusement park, which burned to the ground in 1911.

Dreamland's demise hardly deterred Coney's continued growth. This was made possible by continued advances in rapid transit to the shore. One by one, the Sea Beach, West End, Culver and Brighton Lines—Brighton was last—completed major structural linkages with the shore communities.

By 1916, blueprints had been completed for a massive terminal at Stillwell Avenue, which eventually would service not only all four Manhattan-bound lines, but a trolley service from Coney Island to Norton's Point in Sea Gate. The huge depot was made possible, in part, because earlier in the century, the Brooklyn Rapid Transit had managed to annex all significant lines, while also cementing deals with the Long Island Rail Road, which ran tracks parallel to the Brighton Line, but then curved east near its southern tip to Manhattan Beach. By virtue of one such pact, the Long Island was able to connect its Manhattan Beach service via the Brighton Beach line at Sheepshead Bay station.

Even before the Stillwell terminus made its debut in 1911, the existing depots—Culver, et. al.—opened the arena to more than mere amusement pursuits.

Never considered a twelve-month community lending itself to year-round home-owning, Coney nevertheless found itself a small residential core precisely because of the burgeoning subway connections. But by 1910, dozens of Italian-American families had begun flocking to a three-square block acreage bounded by Neptune and Surf Avenues, and West 15th to West 17th Streets.

As the subway improvements continued, the original two-story stucco houses were adjoined by up to six-story brick apartment houses with elevators, no less! Once the Brighton Line renovation—full, four-track express-local service to the shore—was completed in 1920, it was a signal to developers that it was time to build, build and build some more.

World War I was over and the Roarin' Twenties had arrived. The previously undeveloped streets between the new, ornate, art deco Ocean Parkway Brighton Line station and Coney Island Avenue saw more than two-dozen six-story apartments rise— all with the latest appliances including General Electric refrigerators. (They often were supplied by distributor, Rex Cole, who then affixed a black-on-white sign to each building, proclaiming his latest "score.") The Brighton housing boom coincided with the improvement of living standards for thousands of European Jewish immigrants who previously had lived in lesser-appointed housing.

Thus, those who had become "better-off" became enraptured by Brighton's allure; ocean amenities, reliable transportation and state of the art housing. By the thousands, they flocked to the six-floor palaces.

And by the millions they subwayed to the beach. On a hot summer day in the 1920s it was not uncommon for Coney's attendance to top the million mark—and counting.

With an eye on the subway sensation, the area's planners contributed to the further appeal by designing an arresting Broadwalk that would measure no less than 80-feet wide and almost four miles in length when fully constructed.

Just a short walk from the new housing *and* subways, the Boardwalk, in turn, inspired innumerable new enterprises along its northern perimeter. From Stillwell Avenue to the Steeplechase, one could find the "New" Stauch Baths, a photo shop, Sodamat—the precursor of today's soft drink vending machines—a penny arcade and Bushman Baths.

Along the Boardwalk, three-wheeled rolling chairs—pushed by Coney's version of rickshaw drivers—were available for less than a dollar, tip not included!

Easily, one of the biggest beneficiaries of the new Stillwell subway terminal, was Nathan Handwerker's frankfurter emporium, which one day would become as famous a landmark as the Cyclone and Parachute Jump. Immodestly dubbed "Nathan's Famous," Handwerker's frankfurters were in direct competition with the Feltman's also-famous hot dog, which had launched the trend years earlier.

The difference was that Handwerker undercut Feltman by half, dispensing his juicy and edible hot dachshunds for the same price as a subway ride—a nickel. Better still, Nathan's—unlike Feltman's— was precisely catty-corner from Stillwell's exit. Thus, when you were going to the beach and walked out of the depot, *there* was Nathan's just across the street to the right.

While it may have appeared that the subway's invasion of Coney mostly benefited those to the west of Brighton Beach station all the way to Sea Gate, there remained two other communities which were revolutionized first by the arrival of stream trains and later by the BRT's electrification.

Evolution of Brighton Beach Station

OPPOSITE PAGE, TOP: In its earliest incarnation, the BRT Brighton Beach station was at ground level. Rolling stock took power from overhead wires in a primitive milieu which would dramatically change within the next five years of modernization. The station is on the left in this 1916 photo, and the track on the right is the connection to the Culver Line West End Line and Norton's Point.

ABOVE: Construction of the subway-elevated line to Brighton Beach began in earnest late in the World War I years. The roller coaster is still off to the right and Coney Island Creek is seen on both the left and right. The new elevated structure leading into Brighton Beach station is in the midst of construction. Two sets of tracks of the four-track line have been installed along with third rails. In time, the creek would be filled in and Coney Island Avenue would be paved over on the left, parallel to the tracks.

OPPOSITE PAGE, BOTTOM: With its roller coasters (see right in the distance), race tracks and other amusement attractions, Brighton Beach had become a major rail destination by 1916. This view from the Brooklyn Rapid Transit's Brighton Beach station reveals five tracks leading into Brighton. The two on the left belong to the Coney Island Avenue trolley coming from the race track. The center track is the aforementioned connection. The tracks on the right lead into the Brighton Beach station. By this time the Dual Contracts, written in 1913, had provided for a replacement elevated structure which would carry the subway trains to Brighton and Coney Island.

From the roof of the newly-completed Brighton Beach BRT station, looking west from the station, one can understand how the subway affected a neighborhood's growth. Row upon row of new beach bungalows can be seen to the left (Atlantic Ocean side) of the elevated tracks while new, larger homes are being erected on the right (north side) of the el. Soon after the photo was taken in March 1921, intense building took place on the empty lots to the right.

The Brighton Beach BRT station has just been completed and holds a six-car local at its northbound platform. In March 1921, when the photo was taken, Brighton Beach Avenue, under the el, still had not been developed. Shortly thereafter, stores would sprout under the tracks and the flat land in the foreground would be covered with six-story elevated apartments.

They were Manhattan and Oriental Beaches.

The New York and Manhattan Beach Railroad—a subsidiary of the Long Island Rail Road—operated shoulder-to-shoulder with the competing Brooklyn, Flatbush and Coney Island line.

Once the steam trains reached the Atlantic, Manhattan Beach became a coveted peninsula at the eastern end of Coney Island. Spurred by the railroad connection, developer Austin Corbin organized a Manhattan Beach Improvement Company. In 1877, a 500-acre summer resort was laid out on salt marsh.

The New York and Manhattan Beach tracks ran directly to the opulent Manhattan Beach Hotel which competed directly with the equally fancy Brighton Beach Hotel to the West. As in America's Wild West, where railroad wars were not unusual, the train empresarios serving the ocean had their feuds.

One that led to several legal battles, was between the New York and Manhattan Beach and the Brooklyn, Flatbush and Coney Island. According to rail historian Joe Cunningham, "During one point of the disputes, a fence was erected between the New York and Manhattan Beach and Brighton line properties."

Meanwhile, the area east of Brighton was taking on a luster all its own. The way the rich head for the Hamptons today, is the way they made bee lines for the Oriental Hotel and the Manhattan Beach Hotel, each of which contracted for the top show business personalities as their headliners.

The noted composer and conductor John Philip Sousa not only frequented Corbin's resort, but even composed a hit about it, *Manhattan Beach March.* Patrick Gilmore, who wrote the hit, *When Johnny Comes Marching Home Again,* also was a Manhattan Beach regular.

As long as the three seaside race tracks remained in business, there was an extra, added attraction for the Manhattan Beach *aficionados.* But, the horse business shut down in 1910, at about the time the area was to undergo another dramatic change.

By this time, the electrified Brooklyn Rapid Transit trains had helped turn parts of Brighton into an amusement area—much too close for the bluebloods in nearby Manhattan Beach. On top of that, the suburban sprawl that was spreading south from Flatbush and Midwood now was moving relentlessly toward Sheepshead Bay.

Cognizant of that, Manhattan Beach Improvement created building lots north of the posh hotels thereby dooming them as private resorts. During the World War I years, handsome brochures depicting an ocean promenade—with strollers walking hand-in-hand—were distributed by the realtors.

In their advertising, they proclaimed, *"Swept by Ocean Breezes—Manhattan Beach Estates."*

In a sense, the advertisement was true to its claim. Beginning in the post-World War I era, Manhattan Beach would emerge as one of Brooklyn's classiest communities. It was distinctive in many ways; not the least of which was the naming of its streets—Amherst, Beaumont, Coleridge, among others—in alphabetical order and after English sites.

Relatively easy subway access inspired the Parks Department following World War II to build a public beach in Manhattan—a move that did not go over very well with the posh residents. But it did not significantly affect the twenty tree-lined streets, each of which retained its calm, quiet flavor into the 21st Century.

At the other end of the island, Sea Gate underwent a similar transformation because of railway—and then subway—interests.

The peninsula at the western end of Coney Island had been serviced by ferries from Manhattan in pre-Civil War years and beyond. Once steam trains began serving the island, Sea Gate took on an even more attractive look.

In 1892, Sea Beach Railroad president Alrick Man proposed a blueprint for an upper-class community. Actually, Sea Gate would be *so* high-fallootin' that—unlike any other Brooklyn neighborhood—it would be segregated from the rest of Coney Island to the east by imposing, turreted gates at both the Surf and Mermaid Avenue entrances. No less a designer than Stanford White created two houses which still are on the peninsula.

Ensuring privacy, the Sea Gate Association erected a twelve-foot fence from Coney Island Creek, to West 37th Street, with the Atlantic Ocean and Norton's Point being the other barriers.

Sea Gate's access to rail transport was assured early on when the Prospect Park and Coney Island Railroad (alias the Culver Line) built an extension that served the area. Long after the steam trains departed, Sea Gate received trolley service including tracks that circled the otherwise closed community itself.

However, by the start of World War II, the Norton's Point streetcar service terminated *outside* the gate from where residents would walk past the guard and to their homes. A brief war emergency measure restored the Norton's Point shuttle trolley service, only to be halted by a "nimby"

outcry, as residents complained about the operating noises made by the "hobbleskirt" trolleys.

When all is said and done, Coney Island—from Manhattan Beach on the east and Norton's Point on the west—is what it is today because of, (a) the steam trains and, (b) the electric-powered subway that followed.

One Man's Memories of What It Was Like To Go to Coney Island

To a kid from Williamsburg, Brooklyn, the idea of taking a trip to Coney Island was roughly equivalent to reading a Buck Rogers comic book about his rocket rides to Shangri-La.

Coney Island meant Steeplechase—The Funny Place; Wonder Wheel, The Bobsled, Faber's Poker, Feltman's Pavilion, Milo the Mule-Faced Boy, Tirza and Her Wine Bath and, of course, Nathan's Famous hot dogs, among other attractions.

Not to mention the beach, the Boardwalk, the rolling deck chairs and fishing off Steeplechase Pier with a stopover—if you were old enough—for a beer at the Atlantis (night club) where Mousie Powell's dance band played for an eternity.

For those who liked a beach club within the beach, there was Raven Hall, which had everything from a swimming pool to punching bags, as well as Washington Baths; or at the far end of the spectrum, legendary Brighton Beach Baths; so upbeat it even had live entertainment at night featuring Enoch Light and his Orchestra.

Coney was Christmas in July (August,

The End of the South Brooklyn Lines—
Stillwell Avenue Station

When Stillwell Avenue station was completed after World War I, it served as the terminal for the BRT's (left to right) West End, Culver, Brighton and Sea Beach lines. This picture, taken in March 1921, reveals the several platforms and three different types of rolling stock; two old el cars at the left and a new 67-foot Standard car on the right. The Stillwell station also featured a section for trolley cars which ran to Norton's Point, Sea Gate.

When it came to depots, the Brooklyn Rapid Transit's Coney Island terminal would be regarded as the company's masterpiece, uniting all its runs to the Atlantic playland. By April 18, 1918, it was well on its way to completion near the intersection of Stillwell and Surf Avenues. An engineer can be seen checking blueprints, while a BRT West End trolley idles in preparation for its next run. The Brighton, West End, Sea Beach and Culver lines all would terminate at the elevated station. Some 85 years later, the Stillwell depot would undergo its first major renovation. In its earliest incarnation, the BRT Brighton Beach station was at ground level. Rolling stock took power from overhead wires in a primitive milieu which would dramatically change within the next five years of modernization.

It's May 1944, a few days before Memorial Day, and Coney Island isn't quite "in" season yet. But the resort's hub rapid transit station, Stillwell Avenue, is ready for the anticipated crowds. Coney Island had become the world's hottest amusement area by 1918, thanks in large part to its many subway links. In order to coordinate the rapid transit lines—as well as trolley service—a new terminal was built at Stillwell and Surf Avenues. The ramp on the right connects the West End platform to the new Norton's Point trolley station.

This July 1918 photo shows the steel skeleton of the Norton's Point trolley terminal, adjacent to the subway tracks. During construction of this depot, the Norton's Point el cars in the background actually were trapped in the steel and wood work.

too) and getting there was—at the very least—half the fun.

There was only one "best" way to reach the beach, and that was via the nickel subway ride. It could be the West End, Sea Beach, Culver or Brighton Line; all of them rolled into the vast Stillwell Avenue terminal, which also housed a separate trolley station for the Norton's Point streetcar which connected Coney to Sea Gate.

Riding each line had its virtues, but none could match the surplus of thrills offered by the Brighton run, which boasted two distinctly different sections; one which departed from Times Square, and the other from Franklin Avenue and Fulton Street in Brooklyn.

The best part of the Brighton ride was its rolling stock. If ever there was a Rolls-Royce of subway cars, it was the BMT Standard which was introduced to the Brighton Line during the World War I years and—with improvements over two decades—still was in service when I began riding in the late 1930s.

Long (five-passenger) rattan seats were a feature of its interior along with three sets of wide, sliding doors and large overhead fans that seemed to spin faster than airplane propellers.

By far, the most youngster-friendly item was a tiny, rattan jump-seat situated just to the left of the front window. The seat—about two-feet by two-feet—always was in the open position and almost never was occupied by a passenger.

Even a four-year-old could hoist himself up and onto the jump-seat, which is precisely what I did in 1936 for my world premiere ride on the Brighton Line. Fortunately, designers of the BMT Standard were considerate enough to provide a front window which opened wide enough for a youth to gape at the railroad panorama ahead. The tiny window had a pair of knobs at the top on each side. By grasping and then pressing the knobs with index fingers and thumbs, even a four-year-old could manager to lower the window down each brass ratchet until the opening was wide enough to fit a head, and then some!

Having an open front window available enhanced the ride tenfold, at the very least. First and foremost, I could pretend to be the motorman, while at the same time, enjoying the rush of wind through my hair as the BMT Standard picked up speed en route to the beach.

Since the jump-seat was just across from the motorman's cabin, it was possible to fantasize about being behind the controller and brake used by the operator to move and stop the eight-car train.

The open window also brought me so close to the track itself that I could hear every significant subway sound, from the screech of flange against rail to the special *clickety-clack* of wheels rolling over the rail gaps.

Almost sensuous to the ear, the *clickety-clack* replicated contemporary jazz rhythms, including Gene Krupa's drumming behind Benny Goodman's "After You've Gone"[3] or "The World Is Waiting For The Sunrise."[4] In either case, the rhythms so intoxicated my youthful brain that I soon figured out how to duplicate them with my lips and tongue so that I could actually pretend, while walking down the street, that I was a BMT Standard barreling past the Cortelyou Road local station in Flatbush.

Since we lived on Marcy near Myrtle Avenue, we were nowhere near a Brighton Line station. Two choices were available; either take the Myrtle Avenue elevated line

Enlarging of the Brooklyn System

Before switching to standard subway-type signals, the elevated lines were guided by semaphore signals similar to those used on traditional railroads. A typical semaphore is seen on the left. The station is Marcy Avenue in 1914 on the Broadway Brooklyn line. The tracks at the left and the curved ones in the center head for the Williamsburg Bridge and the Delancy Street station on the Manhattan side. The track on the far right heads to the East River terminal on the line and the ferry station.

The new Brighton Line subway in Brooklyn extended from Flatbush Avenue Extension—at the foot of the Manhattan Bridge—all the way south under Flatbush Avenue, where the boulevard bisects Prospect Park and the Botanic Garden. The photograph, taken from the zoo side of Flatbush Avenue, reveals the southern tip of the Botanic Gardens with Ebbets Field in the background. The trolley tracks cover the northern entrance to Prospect Park subway station.

The BRT Brighton line had proven itself so popular in the early part of the 1900s that a major expansion was inevitable. It came about as a result of the Dual Contracts which provided for a four—instead of two—track main line from Prospect Park to Brighton Beach. To accomplish this, a major upgrading of the Prospect Park-Malbone Street station would be necessary. By June 1917 the project had been well-advanced, including the southbound tracks leading into a 90-degree curve at the tunnel portal. The tracks on the far right were the temporary route of the Brighton Line coming south from Fulton Street and Franklin Avenue. The hole in the center was being constructed as a connection for the subway coming from Manhattan, which still is in use.

The damaged cars involved in the Malbone Street wreck were taken to the Brooklyn Rapid Transit yards for inspection. This car involved in the disaster shows the effects of the collision.

OPPOSITE PAGE, BOTTOM: This photo depicts the entrance to the recently-completed Prospect Park station tunnel at what then was Malbone Street. It was photographed on November 6, 1918, after the November 1, 1918 disaster which cost 97 lives. The trains would come down an incline and into the newly-completed tunnel dug at the right. However, during a strike on November 1, 1918, a replacement motorman lost control of his fleet of wooden elevated cars on the downgrade. The cars crashed into the tunnel after entering the portal. Black marks still can be seen on the left wall five days after the crash. Officials are surveying the route.

Another car involved in the Malbone Street wreck.

The Malbone Street overpass is just to the right of the trolley. Malbone Street suggested such unpleasant memories that the street name was officially changed to Empire Boulevard. Almost three decades later, when this picture was taken, Brooklynites still talked about the wreck. Prospect Park is in the distance, and the entrance to Prospect Park, at the point where the crash took place, is just below the concrete fence beyond the building at the right.

Looking at the south end of the Prospect Park station from the Lincoln Road bridge in June 1916. Enlargement of the Brighton Line, from two to four tracks, had begun and would entail changing from a two-track local operation to four-track express-local runs. Note the tennis courts off to the left.

(a block away) downtown to Flatbush Avenue extension, or take the IND subway (also a block away)—with one change of line—to Franklin Avenue.

The Brighton local stopped at Myrtle Avenue subway station, connecting with the express at Prospect Park, where one could transfer. The fun of this ride was in the speedy underground gallop from Seventh Avenue station to Prospect Park, which was situated in an open cut, allowing the sun rays to reach the tracks.

Nevertheless, the run from Franklin Avenue was preferable on several counts. For starters, this version of the Brighton express actually started its journey from an old elevated station at the corner of Franklin and Fulton Streets. During the winter this was the Franklin Avenue Shuttle, which rolled just a few stations between Fulton Street and Prospect Park. But, in the summertime, BMT officials had the good sense to allow it to run past Prospect Park and all the way to Coney Island.

To distinguish the Franklin version of the Brighton express from the other, BMT dispatchers affixed a large white disk to the front bumper which gave the train an even more important look. To me it was like the Orient Express of Brooklyn.

Easily the most exciting aspect of the jaunt from Fulton to Prospect Park was the incline from the elevated portion to street level and, finally, down to the tunnel portal at Empire Boulevard. It was at this point where the tracks curved sharply to the right and then just as sharply to the left before reaching the Prospect Park station.

Like many other Brooklynites, I knew that this was the precise point where a Brighton Express crashed on the night of November 1, 1918, killing 97 riders. It was known as the Great Malbone Street Wreck and had become synonymous with tragedy throughout the borough. (Family legend had it that a distant relative was on the doomed train and survived, but this never could be verified.)

When the crash occurred, the Brooklyn Rapid Transit was operating fragile, wooden cars which splintered on impact. They lacked the fail-safe "automatic tripper" attached to more modern cars which would have brought the train to a safer halt even though it was traveling an estimated 50 miles per hour in a six miles per hour zone.

Just the idea of riding these same tracks through the same tunnel in which the Brighton Express crashed was both fascinating and exhilarating to me. And the idea of the train being able to negotiate the pair of 90-degree curves was awesome in and of itself.

Getting to Coney Island involved three contrasting aspects of out-of-doors subwaying—the open cut, the dirt embankment and the steel, elevated portion.

From Prospect Park, the four-track open cut was like a railway canyon, extending from the Prospect Park portal past Parkside Avenue station, followed by the Beverly and Cortelyou Road local stops, concluding at Newkirk Avenue, the last express stop in the portal.

Each of these stations was graced with bright, red steel chewing gum machines not seen on either the IRT or BMT lines which featured the more traditional Wrigley's Spearmint or Doublemint flavors. Instead, the Brighton Line stations offered Pulver Chewing Gum in a dispenser that looked more at home in a Coney Island penny arcade than a subway station.

In addition to dispensing three flavors

of gum, the crimson Pulver machine had an extra attraction. Behind a glass cover, a pair of "performers" would swing into motion at the drop of a penny into the gum slot. One was a policeman wielding a night stick, and the other was a robber of sorts. At the moment the machine swallowed its penny, the cop would immediately begin banging the robber on top of the head with his night stick until the stick of gum appeared at the bottom of the red machine.

Heading south from Newkirk station, the BMT Standard ascends a rather steep—for the subway system—hill until it passes Avenue H station, whereupon it seems as if the whole of Flatbush is laid out before you. The embankment—with its straight-away four-track layout—has all the feel of a standard transcontinental railway.

The express run from Newkirk to Kings Highway is long, straight and filled with marvelous sights and sounds. With my head stuck out of the window, I could hear virtually every movement of the wheels over the rails, because the tracks were sitting on dirt; not concrete nor steel. The sound and rhythm was matched in excitement only by the rush of wind on a kid's face as the express virtually leaped past George W. Wingate field on the left and the old Vitagraph Studios movie set on the right.

After a brief respite at Kings Highway, the Standard picked up speed at Sheepshead Bay where the dirt embankment merged with the steel trestle and a totally different—more raucous—sound was produced as the Atlantic Ocean suddenly dominated the landscape.

Suddenly, the *ch-ch-ch* sound of the air brakes signaled that a 90-degree curve was ahead. I never felt quite secure in the knowledge that the trains would be able to negotiate the right turn over Coney Island Avenue and into the Brighton Beach station. But this all was part of the transit melodrama.

The smell of the briny deep penetrated my nostrils as the express headed west over Brighton Beach Avenue toward the concrete art nouveau station straddling Ocean Parkway. It had a massive feel unlike any station on the line.

Then came a puzzle, because the Brighton Line would merge with the Sea Beach, West End and Culver runs. To accommodate the three units, engineers built a two-tiered elevated structure leading into the Stillwell Avenue terminus. And therein lies the puzzlement; which—top or bottom?—el would the Brighton Express take?

It was virtually impossible to tell whether it would be routed down to the lower el or—thrill of thrills—climb to the high el with the most splendid panorama of Coney Island's attractions along Surf Avenue.

Approaching the Stillwell hub, our Express had to negotiate one more screeching curve which heralded our arrival into the land of cotton candy, French fries and frozen custard. Coney Island, I am here!

The Coney of my early youth (1935–age three through 1939–age seven) was far, far different from the contemporary resort. It was much bigger, geographically and image-wise. In 1935, it featured two huge amusement parks, George C. Tilyou's Steeplechase and Luna Park, as well as three major roller coasters, the Cyclone, Thunderbolt and Thompson's Scenic Railway. There were freak shows galore including one that featured Albert-Alberta who allegedly was half man, half woman.

In addition, several bathhouses, such as Raven Hall, not only provided changing

Riding the Brighton Rails

Prospect Park station in August 1963. The D-type Triplex cars are sitting on the express tracks. This is where I would begin my Brighton Line rides either to visit Grandma and Grandpa Fischler in Flatbush or to go all the way for a swim at Coney Island.
William Brennan

The Brighton local slowing down for the Beverley Road station in November 1962. The car is a BMT Type B Standard which was ubiquitous on the Brighton line for decades. If I was visiting my grandparents, I'd be up at the front window, awaiting our destination at Avenue H station. The B Standards—as opposed to the A units—were comprised of three cars linked together.

William Brennan

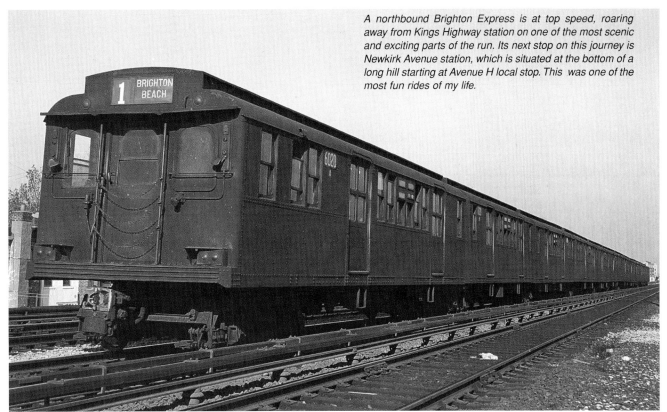

A northbound Brighton Express is at top speed, roaring away from Kings Highway station on one of the most scenic and exciting parts of the run. Its next stop on this journey is Newkirk Avenue station, which is situated at the bottom of a long hill starting at Avenue H local stop. This was one of the most fun rides of my life.

William Brennan

William Brennan

A BMT Brighton local nears the end of its long run from Manhattan as it approaches Kings Highway station. The train is comprised of D-type Triplex cars which were favored—along with the Standards—because the front window could be opened and enjoyed by buffs like me.

A shorebound express of B-Standards and a citybound local of Triplex D-types loading at Kings Highway station. The last south-bound station before Sheepshead Bay and, then, Brighton Beach, Kings Highway always seemed as if it was the prelude to great moments ahead at the Atlantic Ocean.

Sheepshead Bay station on the BMT Brighton Line had a distinctly suburban feel to it; which is not surprising since—for years— many Brooklynites considered the area nothing more than a fishing village. A set of Standards sits on the express tracks. From Sheepshead Bay to Brighton, the tracks move from a dirt-ballast surface to a traditional steel elevated structure leading to Brighton Beach Avenue.

William Brennan

stalls, but everything from swimming pools to punching bags for those who sought a bit of athletics and exclusivity—away from the masses—by the sea.

Coney Island also was home to the world's best handball players, including the omnipotent Vic Hershkowitz, handball's answer to Babe Ruth; and Jack Rudman, who hit the ball so hard he developed a lump that resembled a handball on the back of his hand. Located on Surf Avenue, in the shadow of BMT's Ocean Parkway station, the handballer's haven was just yards from the beach and surf. My father was one of those players and the proof is a photo I coveted since I was a kid of Dad whacking a ball during what appeared to be a fierce game right off the sand. I always believed that my lifelong love of handball began when I first looked at the photo of Ben Fischler hitting a "killer" off the wall at the Ocean Parkway courts.

Starting at Brighton Beach on the eastern part of the island, Coney stretched from Bay 1st Street all the way to Bay Street where the private Sea Gate community's forbidding archway actually featured a gate which opened only for residents.

During World War II, my best friend, Howie Sparer, lived in Sea Gate with his family and the two of us frequented Coney Island from time to time. Since we had a limited amount of money to spend, we usually divvied up our cash between visits to the: (a) Penny Arcade on Surf Avenue, which had an excellent baseball game in which the steel ball came out of a large hole in the umpire's stomach; (b) a ride called "The Whip," which would roll straight for about ten yards and then violently whip around a curve so that you felt as if your *kishkes* were falling out; (c) Skee-ball, a game which produced winning coupons, if you were

really good; (d) the L.A. Thompson Scenic Railway; easily the mildest roller coaster, and (e) The Bobsled, an ultra-modern coaster which originated at the 1939 World's Fair in Flushing Meadows, but was transferred—along with the Parachute Jump—to Coney Island after the Fair closed.

Prior to 1944, when we both were twelve years old, Howie and I made a point of avoiding such attractions as the Cyclone (too scary), Parachute Jump (much too scary), and Faber's Poker—or its equivalent, the Steeplechase Pokerino.

The reason we ignored the poker game was simple; it was too complicated for a kid. For Skee-ball, all you had to do was roll the wooden ball up the ramp and hope that it landed in either the bull's eye hole or the one next to it. Coupons came easily but the gifts were so cheap we were almost ashamed to cash in on them.

By contrast, the poker game featured about a dozen holes in a square; each hole having a card—such as the Jack of Clubs—listed next to it. Since neither of us were poker players, we hesitated to even go near Faber's or Pokerino.

But, one morning, we were strolling along the Boardwalk, planning to buy a Steeplechase ticket good for a dozen rides, including the best of all, what we called "The Horses." On a raised track—something like a primitive monorail—merry-go-round-type horses would speed outdoors around the entire Steeplechase perimeter. One never knew from race to race, which horse would win—or whether or not we'd fall off the horse and get killed. Nobody ever did fall off but the possibility made the ride even more exciting.

One Wednesday morning Howie and I were heading to Steeplechase, ambling along the Boardwalk, thoroughly enjoying life—although our country was in the midst of World War II—as balmy zephyrs wafted in from the ocean.

Just before we made our right turn down the wooden ramp off the Boardwalk, an appetizing sight caught our eyes. About ten yards ahead of us all seven front doors of Steeplechase Pokerino were flung open so that we could see each of the handsome games, fronted by the ubiquitous, round soda fountain-type swivel seats; each lined with a belt of bright chrome.

Ordinarily, we would have passed it by, but just as we began turning toward Surf Avenue, we noticed that Pokerino was empty and that enticed us to walk up to the entrance and peer around. We quickly discerned that the prize list was much more impressive than the one at Skee-Ball.

A salt-and-pepper shaker set, for example, would require ten coupons at Skee-Ball but Pokerino offered the same prize for only one coupon. *Wow!*

Howie and I couldn't resist the temptation, so we walked in and climbed on adjoining red leather soda fountain chairs, dropped our nickels in the slots and down the chute rolled five tennis-size rubber balls.

The idea was to roll the balls into holes that would produce a winning poker hand; which is why it would have been helpful if either of us knew anything about poker. But on this morning, we had something better than Pokerino smarts, and that was beginner's luck.

On our first try we each won a coupon, and that bit of good fortune merely inspired us to continue playing. Incredibly, game after game we were pulling in coupons—one, two, sometimes three at a time—until we had run out of nickels.

Now it was time to cash in and I decid-

HIGHEST SPEED TRAINS

What is the fastest recorded speed of a subway train on the New York system? According to some transit experts the figure is 87.75 MPH. The feat was accomplished on January 31, 1972. On a test run the Transit Authority's 75-foot-long R-44 cars reached that speed, during speed trials on a Long Island Rail Road test track between Woodside and Jamaica.

Eric Oszustowicz

ed that, since my mother might take a dim view of my spending so many nickels on Pokerino, I should select gifts that would directly please her. No stuffed teddy bears; no gimmicks. Items for the kitchen or dinner table would be the thing.

I started with salt-and-pepper shakers, then went for a large pitcher that seemed ideal for orange juice and then the *chef de ouvre,* a magic sugar dispenser. One turn of the gleaming, red cone-shaped cover produced precisely one teaspoon of sugar with every twist of the wrist. *Such a mechanism.* I was convinced that the magic-sugar-shaker would just knock my mom for a delightful loop.

Howie and I collected our booty and decided that it would be prudent to head home with it before we were robbed of our prizes or some other such disaster befell us before reaching safe haven. Since my pal's parents were staying in Sea Gate, he hopped on the Norton's Point trolley, while I headed to the Stillwell Avenue BMT terminal, for what would seem like the longest subway ride of my life.

My main objective was to ensure that my "valuable" Pokerino glassware remained intact from Coney Island to Williamsburg. My secondary objective was securing a spot by the BMT Standard's front window from which to enjoy the trans-Brooklyn hegira.

The trick at Stillwell Avenue station was placement. Since all trains began their northerly trips from Coney, they were empty when taking on passengers. But if too many people already were at the front of the platform, the odds for getting the front window were slim to none.

However, if one allowed the train to fill up and leave, it was possible to position oneself at the exact spot where the next train's doors would open. And that's exactly what I did while balancing the bag full of glassware in my short arms.

When the next Brighton Express arrived, I was in the right spot at the right time. Crowded though it was, I managed to squeeze around the door and up to the open front window before any urchins beat me to the coveted spot.

Of course, that didn't mean that my troubles were over; far from it. The train had filled to a point where standing room was only two stops away. As long as I held position by the window, my aim was to shield the fragile brown bag from the growing crowd.

At last the doors closed and the motorman pulled on his controller. He kept it at the lowest "point" because the tracks over Stillwell Avenue curved sharply to the left for the eastbound run to West Eighth Street station.

Right from the start, the Manhattan-bound run provides thrills. With my head out the window—while nursing the prizes—I bathed in the sea breezes as the first car lurched out toward Surf Avenue. From the top tracks I could see the grand Carousel, Faber's Poker, the freak show and—beyond the Boardwalk—waves breaking in at Bay 16 beach.

By the time the eight cars had negotiated the 90-degree turn, we were approaching Bay Eighth where the Thompson Scenic Railway tracks snaked under the el and then climbed north for the series of hills and valleys that comprised Coney's easiest roller coaster ride.

Not many passengers got aboard, and the doors quickly shut for the downhill run into Ocean Parkway station. After three stops, our car had filled so much that no seats were available. Next stop was Brighton Beach, and I knew this could be trouble.

Still, I was so transfixed with the elevated track work above Brighton Beach Avenue, I hardly had time to concern myself with the valuable goods still well-guarded from the masses.

From Ocean Parkway to Brighton Beach, the trackage widens to six lanes of rails, interspersed with switches. A heavy BMT Standard creates a distinctive *bong-bong-bong-bong* sound as its wheels cross the switches. This subway drum roll is further enhanced as it echoes off the walls of Brighton Beach Avenue apartment houses which flank the railroad. To my ears it was a wonderful sound to hear, until the train braked on entering the next station and I realized a veritable horde of passengers was boarding the express.

Now the train was jammed with standees, some of whom were inadvertently pushing toward my window spot. For the first time, I felt that my glassware was in danger of being crushed because of the sheer volume of passengers.

In a last-ditch attempt to protect my booty, I moved the brown bag into the corner where the motorman's cab wall intersects with the front of the car. Meanwhile, the right side of my body protected—or, at least, tried to protect—my stash.

With all these strategic moves, I still had my head space at the window and exhaled a sigh of relief as the doors closed and the motorman momentarily started us in the direction of Brighton Beach Baths— its handball courts directly in front of us— Sheepshead Bay and Mrs. Stahl's Knishery, which was directly below.

But that panorama suddenly disappeared as the Standard's tracks turned left and negotiated the turn toward Sheepshead Bay station. After a slow start on the el tracks, our Express accelerated over the steel until it reached top speed precisely when the el gave way to the dirt embankment.

Once again the speeding train sound dramatically changed to a softer, more sensuous, *tskuh, tskuh, tskuh, tskuh,* as it barreled into Sheepshead Bay terminal, ready for the big run to Times Square.

By now, I felt secure in the knowledge that not only had I well-protected my coveted gifts, but also was well-ensconced at the window for the remainder of the long ride ahead.

This was as good a day as any for riding the Brighton Express. The beaming sun seemed to highlight the views of Flatbush, and, as we accelerated out of Kings Highway station, I found myself noticing nuances of the embankment that had eluded me before.

I could clearly make out the Long Island Rail Road right-of-way immediately to the east, where once steam locomotives carried passengers from Downtown Brooklyn to the Sheepshead Bay Race Track, as well as such high-class tourist resorts as Oriental and Manhattan Beaches.

Pieces of stone track ballast, which once had seemed to be a blurry, rock mass, now appeared to have a character and shape of their own. The three-tiered signal lights, placed low along the tracks, seemed to be smiling through their sun-protecting visors.

But best of all was the sense of power and speed that the Express exuded along a straightaway that carried through such communities as Downtown, Prospect Heights, Flatbush, Midwood, Kings Highway, Sheepshead Bay, Brighton Beach and Coney Island.

I couldn't imagine having more fun in any place, any time or anywhere but on the Pride of the BMT. However, the best was yet to come.

Just a few yards north of Avenue H local station, the four tracks descend from the embankment to the open cut. The descent represents one of the steepest hills in the entire subway system, and in a strategically advantageous spot, because the Express already is at top speed as it reaches the downhill run, but now will travel even *faster.*

This was one of the most breathtaking moments on the entire system because the motorman still had his controller on its highest point, yet, Newkirk Avenue station was directly below, at the hill's bottom.

By the middle of the hill, our Express' *clickety-clack* was so intense, I questioned

Brighton Line Construction

The new Brighton Line subway in Brooklyn extended from Flatbush Avenue Extension—at the foot of the Manhattan Bridge—all the way south under Flatbush Avenue, where the boulevard bisects Prospect Park and the Botanic Garden. The photo, taken in November 16, depicts construction between the Garden and the park. This hoist is over the top of the Brighton connection to Downtown Brooklyn, from Prospect Park station to Grand Army Plaza.

When the Brighton Line was expanded to four tracks, the Woodruff Avenue local stop seen here simply was abandoned. One can see from the 1916 photo that residential development was extensive in the neighborhood around the tracks. The subway's construction inspired a tremendous increase in population density in this area of north Flatbush.

OPPOSITE PAGE, BOTTOM: Once the meeting of the IRT and BMT subway was completed at Grand Army Plaza, the construction had to be neatly covered over with the neighborhood restored, or—as in the case of the Plaza—made even more beautiful. This photo, taken from Prospect Park's southern entrance, shows the plaza, soon to be adorned with the Soldier's and Sailor's monument. A trolley can be seen in the left background after taking a right turn from Flatbush Avenue on to the Plaza. The IRT and BMT tunnels were simultaneously constructed with both lines serving alternating stations under Flatbush Avenue, north of the plaza.

OPPOSITE PAGE AND ABOVE: Looking first south and then north at the southerly end of the Church Avenue station in the summer of 1916, we see the original place where the Brighton Line expanded. It was from here north to the Prospect Park station that the line was widened to four tracks.

Flat cars fill the express tracks at Church Avenue station on the Brighton Line in September 1918. The northbound platform is nearing completion.

The Church Avenue station in Flatbush. BRT engineers designed an express-local stop still in the open cut. This photo shows the creation of the south-bound platform in 1917, before the station was fully roofed to near-completion in 1918. The station in its original four-track form remains intact today.

whether the motorman would be able to apply his air brakes in time. Finally, as the train leveled off a few feet from the station platform, the *ch-ch-ch-ch* overwhelmed all sounds and the BMT Beauty came to a comfortable stop precisely below the oversized, white number eight sign at the north end of the platform.

That was the chief thrill of the interborough run although there were more directly ahead. Following the Church Avenue stop, the express zipped through a succession of short tunnels, finally arriving at Prospect Park station where the front car actually nosed into the mouth of a tunnel which eventually would lead our train all the way to the Manhattan Bridge which crosses the East River.

I never got that far. One stop before the bridge-crossing was Myrtle Avenue from where I could take the Myrtle el or trolley car directly home. Since the trolley was less crowded—and my glassware still was whole—I opted for the streetcar and arrived in our apartment just as my mother was walking out of the kitchen.

"Mom," I said, barely hiding my excitement, "look what I won for you at Coney Island."

As she gaped at the bag, I pulled out the salt-and-pepper shakers and put them on the table.

"We already have a set," she said, nonplussed.

"But wait," I insisted. And then produced the enormous pitcher.

She hardly blinked: "What do I need that for?"

I knew that the prize of prizes—the sugar dispenser with the magical cone-shaped nozzle that precisely produced one teaspoon per shake—would win her over.

"How about this, Mom?" I exclaimed, showing her how the one-teaspoon-per-turn cone worked.

Mother was conspicuously unimpressed. "I can do that magic with a teaspoon," she said.

I was stunned to the core but also pleased. After all, I had carted the contraband on the subway *all* the way from Coney to the kitchen without breaking one piece of glass!

———————————————

When my father took me to see the Bushwicks baseball team play at Dexter Park, we got off the Myrtle Avenue line (top tracks) at Broadway Junction and changed for the Broadway BMT, which ran on the lower tracks.

CHAPTER TWO

GOING TO

The Ball Parks

Take Me Out To The Ball Game,
Take Me Out To The Park,
Buy Me Some Peanuts
And Cracker Jacks,
I Don't Care If I Never Come Back.

Composer Jack Norworth was passing under the Ninth Avenue elevated line at 155th Street in 1908 when he got the inspiration for the best song ever written about our National Pastime.

Not coincidentally, Norworth—and the el—just happened to be across the street from New York's most famous baseball stadium of that era, the Polo Grounds.

If nothing else, the transit-sporting symbiosis of ball park and subway (or el, as the case may be) was repeated over and over again from the late 19th Century and into the 20th Century.

In most cases, the ball parks—as in Yankee Stadium, Ebbets Field and Shea Stadium—followed the trains.

Which was only natural since—apart from rapid transit—there was no other

means of moving masses on a weekend when crowds of up to 60,000 gathered to watch the Giants and/or Yankees play at their respective diamonds.

Dating back to 1876, the Polo Grounds originally was true to its name; a grounds on which polo was played. Its original incarnation was situated between 110th to 112th Streets, bordered by Fifth and Sixth Avenues at the northeast tip of Central Park.

When New York Giants owner John B. Day acquired the acreage, he summarily dismissed the horsey set and built what rightly should have been dubbed, "The Baseball Grounds." But apparently for sentimental reasons, Day kept it as is and hence Manhattan's first Polo Grounds for baseball lasted a good six years. A short walk from the Third Avenue el's 106th or 116th Street stations was all that was required of straphangers to reach the new stadium.

Unfortunately for Day, he got a taste of eviction first-hand in 1889 when Manhattan's planners decided to designate the original Polo Grounds site for a traffic circle, of all things, at Fifth Avenue and 110th Street; and it still exists.

Like the elevated lines, Day moved north, this time acquiring property bounded by 159th and 155th Streets near the Harlem (East) River. It was a more majestic locale than the original, thanks to unusual rock formations overlooking the land previously owned by one James J. Coogan.

The prairie-like acreage which the ball field would eventually occupy was known as Coogan's Hollow, while the rock ledge overlooking it was known as Coogan's Bluff. Thus, the Giants second Polo Grounds opened on July 8, 1889 with better rapid transit than the original.

Manhattan's Ninth Avenue elevated line had been rebuilt eight years earlier, stretching from South Ferry at the southern tip of the island to 155th Street, the doorstep of Day's diamond! In addition, the Sixth Avenue el connected with the Ninth at 53rd Street in Manhattan and then rolled— on Ninth Avenue el tracks—to the same Polo Grounds terminal. At first, Polo Grounds-bound trains were pulled by tiny steam engines, but in February 1903 the line was electrified, and in 1918 service was extended to the Bronx, via a new Putnam Bridge providing even more potential for filling the stadium.

The el station sat neck to neck with the last stop of the New York and Northern Railroad (later the Putnam Division of the New York Central Railroad), which carried baseball fans to the Polo Grounds from the Bronx and Westchester. Suburbanites therefore had the same easy access to the Giants as the Manhattan and Bronx el riders.

Polo Grounds II thrived until April 13, 1911 when fire razed the grandstands. Within three months it was replaced by a state of the art 38,000-seat concrete and steel structure with a distinct horseshoe shape. It proved to be such a hit that the seating eventually was increased to 55,987.

Until Yankee Stadium was built, the Polo Grounds reigned supreme as the biggest ball park in the city. It was befitting a championship team like the Giants, which had dominated big-league baseball as much as any club in the early 20th Century.

By contrast, the Yankees' home field overlooked the Hudson River on Washington Heights. It was appropriately called Hilltop Park—situated on the highest plot of land in Manhattan—and was to be the first big-league stadium in the city to be directly serviced by a subway line.

Planned at the turn of the century, the original Interborough Rapid Transit line was to burrow north from City Hall, head west at 42d Street, then north under Broadway into Washington Heights. A station was laid out at 168th Street and Broadway within shouting distance of home plate.

When the Yankees opened their first season at Hilltop Park in 1903, the subway was only a year away from completion. The Yanks remained in Washington Heights through the 1912 season, thereby taking full advantage of New York's subway. But the single-deck wooden Hilltop Park was obsolete by 1913, so the Yankees moved their operation, lock, stock and baseballs to the Polo Grounds.

At first the Giants didn't mind the arrangement. Baseball-wise, they owned New York while the Yankees were regarded as second-class citizens. Giants' boss John McGraw was king of the Big Apple's baseball domain and suffered no fears about his tenants until the Yankees obtained Babe Ruth from the Boston Red Sox in 1920.

McGraw sensed that the *Sultan of Swat* would siphon fans away from his Giants and soon there was no sensing; it *was* happening. Ruth had become so big, so fast in New York that Polo Grounds' crowds had become noticeably bigger for Yankee games than the home team Giants.

McGraw figured that if you can't beat 'em in the attendance battle, then evict 'em; which is precisely what he did, successfully urging Giants' owner Charles Stoneham to divide—and hopefully conquer—the Polo Grounds. The Giants divided it by *one* and the Yankees were forced to find a new home.

But where?

Yankees' owner, beer magnate Jacob Ruppert was as sharp in real estate as he was in brewing. When it came to finding a site for his club's *own* ball park, Ruppert merely observed a simple dictum: just follow the new, growing subway.

The subway in question was a new addition to the IRT service in the Bronx. Ruppert knew the route and that it would be heading through an area, Melrose, where land was undeveloped and relatively cheap.

As luck would have it, the IRT's proposed Jerome Avenue Line would be a three-track operation from 135th Street in Manhattan and into the Bronx. After the Jerome Avenue station, the train would climb out of the tunnel and resume its journey along an elevated structure.

While the Yankees still were Polo Grounds' tenants, the Jerome Line was completed. On June 2, 1917, service began from 149th Street-Grand Concourse to Kingsbridge Road in the Bronx. A year later through service from Manhattan was added.

THE DISAPPEARING KIOSKS

Among the handsomest aspects of the first subway were the entrances to the stations. Called kiosks—an Americanization of the Turkish word kushks, or summer houses—the IRT subway entrances were elaborate coverings whose style was borrowed from an earlier Budapest subway. The kiosks were not only attractive but functional. Unfortunately, they were deemed impractical long after the IRT was annexed by the City and the Board of Transportation by the Transit Authority. All kiosks were razed and replaced with pedestrian entrances. Only later did someone in command realize the mistake, and more recently a copy of an original kiosk was erected at City Hall.

At the time, the Bronx traversed by the IRT was, by and large, undeveloped farm land or lots awaiting the arrival of mass transit. The emergence of Yankee Stadium as a significant addition to that once-barren land paralleled the sudden apartment house building boom that followed the tracks north toward Westchester.

Ruppert didn't immediately exploit the available acreage at River Avenue and East 157th Street where his stadium ultimately would be built. Instead he insightfully chose to try a deal with his landlord, Charles Stoneham of the Giants.

The Yankees owner figured that two teams could share the same ball yard but that both clubs needed a new state of the art facility that would handle much bigger crowds than the Polo Grounds.

Putting his cards on Stoneham's table, Ruppert said he would go "halfies" with his counterpart; offering half of what the Polo Grounds was worth in cash, having it razed

Shuttle Off to the Polo Grounds

"See the little puffer-bellies all in a row." This scene at the 129th Street engine terminal of the Second and Third Avenue el duplicates what went on at the engine facility adjacent to the Polo Grounds before 1902.

Here is the 155th Street station, located next to the Polo Grounds in 1914. At this time it was the end of the line for Ninth Avenue el trains. The swing bridge over the Harlem River was for the exclusive use of the Putnam Division of the New York Central and Hudson River Railroad. In fact, its steam-hauled passenger cars can be seen on the opposite side of the platform.

A few months later, change was in the air; a second platform was under construction. Possibly, the increased popularity of baseball was the reason. The second-decking of the outfield grandstand was still a decade away. The open lot in the left foreground was called Manhattan Field. When the Giants first moved here they played at Manhattan Field, which had a grandstand, until their ballpark was built next door.

Before the el service, the steam-hauled Putnam trains curved to the right and descended a ramp to the ground level parallel to the Hudson Division. The Ninth Avenue el's coaling dock and car storage facility is on the right across the river.

In late 1916, a transformation was taking place; a new Sedgwick Avenue station was under construction. It would provide a new terminal for the Putnam branch and a connection to the Ninth Avenue el trains, which would now be able to proceed through a tunnel to the new Jerome Avenue subway line at Gun Hill Road.

By late 1918, construction of the new station at Sedgwick Avenue was almost complete. The west-bound platform was the last piece of the puzzle. The tracks to the Putnam branch had been severed and test trains were already in use. This view is from the enclosed walkway that connects both stations.

The completed Sedgwick Avenue station and overhead connector is on the right. What little that remains of this facility is now directly under the Major Deegan Expressway. Service on the Ninth Avenue el was terminated in 1940, when the city refused to take over its operation. At the unification of the IND, IRT and BMT under the Board of Transportation, the part that extended from the Polo Grounds to Gun Hill Road was converted into a shuttle to continue servicing the ballpark. When the Giants left for San Francisco in 1958, the raison d'etre for this service ended and it was closed.

In 1928, the Polo Grounds had received its outfield upper deck and Manhattan Field had been dug up for the building of the IND Concourse Line.

The IRT Polo Grounds Shuttle rolls over the Harlem River from Manhattan toward the Bronx. The pair of cars were "Steinway" models. The bridge originally was constructed to bring the New York Central Putnam Line rail-road trains to link with the Ninth Avenue el at 155th Street.

and then the two clubs would erect that ball-park-of-all-ball-parks. Ruppert's vision foresaw not only a baseball field but a stadium that also would host boxing, football and whatever else the traffic would bear on the Harlem turf.

Riding high under McGraw's stewardship, the Giants still regarded the Yanks as second-class citizens. Ruppert's offer was dismissed out of hand; so Colonel Jake began biding his time—and looking.

He didn't have to look very far.

In fact, all Ruppert had to do was stand at home plate on the Polo Grounds and face eastward. Just across the river—less than a mile away—was fertile baseball land.

Jake also perceived that it was fertile transit land. He instantly realized the value of having a major subway-el station right across the street from the outfield where it would require a grand total of five minutes for a spectator to walk from his seat to the elevated's steps.

Once Babe Ruth had established his Yankees as *the* premier drawing card, Ruppert and his partner, Cap Huston, headed to the Bronx. The site in Melrose appealed to them as did the price, $675,000.

While Ruth continued to outslug McGraw's Giants, workmen began transforming the Melrose meadow into a steel sports palace. Departing from normal nomenclature, Ruppert chose not to use the traditional names—Field, as in Ebbets, Grounds, as in Polo—for his Yankees. Rather it would be stadium and would become North America's first baseball arena to be called a stadium.

Total cost of construction was $2.5 million in contrast to the $100 million it cost to refurbish the Stadium in 1974-75.

The Yankees played their last game at the Polo Grounds in 1922—against the Giants, no less, in the World Series.

If it was any solace to McGraw—which it was—his *Jints* won the Series, the second his club had won against the now-truly-hated Yanks. But it was of short comfort to Stoneham, McGraw & Co.

As they once watched the IRT's Jerome Avenue Line take shape across the water, now the Giants' general staff could hardly help notice the grandiose ball park taking shape in full view of Coogan's Bluff.

Ruppert couldn't help contain his enthusiasm—nor his disdain for his rivals—when he uttered the deathless line: "Yankee Stadium was a mistake; not *my* mistake, but the New York Giants'!"

And *that* may be an understatement.

But it hardly would be overstating the case to call the Stadium—as millions already have—"The House That Ruth Built."

Even McGraw had to admit that.

It also was the house that the subway built; and on opening day, April 18, 1923, thousands poured through the IRT turnstiles and into the spanking, new grandstands. The official crowd was listed at 70,000-plus but more than 20,000 fans never got into the place because the Stadium already was bulging at capacity.

Meanwhile, the subway had brought new housing to Melrose. Overlooking the centerfield scoreboard were sets of six-story elevator-apartments where farmland used to be and, as an extra-added attraction, apartment-dwellers could watch games—binoculars recommended—from their rooftops in that pre-tv era.

Once the Melrose-Yankee Stadium community grew by the thousands, transit-planners took notice, particularly those affiliated with the City's new Independent Line which already had constructed the Eighth Avenue subway in Manhattan.

The city's IND Line made its debut in September 1932. It conveniently had a stop at 155th Street, within walking distance of the Polo Grounds; which was nice for Giants fans but of no help to the Yankee faithful; unless they were inclined to hike across the bridge to the Bronx.

When the A Line, (IND) proved a success, running express trains from Downtown Manhattan (Chambers Street) to Inwood (207th Street), IND planners pushed for expansion and got what they wanted.

The result was of infinite benefit to the Yankees. Leaving the main (A) line at 145th Street station in Manhattan, the new Bronx extension ran via 155th Street, and then through a Harlem River tunnel and 161st Street station adjoining Yankee Stadium.

Thus, the Bronx Bombers benefited from both the Jerome Avenue subway-el and the new IND terminal at 205th Street, just short of Bronx Park.

Long before the Stadium ever was conceived, an elevated line serviced Brooklyn's professional baseball team, the Dodgers.

Located at Fourth Avenue and Third Street between South Brooklyn and Prospect Park, Washington Park was home to the Dodgers from 1898 through 1912.

The Fifth Avenue Elevated Line, which operated from Fulton Street (Downtown) to 65th Street (Bay Ridge), had a station at Third Street, just a block from the ball park.

Washington Park was dwarfed in size compared to its Manhattan rivals. At best, it could hold 14,000—and often was filled to capacity—but that wasn't enough to satisfy owner Charles Hercules Ebbets.

A George Steinbrenner of an earlier era, Ebbets was given to curious maneuvers. In 1899 he was the first to create a Ladies Day but then cancelled the experiment because men at Washington Park complained that the ladies gabbed throughout the contest and allowed their offspring to further distract the male fans by running around the grandstand.

The grandstands were made of wood and that, too, bothered Ebbets, who realized that Brooklyn deserved a better ball field than its antideluvian specimen.

Where to build it was the question.

One of Ebbets' prime considerations was—you guessed it!—mass transit. Already, the Brighton Line had become electrified, running South from Fulton Street alongside Franklin Avenue.

Ebbets also had a grasp of the original IRT subway's success and learned that August Belmont and the IRT high command were studying long-range expansion of the line into Brooklyn.

When Ebbets discerned that an IRT extension to New Lots Avenue in East New York would run under Eastern Parkway, he decided to buy land nearby and build his new stadium as close to the subway as possible.

His priority was relatively uninhabited land—similar to Yankee Stadium—which could be obtained at a low price.

The answer was Pigtown.

Located in what now is Crown Heights, Pigtown was a ramshackle area near Montgomery Place and Bedford Avenue. It was sprinkled with chicken coops, pigpens and hovels made of wood. (Another Pigtown was on the site of the current Lincoln Terrace Park.) Ebbets chose the Bedford Avenue site but wanted no one but his closest associates to know about his plan.

The Yankees and the Bronx

Here's what River Avenue in the Bronx looked like in 1913 before the coming of the Jerome Avenue el and Yankee Stadium.

A view of the then modern-looking 161st Station of the Jerome Avenue line in 1924, a year after Yankee Stadium had opened.

William Brennan

It was April of 1963, and a new winning season was dawning for the Yankees. Trains like these would spend the summer conveying passengers down into the tunnel on their way back to their homes.

Fearful that others might exploit the area, Ebbets purchased lots, piece-by-piece, until he was satisfied that he had enough for an expansive stadium.

He was equally satisfied to learn that that the Interborough Rapid Transit had begun excavating along Eastern Parkway, paving the way for the New Lots—as well as Flatbush Avenue—Line.

By the time the subway began operating, Ebbets Field was open for business in an area bounded by McKeever Place, Montgomery Street, Bedford Avenue and Sullivan Place. Pigtown was gone and not one, but several subways would be available to transport Ebbets' patrons.

In addition to the Franklin Avenue IRT station on Eastern Parkway, the ball park—which opened its doors in 1913—would also benefit from vast improvements contemplated by the Brooklyn Rapid Transit not far from the grandstand's shadows.

While a part of Ebbets foresight focused on the IRT's arrival in the neighborhood of his projected stadium, another periscope couldn't fail to ignore expansion of the Brighton Line just to the west of Pigtown.

Switching to electricity from steam at the close of the 19th Century, the BRT began expanding all its significant holdings, the most important of which was the Brighton Line.

With a connection from the Fulton Street elevated at Franklin Avenue, the Brighton Line then headed south through Bedford Stuyvesant (Dean Street station, Park Place station) and Crown Heights, beginning its descent from elevated line to ground level at Eastern Parkway (not a station), and downhill toward Consumer's Park station to the immediate west of Pigtown.

Ebbets understood that fans could easily reach his proposed ball park site by exiting Consumers Park station and walking east along Montgomery Street which would adjoin his stadium.

As an alternative for fans coming from Coney Island and other parts south, the Brighton Line also stopped at Prospect Park station, also within easy walking distance to Pigtown and, in years later, to Ebbets Field.

Big Time Charlie finally obtained all his necessary four-and-a-half acres—for a total of $100,000—and secured his architects and designers for what he expected to be a palatial ball park.

If in its final form, Washington Park could hold 16,000 fans, Ebbets deemed that his new diamond would welcome at least 8,000 more spectators in a steel-and-concrete structure unlike few in America—but patterned after one which had opened in Philadelphia for the Athletics in 1909.

Ebbets wasn't afraid to spend. He hired prominent Brooklyn architect Clarence Van Buskirk to design the stadium with a capacity of 24,000. Van Buskirk stressed elegance in the form of a distinctive rotunda through which most fans would enter.

The architect chose Italian marble for the floors with a distinctive baseball centerpiece—crossed bats. Climbing almost 30 feet, the domed ceiling held a large chandelier with a dozen globes shaped in the form of an official National League baseball. They, in turn, were supported by twelve supports in the form of bats.

Total cost of construction was $650,000.

Because of acreage limitations, Ebbets Field took on a bandbox aura—297 feet to the left field foul line and 315 to right field.

In terms of transportation improvements, Ebbets' timing was impeccable. When Ebbets Field opened on April 9, 1913, both the IRT to the north and BRT to the west were either in place—or soon to be in place—with major improvements in store.

Eventually, the BRT—later the BMT as in Brooklyn, Manhattan Transit—redesigned the entire Prospect Park station, which heretofore was all outdoors with a trolley loop connecting the streetcars to the station.

By the end of World War I, Prospect Park had become the station of choice for Ebbets Field-bound passengers and would continue to be so, although many fans would eventually connect to the ball park from the IRT Line under Eastern Parkway starting in August 1920.

The subways—and Ebbets Field—contributed to the demise of Pigtown and the total revitalization of the neighborhood which, from Eastern Parkway south to Empire Boulevard, became known as Crown Heights.

Six-story, elevator apartment houses emerged immediately beyond the right field scoreboard along Bedford Avenue. From Bedford Avenue east to Kingston Avenue and from Eastern Parkway to Empire Boulevard, the neighborhood grew into an upper-middle class collection of stately one and two-family homes, most of which had easy access to the IRT or BMT and a number of connecting trolley lines.

Ebbets Field remained the most beloved of the major league ball parks until the Dodgers moved to Los Angeles in 1958.

Four years later, a New York lawyer named William Alfred Shea organized a group which obtained a new Big Apple baseball franchise, the Mets, which would temporarily play home games at the Polo Grounds until a suitable park could be erected at a new site.

Shea and his associates had a difficult equation to solve; the new stadium would have to be on available land but also in proximity to rapid transit. The land they selected was near the Flushing Meadow site of the 1939-40 World's Fair, which had been served by the IND, BMT and IRT lines.

But by the early 1960s only the IRT's Flushing-Times Square route serviced the somewhat barren community. Nevertheless, there *was* a significant station available—Willets Point Boulevard—and eventually it proved a part of the equation.

Willets Point Boulevard station originally opened on May 14, 1927. Shea Stadium was completed in 1964, when the next New York World's Fair made its debut. All stations on the line were repainted

To this day, the IRT Flushing Line remains *the* way to go to see the Mets play their home games.

POSTSCRIPT:
About Dexter Park

Although it never could boast of having a major league team as a tenant, Dexter Park—on the Brooklyn-Queens border—was as popular a stadium, in its own miniscule way, as Ebbets Field, Yankee Stadium and the Polo Grounds.

Home to the Brooklyn Bushwicks—actually just about *everyone* simply called them "The Bushwicks"—Dexter Park was never directly linked with a subway line *per se*, but it was so intrinsically intertwined with a major elevated line that we thought it worth mentioning here.

When conceived in the latter part of the 19th Century, Dexter Park sat in an uninhabited section of what later would be Cypress Hills and Woodhaven.

It began as something of a rural resort, replete with a merry-go-round, hotel and other amusement attractions that included a picnic area and dance hall. Dexter Park, then, had no formal baseball connections and there would be none until a Hungarian immigrant named Max Rosner organized a semi-pro team in 1913.

Five years later Rosner moved his Bushwicks to Dexter Park for very sound transportation reasons.

Until 1917, the Broadway Brooklyn elevated line had terminated at a station located on the corner of Crescent Street and Jamaica Avenue. Operated by the BRT, the Broadway Line was extended eastward to Jamaica in 1917 with a brand, new stop at Elderts Lane, directly across the el tracks from Dexter Park.

Rosner now had a convenient means for his fans to reach the ball park; so convenient, in fact, that capacity crowds became the norm. In response, Rosner rebuilt Dexter Park in 1922, adding a concrete and steel grandstand that made it the envy of every semi-pro stadium in America.

After the BMT succeeded the BRT, service along the Broadway-Jamaica Line was embellished with 67-foot Standard rolling stock, by far the best on any rapid transit system in the world at the time. Thus, one could get to Dexter Park quickly, comfortably and efficiently for only a nickel.

The Broadway Brooklyn el is still operating to Jamaica but the Bushwicks are long gone. They folded in 1951 and Dexter Park was razed five years later!

One Man's Memories of What It Was Like To Go to the Ball Parks

The beauty of being a poor kid who also happened to be a baseball fan in the late 1930s and early 1940s was that you never needed an automobile to get to the ball parks.

And that included Ebbets Field (Dodgers) in Brooklyn; the Polo Grounds (Giants) in Harlem; Yankee Stadium (Yankees) in the South Bronx; and the best semi-pro field in the entire city, Dexter Park (Bushwicks), situated right on the Queens-Brooklyn border of Woodhaven-Cypress Hills.

Some of the trains—such as the IND A Line—would take you right up to the stadium's doors. In fact, the steps coming down from the Polo Grounds' clubhouse ended just a few yards from the IND's 155th Street station entrance.

Others, like Ebbets Field, were situated a short walk from the stations, but never more than a five-minute stroll, tops.

As a native Brooklynite, I started my baseball rooting career at Ebbets Field, which was situated on Sullivan Place at the very bottom of Crown Heights. The ball park, dating back to 1913, overlooked the Botanic Gardens and Prospect Park to the west and Empire Boulevard (originally Malbone Street), which separated Flatbush from Crown Heights, to the south.

Three distinctly different subway lines converged on the Dodgers' home park. The IRT's New Lots Avenue run operated under Eastern Parkway. To reach the ball park, I'd occasionally get off at Franklin Avenue station and walk down the hill along Franklin to the stadium.

I rarely used that route because (a) I wasn't an IRT fan, and (b) The walk was longer than the others.

Two BMT lines took you a lot closer to the famed Ebbets rotunda. The Franklin Avenue Shuttle had a Botanic Garden stop, while the Brighton Line let you off at Prospect Park express station, which was the one used by most Dodgers fans. Each of the BMT stations was a five-minute walk from the ticket wickets.

It was a fun walk because of the sights and smells that abounded Prospect Park station. The moment I reached the top of the stairs, I inhaled the sweet smells emanating from Bond Bread's huge bakery on Flatbush Avenue. Once I crossed to Empire Boulevard, hot peanut vendors lined the route along with *Brooklyn Eagle* newsboys, hawking copies of the newspaper as well as free scorecards for the day's game.

Ebbets Field's rotunda—at the corner of McKeever Place and Sullivan Place— swallowed the incoming fans, who then purchased their tickets, entered the turnstiles and then climbed the long, concrete ramps to the grandstands and boxes. (A separate bleachers—or pavilion—entrance was around the corner on Bedford Avenue.)

My mother took me to my first Dodgers' game in 1937 when I was five years old. Apart from the game itself—Dodgers vs. Pittsburgh—which I loved—I learned for the first time that hot dogs could be served without being grilled. For some reason, Ebbets Field frankfurters were *boiled,* a technique that I found particularly strange. Since then, however, I became a big fan of boiled hot dogs.

I also liked running up and down the long concrete ramps and watching the numbers changing on the big scoreboard in right field. Brooklyn didn't have a very good team in those days but I really didn't care. The scene in that bandbox of a ball park was so engaging that the score wasn't an issue at that time.

My father was *the* sports fan in the family, and when he escorted me to Ebbets Field, it was an *event*. Dad would wear a jacket and tie and treat a ball game as a high-class social event.

Easily the most memorable moment of my first Ebbets game with Pop came during the traditional seventh-inning stretch. As my father prepared to sit down, there was an unceremonious *plop!* whereupon I noticed that a passing pigeon's droppings had landed square on the left shoulder of dad's jacket.

Naturally, I expected him to be both angry and embarrassed but, instead, a smile curled across his face. "What's so funny?" I inquired.

"Oh," my father replied, "that's a sign of good luck!"

(I've spent the rest of my life waiting for a bird to crap on my shoulder.)

Trips to the Polo Grounds were less frequent since we were not Giants fans and, besides, the horseshoe-shaped stadium not only was in another borough but 'way up in Manhattan's northern tier.

That was the bad news. The good news was the subway ride on the Independent System (IND), the first built by the city after the IRT and BMT were privately operated.

The trip to the Polo Grounds was special. It included one of the longest—and fastest—non-stop runs on the entire system, from 59th to 125th Street, under Central Park West, and then another neat sprint, from 125th to 145th Street under St. Nicholas Avenue.

I started the Polo Grounds jaunt at my

ENDING THE CLICKETY-CLACK

The installation of welded rail through most of the system produced some of the most pleasant runs in the history of the subways. None is smoother than the downhill from 122nd Street (over Broadway) south to the 116th Street Station on the IRT West Side Local. The train comes off the steel-based elevated structure on to concrete-embedded ties installed in 1993. The combination produces a hitherto unattainable glide punctuated by a soft yet lyrical curve just inside the tunnel portal.

home station, Myrtle-Willoughby on the GG, Brooklyn-Queens crosstown line and then changed at the vast, six-track Hoyt-Schermerhorn terminal in Downtown Brooklyn.

The IND cars operating in the years through World War II were part of the R-1 through R-9 rolling stock. They were supposed to be an upgrade on the BMT Standard and, in some ways, were better; but certainly *not* from a train buff's viewpoint.

For while there was a large, front window out of which to peer, it lacked the Standard's special feature; it could not be opened and that was a crusher. On the other hand, the IND's pane of glass was considerably larger than that on its BMT counterpart, which made it easier for more than one person to scout the track ahead.

Easily, the best part of the trek began at High Street station in Brooklyn where the squarish-designed tunnel gave way to the circular tubes that snaked under the East River to the Manhattan side. This was the first opportunity for the A Express to free itself from the twists and turns of Brooklyn

and go full tilt underwater. I considered every trip from High Street to Broadway-Nassau Street station in Manhattan a special thrill.

It all had to do with a *Sub-Mariner* comic book I had read in my very early years. One chapter told about an enemy plot to sabotage the East River subway tunnel and—with vivid drawings—depicted the underwater tunnel being pierced by an explosion, whereupon the subway trains were flooded on the river bed.

The question I posed to myself as the A train began its descent under the river was this: Would the tunnel somehow be damaged, and what would happen if the gallons upon gallons of water crashed through the tunnel while my train was destined for Broadway-Nassau?

If nothing else, it made for a melodramatic ride!

Once in Manhattan, the A took its time about being a *real* express. There were a couple of short dashes—past Spring Street and later, 23rd and 50th Streets—before Columbus Circle; but nothing compared to what would come after 59th Street station.

Designers of the original Eighth Avenue (IND) Subway had a two-tiered arrangement of express and local trains running under Central Park West. Uptown trains ran on the upper level while the Downtown local and express operated below.

This made for most interesting train-watching since we were accustomed to four-track operation on one level where expresses and locals plied the same route rather than a pair of tracks atop the other.

On my first solo trip to the Polo Grounds, I was enthralled by what seemed to be a never-ending run north from Columbus Circle. By the time we had reached the 72nd Street local stop, the A was up to speed and making no bones about it.

Since IND tracks were laid in concrete—as opposed to dirt and ballast for the IRT and BMT—the decibel count was significantly higher for the A Express. As the Express passed 86 and 96 Street stations, it had created a thunder all its own which, combined with the speed, made it one of the most arresting experiences for any subway fan.

Adding to the kick of it all was the manner in which it changed from two-track express-local to a traditional four-track at 110th Street-Cathedral Parkway, which was situated at the very northerly tip of Central Park.

By the time the A train had burst through 116th Street station, it was time for the motorman to hit the brakes, and we glided into 125th Street; myself sensing that the Express was as exhausted by the 66-block race as I was having endured it.

At 145th Street, it was necessary to detrain and change to the Bronx-bound D Express which switched to the right at 149th Street and stopped at 155th Street and Eighth Avenue before another underwater trip—this time it was the Harlem River—brought the train to Yankee Stadium.

Originally located at 110th Street and Fifth Avenue, the Polo Grounds moved to 155th Street and Eighth Avenue in 1889. Its odd, horseshoe-shape was much better suited for football than baseball but that hardly detracted from its appeal as a stadium. In fact, the geographic oddity of its layout actually lent an intriguing feel to the Polo Grounds, especially since polo never was played at the transplanted, uptown ball park.

Once the scourge of the National League, the Giants had lost considerable prestige by the time I had made my first trip to their Harlem home. Still, having been accustomed to tiny Ebbets Field, I was awed by the 55,000-seat Polo Grounds once I climbed out of the subway and into the stadium.

For my first trip, I hiked to the upper right field grandstand because of a tip I had gotten from a schoolmate, Harvey Mandel, one of the few Giants' fans in the entire community of Williamsburg.

"Get there before batting practice starts," Mandel urged, "and go to the upper stands. Stay close to the foul line. When Mel Ott comes up for his swings, get ready to go after the balls."

Ott was Mister Giant in those days; a long ball hitter whose trademark was lifting his right leg before taking a swing. And what a swing it was.

What made the Polo Grounds even more attractive to Ott was its short right field. The distance from home plate to the right field foul line was only 257 feet, small potatoes for a slugger like Ott.

Just as Mandel had advised, I arrived in time for batting practice and prepared for some genuine baseball-chasing. And, as billed, Ott stepped up to the plate and began booming the horsehide in my direction.

The first ball that cleared the lower deck landed about six yards in front of me and then bounced up a few rows. At first I had the feel that it had been shot out of a cannon and immediately regretted that Harvey neglected to advise me to bring a baseball glove along.

Not every one of Ott's clouts reached the upper deck but enough of them did to convince me that I could wind up with a souvenir ball if I played my angles right.

Unfortunately, I never quite landed the Official National League Baseball. Whenever the slugger put one in my direction, my first concern was my life; so I ducked until the ball landed and then started following its bounce. But by that time, other kids braver than I had already been on its trail and snagged the sphere.

Of all my subway trips to the Polo Grounds, two stand out for sheer enjoyment; one involved a game between the Giants and St. Louis Cardinals, and the other, a World Series match against the Yankees.

Following the calamitous 1941 World Series Mickey Owen blunder on a third strike in the ninth inning that led to the Yanks beating the Dodgers, I was so disgusted with the Bums that I switched allegiance to the Cardinals.

The year 1942 was a super season to be a Cards fan. Stan (The Man) Musial was a sensational rookie, the brothers, Mort and Walker Cooper, comprised a pitcher-catcher battery and such wondrous characters as George (Whitey) Kurowski, Marty (Slats) Marion and Enos (Country) Slaughter patrolled third base, shortstop and center-field, respectively.

I remained a Cardinals' fan through the World War II years, and by 1946, had found a new idol. His name was Vernal—great name!—Jones. He played first base and carried the monicker *Nippy* for reasons I never did discern.

Although I knew little about Nippy Jones, I liked everything about him: the way he hit; the way he patrolled first base; and, most of all; his name, Nippy Jones. Nice. The only other Nippy I ever knew was Norman Birnbaum, kid brother of my neighborhood pal, Gilbert Birnbaum. Nippy Birnbaum never sounded as romantic to me as Nippy Jones.

On a bright, sunny day in late August 1946, I subwayed up to the Polo Grounds to watch a double-header between the Cards and Giants.

St. Louis still was a fun team for which to root. Musial and Slaughter still were around not to mention some awfully good pitchers—and Nippy Jones, my newest hero.

If ever one of my idols justified the adoration, it was first baseman Jones facing the Giants. For all I know, it was the best day at the plate he ever had. Singles, doubles, triples were flying everywhere. He must have gone five-for-six in the opener, won easily by the Cards.

For an encore, remarkably, Jones was just as good, and by the time the second game had ended, Jones had gone something like ten-for-twelve and St. Louis emerged with two resounding victories.

My happiness was doubled in value as I headed for the 155th Street subway station. Once the players had gone into the respective clubhouses in deepest center-field, fans were allowed on the field to exit via the Eighth Avenue side of the ball park.

Savoring every moment, I took my sweet time, enjoying the post-game *ambience* and finally arrived out on Eighth Avenue, where the clubhouse steps and the subway entrance meet.

A rather large crowd had gathered around the two—one for the home team the other for the visitors—long staircases that led from the clubhouse to the street.

One by one, players began drifting out and the fans, of course, clamored for autographs. I wasn't sure I wanted to hang out because of the long ride back to Brooklyn, but I decided to stick around for a few minutes—and then it happened.

A tall man with jet black hair—still wet

from the showers—stepped out of the Cardinals' side and began down the steps. At first I did a double-take. I couldn't believe my eyes but there was my hero, Nippy Jones, heading right in my direction. I quickly grabbed my scorecard and positioned myself at the bottom rung.

Jones already had been signing autographs and I couldn't help notice that he wore a broad smile and was as handsome as my favorite actor of the time, Robert Preston. At last it was my turn. Nippy graciously signed for me and I believe some words blurted out of my mouth, but I can't remember what they were. I was too much in awe at that moment.

I don't remember much about the ride home other than the fact that it seemed to take no time at all. I had spent just about every second thinking about the wonderful ball game Nippy Jones had played, and then the autograph he had given me.

Traveling to Yankee Stadium was more of a hassle. Even though it was just across the East River from the Polo Grounds, it seemed far, far away. That feeling stemmed from the fact that the Yanks always seemed to be winning World Series and gave the impression of coming from Superman's planet Krypton. And, let's face it, the Bronx *is* far from Brooklyn.

A trip to the Stadium usually was unpleasant because we always rooted *against* the Yankees and they always won. But the redeeming aspect of the excursion was that it would provide one of the few opportunities to ride what I considered the quaintest of our three subway lines, the IRT, known formally as the Interborough Rapid Transit.

Everything about the IRT was outlandish to me. To begin with, its subway cars were conspicuously thinner than

those on the other two lines, and the tunnels also had a smaller look. In the late 1930s, when the IRT still was privately-operated, its standard car was called the Low-V—as in Low Voltage—and dated back to 1916.

The Low-V was idiosyncratic in several ways. For one thing, its motors groaned considerably louder than those on the IND or BMT. When a Low-V approached you had the distinct impression you were standing outside an *abbatoir.* At times, it was almost painful to be assailed by the noise.

It had three doors which, unlike other cars, slid from side to side instead of meeting at the middle. A huge hunk of rubber covered the end of the door, making it very easy for one to keep it from completely closing should you want to hold it open for an oncoming passenger.

For front window-viewing purposes, the Low-V was a treat because even though the window didn't open, there was a secondary viewing position on the far left side of the platform, which meant that at least four train buffs could enjoy the view.

When embarking for Yankee Stadium, our connecting station was Broadway-Nassau, where we changed from the IND A train to the Jerome-Lexington Avenue IRT Express. Like its West Side counterpart, the Lex provided several good runs—such as 14th to 42nd Streets; 42nd to 86th; and 86th to 125th—but none as lengthy as the Eighth Avenue's Columbus Circle-125th Street gallop.

The beauty part of any trip to Yankee Stadium came at the very end. Just before reaching the elevated 161st Street station, the Express negotiates a long right-handed curve out of the tunnel, passing directly behind the outfield wall.

Ever since the Stadium was completed in 1923, the elevated line has been part of the woof and warp of the ball park's landscape, and remains so until this day.

Easily the most gratifying subway trip from Brooklyn to the Stadium took place in 1962. The Yankees were playing the San Francisco Giants in the World Series, and I had been working for the *New York Journal-American* newspaper at the time. Thanks to my connections, I secured a pair for Game 4 on a magnificent Autumn afternoon.

There was only one problem. That evening the most holy of all Jewish Holidays, *Yom Kippur*, would begin with the sacred *Kol Nidre* services. It was a ritual that we would never miss—ever!—and certainly we wouldn't dare come late to services on this date.

But there was an important baseball game to be played and the IRT got us there with plenty of time. Now, the question was whether the nine innings—Heavy forbid that it would go into extra innings!—would be played fast enough to allow Dad and I to remain for the full nine frames.

What also made the date special was the fact that Dad and I were rooting for the same team for a change. Ben Fischler disliked the Yankees as much as his son and, after many early disagreements which we had had, this mutual rooting interest against the Yanks provided a *camaraderie* which had been missing too often in the earlier years of our relationship.

Everything worked out well. The game itself was a classic of sorts with the Giants playing superbly behind the pitching of Juan Marichal. While the contest was not played at record speed—we did check our watches every few innings—it moved along fast enough for us to feel comfortable staying the entire nine.

Of course none of this would have been possible had there not been two separate subway lines—IRT and IND—next to the Stadium to carry us home.

The Giants won 7-3; we jumped on the IND D Express and made it to Temple Shari Zedek for *Kol Nidre* with time to spare.

When it came to baseball, Dad and I had our most fun on Sunday afternoons when the Dodgers were on the road and we trained out to one of the most pleasant ball parks in America.

That was the home of the (Brooklyn) Bushwicks, known as Dexter Park. It was located shoulder to shoulder with Franklin K. Lane High School on the Brooklyn-Queens border. Cypress Hills was on the Brooklyn side, and Woodhaven was on the Queens side. I believe the county line ran directly through home plate, second base and centerfield.

Of all the stadia in New York City, Dexter Park was the most scenic to reach by rapid transit. The reason being that, from Williamsburg to Cypress Hills-Woodhaven, the entire trip was done *above* ground and on some of the most unique track beds.

I started going to Dexter Park with my dad in the late 1930s and continued making the journey through the end of World War II. For some reason I *always* went with my father; as if it was a family ritual.

The Bushwicks comprised what then was called a "semi-pro" team although today it would be recognized as Double—or even Triple—A minor league ball.

Double-headers were played every Sunday afternoon; usually against teams from the Negro National League or the Negro American League. Such legendary African-American ball clubs as the

COLUMBUS CIRCLE,
A RAILROAD AND THE SUBWAY

One of the most difficult engineering aspects of the first subway built in New York centered on the area where Eighth Avenue, Broadway and 59th Street (Central Park West) converge.

In 1892, the intersection was named Columbus Circle, thanks to a memorial to the explorer which was placed there by natives of Italy residing in the city.

At first the Columbus memorial consisted of a marble rostral column, to which a statue of Columbus was added in 1894.

When the IRT's construction crews began work at 59th Street, extra special care had to be taken so as not to disrupt the statue. That succeeded without mishap.

Once the Columbus Circle station opened for business in 1904, the area rapidly developed. In 1913, a monument was erected at the entrance to Central Park, honoring sailors killed in the Spanish-American War battleship Maine disaster.

By the start of the Roarin' Twenties, night clubs were sprinkled throughout the area.

Still later, the Baltimore and Ohio Railroad established a terminal of sorts directly above the IRT subway station's northern exit.

Since the railroad lacked a Manhattan terminal, it would transfer passengers to streamline buses at 59th Street and carry them directly to its New York station across the Hudson River in New Jersey.

B&O-bound passengers would reach the trains by taking the IRT to Columbus Circle, checking in at the waiting room and eventually boarding the blue buses for the trans-Hudson trip to New Jersey.

Homestead Grays, Kansas City Monarchs, Baltimore Elite Giants and New York Black Yankees were regular visitors to Dexter Park.

Which meant I was fortunate to see Black baseball immortals Jackie Robinson (Kansas City), Roy Campanella (Baltimore) and Josh Gibson (Homestead-Pittsburgh) on a reasonably frequent basis.

In addition there were a number of all-white teams that also had strong followings. One was the Bay Parkways—on which Sandy Koufax later played—the Sanitation Department All-Stars, featuring future major-leaguer Tony Cuccinello and the House of David, a squad which had nothing but bearded ball players.

Dexter Park had a long and colorful history. The Bushwicks began playing there in 1918 and in 1922 the stadium was modernized so that it comprised a roofed, single-decked grandstand. Max Rosner, a Hungarian by birth, was the George Steinbrenner of the Bushwicks. He owned the team for its 38-year life and was responsible for such innovations as night lights which he installed in 1930, eight years before they were inaugurated at Ebbets Field.

Although games also were played on weeknights, my father preferred the Sunday double-bills because it cost only a half-a-buck to get in (a quarter for a kid) and we could spend a half day in the sun.

The subway—or, in this case the elevated line—was the best way to get to Dexter Park. Dad and I would walk a half-block to Myrtle Avenue and then a full block underneath the Myrtle Avenue el to Tompkins Avenue.

One of the oldest elevated lines in New York, the Myrtle route had a charm all its

Jerome Avenue Line

The IRT tracks leading to the el station at 161st Street in the Bronx have been laid and the concrete portal still has a spanking, new look in April 1917. Piping along the center tracks and implements along the side wall suggest that some work still has to be done. Completion of the line would inspire the New York Yankees management to build their new stadium adjacent to the IRT. Notice the rural nature of the surrounding area, which contrasts with the congested nature of the same neighborhood today.

William Brennan

A Woodlawn-bound set of IRT Low-V cars emerge from the same portal 46 years later. Notice the proximity of the apartment houses to the subway and the aforementioned congestion.

The skeleton of the IRT Jerome Avenue el is in place but much work needs to be done. The steelwork begins to cast a pall on this extremely rural Bronx scene. The summer of 1917 was warm enough on this day for a supervisor to be wearing a straw hat.

Landscaping around the IRT's almost pristine Mosholu Parkway station in the Bronx suggests a railroad station rather than a New York City subway stop. Note the modern, concrete el stop; a far cry from earlier el station designs on Third Avenue and Ninth Avenue in Manhattan.

The old and the new in rolling stock, circa May 1966, pass each other at 205th Street in the Bronx.

William Brennan

William Brennan

A set of northbound IRT Low-V cars depart the Bedford Park Boulevard station in the Bronx near Lehman College.

William Brennan

IRT Low Vs occupy center-track stage at Kingsbridge Road in the Bronx, June 1963.

own. Rolling stock dated back to the 19th Century. Cars had open platforms at each end with conductors manning steel gates between each car. When the last car's conductor was ready to flash his "all-clear" signal he pulled on a cord which rang a bell for the conductor straddling the cars ahead of him. This was repeated until the bell rang in the motorman's compartment and another run began.

No less unique were the stations themselves. One had to climb two sets of staircases to reach the changemaker's booth. Like a miniature waiting room on a rural railway, the Myrtle station featured everything from pot-bellied stoves to ancient turnstiles adjoining the change booth. During harsh winters, the stoves generated an amazing amount of heat.

Outdoor platforms were made of wood with steel beams holding up the roof. When trains approached, the entire station seemed to tremble, leading me to wonder when the whole shebang would simply collapse onto the street below. (Of course, this never happened.)

Myrtle's el had a distinct rhythm to it, which was a function of the rail gaps and the train speed, which fluctuated between very slow and languid. Since stations were usually spaced only two blocks apart, it would have been difficult for any subway car to pick up much speed.

The percussive rail sounds almost could be equated with a waltz tempo, *ta-ta-ta-ta...ta-ta-ta-ta,* which increased in tempo as the ancient cars accelerated toward the next station. But after one block's worth of momentum, the motorman was compelled to shut down his controller and begin braking to a stop.

Like the BMT Standard, Myrtle's unique cars had several extra, added attractions for train buffs like me. The open platform between the cars was a treat because it allowed a passenger to stand outside and watch the passing parade on the street below, not to mention fascinating sights through the windows of second-story apartment buildings; not that I ever saw anything *that* interesting.

During the summer—which was when we went to see the Bushwicks—the BMT operated cars with open sides that allowed cool breezes to flow through the cars. Although the window on the front car did not open, the door did. That meant I could actually stand by the door opening—the platform was still ahead—and look out at the tracks before me without *any* encumbrances whatsoever. The fact that the Myrtle line didn't go very fast hardly mattered; in fact, the slow speed actually was a virtue in this case because there was so much to see, and, the slower the train, the more to view.

In any event, our ride on the el took only a few minutes because we got off at Broadway (Brooklyn) junction after previously stopping at Sumner Avenue station. Broadway was a major intersection of two lines. The Myrtle continued east to Metropolitan Avenue at Lutheran Cemetery in Ridgewood, while the BMT Broadway Line had crossed the Williamsburg Bridge from Manhattan's Delancey Street and was proceeding (over Broadway, Brooklyn) to its terminus in Jamaica.

While Myrtle Avenue was a two-track line, the Broadway run included two local tracks on the outside and a single express track in the middle. During the morning, weekday rush-hour, the express ran west to Broad and Wall Streets in Manhattan. In the late afternoon it would reverse itself and run east to Jamaica. However, on Sundays there was no express service, so I had to be content with the long—but very scenic—local ride.

Built in 1908, the Broadway el began its run in the financial district, proceeded to Delancey Street on the Lower East Side and, after crossing the East River, rolled past Williamsburg and Bushwick *en route* to a monstrous meeting of the rails at Eastern Parkway-East New York junction.

An earlier, interesting rail-meeting preceded Eastern Parkway by about a mile. The venerable Lexington Avenue el, which began its run at City Hall (Park Row Station), Manhattan, crossed the Brooklyn Bridge and then proceeded along Myrtle Avenue, was a transit curio.

From Myrtle Avenue in the Clinton Hill section, the Lex switched right on to Grand Avenue and then left on to Lexington where it proceeded east toward the Broadway el.

The meeting of two lines—in this case Broadway and Lexington—invariably arrests the attention of subway fans because it entails intricate track crossovers including a "diamond" where the Lex rails intersperse with the Broadway middle express track.

At sections such as these, the *sound* is the thing. As the train trucks lumber over the crossing, a most pronounced *thunk-thunk-thunk-thunk…thunk-thunk* thunders over Broadway and Lexington as the switch almost defies the train to hold fast to the tracks.

Of course, it does and then proceeds to Eastern Parkway-Broadway junction where the BMT Canarsie Line exits its tunnel portal and climbs above the Broadway in a magnificent knot of steel girders and tracks.

Once past the junction, our Broadway local moves on to East New York above Fulton Street where once Dutch farmhouses dotted the rich terrain. The Dutch heritage is retained by such stations as Van Siclen Avenue and nearby Schenck Street.

When the el reached Crescent Street station, it was staring ahead to Fulton, although the tracks curved sharply to the left toward Cypress Hills. I always found myself fixing a glance at the distinguished looking Hamburg Savings Bank building which sat at the intersection of Crescent and Fulton Streets. The bank caught my eye because as the train screeched around the 90-degree turn, it passed over the building. I figured that if the motorman ever allowed his consist to get out of control, the train would plunge right on top of the bank roof. It made for an exciting turn, anyhow.

Three blocks to the north, the Broadway local executed another 90-degree turn, this time to the right over Jamaica Avenue and Cypress Hills station. To the right was a rather large, private club with a gigantic pool and an equally long slide that deposited swimmers into the water. I longed to go down that slide but was assured by my father that we would not be welcomed in Cypress Hills.

Our trip ended at Elderts Lane station. I fairly well danced down the steps in my anticipation of getting to the ball park. We crossed Jamaica Avenue under the el, along a dirt path to the wooden ticket windows, where dad plunked down his three quarters.

A news hawk sold us a program and then we proceeded to the third base grandstand, although Dexter Park also had open bleachers past first and third base. There also was a handful of bleacher seats in left

Gatecars on the Myrtle and Broadway Els

Many el cars were equipped with trolley poles on their roofs. This one is operating on the Broadway-Brooklyn line at Myrtle Avenue, as viewed from the Myrtle Avenue station platform in 1914. Chambers Street in Manhattan is its destination.

After electrification, coaches that had been hauled by steam engines could operate on their own. Even after stations were modernized, the old el cars were able to adapt. This set of Myrtle avenue el cars is seen on Knickerbocker Avenue in May 1940. (Please don't disturb the lady in the center car, thank you!)

My favorite elevated line, the Myrtle Avenue route, featured a conductor between every car. Among other chores, his job was to pull on the iron levers which opened and closed the gates. Hidden from view is the rope he would pull twice to ring a bell notifying the motorman that his gates were closed and the train could continue its journey. This photo was taken on March 24, 1939, seven days before my seventh birthday, at Washington Avenue station, about two miles from my house.

One of the city's oldest elevated lines, the Myrtle Avenue route featured wood-platformed stations that complemented its wooden cars. This photo at the Vanderbilt Avenue (and Myrtle) station, taken in September 1946, connotes some of the romance of the els.

and center fields, but we always sat in the third base grandstand.

For no particular reason that I can deduce, there was a curious segregation at Dexter Park. Just about all the white people from East New York sat on the first base side while on the third base side, there was a homogenous mix of African-Americans, and whites who had come from areas other than East New York.

Perhaps, this was because the sun shone on the first base side for most of the afternoon while the third base side got the shade after 2 p.m. I never thought twice about our sitting with the black fans. We all got along fine, as well as the home-owners whose backyards faced the ball park. Those residents conveniently built decks which enabled them to comfortably watch the games from above and behind the right field wall.

And speaking of that wall, it contained what I consider the most amusing billboard of any stadium anywhere in the world. In bold letters it read:

DON'T KILL THE UMPIRE—MAYBE IT'S *YOUR* EYES;

SEE GOLDBERG, THE OPTICIAN!

The only ball park billboard roughly equivalent in terms of humor was the Abe Stark Clothing sign at the base of Ebbets Field's right field scoreboard. Reading from left to right, it proclaimed:

GGG HIT SIGN, WIN SUIT ABE STARK 514 PITKIN AVE.

The three Gs was the name of a suit manufacturer and there was no particular humor in that. More amusing was the fact that the billboard measured about 40 feet wide but only about four feet high. With Carl Furillo patrolling right field it was almost impossible for *anyone* to hit the sign with a fly ball. The ball either would

be caught by Furillo—or whoever happened to be playing right field—or hit at least ten feet *above* Abe Stark's sign.

Hence, I know of no ball players who ever won a Three G suit from clothier Abe.

Like the colorful Dodgers' manager Leo (The Lip) Durocher, the Bushwicks featured an equally volatile manager. His name was Joe Press and he became legendary in the semi-pro world, much in the manner that Casey Stengel and Durocher did in the majors.

Press usually was surrounded by a flock of good minor leaguers because owner Max Rosner wouldn't have it any other way. Rosner made a point of signing former major leaguers who were in the twilight of their careers; among them were ex-Giant Jeff Tesreau, former Dodgers favorite Dazzy Vance and Waite Hoyt who pitched for the Yankees and Brooklyn.

My favorite ex-big-leaguer-turned-Bushwicks-star was a native New Yorker named Francis Joseph Nekola. After brief major league stints with the Yankees and Tigers, the left-hander was signed by Rosner and became the most popular Bushwick in the late 1930s.

Apart from the fact that he was above-average in that *milieu* , there were two other reasons for Nekola's popularity. He possessed an arresting wind-up whereby he would kick high and then hide the ball behind his hip; then in one motion the fastball would come down the pike. The Dexter Park faithful just loved Nekola's "hidden-ball trick."

They also were intrigued by his nickname—Bots. Where else in baseball was there a player nicknamed Bots? Nowhere but at Dexter Park.

I saw Nekola go head-to-head with the inimitable Satchel Paige, when the latter

Riding the Jamaica-Myrtle Lines in the 1960s

A BMT Standard at Chambers Street in Manhattan, preparing for a journey to Brooklyn over the Williamsburg Bridge. William Brennan

William Brennan

After the open-ended gate cars were retired from the Myrtle Avenue el, they were succeeded by Q-cars, which were repainted and upgraded. The Qs remained in Myrtle Avenue service until the older portion of the el was razed. This photo was taken at Wyckoff Avenue station, which still is in use.

William Brennan

Crossing the Williamsburg Bridge, heading for Brooklyn, a train of R-27s will be next stopping at Marcy Avenue station, en route to Jamaica.

William Brennan

The Myrtle Avenue Line terminates at Metropolitan Avenue station as it did decades ago. The still-partially rural area was then inhab-
ited by the el's Q-cars, successors to the open-ended rolling stock which dated back to the turn of the century.

starred for Kansas City in the Negro National League before moving up to the Cleveland Indians in 1948 on his 43rd birthday. Bots held his own against Satch in what amounted to a battle of the semi-pro pitching giants.

The subway—el in this case—played a major role in our post-double-header summer Sunday rituals. Following the second game, dad and I would board the Broadway Line and take it back to Myrtle Avenue, where we'd get off on the lower, Broadway Line, platform, and then climb a flight of stairs for the Myrtle el heading to Downtown Brooklyn.

I'd stand at the back end of the platform and peer eastward, down the tracks until the open-ended trains hovered into view. Instead of going straight home, dad and I would remain on the local, bypassing Tompkins Avenue, Nostrand, Franklin, continuing all the way Downtown to Fulton Street. This meant I had the luxury of standing by the open front door as the train moved through Williamsburg Clinton Hill and the Navy Yard district before crossing the long, steel Flatbush Avenue Extension trestle that signaled we were Downtown.

The target of our late, Sunday afternoon jaunt was the Automat, a popular cafeteria run by an outfit called Horn and Hardart. The Automat was renowned for its inexpensive items, such as creamed spinach, mashed potatoes, baked beans (in a glazed, brown bowl with a slice of bacon thrown in) and mashed turnips.

On Fulton Street the Automat was a huge edifice with a large front window and a revolving door in front. Upon entering you were immediately facing a cashier's counter with at least two women behind the ivory table. As quickly as you'd put a dollar bill on the counter, the change-makers would unerringly toss back the correct number of nickels, flawlessly rolled out in abrupt sets of five.

In the Automat, the nickel was king. If you wanted coffee, you went over to the dragon-shaped coffee spouts, put your nickel into the slot and pulled on the gleaming silver handle and the brown liquid poured out of the dragon's mouth.

All manner of food, including baked macaroni in elliptical dishes, was found behind glass compartments, each of which had slots to receive the nickels. Although the Automat was a food chain—and an inexpensive one—the food had a unique quality to it. Hot chocolate—also out of the dragon's mouth—was full-bodied and rich. The creamed spinach was so tasty, even a spinach-hating kid had to love it. And I did!

Instead of taking the Myrtle Avenue el home, dad and I walked along the Fulton Street shopping center, passing such major department stores as Abraham & Straus, Namm's and Frederick Loeser's, which was located diagonally across from the magnificent RKO Albee Theater near DeKalb Avenue.

Loeser's Department Store had a special entrance leading to the IND's GG (Brooklyn-Queens Crosstown) Line that sped directly to our home on Marcy Avenue.

It always was fun to ride the GG from Downtown Brooklyn because the primary subway station in the shopping center was Hoyt-Schermerhorn, which was a massive six-track terminal. Not only did it serve the GG; but also the A Express; as well as a two-station Court Street Shuttle, the HH; which connected Fulton Street with a station at Boerum Place and Court Street.

The Shuttle was part of several grand plans which the IND had devised during the Depression years, but never were realized because of fiscal constraints. The blueprints envisioned additional lines heading south through Brooklyn, and that Court Street would be the first stop South on the line-that-never-happened.

After all the fun of the Broadway and Myrtle rides earlier in the day, the GG trip home was rather prosaic. I peered out of a closed window and heard none of the wonderful track sounds available on either of the els. Completed in 1937, the GG—like most IND lines—had its track embedded in a concrete road bed.

This tended to muffled the *clickety-clack* which was so audible—and delightful to a rhythm-minded youngster—on the Myrtle and Broadway lines. On the other hand, I loved the newness of the GG. In 1939, when I was only seven, it was only two years old.

Station tiles still gleamed in their green, blue or red colors. The platforms had the newness of freshly-poured concrete and the platforms were so long they could handle up to ten cars; something that neither the Myrtle nor Broadway lines could do.

From Hoyt-Schermerhorn, the local stopped at Fulton Street, Clinton-Washington, Classon and Bedford-Nostrand before reaching our home station at Myrtle-Willoughby.

Bedford-Nostrand was another interesting stop because it contained a third—middle—track which never was used. That, too, was to integrate into a super-express line under Bedford Avenue which also was never built. I always had hoped to see some train—any train!—use the middle track but it never happened.

We closed our baseball day climbing the stairs at Myrtle and Marcy, walking the half-block to our house at 582 Marcy.

It was a wonderful day—as most of those baseball Sundays were—and none of it would have been possible without the el, which we called our subway.

The Sixth Avenue El

At some points along the Sixth Avenue el, the stations and tracks were so close to adjacent buildings, they appeared to be attached to them. The photo was taken from the Northbound IRT platform at Park Place in March 1927. Yuban Coffee and Mennen Skin Balm are prominently billboarded under the southbound platform.

At sharp curves—this one is at West Broadway—the el structure snakes around the corners of houses with little space between the brick siding and guard rail.

Looking west on West 53rd Street, we note the contrast between a street without an el and with one. The Sixth Avenue line turned west at West 53rd Street before linking up with the Ninth Avenue el. A southbound local can be seen approaching the 90-degree curve at 53rd Street and Sixth Avenue. In 1927, nobody had dreamed of calling Sixth Avenue the Avenue of the Americas.

A Sixth Avenue el train can be seen taking the curve in Greenwich Village, high above the just-completed Independent Subway. The new subway grates are visible at the bottom center of the photo, a part of the freshly-paved sidewalk along Sixth Avenue, near West 8th Street. You know the future of this el is as gloomy as the streets underneath it.

Nearly two decades after the Times Square digging had begun, The Great White Way had become the world's entertainment center—thanks to the subway. By October 1921, at least one theater can be found on virtually every block.

CHAPTER THREE

GOING TO

The Theater District—and The Garden

Give My Regards To Broadway,
Remember Me To Herald Square;
Tell All The Gang
At Forty-Second Street
That I Will Soon Be There!

Composer-actor-song-and-dance man George M. Cohan wrote the words to "Give My Regards To Broadway" all because of the subway.

"The IRT Subway," as New Yorkers liked to call it.

And *because* the brand-new Interborough Rapid Transit line was *the* reason why New York's theater district was moving uptown from its former home at 34th Street, to one centered at the intersection of Sixth Avenue and Broadway.

To New Yorkers, the crossroads is known as Herald Square because the newspaper, the *New York Herald* was quartered in a two-story, arcaded Italiante structure on 35th Street. Horace (Go West Young Man) Greeley was its editor, explaining

why a section of Herald Square is named Greeley Square!

Before the trains came, Herald Square was of no particular consequence since the city's center, prior to the Civil War, was located farther south, toward City Hall, or, as New Yorkers like to say, Downtown.

In the immediate post-Civil War years, Manhattan's theater district was centered around 14th Street where such "in" places as Tony Pastor's concert saloon packed in the entertainment seekers.

But Manhattan was growing in a northerly direction and the transit interests followed.

A major thrust northward was initiated by the Metropolitan Elevated Railway Company (a.k.a. Gilbert Elevated Railway) which began construction of the Sixth Avenue Line, starting downtown at Morris Street and moving uptown to 58th Street.

In June 1878, the Sixth Avenue el was open for business—and so were land speculators—not to mention entertainment

"Give My Regards to Broadway" (Little Johnny Jones), words and music George M. Cohan, F.A. Mills, © 1904

moguls. Since the brand-new means of rapid transit had a station serving Herald Square, theater-owners were enticed to build new vaudeville and minstrel houses within walking distance of the el.

The el's magnetism was apparent in many ways.

For starters, it looked good, very good.

Rolling stock had the *imprimatur* of major railroads. Expensive woods were used on the insides of rolling stock. The trains not only featured carpets, chandeliers and a two-tone green paint job but also ran reasonably on time.

In short, the el became the way to travel in Manhattan, uptown or downtown. And it certainly was a terrific mode of travel for one who wanted to see the plays and musicals of that epoch.

Even before the Sixth Avenue el had become electrified late in the 19th Century, Herald Square had become the Big Apple's new theater district and home to the Manhattan Opera House, McAlpin Hotel, Herald Square Hotel, not to mention innumerable restaurants and dance halls and theaters in which the likes of George M. Cohan would perform.

There was nothing in the world quite like the corner where Broadway met 34th Street and Sixth Avenue.

At least not for a while.

Or, to put it more succinctly—and accurately—not until New York's first subway was built just after the turn of the century.

As originally laid out by August Belmont, his chief engineer and others in the Interborough Rapid Transit general staff, the IRT's original line would begin at City Hall, proceed north to Grand Central Terminal, then turn left (west) under 42nd Street until it turned right (north) at Times Square. From there it tunneled north under Broadway.

During the era when Herald Square held forth as the song-and-dance center of the city, Times Square wasn't even Times Square.

Originally it had been known as Long Acre Square, a surprisingly busy part of town in the pre-automobile era because William H. Vanderbilt's American Horse Exchange was located there, among other businesses.

Another prominent family was John Jacob Astor's, some of whom purchased acreage in the Times Square area between 1830 and the years immediately preceding the Civil War.

While Herald Square flourished as a theatrical center, Long Acre Square was transformed into a society family's paradise. As William R. Taylor noted in *The Encyclopedia of New York City,* "The Astor Family built a neighborhood there that remained exclusive until the 1890s."[5]

Exclusivity ended when construction on the first IRT subway began. So ended the centrality of theater life downtown.

Taylor: "The area surrounding Union Square was given over to dime museums, film studios and movie theaters."

Likewise, as Cohan noted in his evergreen, "Give My Regards To Broadway"—composed in 1904 when the IRT subway premiered—Herald Square was about to become *passé.* Forty-second Street was about to be "in." Which explains what he meant by, "Tell all the gang at Forty-Second Street that I will soon be *there!*"

And the subway did it.

Anticipating the opening of the new line, theater-owners and builders entered an unprecedented era of construction even as the streets were being ripped open to construct the IRT tunnel.

For example:

* REPUBLIC THEATER—207 West 42nd Street, 1900.

* NEW AMSTERDAM THEATER—214 West 42nd Street, 1903.

* HUDSON THEATER—139 West 44th Street, 1903.

* LYRIC THEATER—213 West 42nd Street, 1903.

* LYCEUM THEATER—149 West 45th Street, 1904.

* LIBERTY THEATER—234 West 42nd Street, 1904.

* WALLACK'S THEATER—254 West 42nd Street, 1904.

Arguably, the best theatrical exploitation of the new electrified subway and el lines was completed as the new IRT put the finishing touches on its tilework and mosaics.

Along Sixth Avenue, from 43rd to 44th Streets, the world's largest legitimate theater, the Hippodrome, was being built under the shadow of the el and a two-minute walk to the IRT.

(A reproduction of a Hippodrome picture postcard can be found on page 476.)

Not one, but two rapid transit lines would serve this monster entertainment complex which would seat up to 5,200 patrons of the arts.

A huge sign over the front entrance proclaimed, "THE GREATEST SHOW ON EARTH" when the circus was in town, but the Hippodrome ran the entertainment gamut, from plays to aqua extravaganzas.

Historian Lawrence Ritter called it one of the city's best-known entertainment centers.

"The great stage was 200 feet wide," noted Ritter in his book, *East Side, West Side,* *"and 110 feet deep, including a semicircular 'apron' that extended 60 feet into the orchestra.*

"Under the stage, on various levels, were storage areas large enough for chariots and hundreds of costumes; dressing rooms for human performers and stables for horses, lions, tigers and elephants; a labyrinth of warrens and passageways for use by busy stagehands, excited animals and anxious performers; and a complex of water tanks and hydraulic pumps capable of producing gushing fountains or creating flowing rivers or placid lakes.

"For the year 1905, it was heavy stuff."[6]

So was the new subway—*and* Times Square.

The Astor's erstwhile Long Acre Square silk stocking district had given way to the Great White Way, as Times Square became known.

Even the newspaper industry followed the subway.

Once located in a cluster of buildings across from City Hall at Park Row, the journalistic junction also headed uptown.

The *New York Times* built a skyscraper on the corner of 42nd Street- 43rd Street at the intersection of Broadway and Seventh Avenue. And it was directly above the subway station.

Long Acre Square was no more; Times Square, it was—and is!

Vocalists soon were touting the subway in song. Maude Raymond made a hit out of *The Subway Glide* while May Yohe followed with another winner in *Down In The Subway.* (See pages 477 and 479 for reproductions of the original songsheets.)

Publisher William Randolph Hearst thought enough of *Down In The Subway* that his two newspapers, *The New York American* and *New York Journal* distributed the sheet music in separate music supplements to the papers on Sunday,

March 5, 1905 when the IRT was only five months old.

Before the IRT had reached its ninth birthday—and clearly was a five-star hit—one of the most famous theaters was to be built three blocks from its 50th Street station.

Founded by show business impresario Martin Beck, the Palace Theater lifted the curtain on its first vaudeville show in 1913 and soon became known as the show business Taj Mahal for such legendary performers as Burns and Allen, Smith and Dale, Jimmy Durante and Eddie Cantor, to name just a few.

If you played the Palace, you had reached the apex of vaudeville, which remained a leading form of entertainment until it gave way to movies that not only talked but played music, as well.

Tin Pan Alley—the music publishers and composers part of town—also followed the underground tracks. During the late 19th century, Tin Pan Alley was concentrated at 14th Street and Broadway.

The music business, quite naturally, followed the theater people, and as musicals moved into new Times Square theaters such as the New Amsterdam and Hippodrome, Tin Pan Alley shifted its headquarters to 42nd Street and later, the Brill Building, which was erected at Broadway and 49th Street in 1931.

Perhaps the definitive example of the subway's pull on theater people can be shown in terms of the Lambs Club, one of the earliest organizations for theater people.

Before the subway was built, the Lambs headquarters was at 34 West 26th Street. But with the northward theater movement, and the IRT construction, the Lambs went along for the ride.

Noted architect Stanford White designed a new clubhouse at 134 West 44th Street, just off Times Square. It opened just three months after the IRT made its debut.

So successful was the original IRT that it became evident to citizens and politicians alike that more would have to be built as quickly as possible—and to as many different locations heretofore untouched by the tunnels.

What became known as the Dual Contracts provided for an enormous boom in subway construction; some of which further affected—in a positive way—theater interests as well as the sporting fraternity.

The IRT's original line was deemed insufficient so an extension was blueprinted for the East Side whereby the line which turned west at Grand Central Station would be extended north under Lexington Avenue and reach into the Bronx.

Likewise, the west side portion under Broadway would also be extended. This time the tracks would head south from Times Square and continue downtown under Seventh Avenue before eventually tunneling to Brooklyn.

What's more, another subway would parallel the IRT in Times Square; only it would be operated by the BRT, later to be known as the BMT.

The Dual (IRT, BRT) Contracts led to massive underground construction from 1914 through 1923 including a BRT line which was dug under Broadway and ran south to Whitehall Street-South Ferry at the tip of Manhattan and north to 57th Street. From there it tunneled under Central Park South (59th Street) to Fifth Avenue, Lexington Avenue and terminated at Queensboro Plaza.

In terms of its significance to the theater district, the BRT's Broadway Line had major stops at Times Square (express-local), 49th Street (local) and 57th Street (express).

While its opening didn't have the importance of the original IRT subway debut in 1904, the official launching of the BRT Broadway Line on January 5, 1918 had the trappings of a major civic event.

Officials from the Broadway Association as well as the Public Service Commission and Brooklyn Rapid Transit traveled in a special BRT train which ran from Times Square to Rector Street in less than eighteen minutes!

The BRT heralded the success of its latest venture with bold newspaper advertisements:

NEW SUBWAY IN BROADWAY— THROUGH THE HEART OF BUSINESS, COMMERCIAL AND THEATER DISTRICTS.

Broadway's theatrical empires never had it so good, transit-wise. By the time the BRT's newest line was fully functional, the Great White Way not only featured two, four-track (express-local) subway lines operating through Times Square but also the older—but still dependable—Ninth Avenue and Sixth Avenue elevated lines within easy walking distance of the theaters. (Plus, the Second and Third Avenue els also were in business.)

Theater-building kept pace with the new subways, and when silent movies gave way to "talkies" at the end of the 1920s, transit in and around Times Square never was better for a New Yorker. In addition to the two subways and four elevated lines, a streetcar ran along Broadway, and a brand new subway was being dug under Eighth Avenue with stops at 42nd Street, 49th-50th Streets as well as Columbus Circle (59th Street).

This convinced show business people in the know that Times Square *still* was the place to build—and build they did.

Backed by another colorful Broadway character, Samuel (Roxy) Rothafel, the movie theater that went up in 1927 on 50th Street and Broadway was reverentially described as "the cathedral of the motion picture."

Designed by the architect W.W. Ahlschlager, the theater was immodestly named The Roxy by promoter Rothafel. Ostentatious in the best show biz tradition, The Roxy could seat 6,000 and offered both films as well as stage shows.

The Roxy sat right atop the IRT's 50th Street station and one block from the BMT's 49th Street stop.

Were it possible to outdo the Roxy Theater for attractiveness, Rothafel was the man to orchestrate such a move; and so he did.

Five years later, he moved down the block to 50th Street and Sixth Avenue— right under the el and up a few blocks from the Hippodrome—to preside over the *ultimate* in theaters, Radio City Music Hall.

When completed in December 1932, the Music Hall was America's largest theater and, in the opinion of many, the most opulent.

Rothafel didn't provide as many seats (5,874) as his Roxy, but its art deco designer, Donald Deskey, offered just about everything else, including a huge stage that would feature a soon-to-be legendary dance troupe known as the Rockettes.

The only sports arena to benefit from early subway construction was St. Nicholas Arena, one block away from the IRT's original 66th Street (Broadway) subway station.

Times Square Under Construction

Longacre Square, before the Times Tower was a thought, hardly resembled a "Crossroads of the World" in this 1901 photo. Serious digging has taken place on Seventh Avenue on the right and Broadway on the left for the original IRT subway. The New York Times' Building will replace the old four-story structure in the center.

OPPOSITE PAGE, TOP: One of the most remarkable aspects of New York life always has been the ability of Big Apple residents to adapt to the hectic construction going on around them. This was true in August 1915 at the height of subway work at Times Square (Seventh Avenue and 43rd Street), where the IRT is being extended southward along Seventh Avenue below Times Square. The impact of the subway had brought the entertainment district to Times Square. This is evidenced by such theaters such as the Vitagraph and Loew's New York.

OPPOSITE PAGE, BOTTOM: As digging along Time Square progressed, northeast trolley tracks had to be supported in some places by wooden beams. Once the subway was completed here at the corner of 45th and Broadway, theaters would rise on both sides of Times Square. But when this picture was taken in February of 1903, Manhattan's entertainment center was a dozen blocks south at Herald Square.

In order to build the BRT Broadway subway, Times Square had to be dug up again simultaneously. This view, looking north from 43rd Street, shows the Astor Hotel in the left background and the three-story crane platform in the foreground. The building in the center provided access to the construction site and the bringing down of supplies, along with the removal of earth.

Two years later, work on the BRT Broadway line had extended to the Seventh Avenue-Broadway junction, near 47th Street. Looking south, one can detect the famed Palace (vaudeville) Theater on the left. The Times Tower in the distance had been constructed by now, and Times Square had replaced Longacre Square. On Seventh Avenue (below) are two Hedley "Hobbleskirt" streetcars. They were nicknamed "Broadway Battleships" and ran for eleven years, but were scrapped in 1915 because they could not be converted to a one-man operation. Their fate, like the subway Redbirds, took them to the bottom of the ocean to form reefs.

Madison Square Garden II, designed by Stanford White, still was a relatively new arena when the original IRT made its way north from City Hall in 1901. The Garden would be serviced by the Interborough until it was razed in 1925 and replaced by Garden III at Eighth Avenue between 49th and 50th Streets.

Situated on the northeast corner of 66th Street and Columbus Avenue, St. Nick's actually preceded the subway opening by eight years. It remained a combination ice rink, sports arena in the early part of the 20th Century, but was not big enough to be certified as a major league arena.

That label belonged to Madison Square Garden.

In its original garb, the world's most famous arena was a railroad station near Madison Square Park. At the time there were two different stations—the New York and Harlem at 26th, between Fourth Avenue and Madison Avenue, and the New Haven at 27th, between Fourth and Madison. A roof was put over the latter and it was converted into a showplace for the likes of P.T.

Barnum. The three-story converted train terminal became the focal point for circuses and flower shows. After Barnum moved out—the original railroad station was unheated and not hospitable to animals—entrepeneur Patrick Gilmore did so well with his flower show, he renamed it Gilmore's Garden. Hence the name Garden.

When its usefulness was exhausted, Madison Square Garden II was constructed in 1890 at Madison Avenue, 26th to 27th Streets and Fourth Avenue, now called Park Avenue South.

Designed by Stanford White, the second Garden was impressive in every way, from its Spanish Renaissance architecture to its 13,000-seat sports arena. In addition, it sported a theater, concert hall, restaurants and an arresting 341-foot tower which then made it the second tallest building in New York!

The second Garden flourished through the post-World War I years until it became apparent that obsolescence was creeping in as well as the fact that New York's entertainment kings had long ago followed the subway uptown.

In 1924, the company that held title to Madison Square Garden II—the New York Life Insurance Company—announced that it would replace the arena with a sky-scraper.

Garden officials, led by George Lewis (Tex) Rickard, its top banana and chief spokesman, had to find another site on which to build an arena which would be the sports showplace of America.

By no small coincidence, in that same year, the New York City Board of Transportation took office. The BOT—as distinct from the privately operated IRT and BMT lines—was to preside over the city's own subway, the Independent System.

Well-connected in city politics, the gregarious Rickard discerned that the city's original subway would be called the Eighth Avenue-Central Park West line and would ply a route between Lower Manhattan and Washington Heights.

More important to Rickard, the tracks would be laid only a block from Times Square under Eighth Avenue and ground-breaking would take place early in 1925.

Rickard and his 600 investment pals— he called them "My 600 millionaires"— rounded up six million dollars to build the super-arena. But where?

Convenient transportation was necessary and the subway fare still was a nickel. Rickard wanted his new arena near Times Square on the one hand and with immediate subway access for another.

Upon learning that the new Eighth Avenue subway would have dual entrances at 49th and 50th Streets, he ordered his advisors to check out the site.

As it happened, an old trolley car barn belonging to the 8th and 9th Avenue Railway Company was situated precisely where Rickard & Co. chose to build Madison Square Garden III.

The 600 millionaires swung a deal for the property, and on January 9, 1925 more than 400 demolition workers descended on the onetime house of streetcars and began hammering it to the ground.

On November 28, 1925 Madison Square Garden III opened amid appropriate pomp, circumstance and a professional hockey game between the New York Americans and the Montreal Canadiens.

Meanwhile, construction workers of another sort kept digging away in front of the Garden's Eighth Avenue entrance and, in 1932, the Independent System's first subway opened. It operated right under the Garden and encompassed a route that extended along Manhattan's spine from Chambers Street in the southern tier to 207th Street, Inwood at the northern tip.

The subway entrances and exits were only about 40 steps from the Garden box offices. It doesn't get any better than that, in terms of moving the millions who would pass through the arena in a season.

The last—and in many ways most impressive—subway to serve the Garden as well as the theater district was constructed as the Sixth Avenue elevated line was then being destroyed.

Mayor Fiorello LaGuardia had become an outspoken critic of the elevated lines, and in particular, the ancient Sixth Avenue route. The el was considered an eyesore; not to mention a real estate debit considering

INTERBOROUGH RAPID TRANSIT COMPANY

I·R·T LINES SERVE THE NEW YORK WORLD'S FAIR

The Subway Sun

THE SAFEST RAILROAD IN THE WORLD

VOL. XII No. 22 — THOMAS E. MURRAY ~ Receiver — 1940

With best wishes!

Mr. Receiver

Mr. Mayor

I·R·T

Unification ~ June 12, 1940

that the new Rockefeller Center complex was rising along Sixth Avenue, and its first group of buildings would open in 1939.

Replacing the Sixth Avenue el was the most modern subway the city could build—and the most complicated.

Unlike the original IRT, the Sixth Avenue route had been developed with office buildings and theaters already in place for almost its entire route. In addition, it would cross existing subway lines in many areas and run side by side underground along a portion of Sixth Avenue with the venerable Hudson and Manhattan Railroad, otherwise known as the Hudson Tubes, now PATH.

Despite the innumerable engineering obstacles, the Sixth Avenue subway—costing $59,500,000—opened December 14, 1940, almost a year before the Japanese bombed Pearl Harbor. Connecting Queens and Brooklyn via Manhattan, the Sixth Avenue subway delivered straphangers to the Times Square theater district as well as Radio City Music Hall and the Center

Theater—which featured ice shows among its entertainment package—not to mention Madison Square Garden, which was two blocks east of the IND's 50th Street station on Sixth.

When Madison Square Garden III closed early in 1968, its successor was erected in what, arguably, is the best mass transit site in the world.

Sitting atop Penn Station, MSG IV is flanked by the Seventh Avenue IRT at its east end, the Eighth Avenue IND on the west as well as the Long Island Rail Road and New Jersey Transit commuter trains and Amtrak operating out of Penn Station.

In addition, both the BMT Lines under Broadway as well as the PATH trains have stations only a block away at 32nd Street and Sixth Avenue. Plus, the IRT Flushing Line is a short walk away at Times Square where the Grand Central-Times Square shuttle also operates.

No other arena can make that—transit—statement!

This is Marcy Avenue in Williamsburg—some call it Bedford-Stuyvesant—in Brooklyn. It's my block. You're looking at it—viewing northward—from the corner of Willoughby Avenue. The next block north is Vernon Avenue, a dead-end street on which we played punchball, hide-and-go-seek and other neighborhood games. Our house, 582, is the third brownstone of the white-looking houses to the left, in front of the four-story tenement. The Myrtle Avenue el is in the distance, framing a Marcy Avenue trolley. A drug store—with soda fountain! —is on the far left and Konowitz's grocery on the far right. The subway significance of the picture is this: On March 16, 1931, when this photo was taken, planners were laying out the Brooklyn-Queens Crosstown IND (GG) line. It would run under Marcy Avenue and eliminate the need for a trolley. I watched the subway being built, and directly underneath our house was the Myrtle-Willoughby local station, which opened when I was five years old, six years after the picture was taken.

I'm the one on the right, standing directly above the Myrtle-Willoughby subway station (GG). My other pals are Gil Birnbaum (left) and Howie Sparer. The sinister-looking fellow in the rear was "Anthony," not one of our favorite neighbors, but none of us would dare tell him he couldn't get into the picture,

This view looks north on Marcy Avenue from my house. It's the corner of Marcy and Floyd Streets, also indicating where the GG line eventually would run. On the right, in front of the parked car, a German bakery specialized in Dresdener stollen, a delicacy if ever there was one. In the distance, a pair of Marcy Avenue trolleys are meeting at Flushing Avenue. Once the subway was completed in 1935, the streetcar tracks were removed.

What It Was Like
To Take the Subway
to the Theater District
and Madison Square Garden

At the age of three I became intrigued—as much as a three-year-old *can* be intrigued!—by workmen digging in front of our three-story brownstone located at 582 Marcy Avenue in Brooklyn.

Little did I know it at the time but an outfit called the Board of Transportation had designated my block—*my very own block!*—to be the route of a brand-new subway in Brooklyn.

They were to call it the Brooklyn-Queens Crosstown Line; known alphabetically as the GG Line.

Since my mother and father—as well as grandfather, grandmother and aunt, who also shared our three-floor brownstone—never had a car, we were obliged to take cheap mass transit wherever we had to go.

In 1935, when workers began digging for the GG Line, that meant walking a block to the Myrtle Avenue el that traveled either to Downtown Brooklyn or 'way out to Fresh Pond Road and Metropolitan Avenue in Maspeth, wherever that was!

Or, we could take any one of a half-dozen trolleys. They included the Tompkins Avenue, Nostrand Avenue, Lorimer Street, DeKalb Avenue, Franklin Avenue or Flushing Avenue lines.

But none of them went to Times Square or to Madison Square Garden.

In those antideluvian, pre-GG days, if one wanted to get to a Broadway theater such as the Strand, Capital or Loew's State, it was necessary to ride the el to Broadway-Myrtle station. Then, we had to transfer to a Broadway Brooklyn train that ran over the Williamsburg Bridge to Canal Street and *then* transfer to the BMT Broadway Manhattan line that sped to Times Square.

To say the least, it was a hassle.

To say the most, the trip took about an hour and change.

And *that* was too long by half.

Which explains why we eagerly awaited completion of the Brooklyn-Queens Crosstown local. It would connect in a matter of minutes with the A Express which rolled *directly* to Times Square without further need to change trains.

That, to us, was a transit bonanza.

I was all of five years old when the GG opened for business on July 1, 1937.

How great was that!

Our home station, Myrtle-Willoughby was directly under our house, and the subway grating was on the sidewalk in *front* of our house.

Station entrances—one at Myrtle and Marcy; the other at Marcy and Willoughby Avenue—were a half-block one way and a block-and-a-half the other way from my house.

It was as good as it could get.

And *everything* was brand new.

The green-and-white station tiles could take your eyes out, they were so pretty. This was no accident. Designers had agreed that each platform should be adorned with a specific color surrounding the station's name. And each color would be different from the one at each of the surrounding stations.

You could eat off the concrete station floors, they were so clean.

Each station entrance was adorned with squarish light fixtures; one white, the other light green. At night they looked beautiful.

But best of all were the brand-new trains.

Big, long, electric trains; better than the Lionel set my uncle Ben bought me for my birthday!

The Board of Transportation studied extensively before selecting its IND rolling stock. First, the BOT examined the available cars on the IRT (51-foot-long Low Voltage steel cars) and the BMT (67-foot Standards as well as an articulated, three-section car which was known in the trade as the Triplex; it was 137-feet long).

Out-of-town lines such as Boston and Philadelphia also were inspected for the quality and design of their respective trains.

And when all the checks and balances were completed, the IND came up with a design all its own. *That* would be the car on my line—the R-1.

For a kid like me, it was a bad-news-good-news situation. The bad news was that IND engineers failed to copy the front window style used on the Standards and the Triplex; each of which had manually-operated windows *that opened!*

That meant cool breezes, the ability to pretend to be the motorman while sticking your head *out* of the window and to see and hear all the necessary sights and sounds of the subway train as it rolled over the rail gaps.

But there also was good news.

Unlike either the Standard or Triplex, the R-1's front window was *huge*.

This meant that a little kid, like me, actually could see out of it merely by standing on his toes while holding on to the gold, brass door handle on the right, near the motorman's cabin.

The R-1 window was so big that it easily could be shared with at least one other youngster, two in a pinch. Granted, there

was nothing like the wide-open window breeze that the BMT's dandy cars provided, but wisps of wind would filter through the tiny openings between the door and its frame so, at least, there was a *feel* of wind.

In a sense, the R-1 looked like a trim version of the BMT Standard. It was seven-feet shorter but the same width, with strikingly similar contours as the Triplex. R-1 had four doors on each side of a car—Standard had three—and what was described as a safer door operation than its predecessors.

Light bulbs looked like any others except that the bulb's screw was left-handed which meant that the fixtures were of no interest to bulb-snatchers. After all, what would one do with a left-turning light bulb in a right-turning socket?

The tracks were different from those on the BMT and IRT, where full wood ties ran from one side of the tracks to the other. On the brand-new IND the ties were short and embedded in concrete. Between rails, a concrete drainage trough ran the length of the track, giving the IND a much more modern look.

Because of the trains' newness, virtually no motor noise could be heard, and since the rails were set in concrete, the normal *clickety-clack* of wheels over rail gaps could hardly be heard, if heard at all.

There were two routes for us to take to Manhattan. We could take the GG local that headed south toward its last stop at Smith-9th Street. That required us to change for the Manhattan-bound A Express at Hoyt-Schermerhorn station.

Or we could head in the other direction to Queens-Plaza, change for the Manhattan-bound E train there, and continue on to Times Square from a totally different geographic perspective.

WHEN THE CHAIRMAN
GOT DOWN TO THE RAILS

When he was TA Chairman in the late 1950s, Charles Patterson enjoyed touring the various lines to get a first-hand view of operations. One day when he was in the IRT Union Square Station, Patterson discovered that a train was stuck at the platform. He approached the motorman and asked him about the problem. Not realizing who had approached him, the motorman demanded to know who he was. Patterson explained and then produced his I.D. for good measure. The motorman explained that one of the car motors had broken down and the train had to be uncoupled before removal to the yard. "Tell me where," said the chairman, rolling up his sleeves. The motorman pointed out where the cars had to be uncoupled. Patterson, a veteran railroader, headed down the platform and then down to the tracks. He uncoupled the cars and waved the motorman on his way.

Either way, it was an interesting ride, especially for a five-year-old riding the fresh subway for the first time.

My mother took me on this particular inaugural trip and it was a big one. We were going to the Paramount Theater (on Broadway between 43rd and 44th Streets) to see a movie and a stage show.

The movie was "Buck Benny Rides Again," starring Jack Benny, one of my mom's favorite (radio) comedians, and his sidekick, Andy Divine. The latter had one of the strangest, funniest voices I had ever heard—sort of a cross between the *naying* of a horse and an opera diva reaching C above high C. In any event, I thought Andy Devine was funnier than Benny.

But the movie was secondary.

Our main purpose was to catch the stage show which, among other things, featured Gene Krupa and his Orchestra.

At that time Gene Krupa was the world's most popular big-band drummer, and I just loved drumming, even though I was only five-years-old. The idea of seeing Krupa in action was—for me—beyond all belief.

But it wasn't going to be easy. For one thing, thousands of other New Yorkers were just as awed by Krupa as I was and for another, Benny was at the apex of his popularity, so it was not going to be easy to get in.

I couldn't have cared less.

My thoughts were consumed by riding the new subway that ran directly under our house, and I practically danced down Marcy Avenue toward Myrtle—while my mom lagged behind—enthusiastically heading for the station entrance.

Since we had to cross the Myrtle Avenue trolley car tracks to reach the entrance, I had to wait impatiently for my mother to catch up to me. (I was not allowed to cross a major thoroughfare like Myrtle by myself in those days.)

Mom and I waited for the light to change and then walked across the tracks to the other sidewalk. Mom stopped at William Davis' news stand to pick up our newspaper of choice, *the World-Telegram.* Then, we headed down the steps and into the station.

My mother went up to the black change booth, gave the man behind the bars, a quarter and got five nickels back. "You go under the turnstile," she whispered. "I'll be right behind you."

That didn't sound *kosher* to me, but since the words came out of my mother's mouth, there was no challenging them. And so, for the first time, I cheated on a fare. (At age five, I was still small enough to get away with it!) Once inside the station, I was dazzled by the sparkle and the size.

Unlike the IRT, which, in its original form, only provided for four-car locals, the IND local stations could hold up to eleven cars. In fact, the station platform was two blocks long, extending from Myrtle to Willoughby Avenues under Marcy.

My mother walked me along the platform, past the shiny chewing gum machines—a penny got you a Juicy Fruit or Spearmint—and the big, round glass containing peanuts, salted and without shells.

The train would be coming south from Flushing Avenue station on a direct line. By leaning over the end of the platform—a move my mom didn't like—I could see the lights of the local.

In those days, none of the subways carried the high-beam, automobile-type headlights in use on all of the contemporary cars. As a result, the GG at Flushing Avenue could only be seen faintly until it actually left the station and made its way over the six-block route to Myrtle-Willoughby.

As the R-1 thundered into the station, it still bore the new-car look. The paint job was fresh and no steel dust had accumulated on the frame. Why, it even *smelled* good.

Since we were riding at an off-hour, the car was less than half-full. As soon as the door opened, I made a sharp right turn, hurrying over to the window. As luck would have it, nobody was there.

I grabbed hold of the muscular door handle, pulled up on my toes, and there before me was the black hole of the tunnel.

Meanwhile, the doors had closed and the adventure was ready to begin—in earnest.

The motorman pulled on his controller and, in five seconds, the front car had entered the semi-dark tunnel. Since the next stop was Bedford-Nostrand, the GG had to take a 90-degree curve moving under Lafayette Avenue toward Downtown Brooklyn.

As the wheel flanges, rubbed against the inside of the rails, the friction caused a deafening—and seemingly endless—*screeeeeeeeeeeeeeeech*—that was piercing enough to make me wonder whether the ride was really going to be that much fun.

But the decibel count soon lowered and the local lumbered over a switch, swung right and into Bedford-Nostrand station. The platforms were striking because—unlike the usual local stops—Bedford-Nostrand had a middle "third track" which appeared to be unused. I later learned that an extension to a proposed-but-never-built express line explained the middle track.

From Bedford-Nostrand, the local next stopped at Classon Avenue, which was totally bland and then Clinton-Washington, which had a certain class about it.

Fulton Street followed, after which the GG met its express partner, the A train, at Hoyt-Schermerhorn Street station, which had no less than six tracks. Wow!

The A train already was in the station, awaiting us, so we dashed across the platform and entered; only this time we were two cars from the front. (The GG was running four-car trains then and the A six-car trains.)

I begged my mother to take me up to the front. Very bravely (I thought) we made our way between the cars as the train proceeded to the next stop, Jay Street-Borough Hall.

How exciting! We actually were standing *outside* the cars as the train bobbed and weaved across switches, sharp curves and snaked toward Jay Street. Mom held me tighter than I ever remember her doing, but we successfully negotiated the two crossings and made it to the front car.

Being at the front window of an express as compared to that of a local is about the same difference as sitting in the front row of a Broadway musical rather than the last row of the balcony. This was *special!*

The best runs of the A Train—I would later learn—happen north of 59th Street; nevertheless there are some nifty aspects to the crossing from Brooklyn to Manhattan.

One of the best was the underwater tunnel, linking the High Street-Brooklyn Bridge station in Brooklyn with Broadway-Nassau on the other side. This tube was completed in 1933, when I was a one-year-old. Later I learned it was a tremendous year for the IND, spreading its wings through Manhattan, Brooklyn and Queens.

When the A train entered High Street-Brooklyn Bridge station, everything changed from the front-window-watching cockpit. Previously, the tunnels were squarish and somewhat dull. But as the express entered High Street, the tunnel evolved into a curved tube and the station itself had that roundish—London *Underground*—kind of look.

After rolling out of High Street, the A plunged under the East River—down, down, down—to the river bed. The closeness of the tunnel walls made it all seem a bit claustrophobic, while the sounds of the wheels were all the louder.

Once we hit mid-point between Brooklyn and Manhattan, the express began its upward climb with plenty of momentum to carry it speedily into Broadway-Nassau station. I felt a great sense of accomplishment once the doors opened in Manhattan.

By far the best part of any express run occurs when it passes a local station *and* there happens to be a local stopped there. This is the race track aspect of train-watching. The express is like the horse coming up from the rear and catching the leader down the stretch.

As luck would have it, the first local stop we passed on the uptown run was Spring Street. The A barreled through—at about 40 miles per hour, I would guess—but, alas, there was no local there.

But when we stopped at the next express station, Canal Street, I noticed an amber light at the head of the local platform. That signaled to me that the local could not be far ahead. The questions were: (1) How far ahead? and, (2) Would we be able to catch it?

The A arrived at 14th Street—another express-local stop—and, sure enough, the local signal was amber again; which meant there still was a chance.

Pulling out of 14th Street, the express accelerated smartly and had arrived at top speed by the time the lights of the 23rd Street local stop shone ahead.

I pressed my nose firmly against the window, trying to discern signs of the local. As I peered to the right, I noticed that the local signal now flashed red.

Hot stuff! Our prey could not be far ahead.

And it wasn't.

Just yards from the outskirts of the platform, I could see the four bullseye red signal lights and the big lettering—AA—above the rear window.

The local had just discharged its passengers and had begun pulling out of the station. It couldn't have be moving more than five miles per hour as we pulled up to it and began passing the "enemy's" cars—one, two, three, four, five, six—and finally left it behind us, for the moment at least.

When we arrived at our next stop, 34th Street, the local pulled up right behind us, and the conquest was complete. One more station, 42nd Street, and we were out of there and my day was made!

Mom and I walked from 42nd Street and Eighth Avenue over to 43rd and then east to Broadway. The Paramount Theater's curved marquee stunned me with its size and glitter. But I was even more stunned by the hordes of people curling from the box office along Broadway and around onto 44th Street.

"We're going to have to wait on line," my mom intoned not too happily.

I didn't mind. The mid-winter winds were blowing off the Hudson River and down 44th Street, but a little cold wasn't going to bother me. Times Square was abuzz with people and sights.

A trolley car rolled along Broadway—but it didn't have a trolley pole. I wondered to myself: how could a trolley car not have a trolley pole? Mother explained that in Manhattan—unlike Brooklyn and the Bronx—streetcars take their electric power from an underground source. All the Manhattan trolley tracks also had a center "rail" with a conduit opening in the middle rail, from which the car drew its energy with a plow-type apparatus.

Even after the explanation, I found it hard to figure *how* the car managed to move; it all seemed so magical; so did the galaxy of billboards we faced once the line moved down 44th Street and around to Broadway.

Just getting inside from the cold was accomplishment enough, but the comfort of this amazing theater was secondary to its size.

I had never been in a movie house *that* big. Our local movie theater in Brooklyn, the *Kismet,* was miniscule compared with this palace.

Built in 1926, the Paramount had 3,900 seats, a huge stage and an organ loft where a chap named Dick Liebert emerged between the stage show and film to entertain the new patrons.

It was all so wonderful to me; the organ magically coming out of a wall just in front of the left loges and Liebert energetically pumping away at the console a rendition of Mitchell Parish and Cliff Burwell's "Sweet Lorraine," which, to this day, is one of the sweetest tunes I've ever had the pleasure of hearing.

Liebert played a half-a-dozen songs, which was just enough to get everyone—and I do mean *everyone,* since the theater was packed to the gills—seated. Then, the houselights dimmed and Paramount's "Buck Benny Rides Again" appeared on the screen.

It was as funny as I had hoped—especially Andy Devine—but the treat-of-the-treat was what followed.

First another set of Liebert tunes charmed us, whereupon the curtain opened and a bandstand suddenly emerged from the depths, climbing from somewhere in the bowels of the Paramount, square in front of us.

Krupa was sitting on an upraised platform, *rat-a-tat-tatting* on the drums, bouncing his sticks from the *snare* to the *tom-toms* to the *cymbals,* all in one fell swoop.

The stage show also featured a comedian, dance act and Krupa's singer, but they all faded from memory because I was so fixated on the drummer man and his amazing speed and dexterity.

When Krupa finished his set, I turned to my mother and said with as much emphasis as I could, "Ma, I wanna be a drummer when I grow up!"

She smiled never thinking that her young son one day *would* get paid to play the drums; albeit not as handsomely, nor as well, as Gene Krupa.

Our expedition to Times Square would be the first of endless visits to the legitimate theaters, movie houses and, of course, Madison Square Garden—all for a nickel—all by subway.

My first experience with a stage play—or musical comedy, if you will—was "Let's Face It," in which a young, rising comedian-dancer-singer named Danny Kaye was the star.

Kaye had special meaning to our family because he—like my father—was an East New York boy who went to the same elementary school (P.S. 149) as Dad. In fact my pop would tell me about how Danny Kaye attended P.S. 149 reunions and dad actually *talked* to Danny Kaye!

The thrill of seeing a legitimate show was almost—but not quite—as exciting as the first trip to the Paramount. But this time it was at night, and that in and of itself was special.

Having never before seen a stage play, I was taken aback by "live" theater. Even though there was lots of humor that went clear over my head, I got into the swing of things, laughing along with the audience.

And even though I was as far as possible from being a *connoisseur* of talent, I could tell that Danny Kaye was a very special funnyman. The song-and-dance routine was highlighted by a form of *git-gat-gittle* double-talk that reminded me of the *clickety-clack* sounds of the Myrtle Avenue el.

Times Square's sites were a show unto themselves.

My favorite was an enormous billboard that hung on the side of the Hotel Claridge at Broadway and West 44th Street (Southeast Corner), diagonally across from the Paramount Theater.

Erected in 1941, the billboard featured a man's head with opened lips, through which a large round pipe was inserted. Every three seconds giant smoke rings would be blown out of his mouth.

To his left was a pack of Camel cigarettes. To his right was a slogan that just about everybody in town seemed to be uttering, I'D WALK A MILE FOR A CAMEL.

No less riveting was the Times Tower at Broadway and West 42nd Street (Northwest Corner), which had opened in 1904. A handsome building, the Tower's most intriguing feature was the world's first "moving sign," which began on November 6, 1928 and delivered all the latest news as it was breaking.

There were endless movie houses; Loew's State and Loew's Criterion were across from the Paramount. Farther up Broadway was the Strand, which featured first-run Warner Brothers' films, and past the Strand glowed the Capitol Theater on the Southwest corner of West 51st Street.

In show business terms, the Capitol was famous for more than its lavish appointments. Its historical importance actually was related to the early days of radio. *Major Bowes' Original Amateur Hour,* an audience-in-theater show, was one of radio's most popular. It played the Capitol before locating to its own studio theater.

The theater also made history when I was seven years old. *The Wizard of Oz,* starring Judy Garland, premiered at the Capitol on August 17, 1939. I wasn't there for the first night, but everyone in New York knew that Judy—appearing live on stage with her occasional movie sidekick, Mickey Rooney—sold out the theater for days between showings of *The Wizard.*

For atmospheric reasons, I never liked the Capitol, and my antipathy was rooted in one afternoon subway trip there.

My grandmother, Etel Friedman, who often took care of me when my parents were working, decided to take me to see a film called *The Magnificent Ambersons.* I had gone to lots of movies with Grandma and usually enjoyed the flicks, but this one—to a nine-year-old—was the worst!

It was boring beyond belief; which was bad enough. But, for some reason, the Capitol was not yet air conditioned. Remember, in those pre–World War II days, not every major theater was air cooled.

And it was blazing hot that afternoon. The combination of heat and lousy movie turned me off the Capitol forever. I never returned there to see a movie—with or without Grandma.

Actually, by the time America was immersed in World War II, my parents considered me old enough to travel to Times Square without adult supervision. Usually the subway trips were made on Saturdays with my friends; either Howie Sparer, with whom I traveled the most, Larry Shildkret, Neil Brown or one of the many pals from Vernon Avenue or Public School 54.

Our favorite theater, by far, was the Paramount because it always seemed to have the hottest bands on stage as well as the best comedians and singers. (Frank Sinatra broke records at the Paramount on

NATURAL LIGHT UNDERGROUND

When the original IRT was built, designers arranged for a number of areas along Broadway where open grates would allow sunlight to pour into the tunnels below. This system of natural lighting can still be found on the Upper West Side, among other places. It should be noted that the openings not only allow light to reach the darkness but snow and rain as well.

December 30, 1942.) In addition, Paramount movies always seemed to be my favorites.

Oddly enough, one of my most memorable subway trips to the Paramount turned out to be one of the worst days of my young life.

It began on a Saturday morning when I found a light brown wallet on the street that, remarkably, had a ten-dollar bill inside but no identification page. What's more, the wallet appeared to be brand new.

When Howie and I met in front of my house, I told him about my good fortune.

"Why don't you find out who it belongs to?" Howie demanded.

"How can I?" I shot back. "There's no name in it."

I showed the wallet to Howie, but he didn't appear convinced.

What could I do?

I stashed the wallet in my back pocket, and we headed to the Myrtle-Willoughby station. I generally used the Myrtle Avenue entrance, but every once in a while, we walked over to Willoughby because there was a drug store on the corner of Marcy and Willoughby, run by two elderly ladies.

This was in the era when it was customary for drug stores to have soda fountains. The ladies were aces when it came to making a chocolate ice cream soda, which, to this day, is my favorite drink, non-alcoholic or otherwise.

We'd stop in to see the ladies, fuel-up, then head down to the subway. Because it was so little used, and so eventually was closed, the Willoughby Avenue end of the station retained its newness long after the Myrtle part. In fact, it was *so* different and distant from Myrtle it seemed like another part of our subway world.

Howie and I shared the front window, although he never seemed to enjoy track-watching with my enthusiasm. He couldn't have cared less whether the express ever caught the local, while I regarded the event as the high point of our trip.

Still, it was a fun ride, and on this Saturday, the Paramount featured Tony Pastor's band. Before going out on his own, Pastor had played tenor-saxophone and was also a vocalist with Artie Shaw's greatest orchestra of the late 1930s. Pastor's vocals—very much in the Louis Prima *genre*—exuded joy and gladness. Anytime I listened to Pastor singing that wonderful tune "Rosalie," I felt a lot better about *everything.*

As anticipated, Howie and I were smitten by the matinee. I can't remember the movie, it was that insignificant, ending at about 4 o'clock in the afternoon. We walked out of the theater into the daylight of Times Square, turning left toward the Hotel Astor at 1515 Broadway, one of the oldest and classiest buildings in the entertainment district.

When we reached the corner, I decided to get a hot dog at the orange drink stand under the Camel's smoke ring billboard. I reached to my back (left) pocket for the wallet, but there was nothing but my left buttock where my wallet should have been bulging out.

Panic-stricken, I didn't know whether it was worse losing the new wallet or the ten-dollar bill, which was a *huge* amount of money for a kid at that time.

"We gotta go back to the Paramount," I said as urgently as possible. "Maybe I dropped it when we got up to go out."

I vaguely remembered having a tight squeeze moving past the seats to reach the aisle. Maybe that's when it fell out of my pocket.

So, we went back to the theater and were graciously allowed in by the manager. The movie was on so it wasn't easy to make out where we had been seated but I crawled around a few places, groping with the aid of an usher's flashlight.

Nothing doing.

I was crushed beyond belief and moped my way home, for the first time paying no attention whatever to the A train or the GG for that matter.

The moment I got to our house, I went straight to my room and began thinking. It didn't take long to figure it out. There was a reason why this happened; I shouldn't have kept the wallet in the first place; nor the ten dollar bill. Somebody up there was punishing me for the deed.

From that Tony Pastor day on, I instinctively reach behind to make sure that the wallet is secure in that back, left pocket. It was a ten-dollar lesson worth learning.

Another memorable Times Square subway trip involved the first time I ever took a date by train to a legitimate theater. (A taxicab was out of the question.)

Marilyn Wurtzel was my date of choice; although not what you would call a true "girlfriend."

Second trombone in the Eastern District High School band, Marilyn was an infinitely better looker than she was a musician. She was, as we were apt to say in the lexicon of 1949, Brooklyn, "built like a brick shithouse."

Her breasts, as the Lucky Strike cigarette ad liked to proclaim, were "so round, so firm and so fully-packed," though not necessarily as the ad continued, "so free and easy on the draw."

As first trombone, I sat immediately to Marilyn's left in the band and since my right elbow would thrust out when pulling in the slide for a B-flat, I occasionally had an exceptionally good "feel" for Miss Wurtzel's left boob.

If this ever bothered her, she never let on, and so my motivation for playing John Philip Sousa's delightful march, "On Parade," was even further enhanced.

Not necessarily stunning, Marilyn nevertheless had a certain charm about herself that extended well beyond her bust. The problem was that she was my age and tended to travel—as the girls in our senior class were wont to do—with college guys, not us high schoolers.

That's why I was pleasantly surprised when Marilyn accepted my invitation to see Ethel Merman starring in "Annie Get Your Gun."

Irving Berlin's musical already had been running for three years, so it was easy to get tickets, albeit expensive—for me—even though we'd be way up in the balcony.

But Merman was special. My family loved her because she was a native New Yorker (born in Queens) and a dynamo. She had a powerful voice and was funny in a good-humored sort of way.

To this point in my life, the Marilyn soirée was *the* most important date imaginable and I planned hard for it. First, we'd go to the show and then we'd do something really neat after that; I knew not what.

Naturally, all of this would be done via rapid transit.

There was, however, a major subway difference; Marilyn was not an IND person. Unlike myself, who lived on the outer fringe of "the Burg"—as we liked to call Williamsburg—she was a resident of Ross Street, right in its heart.

No IND station was nearby, but there was the BMT—specifically the Marcy Avenue stop—the first station over the Williamsburg Bridge coming from Manhattan.

This meant that we would walk from Ross Street up to Marcy and then left until we met the elevated line. Marilyn had absolutely no interest in the ride, but it excited me on several counts.

For one thing, I always got a kick out of historic routes, and this definitely was one of them.

Williamsburg was one of Brooklyn's first settlements and later would become a city unto itself until it became part of Brooklyn's incorporation as a metropolis during the late 19th century.

The Williamsburg Bridge, over which we would ride, was a classic built in 1903. And to top it all, the elevated line at Marcy Avenue had a distinction of its own.

Before the bridge had been built, the primary link with Manhattan was a ferry which landed on the Brooklyn side, at the western tip of Broadway. The Broadway elevated line originated at the lip of the East River, and then proceeded east with its next stop being historic Marcy Avenue.

The Broadway Ferry Landing station

The Manhattan Park Row Terminal
of the Brooklyn Els

Not long after its completion, the Brooklyn Bridge became a primary artery for rapid transit. At its zenith, the span carried both trolley and el tracks from Manhattan to Brooklyn. Each end of the bridge housed a massive terminal shed. The views here show the Manhattan side with City Hall hidden behind the depot roof. The Park Row terminal had two levels; the top level, shown here, was the exclusive depot for the Lexington Avenue (Brooklyn) trains after 1940. Only the two center tracks were used for regular service. The lower level served trolley lines which crossed the bridge from Brooklyn.

Inside the shed, we see three platforms and tracks. This design allowed for the separation of arriving and departing passengers. First, the conductors opened gates on the outside platforms to unload, and then proceeded to open gates facing the center platform for loading. Apart from improving the traffic flow, it also prevented passengers from taking a round-trip without paying an additional nickel.

The Lexington Avenue el crossed the Brooklyn Bridge, terminating its run at the vast Park Row-Brooklyn Bridge depot, opposite City Hall. This is a view of the BMT station, looking northeast from the west side of Park Row and south of the Brooklyn Bridge approach. Also in view is the IRT City Hall station. At one time, both the Third Avenue el (upper level) and the Second Avenue el (lower level) used the station. (The photo was taken in 1943.)

opened, as did the Marcy Avenue stop, in August 1889, long before the line was to be electrified. It would continue, with steam operation, all the way to East New York.

I felt a twinge of excitement, climbing the el steps, and was tempted to explain the wonderful background of the Broadway Line to Marilyn, but I sensed that she had no interest in it, any more than she would want to stand with me by the front window.

No matter; there was another aspect to the BMT Standard that made it more comfortable than the other cars: it had some awfully big seats. Designers had created four sets of cross seats measuring 54 inches which could comfortably hold three passengers. And, when it wasn't rush hour, a couple on a date could easily stretch out on the three-seater and feel as if they were in a limousine.

Marilyn and I found such a seat with a wide window view. We were on the right side so it was easy to follow the tracks as our local swerved right, cruising slowly toward the span, providing us with a panoramic view of Greenpoint to the north and Williamsburg Bridge Plaza—which still had a major trolley terminal—directly below. Landmarks, such as Peter Luger's Steak House and the Williamsburg Savings Bank Building on Broadway, could be seen out of the left side.

Soon, the eight-car consist of Standards eased to the left, bringing a full view of the East River to our eyes. I gaped at the huge Domino Sugar refinery complex sitting on the water's edge to our right, as the train sound abruptly changed as we rumbled on to the bridge.

I was only half-enjoying the sights because, after all, this *was* a big date and there was conversation to be made other than to point out that on the Manhattan side, as we entered the tunnel, a magnificent trolley terminal still was in operation under Delancey Street and remained so through 1948, her lack of interest notwithstanding.

At Canal Street we switched to Manhattan's Broadway BMT Line, which carried us to Times Square, from which it was a short walk to the Imperial Theater and "Annie Get Your Gun."

Ethel Merman's performance knocked us both out; particularly her renditions of Irving Berlin's "You Can't Get a Man With a Gun" and "They Say That Falling In Love Is Wonderful."

I was very pleased that Marilyn enjoyed the show, and I wanted very much to follow up with something else that would make her think I was *quite* the guy.

It had to be a nice place to eat since I was in no position to do a night club or even go dancing; although the latter was a distinct possibility, until I discovered that dance lessons at the Arthur Murray studio were 'way too expensive.

Where to go? That was the question.

"Are you hungry?" I asked.

"Definitely," Marilyn replied with no hesitation.

So, we walked to Broadway and then turned right past Jack Dempsey's Restaurant. Like everyone else, we peeked in the windows to see if the Champ was there. Dempsey's and McInnis of Sheepshead Bay, the seafood restaurant, both were tempting, but a bit out of my price range. So, we kept walking until I noticed a big WALGREEN sign.

I remember my mother having taken me to Walgreen's in Times Square. It really was a gigantic drug store but also featured a luncheonette counter as well as booths.

"How about we try this?" I suggested, never thinking that Marilyn would refuse. And why should she? We both came from relatively poor families and I never felt there was anything terribly snobbish about the Wurtzel family.

Marilyn nodded and in we went.

Walgreen's was packed with the after-theater crowd but we found a booth. I ordered a bacon-and-tomato sandwich on toast—with mayo!—and a chocolate ice cream soda.

I have no recollection of what Marilyn ordered because I spent most of the time trying to figure out what kind of future I had with her. We both would soon be graduating. I was going to Brooklyn College and she was going elsewhere. Was this the beginning of the end?

We rode home on the BMT, chatting amiably about Ethyl Merman and school and friends. The conversation was a bit heavy because I completely ignored my favorite subway things.

After descending the steps at Marcy Avenue station, we walked past *Kitzel* (petting) park, a triangular oasis with benches that was notorious in Williamsburg for "hot" sexual adventures during the summer.

But neither the weather nor Marilyn seemed conducive for any *kitzeling* and by the time we reached Ross Street, I got the distinct impression that our date was more of an opportunity for Marilyn to enjoy the talents of Ethel Merman than Stanley I. Fischler.

Her good-night kiss—if you can call it that—confirmed my thinking.

It was my first and last date with Marilyn Wurtzel—but, heck, it cost me only forty cents for transportation!

The subway fare, which had been a nickel since its inception in 1904 climbed to a dime in 1948. Until then, the five-cent ride was one of the world's best transportation bargains because one could travel from Times Square to Coney Island for only a nickel; or from Van Cortlandt Park to Flatbush for the same price.

Of course, there were times when a ride was free, although not exactly *legally* free.

A good example would be the trips my P.S. 54 pal, Larry Shildkret, and I would take to see the hockey games at Madison Square Garden.

During the World War II years, the Rangers—New York's major league hockey club—had a New York farm club called the Rovers.

While the Rangers played home games on Sunday and Wednesday nights, the Rovers specialized in Sunday matinees at 3:30 p.m., preceded by a Metropolitan Hockey League game at 1:30 p.m.

My mother, who had done some volunteer work for the Police Athletic League's 79th Precinct, often would bring home free PAL tickets which Larry and I would use almost every Sunday.

The trick, for us, was to reach the Garden—then on 49th Street and Eighth Avenue—by noon, so that we would be either first, second or third in line when the balcony doors opened at about 12:45.

In this way we were in good position for the "race" up the balcony stairs and had a good chance of getting seats in the front row.

Larry, who lived three blocks away on Hart Street, would ring my doorbell at about 11 a.m., by which time my mom had completed my "hockey lunch," comprising a cream cheese sandwich with grape jelly—or a bologna with lots of mustard on

When Fulton Street Had a Ferry

With the Brooklyn Bridge in the background, the "Rutherford" prepares to leave its downtown Brooklyn slip for its cross-East River trip to Fulton Street in Manhattan. The scene from the edge of Fulton Street, Brooklyn, also reveals the Fulton Ferry elevated structure in this May 1914 scene. Note the passengers lounging on the ferry's deck chairs! Ferry riders knew how to do it in style in those pre-World War I days.

As the "Rutherford" pulls away from its dock, there's a clear view of the ferry's elevated station, which lasted until May 31, 1940, when the city refused to take title.

rye, four black olives and two tangerines. On a very good day, she would toss in a chocolate malomar cookie as a bonus.

Shildkret and I always took the Queens route to the Garden; which meant that we entered the subway on the northeast corner of Marcy and Myrtle Avenues, right next to the huge Cascade Laundry building.

The significance of this entrance was that it didn't have a normal change booth, but rather an automatic entrance. It was a five-foot revolving steel panel designed to keep anyone from climbing over to get a free ride.

You put your nickel in the slot and pushed against the panel which slowly turned until you came out on the other side at the subway platform. Larry and I figured out that there were two ways to "beat" this prison-like turnstile:

At the bottom of the steel "door" there was about a foot of "air," which would allow a youngster to sneak under if he was relatively thin. It required a crawling maneuver that could mess up a kid's shirt since his stomach was rubbing against the ground.

Our more favored procedure—a two-for-a-nickel deal—involved the pair of us jamming ourselves into the area meant for one person and then pushing forward in the hopes that, somehow, the revolving steel plate wouldn't jam. (It never did.)

When emerging on the subway platform, we always were in danger of being spotted by the change-maker in his cubicle directly across the way.

This happened once—and it *was* scary—but there was little the man could do, since we were on the other side of the tracks and there was no policeman in sight.

Breaking the law for a nickel did not exactly fill us with guilt, but rather with a sense of excitement in having beaten the shadowy Board of Transportation out of five cents.

Riding to the Garden via Queens Plaza on the GG offered little in the way of thrills. It was a two-track line whose tunneling was square until the subway went under Newtown Creek, crossing from Brooklyn into Queens, whereupon the round, underwater shape took over.

Even though it wasn't as long a run as the A train's beneath the East River, the Newtown Creek dash had its moment of fun, especially when the train entered an air pocket with a *whoosh* that could be felt deep into one's ears.

At Queens Plaza, we climbed the steps over to the Manhattan-bound express platform where the E delivered us to the 50th Street station, directly beneath Madison Square Garden.

We flew up the steps, two at a time, practicing for the more challenging race to the Garden balcony an hour or so later.

Larry and I always hoped against hope that one day we would actually *meet* a hockey player riding the subway to the Garden, but it never happened. However, years later—1954-55 to be exact, when I worked for the Rangers—my mother and I were riding the E train when, whom should we see minding his business on the express, but Lorne (Gump) Worsley, goaltender for the Rangers. We had a nice chat before leaving him at 50th Street.

I always regarded the IND's 50th Street station as a weird one because of the manner in which it accommodated both the Washington Heights (Eighth Avenue) A and AA lines as well as the Queens E route.

When the A train originally was built,

the 50th Street station had only one level. However, when service on the IND was extended to Queens, the 53rd Street Queens line ran along the original Eighth Avenue tracks until 42nd Street. At that point it switched to a separate section and a lower level station at the Garden.

The lower level Queens service opened in August 1933, and still was relatively new when I began riding it. What intrigued me was our ability to stand on the upper AA local platform and still be able to see parts of the lower E track through apertures worked into the design. For some reason, I always was surprised when I noticed that at the Garden station, one pair of tracks was atop another pair, although this was commonplace on other lines such as the A and the AA north of Columbus Circle. The difference here was that you could actually see down to the E.

Returning home from a Sunday afternoon double-header at the Garden, Larry and I invariably stayed with the upper level AA local heading downtown through Manhattan.

You see, there was no point in going through Queens Plaza. We couldn't do our two-for-one cheat at 50th Street station because there were none of those big, black turnstiles.

With clear consciences—and our eyes riveted at the big, front window—we returned to Myrtle-Willoughby.

Total cost was fifteen cents for both of us; and no charge for the hockey tickets or sandwich-tangerine-malomar lunch.

Neither Times Square movies, theater, nor hockey could have happened for me without the subway.

Sands Street Terminal,
the Crossroads of Brooklyn Elevated Transit

The Brooklyn Bridge el terminal remained operable on the Brooklyn side through the World War II years. It was even more extensive than its Manhattan counterpart. Over the years, such lines as the Myrtle Avenue, Fulton Street and Lexington Avenue els all
plied the bridge tracks, stopping, of course, at the Sands Street depot on the Brooklyn side. The configuration of the bridge surface
was different when the el trains used the span. In this post-1940 view, passengers from the terminated Myrtle Avenue el train wait
for a Lexington Avenue train on the other side to take them the rest of the way to Manhattan, over the Brooklyn Bridge.

The upper level loop, abandoned only a week earlier than when this photo was taken, was used by trains not going to Manhattan. Below the loop are the remains of the Fulton Street el's station.

Reaching Canarsie was a long subway trip from virtually every part of Brooklyn, especially this downtown terminal at Sands Street. This photo depicts the east side of the building, showing the loading platform of the upper loop that was taken out of service the week before.

CHAPTER FOUR

GOING TO

Canarsie

Long Ago And Far Away,
I Dreamed A Dream One Day

During the halcyon radio days of the 1930's and 1940's, the surest way to get a rise out of a quiz show audience was to have a guest reveal to the crowd that he was "from Brooklyn."

For some reason—probably the daffy Dodgers or even the daffier Brooklyn accents—Brooklyn, to the rest of the civilized American world, was funny.

But, to Brooklynites, the funniest geographic name of all, was located in the borough itself—Canarsie.

At the very least, if the name "Canarsie" came up in conversation, a smile would cross the listener's face, sometimes accompanied by an outright roar of laughter.

For borough residents who lived from the Flatbush community and north, Canarsie was some far away place. So far, in fact, that in Yiddish, it was called *yenevelt,* or another world.

Going to Canarsie, to some of us, had the same feel as if it were announced that we were en route to Montana. It just *seemed* that far away.

And, if you check a map of Brooklyn, you can see why: Canarsie sits on Jamaica Bay's shores in the far eastern section of Kings County.

It is named after the Canarsee Indians, who populated the shore area that now includes Coney Island, Brighton Beach, Manhattan Beach and Flatlands, as well as Canarsie.

Technically, it is bound by Jamaica Bay to the east; East 108th Street to the north; Fresh Creek Basin to the east; and to the south and west by the Jamaica Bay, Paerdegat Basin, Ralph Avenue and Ditmas Avenue.

When the Dutch—and later the English—settled there in the 17th century, they found the seacoast hospitable for both farming and fishing. It was quiet and distant enough from Manhattan's relatively

"Long Ago and Far Away" (Film: Cover Girl), words Ira Gershwin, music Jerome Kern, Crawford Music Corp., © 1944 by Jerome Kern

maddening crowds to remain undeveloped except for the occasional vessel which would drop another anchor along the shore.

But Canarsie would not remain quiet for long. It could thank the steam engine and, later, the subway for that.

During the decade preceding the outbreak of the Civil War, Canarsie was "discovered," so to speak, for its virtues as a seaside resort.

At the time, steam railroads had established themselves as the best and most efficient land carriers, and many already were using Manhattan as a terminus for trips north, east and west of the city.

Brooklyn would not be far behind.

The first such steam railroad to cross Kings County, surprisingly, did not go to Coney Island, but rather Canarsie, of all places. The line was called the Brooklyn, Canarsie and Rockaway Beach Railroad. Its "downtown" terminal was near Fulton Street and Atlantic Avenue, from where it headed Southeast to a depot on the coastline in Canarsie.

Service was inaugurated on October 21, 1865 with a single track traversing the still relatively undeveloped community.

At the time of its opening, the Brooklyn, Canarsie and Rockaway Beach Rail Road was a subsidiary of the Long Island Rail Road, which, to this day, stands as the third-oldest railroad in the country, having inaugurated its first run on April 18, 1836.

The Canarsie line's link to Rockaway Beach was via ferry from Canarsie Landing. Thus, two of the first seacoast resort areas were in business; at Rockaway and Canarsie.

More importantly, from a development viewpoint, the gamble that was the railroad, soon would pay off handsome dividends. Passengers began riding the steam line not merely to enjoy the Atlantic Ocean's virtues but also to settle—and live—near the water.

Immigrants from Germany were among the first to populate Canarsie—coming by train, of course—followed by Irish and Scottish home-builders. The more they came—including a second wave of immigrants from Holland—the more demand for better rail service.

The Long Island Rail Road responded by adding a second track to satisfy Canarsie business which continued to grow. This was accomplished in 1893-1894, nearly three decades after New York's first railroad-to-the-sea began steaming south.

By this time, the trip from Downtown Brooklyn to Canarsie started with a ride on the Long Island Rail Road's main line with a connection at the LIRR's East New York terminal.

From there the Canarsie line stopped at New Lots station—eventually to be a terminal on the IRT subway—followed by Canarsie Village station and, finally, Canarsie Landing.

It should be noted that the LIRR's other two subsidiary lines running at that time in Brooklyn included the New York and Manhattan Beach Rail Road as well as the New York, Bay Ridge and Jamaica Rail Road.

By the turn of the century, Canarsie was taking on some of the aspects of Coney Island as an entertainment center as well as a place to live or simply stay a week at a posh hotel.

Although Canarsie never did achieve the fame nor fortune of Coney as a resort, it greatly benefited from electrification of the Canarsie Line.

Equally significant was the fact that the Brooklyn Canarsie and Rockaway Beach route gradually became assimilated into the greater New York subway system, which means that a trip to Canarsie—just like the ride to Coney—would cost only a nickel.

The transformation began in earnest after electrification in 1906. Streamlining its operation, the LIRR leased the BCRBRR to the Brooklyn Union Elevated Railroad, a subsidiary of Brooklyn Rapid Transit.

During the late 1890s and early 1900s, the BRT moved swiftly to become a major power broker among the city's movers of millions. Starting as a securities holding firm, the BRT enlarged through a series a mergers and leases involving many of the original Brooklyn steam lines and horse car companies.

In short order, the BRT acquired the Brooklyn Union, Kings County, and Seaside and Brooklyn Bridge elevated lines. In addition, the Sea Beach, West End and Brighton lines soon came under the BRT umbrella.

Pivotal, however, was a traffic-sharing deal with the LIRR which allowed the Long Island to run transit lines in Queens. On the other side of the pact, the BRT was able to assume control of former LIRR routes in Brooklyn such as the South Brooklyn and Culver lines.

Thus, in 1906, the Canarsie Railroad was just one route among the many BRT-controlled operations. Lumped together, the lines enabled the BRT to control nearly all elevated and street lines in Brooklyn.

For Canarsie, electrification meant expansion of the resort and the seaside transit facility.

One of the largest resorts, the Diamond Point Hotel, was situated right on the waterfront. It featured a long pier and dock at which steamships moored after their voyage from Manhattan. By the end of

THE LONGEST RIDE

If one were to take a taxi from Far Rockaway in Queens through Brooklyn and up to 207th Street in upper Manhattan, the cost would top $50, not counting the tip. That same 31-mile run—longest of all subway rides in the city—costs only $2.00 on the A Train.

World War I, the Diamond Point Hotel—under the proprietorship of Adam J. Stahle—had become a sprawling enterprise which even included an airship floating over the acreage as part of its promotional package.

The White House Restaurant had become one of Canarsie's many outstanding eateries, while the Gold City Amusement Park—opened in 1907—had all the trappings of Coney's Steeplechase a few miles to the west.

Canarsie's train terminal rubbed shoulders with a roller coaster and included a storage yard with five tracks which extended south from Skidmore Avenue.

Visitors to Canarsie hotels and amusement areas would debark the trains at the terminal (Rockaway Parkway), where a free transfer was obtained to a trolley which ran to the Jamaica Bay shore.

Described by Brooklyn historian Elliot Willensky as a "Toonerville-type trolley," the streetcar "took its own littered route through the tall grass, phragmites, and reeds to the beach" with its many attractions.

In the years prior to World War I, Canarsie was regarded by transit planners as a boom area in the making. The Transit Committee of the Public Service Commission and the Board of Aldermen issued

When the Canarsie Line Was Not Whole

In April 1917, you could get your suits sponged and pressed for only forty cents. Note the double-decked express-local elevated station along Second Avenue, as well as heavy streetcar traffic and the Third Avenue el station in the distance. The pile of wood planking along the sidewalk signifies the beginning of Canarsie line subway work.

When do you expect to find a brand-new subway car in the streets of Brooklyn? When there are no subway tracks to put it on, of course! Seriously, a problem arose when the first portion of the Canarsie line was ready to be opened in 1924. It had no track connection to the rest of the BMT system. Cars had to be delivered through a temporary ramp and hole in the street.

Here, everyone stops on the ramp in Greenpoint for picture-taking with the latest example of subway car development, the BMT Standard. Note the cable on the left, used to control the car's descent since a third-rail was not available.

a report in 1911 which included Canarsie as part of a mammoth transit plan.

Dubbed "The 14th Street Eastern District Line," the expanded route to Canarsie would begin as a subway at Sixth Avenue and 14th Street in Manhattan. The two-track line would tunnel under the East River to Brooklyn and eventually become an elevated line before reaching Canarsie.

Despite the modernization blueprints, transit officials still treated Canarsie as if it were a rural stop. This was evident before the route reached its final destination. Instead of being taken into the terminus as a subway—as it was done on the IRT line to Flushing—the trains rolled into Canarsie at ground level.

Where 105th Street intersected with the tracks, BRT engineers erected a railroad-style crossing gate replete with an operator who would raise or lower the gates manually! This system remained in vogue until 1983.

Unlike most of the major (Dual Contract) transit works completed during or after World War I, the Canarsie project was bedeviled with delays, many of them caused by transit-hating mayor John F. Hylan, who served from 1917 to 1925.

Hylan railed against several subway projects, but managed to delay the Canarsie line more than any. It finally was completed on July 14, 1928, setting the stage for development in the form of apartment house construction as well as smaller units.

While the subway inspired an influx of new home owners and apartment-dwellers, it could not help what once was a thriving industry now on the wane.

Uncontrolled pollution of Jamaica Bay destroyed the fishing and oyster industries, many of which were operated by Italians and Jews who made their livings working the oysterbeds of the Bay.

Canarsie's entertainment sector took a hit during the Great Depression, especially when the Golden City Amusement Park burned down in 1934.

Once World War II had ended—and with it The Great Depression—Canarsie began taking full advantage of its rapid transit link with northern Brooklyn and Manhattan.

In the immediate post-World War II years, marshes adjoining Canarsie were filled and new housing went up with the promise of easy transit access. The area became a predominantly Italian and Jewish community replete with corner candy stores, delicatessens and Chinese restaurants.

All that remained of the halcyon days of Golden City Amusement Park was Canarsie's pier which, somehow, avoided the razing that followed construction of the nearby Belt Parkway in 1939.

Eventually, the Canarsie trolley's run-through-the-reeds ended in 1942 when new track connections were installed on Rockaway Parkway. All that remained from the "old" transit days was the manually-operated crossing gate at East 105th Street.

An attempt by the Transit Authority to have the gate-operator removed and replaced by an automated gate was successfully fought in the late 1950s by local residents, but even the gate-operator lost out to "progress" when the authority finally eliminated the crossing gate in 1983.

The subway-inspired growth became more evident with construction of high-rise apartment complexes as well as one and two-family homes, many of which were lavish in their appointments. Canarsie even got its own public high school.

A later influx of Russians, Chinese, African-Americans and Caribbean Blacks added to Canarsie's racial mosaic. Like their predecessors, they were attracted by the subway access as well as the shore attractions such as Canarsie Park and Canarsie Pier which still stands.

The change has been so dramatic and successful that nobody laughs at the mention of Canarsie anymore!

One Man's Memories of What It Was Like To Go to Canarsie

Canarsie was the impossible: North Dakota, maybe; Mount Everest, on a dare.

But Canarsie, for trip purposes, simply was out of the question for a kid like me, growing up in Williamsburg; unless two factors intervened.

One was a relative.

The other was a date; but definitely *not* a blind date:

As it happened, my relatives living closest to Canarsie included Uncle Julius, the lawyer, who was my father's younger brother; as well as Aunt Ceil and cousins, Daisy and Judd.

They, fortunately, lived at 469 Miller Avenue in East New York, which still was plenty far—as most places were—from Canarsie.

That eliminated one excuse to go to, what we called, *yenevelt* because Canarsie really did seem like another planet to us.

By the time I had started high school, I had begun to date. Had somebody fixed me up with Miss America, and had she happened to live in Canarsie, I *might* have given it a second thought; but that, too, never happened.

Hence, no reasons to go to that far away place which we equated with stinking dumps. That was because of the fact that Canarsie was then surrounded by dumping grounds, euphemistically passed off as "ground-fill," although it never fooled us.

Reaching Canarsie by subway wasn't that difficult; it just *seemed* that way; mostly because the BMT's 14th Street Line—the only one that went there—was like a forbidden route to us Williamsburgers.

Not that it was dangerous in any way; but it ran to places to which we never wanted to go—Sixth Avenue and 14th Street—its Manhattan terminus being one of them.

So, I actually survived the first twenty years of my young life without, (a) ever visiting Canarsie; and, (b) meeting anyone who lived there.

However, in the spring of 1950, at age 18, I began my four-year *tour de force* of Brooklyn College. And as luck would have it, my first semester curriculum included a course called "French 01," otherwise known as Beginners' French.

My pal from Public School 54 as well as Eastern District High School, Neil Brown, was a classmate in French 01 under the aegis of a rollicking sort of fellow named Professor Bobé.

Brownie and I would sit next to each other, and, when we weren't paying *close* attention to Professor Bobé, we played a running game that could loosely be called "Let's Keep Track of Who Gets Called On The Last."

For some strange reason, we got it down to a pair of finalists. One was an attractive lass sitting in the front row whom we only knew—thanks to Professor Bobé—as "Miss Friedman."

East New York Junction—
The Other Brooklyn El Meeting Place

OPPOSITE PAGE, TOP: The Dual BRT-IRT Contracts of 1913 not only resulted in massive subway construction but significant improvements on the elevated side. One of the most ambitious projects of all involved the Eastern Parkway-Atlantic Avenue interchange, originally named Manhattan Junction. Several BRT el lines—Broadway-Brooklyn, Lexington Avenue, Fulton Street and 14th Street-Canarsie—met at the outskirts of East New York. The three photos, taken in 1918, reveal the intricate steelwork required to bring the assorted lines into one terminal. Before the Canarsie Line was built, the lines met in an "H" formation. In order to accommodate the 14th Street-Canarsie subway-el, the intricate multi-level steelwork had to be constructed.

Looking west along the reconstructed Fulton Street el in Brooklyn.

OPPOSITE PAGE, BOTTOM: The track in the foreground connects the Fulton Street el to the yard and the Broadway (Brooklyn) Jamaica el. The Canarsie line vaults over the top.

William Brennan

Here, in 1963, a BMT Standard ascends from the Canarsie line tunnel into Brooklyn's Broadway-East New York station.

Although she never knew it, her "opponent" was a chap who sat directly behind me; one Jack Goldstein.

Born and bred in Canarsie, Goldstein had only recently moved to Williamsburg where his father, Morris—also known in the trade as "Moe"—operated a luncheonette-candy store.

Jack was an avid student, but since he often had to work long hours at Goldie's Emporium, it was difficult for him to keep up with classwork. Early in the semester, Jack introduced himself to me and requested an academic humanitarian gesture.

When Professor Bobé would give one of his classroom quizzes—rather often—it was suggested by Jack that I sharply drop my right shoulder so that he could have a clear view of my exam paper.

Shoulder-dropping was not a difficult task, so I agreed. And that's how Jack passed French 01 and we became good friends over a half-century.

From time to time, he would tell me stories about Canarsie, but I never got to see it firsthand until June 1950.

Playing professionally for the first time in a dance band, I had the good fortune to take my drums up to the Helderberg Mountains (near Albany), where I played in a quartet. The piano man, Mel Smith, was a bandmate of mine at Eastern District High School, but the other two musicians were all new to me.

The saxophone player—a very funny fellow—Len Solomon, was from Canarsie, as was Harold Braunstein, who played what he called the "electric Spanish guitar."

We worked at Farley's Thompson's Lake Hotel that Memorial Day weekend of 1950, after which Braunstein and Solomon invited me to visit Canarsie. One Saturday in June 1950, I took them up on the invitation.

Not having a car, I had the wonderful opportunity of getting there by train, and since I was thoroughly new to the 14th Street Line, I decided to take it to the end; from Sixth Avenue in Manhattan to the terminal in Canarsie.

To do so, I first had to hustle the GG at my home station, Myrtle-Willoughby, then connect with the A at Hoyt-Schermerhorn; quickly change to the (Sixth Avenue) F train at the next stop, Jay Street and get off at 14th Street, where a short walk took me to what everyone in Brooklyn called "The 14th Street-Canarsie Line."

I always got a kick out of starting a subway trip at the very first station. It reminded me of visiting my Aunt Hattie, Uncle Paul and cousin Ira in Albany. I always left from Grand Central Terminal, the first stop. It had a formality about it that differentiated from waiting on a platform for an oncoming train. At the first stop, the train was *there*, waiting for you. Usually, it hung around for a while before closing its doors. There was no rush, no hustle.

There was *especially* no hustle on the 14th Street-Canarsie Line. It reflected the slow-paced *ambience* of far-away Canarsie. This was the local's local; slow in starting, slow in moving, slow in stopping.

No matter. I couldn't have cared less. In 1950, there still were plenty of BMT Standards—also known as the ABs to transit folk—and the front windows still opened.

After more than a dozen years experience, I knew all about annexing the front window. This was easy at Sixth Avenue depot because it was the first stop, and it was Saturday, with few people heading to or from work. I had it made.

Finally, the motorman arrived, keyed open his compartment door, placed his brake handle on top of the notch and inserted his reversing key, putting everything in gear, so to speak.

The motor immediately began humming, the doors closed and we were off to Canarsie; next stop Union Square, followed by Third Avenue and First Avenue, before we ducked under the East River. By 1950, some of the Standards were a good 35 years old, but were holding up well; as sturdy as could be with their overhead fans spinning like airplane propellers.

Once we got to Montrose Avenue, the first stop in Brooklyn, the trip got more interesting.

Montrose intrigued me because of its historic significance in relation to subway-hating Mayor John Hylan. As the BMT attempted to extend service to Canarsie, Hylan kept sabotaging the plans.

True, the link between Sixth Avenue, Manhattan and Montrose in Brooklyn was operating in the early 1920s, but Hylan would not permit any city money to be used for the necessary extension through the borough because of what he termed the "wicked interests" of BMT.

This meant that at both the Manhattan terminus (Sixth Avenue) and its Brooklyn counterpart (Montrose) there were dead ends and, therefore, no means to easily deliver new cars to the line.

When new 67-foot Standards were ready for delivery to the Canarsie Line, some means had to be established to install them on the subway track.

The solution was clever, to say the least. First it was established that the cars should be brought to the Long Island Rail Road Bushwick yard, within reasonable distance of Montrose Avenue. Next, a special track was laid from the LIRR yard—across city streets—to Montrose station.

"At one end of the station, a ramp allowed cars to be dropped into the subway,"[7] noted Joseph Cunningham and Leonard De Hart in their book, *Rapid Transit In Brooklyn*.

Cunningham-De Hart: *"On June 17, 1924, two cars were lowered by a winch and pulley. Six more followed on June 19, while nine more were added on June 22. A temporary service area was located in the Montrose Avenue station."*

As we pulled into Montrose Avenue station, I began picturing what it was like to actually slide those huge BMT Standards from the street level down and into the tunnel, but twenty-six years later, I could find no evidence of the ramp nor the service area to which Cunningham and De Hart referred.

Proceeding to Canarsie, I continued to note arresting aspects of this curio of a line. One was that the track climbed to surface level when we reached Wilson Avenue. (That, as Cunningham and De Hart noted, was to "avoid a cemetery.") Then, the train climbed to the steel ganglia that comprised the vast Broadway Junction intermingling of all manner of elevated lines.

At one time—before the Fulton Street el was razed—Broadway Junction played host to the 14th Street Line as well as Fulton Street's el and the Broadway-Brooklyn run to Jamaica.

To me, the interesting steel work was reminiscent of an oversized roller coaster, curving in and around, up and down.

It's always fun—if you're a subway-watcher—to follow the trains as they roll into or out of the stations, particularly when it happens to be such a complex depot as Broadway Junction.

The remainder of the meander to Canarsie was uneventful until the local dipped to ground level and I actually could see the railroad crossing gates lowered as we approached East 105th Street.

"This Canarsie place really *is* different," I muttered to myself.

Harold and Lenny were awaiting me at the station platform once the BMT Standard emitted its final *chow* blast of released air at the last stop.

"You wanted to see Canarsie," Braunstein said, almost boastfully, "well, here she is!"

There were no thatched huts; nor gorgeous women, such as Dorothy Lamour, running around in sarongs. As a matter of fact, Canarsie looked a lot more "normal Brooklyn" than I had expected although there *was* a suburban feel about it.

In a sense, it reminded me of visits during the early 1940s to my grandmother's sister, Regina—also known as "Aunt Ray"—who lived with her husband, Adolph, in Dover, New Jersey.

Dover had a theater, just as we did in Williamsburg, and it had a grocery store and a tailor and other shops but, no matter how you shook it, Dover was The Sticks. Likewise, Canarsie was The Sticks of Brooklyn, no question about it.

After touring the area, we wound up at a corner housing a dark, tan brick one-story building, with a number of shops. On that very block was a candy store in which we all had chocolate malteds.

That done, we walked around the corner where I instantly sensed there was "action"—Canarsie-type action.

About a dozen young adults were hanging out at the back side of the candy store where there was only brick wall and sidewalk. The game which they were so assiduously playing was called "Pitching Pennies."

According to the Brooklyn—also

THE DEEPEST TUNNEL

Digging deep for a subway is one thing, but the sandhogs seemed to overdo it when they built the 191st Street IRT Broadway Line Station in northern Manhattan. It is 180 feet below the sidewalks of Inwood, which automatically qualifies it as the deepest platform on any of the three systems. It's on the Number One route.

Bronx—version of the game, players lined up on the curb at the edge of the sidewalk, each with a penny in his hand. Then, one at a time, the fellows would flip the coins toward the wall. After all tosses had been made, the player whose penny was closest to the wall would win the pot. Higher stakes versions included nickels, dimes and, sometimes, quarters.

I was intrigued by the crowd surrounding the players and the assortment of different "pitches" employed. One would hold the coin between the edge of his thumb and the inside of his index finger and then *flip,* whereupon the penny would describe a high arc before landing on the sidewalk and roll toward the wall.

Others would hold the copper flat between the inside of their right thumb and tip of their index finger. In this case, the motion was more of a *toss* than a *flip* and quite often the penny would fall flat rather than roll.

Obviously, there were masters at work here and I merely shook my head when Braunstein wondered whether I wanted to enter the gambling den.

My reluctance was based on ineptitude more than anything else. I didn't want to be shown up by the Canarsie sharpies. Penny-pitching was not my *forte* and, besides, I was having more fun just watch-

Canarsie-Bound on the 14th Street Line

William Brennan

A set of Standard (B) cars leads a long Canarsie train into the Sutter Avenue station in 1962.

For an old-time, rural touch on the vast New York subway system, nothing could beat the East 105th Street crossing in Canarsie. The BMT's multi (trio)-trains have arrived with the result that the venerable railroad-style gates have lowered. The Eighth Avenue-bound train is operating in the only remaining rural area of Brooklyn, where crossing at grade—Toonerville Trolley-style—was possible.

William Brennan

Many years later, a Canarsie-bound BMT Standard makes use of the same crossing gates.

Before 1928, this Rockaway Boulevard (Rockaway Parkway) station was not the end of the line for Canarsie-bound commuters. Also, 1928 marked the end of overhead-powered el cars which operated all the way to the Canarsie Pier. Trolley cars then substituted for the trains. Note the station also featured an Armstrong interlocking tower connected to the switches and signals by pipes.

A small yard occupies the area east of the Rockaway Parkway station filled with the BMT's finest (Standard) cars in June 1963.   William Brennan

THE SUBWAY IN SONG

New York City has been celebrated in song with such classics as Richard Rodgers and Lorenz Hart's "Manhattan" and Louis Alter's "Manhattan Serenade," so it was inevitable that someone would pen a tune about the subway.

The music industry—otherwise known as Tin Pan Alley—wasted no time getting into the act. While the shine of fresh paint still gleamed underground, "Down In The Subway" (see page 477) was being sold in music stores throughout the city.

May Yohe, a star vocalist in 1905, popularized the tune, which got a sales boost when publisher William Randolph Hearst featured it in both of his papers, the New York American and New York Journal.

Lyricist Jack Norworth also was inspired by the subway. In 1908, he collaborated with vaudeville partner Nora Bayes on a classic, "Shine On, Harvest Moon."

Shortly thereafter, Norworth was riding the IRT when he noticed an advertisement for a New York Giants baseball game at the Polo Grounds. Inspired by the ad, he jotted lyrics down on a piece of paper while the express swung toward Harlem. The result was another classic, "Take Me Out To The Ballgame," for which Albert Von Tilzer wrote the music.

Seven years after "Down In The Subway" made its debut, lyricist Arthur Gillespie was so smitten by his IRT journey that he penned "The Subway Glide" (see page 479). With the aid of composer Theodore Norman, the tune became another underground hit.

Its opening lines went as follows:

> *"Ding-a-ding, hear the bell,*
> *Come along, Isabella, for a ride.*
> *Just room enough for two,*
> *Hurry up, come and do the Subway Glide."*

The New York Daily News' excellent series, "Big Town Songbook," mentioned "The Subway Glide" in a piece by Fergus Gwynplaine MacIntyre on May 6, 2004.

MacIntyre noted that Eli Danson—a song-plugger by trade—was featured in a photo on the cover of the sheet music. Furthermore, Danson actually performed on stage in a vaudeville act, singing the subway tune.

"Dressed in a motorman's uniform," wrote MacIntyre, "Danson came onstage leading a troupe of dancers costumed as subway riders. These commuters began the Subway Glide squashed up together like sardines, and finished the song tumbling across the stage."

ing the action, as one would *kibitzing* a game of poker.

In the end, my reluctance inadvertently spared me some quality time with the New York City Police Department. Here's how:

About twenty minutes into the penny toss, the game suddenly was interrupted by the wail of two sirens accompanied by flashing lights and the *screeching* of brakes. *New York's Finest* had arrived to bring justice to Canarsie.

As I froze in my position at the outer fringe of the crowd, three officers climbed out of their vehicles with the most no-nonsense attitude I had ever seen from lawmen in my life.

"All you guys stand against the wall," the lead cop demanded.

I wondered whether little, ole me was included in that "All you guys," order. It took me about two seconds to figure that out.

"I said *everybody*," the head of the Canarsie Anti-Pitching Pennies Crime Unit added, in case someone didn't get it the first time.

Now, for the first time in my eighteen years, I was in a police lineup, so to speak.

In no time at all it became evident that the cops knew who the *real* culprits were and had been through this drill before. They hustled four of the key players into the two cop cars, slammed the doors as if to put closure on the raid and motored off to the Canarsie precinct.

I couldn't even begin to describe the relief I felt at not being carted off to the police station—and possibly even jail. Visions of my mother and father being phoned by the precinct captain intermingled with thoughts of my Uncle Julius, the lawyer, having to represent me in what surely would have been the first pitching-pennies case Julie ever tried.

But as the cops faded into the distance, I said to myself: "You're free, I tell you, *free*!" There was no happier person in Canarsie at that moment than Your's Truly.

Braunstein and Solomon were less shaken than I; which only proved that they had been at penny-pitching raids before—and escaped unscathed.

Once the tumult had subsided, we went into the candy store, had a few egg creams, after which they walked me to the Canarsie BMT terminal.

I enjoyed my visit to Canarsie, much as I used to love going to Dover, New Jersey; the difference being that *nobody* pitched pennies in Dover, possibly because there were so few sidewalks in town.

Braunstein and Solomon were great company; particularly Lenny, who was one of the funniest people my age I had ever met. I hoped we would be friends for life, but our relationship ended—mostly via letter—after a couple of years when he disappeared somewhere in the teaching realm, never to be seen by me again.

I played a couple of gigs with Braunstein, but guitar was never an instrument of choice in my bands, and eventually we, too, drifted apart.

After boarding the 14th Street local, I moved into my preferred window position and gaped at the lights of Canarsie while the train meandered past the railroad crossing gate *en route* to Broadway Junction and Montrose Avenue.

At night the trip seemed longer and less fascinating, particularly because there was so much less to see. Nevertheless, the 14th Street Line was new and different to me; all of which made the ride back worthwhile.

When I got home, my grandmother was sitting on her living room chair and greeted me as I plopped down on the couch opposite her.

"Where were you?" she wondered.

"Gram," I replied, "I was all the way out in Canarsie."

"Canarsie?" she said incredulously.

"Yeah, Gram. And do you want to know something?"

"What?"

"It is *'yenevelt'!*"

Newly modernized IRT subway cars for use on the Flushing line await the opening of the Fair, February 14, 1939.

CHAPTER FIVE

GOING TO

The World's Fairs, 1939–1940 and 1964

"Hi Ho Come To The Fair " —
The New York World's Fair
In 1939 And 1940.

The New York World's Fair of l939 at Flushing Meadow in Queens was arguably the biggest, most artistic, most esthetic and widely acclaimed international pageant in history.

Writing in the *Variety Music Cavalcade,* Julius Mattfeld called the New York World's Fair "a stupendous, colorful affair in which sixty nations took part."

Time magazine described it as "the greatest show of all time."

Author David Gelertner (*1939, The Lost World of the Fair)* called it "one amazing show."

And even these may be understatements.

It inspired songs, books, inventions and even brand-new roller coaster rides.

But none of this would have been possible without the subway.

In fact, the Fair's site—much like that of Yankee Stadium—was determined by the geography of the combined IRT-BMT Flushing Line which connected Times Square with distant Queens.

Joseph Shadgen, a 43-year-old Luxembourg-born engineer, conceived plans for a World's Fair which would "augment New York's civic pride and city-mindedness."

Shadgen's idea inspired the city's power brokers who, one-by-one, hopped on his band wagon.

Deciding where to put it was not easy.

When Yankee Stadium was conceived immediately after World War I, there was abundant land in the Bronx for development. But two decades later, as Shadgen surveyed the five boroughs for the best fair location, the Bronx had been over-built along with Brooklyn and Manhattan.

Staten Island was too distant, which left Shadgen with Queens as his choice almost by default.

He needed ample space as well as

"Come to the Fair!" words Helen Taylor, music Martin Easthope,
Enoch & Sons, © 1917

direct mass transit connections. Flushing Meadow fulfilled the equation on each count. It boasted ample acreage, and not only was next to the Willets Point Boulevard elevated station on the IRT-BMT line to Flushing, but the Port Washington branch of the Long Island Rail Road.

Better still, the city-owned Independent System was digging a four-track subway under Queens Boulevard not so far from the proposed fair grounds that a spur of some kind could be built.

If such a connection could be made, the fair then would be serviced by three major rail systems, each with a Manhattan connection.

Gradually, all the necessary elements fell into place. The land purchased in Flushing Meadow comprised 1,100 acres, a good portion of which were swampy marshes. A tidal expanse covering 1,216 acres, the site also was affectionately known as the "Corona Dumps."

After considerable backroom politicking, an official announcement about the fair's development plans was made on September 22, 1935: "The 150th anniversary of the establishment of the government of the United States under the federal constitution." Simply translated, it was the 150th anniversary of George Washington's inauguration as the country's first president.

In addition to the subways, the fair would be served by boats, which would dock at Flushing Bay, highways and two airports, Flushing and Holmes Airport.

By far the biggest boosts, in terms of crowd-management, was the Independent System's decision to deliver direct service to the fair via a new spur to be built from the Kew Gardens-Union Turnpike station to Flushing Meadow as well as plans to greatly enlarge the Willets Point local station and make it an express stop as well.

Once all the land parcels were assembled, the grounds measured a mile wide and three-and-a-half miles long. In many sections it was littered with ashes which had accumulated during the property's years as a dumping ground for the Brooklyn Ash Removal Company. When all was said and done, no less than 8,000,000 cubic yards of fill was dumped in the process of converting the wasteland into a glittering fairgrounds.

Although visitors could reach the fair by all means of transit—there even was a trolley line running along Flushing Avenue in Brooklyn that went to the fair via Williamsburg and Ridgewood—the subways and the Long Island Rail Road would bear the brunt of the traffic.

With the IRT-BMT Flushing line already in place, all that was necessary—not that it wasn't a major project—was reconstructing Willets Point Boulevard station into a mammoth entrance-exit as well as a hub for both expresses and locals.

The more complicated subway project involved the Independent Line, which had branched into Queens earlier in the decade.

Once the primary IND Eighth Avenue work was completed in Manhattan, Queens received subway attention and, in August 1933, the borough received its first service on the city-owned system.

Its main line comprised a four-track route from Queens Plaza to Roosevelt Avenue in Woodside and on to Union Turnpike. Service to that Kew Gardens hub was inaugurated in December 1936 at a time when World's Fair planners were preparing to get serious about rapid transit connections to Flushing Meadow. Meanwhile, the Queens Boulevard line was pushed farther east under Hillside Avenue to Parsons Boulevard and 169th Street. All in all it was an impressive looking line; by far the most modern of the entire system, BMT and IRT included.

What still had to be determined was the manner in which the Queens IND could connect with the proposed fair-grounds. Or, *if* such a spur even would be approved.

Not surprisingly, the primary power broker—*and* power behind the fair—Robert Moses adopted a stance that was to be repeated over and over again during his long stint heading several city agencies, including the Department of Parks; he opposed subway construction!

In this case, Moses argued that the proposed $1,200,000 cost of building a spur from Union Turnpike to the fair was excessive. Fortunately, Mayor LaGuardia endorsed the IND plan as did key members of the state senate and assembly; not to mention Governor Herbert Lehman, the most powerful Democrat in the state.

Before the summer of 1938 had arrived, the legislature had given the green light to the IND fair line and blueprints were drawn. Designers had one advantage right from the get-go. Once the Forest Hills (Continental Avenue) station was complete, it included trackage that swerved left (northward) under the 75th Avenue local station and headed on four tracks in the direction of Grand Central Parkway.

Just north of a new set of six-story apartment buildings being built to complement the Queens Boulevard subway, the tracks emerged from a tunnel portal at Grand Central Parkway. They then mounted a trestle crossing the highway. From there, the tracks led to the newly-con-

MAPS, AND MORE MAPS

In April 1993, New York City Transit created a subway-el map for the visually-impaired. Produced in Braille, the map not only covered the entire system but provided extra maps for heavily-used lines. After years of complaints about hard-to-read maps, the TA produced a "modern" bit of geography, created by chief map designer John Tauranac, and introduced it on June 23, 1979. Tauranac later improved upon his original concept and, in the 1990s, produced and marketed his ultra-modern edition, which became available in bookstores and other outlets. Many critics regard Tauranac's updated version as the best New York subway map ever designed.

structed Jamaica yards where the fresh R-1 rolling stock was stored when not in use.

In a sense, the tracks to the storage yards would eventually prove to be the first leg of the spur-to-the-fair. From four tracks, the extension would be reduced by half and continue past Flushing Meadows Park for almost two miles to a terminal that would be erected at Horace Harding Boulevard, now part of the Long Island Expressway. The entire spur would measure 4.13 miles.

Despite the many advances in subway construction since the early 1900s, the World's Fair Railroad would present unique challenges to its builders. The swampland of Flushing was not a stable foundation for tracks.

"The tracks would be laid on a pile trestle roadbed," said Frederick A. Kramer, who wrote a definitive work on the subject, *Subway to the World's Fair.*

Although construction crews were on a tight deadline (22 months), work moved

The Steinway Tunnels to Queens Plaza

Among the strangest segments of the early subway system was the Steinway tunnels connecting the Flushing Line's tracks in Manhattan with Queens. Originally built for trolley operation, they were rebuilt in 1915 for IRT operation. The essential tube still is used by the Number Seven train running between Main Street and Times Square. Notice that the tunnels are unusually tall to provide room for the trolley poles and overhead power line which was planned for the original underground streetcar line.

OPPOSITE PAGE, TOP: Here, in 1915, we see construction of the Flushing Line station at Grand Central in Manhattan. The original tunnel only provided for a small low-level trolley stop located under the current platform near the Lexington Avenue stairs at the east end of the station. Immediately west of the current station, the remains of the trolley loop still exists.

William Brennan

A Flushing-bound set departs Grand Central stop in 1964. The western-flared end of the platform exists because the eastbound track follows a portion of the long-defunct trolley loop.

Between February and May 1914, the Queens side of the Queensborough Bridge would dramatically change. During the winter, no evidence of alteration of the bridge could be seen. But only three months later, steelwork for the Second Avenue elevated trains began to be put into place. Notice there were four trolley tracks on the bridge; two in what would be the center roadway and two on the more familiar outer roadway.

The first steel for the new Queensborough Plaza multi-level elevated station is seen at the 59th Street Bridge's entrance.

When the Queensboro Bridge was designed, provisions were made for an upper level rapid transit line as well as walkways. Here, in 1917, we see the finishing touches made on the tracks curving off of the Second Avenue el and heading for Queens. The kiosks (they still exist) for the below-ground trolley terminal can be seen below the el structure.

On the Queens side of the bridge, the el's connection to the Queensborough Plaza el station is almost complete. In the 1930s, increased road traffic resulted in the removal of the walkways and the relocation of the tracks to the north side of the bridge and a roadway installed. In 1942, el service ended and an additional roadway replaced the tracks.

Looking from Ely Avenue into the steelwork of the four-platform eight-track station in 1915.

Looking at the other side of the station on the same 1915 day.

From the end of the upper platform in 1917 that's still in use, we see the almost completed eastern end of the station. What differs from today is that the track on the left side of the platform was for Astoria-bound Second Avenue el trains, not trains from the 60th Street tunnel. The double crossover gives dual service trains a choice of routes.

The east end of Queens Plaza was a major trolley terminal before the coming of subway service from Manhattan to Long Island City. This is where Jackson Avenue (Northern Boulevard) meets Diagonal Street (Queens Boulevard).

The Queens Plaza service was completed here in 1923 with the connecting ramp from the 60th Street subway tunnel to the Plaza station. Note how empty the area around the bridge was at that time.

The steel skeleton of the Astoria Line emerges over the top of the trolley depot on December 31, 1915.

Queensborough Plaza—known on the IND as Queens Plaza—emerged as the transit hub of the borough. This was due to the fact that trains (Second Avenue el) not only arrived via the Queensborough (59th Street) Bridge but also via subway and elevated tracks. This is a view of one platform servicing the IRT's Second Avenue el and the BMT subway which arrived through the 60th Street tunnel. Prior to 1950, the original Queensborough Plaza el station had eight tracks and four platforms to accommodate the three lines and five routes. Here we see a Second Avenue el train occupying the track used today by the BMT. The removed portion on the left handled the BMT trains.

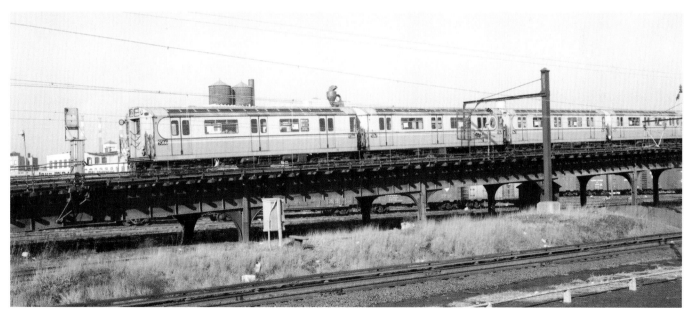

A World's Fair-bound set climbs out of the Steinway tunnel and climbs to the Court Square station in Long Island City.

William Brennan

John Henderson

Forty years later, a set of "Redbirds" in the same location as the previous picture. Notice the new foliage that has taken over the now-abandoned Long Island Rail Road yard. In 2003, the last of the beloved Redbirds were removed from Flushing Line tracks and transported to the Atlantic Ocean, where they were dumped to be used as reefs.

Rushing back from the el, this set of R-33-36 cars rounds the curve into the Court Square Station.

William Brennan

William Brennan

Astoria-bound Standards pass through the double-crossover located just east of the upper level platform. At one time these crossovers were used to separate Astoria-bound from Flushing-bound trains. Today it exists to provide the only physical connection between the Flushing Line and the rest of the system.

along without any traumatic hitch. By April 1938, the completed trestle was in place, well before many of the most important fairgrounds buildings were finished.

Likewise, expansion of the el station had been virtually trouble-free as well, and by July 1938, the new platforms and ramps—along with track extensions—were shaping up as well as the construction companies could have hoped.

The City's Board of Transportation pitched in by replacing old signaling, adding power facilities and adding a center (third) express track so that the line could handle 40 trains an hour, carrying about 40,000 riders. To Queens residents, the express service was as cherished a gift as the rebuilt Willets Point station.

Meanwhile, battles over the fare structure raged among the politicians, some of whom believed that it was necessary to double the fare to a dime in order to cover all expenses.

However, competition from rival transit groups—whose marketing skills were sharp—gave the city fathers pause. For one thing, the Long Island Rail Road, which had a lot to offer in terms of train speed from Pennsylvania Station in Manhattan, was charging only ten cents, which was a bargain price for that route.

"The World of Tomorrow in ten minutes for ten cents," was a Long Island Rail Road slogan that caught the fancy—and dimes—of thousands who climbed aboard at Penn Station and wanted a quick, easy ride to Flushing Meadow.

In addition to the rail routes to the fairgrounds, there were private bus companies and tour boat outfits galore eagerly awaiting the tourist potential.

Even the venerable Hudson River Day Line—better known for its excursion boats to Bear Mountain—got into the act with a run from its 42nd Street dock to a Whitestone pier from which buses would carry passengers to the jubilee.

More prosaic transit forms than the 75-minute Day Line cruise, included the Fifth Avenue Coach Company buses as well as keen competition from the North Shore Bus Company, which bragged of an air conditioned fleet, and the W.F. Transportation Company, which charged a half-a-buck for a round-trip.

With these factors in mind, the subway fare was held to a nickel, making it the bargain ride of them all.

The low price was not its only attraction. IRT, IND and BMT operators fully understood that handsome rolling stock also was a necessity to lure customers. Interestingly, each went about the business of creating its special World's Fair subway trains in a different way.

For the IND it was a simple matter. The Independent's original R-1 design had been successful and constantly improved under new contracts—153 new cars were delivered as late as 1940 as part of contract R-9—so the IND merely placed an improved version of its first Eighth Avenue subway train on the Fair run.

Renowned for its innovative experimental cars such as the *Zephyr, Green Hornet* and *Bluebird,* the BMT might have been expected to come up with another ultra-modern design.

Instead, its "futuristic" rolling stock actually went back to the past.

Engineers re-designed the old fleet of vestibule elevated cars which had run on the Flushing and Astoria lines using Queensborough Plaza as its terminal. Because of their relatively fragile composition—as opposed to the all-steel R-1 to R-

9s—the 30-year-old wooden cars had not been permitted in subway service.

However, the remodeling changed all that, and they would be allowed to operate into the underground Main Street, Flushing station.

Where once there were open platforms at each end of the wooden el cars, there now were closed ends following the pattern of all other subway rolling stock. The old iron gates, manually operated by conductors who stood between the cars, were replaced by pneumatically-operated sliding doors, two on each side. The motorman's cab was relocated and the rolling stock was dubbed Q—as in Queens—cars.

Aesthetically, the re-designed trains lacked *panache,* but they nonetheless had a peculiar attractiveness about them. On the one hand, they couldn't completely eschew their ancient lines, but on the other, there was a certain "newness," embellished by an arresting color scheme which captured the World's Fair orange-and-blue theme.

The paint scheme was so outstanding, it tended to overshadow any of the "old" aspects of the cars—plus—they worked!

By contrast, the IRT had a *total* face-lift for its fleet. Previously, the Flushing Line featured wooden cars dating back to the 19th century when they were hitched to steam locomotives. When they were electrified in 1902, the rickety rolling stock plied the Queens-Manhattan run over the Queensborough Bridge.

Signing a pact with the respected St. Louis Car Company, IRT moguls designed a car that from the front appeared to be a kid-brother to the IND's R-1 through R-9s, except for a "turtle roof" which lyrically curved downward, as opposed to the more squarish IND look.

Simple in its overall design, the IRT cars had one thing over their counterparts on the IND and BMT; they were completely new, top to bottom. St. Louis Car Company delivered fifty of what were called "World's Fair Cars." Total cost: $1,539,330.

Commenting on them, Frederick A. Kramer, observed, "As a practical matter, they were specified to be mechanically and electrically compatible with the hundreds of cars the IRT had bought since 1915."

The first new IRT cars were delivered from St. Louis in September 1938 and were greeted with delight by train buffs merely for their particular characteristics which included enclosed marker lights, an illuminated end sign as well as three sliding doors on either side.

Neither the Fair nor the subways totally transformed Queens, but aspects of the IND construction *did* have a conspicuous effect on the borough's changing topography.

Originally occupied by American Indians, Queens had considerable attractiveness to the Native Americans. With access to the Atlantic Ocean, Queens' first inhabitants also made good use of, what now is, Newtown Creek, Jamaica Bay, Little Neck Bay and Flushing Bay, among other waterways.

The Dutch and English followed in the 17th Century and eventually Queens was divided into several towns, including Newtown, Jamaica and Flushing.

It wasn't until the Civil War era that urbanization was felt in an area that essentially had been a mix of farmland and towns. But once the Long Island Rail Road began spreading its tentacles in an eastward direction, the population increase was marked, and by the late 19th Century, it had climbed to 152,999.

Once the Pennsylvania Railroad, owners of the Long Island Rail Road, completed its monumental East River tunnels in 1910 and electrified the LIRR (starting in 1905), a bonanza was created for land speculators.

Meanwhile, the Brooklyn Rapid Transit helped development of southern Queens with its Liberty Avenue elevated line which stretched to Richmond Hill in 1915. As well, the BRT's Broadway Brooklyn el reached Jamaica at the close of World War I. A further catalyst was the finished IRT Flushing Line which terminated in a subway station at Main Street, Flushing in 1928.

Considerable apartment-building followed much of the subway construction along with smaller residential homes.

Although LIRR stations at Forest Hills and Kew Gardens opened those communities for apartment construction, it wasn't until the land along Queens Boulevard was excavated in 1931 for the new IND line to Jamaica that the housing boom reached its peak.

Modern apartment dwellings sprouted in the Queens Boulevard environs all the way to the Kew Gardens-Union Turnpike station and then beyond.

Yet, with all the Queens construction, the borough egregiously lacked a landmark structure comparable to Manhattan's Empire State Building or Brooklyn's Williamsburg Savings Bank tower at Hanson Place near the Fulton Street shopping center.

This would change as construction crews completed their work on the World's Fair Train in 1938, and the Fair acreage began to take shape, looking more like a gigantic exhibit than a dumping ground for ashes.

A good example of progress took place in January 1938, when notables such as Parks Commissioner Robert Moses, Mayor Fiorello LaGuardia and Queens Borough President George Harvey presided over the cornerstone-laying ceremonies for the New York City pavilion; one of the few edifices to survive to this day. Likewise, work had begun on two other structures which would become unequivocally synonymous with the Fair.

A pair of architectural marvels—the Trylon and Perisphere—became the Fair's twin symbols and household words throughout New York. For example, a Trylon movie theater was erected along Queens Boulevard about the time that the genuine Trylon was being constructed at nearby Flushing Meadow.

Designed by architects Andre Fouilhoux and Wallace Harrison, the three-sided obelisk and incredibly large sphere were stunning contrasts in design. Appearing like a giant, white bowling ball, the Perisphere—according to Harrison—was inspired by the domes of Saint Mark's in Venice.

The Trylon originally was supposed to tower 700 feet above the fairgrounds, but fiscal constraints limited its height to 610 feet. Tall, thin and coming to a point at its apex, the obelisk proved the perfect counterpoint to its circular sister; so much so, that images of them appeared on every conceivable World's Fair souvenir, from drinking glasses to thimbles, not to mention radios, cameras, typewriters, carpet sweepers, and spoons.

In describing the Fair, one guidebook of the era could well have been describing the Trylon and Perisphere itself when it offered: "The Fair is so stupendous, gigantic, super-magnificent that one could write a whole book about it."

BYE-BYE REDBIRDS

One of the most popular cars on the system was the 1964 World's Fair Car. In later years, they were nicknamed Redbirds for their crimson paint job which lasted through 2003. They were eventually replaced by a new fleet of high-tech, stainless steel cars. The oddity is that the old cars were dumped off the Atlantic Coast to create artificial reefs. More than 1,100 were dropped down to Davey Jones' locker. By the way, the Redbirds weren't originally red when they arrived to serve the World's Fair of 1964. Originally, the cars were blue-and-cream colored. Another interesting note is that the cars, which once had special World's Fair lettering in 1964, also had a unique paint job when the Yankees and Mets collided in the World Series of 2000. This time a sign read: Subway Series 2000, on the side of the car.

If the Trylon and Perisphere architecturally symbolized the Fair, Grover Whalen was its human personification.

Known to most New Yorkers of the time as its "Official Greeter," the moustacheoed Whalen was given to *homburgs* and was said to be the father of the ticker tape parade. Officially, he was president of the Fair Corporation and also was fondly remembered as The Big Apple's police commissioner during the Prohibition era.

Between Whalen, the Trylon and Perisphere and the burgeoning new subway, the Fair had a headstart on capturing the public's imagination before the first 75 cent ticket was purchased.

Signing a pact with the renowned and respected St. Louis Car Company, Interborough moguls chose to altogether remove its wooden el trains, some of which once had been 19th century coaches pulled by steam locomotives. They had been electrified in 1902 and worked the Queens-Manhattan run via the Queensborough Bridge.

Meanwhile, construction of the Fair kept pace with the subway improvements designed specifically for the pageant. The steel lattice that formed the Trylon's skeleton could be seen from the newly completed ramp from Willets Point Boulevard IRT station during the summer of 1938. Steelwork for the Perisphere lagged a bit behind.

As for the Independent's fairgrounds spur, its wooden trestle was completed in April 1938 at a time when several of the pavilions were taking shape. These included the Heinz Foods exhibit; the Life-Savers Parachute Tower—later to be moved to Coney Island; the Railroad Building; and Ford's Road of Tomorrow.

In addition to the two-track right-of-way, the World's Fair Train required a two-story signal tower with an interlocking console. A chain-link fence was erected to separate the tracks from the fairgrounds itself. As luck would have it, the soon-to-be-heavily-used amusement area rose adjacent to the IND tracks; which would prove to be a boost, since the parachaute jump, Bobsled and other rides were extremely popular and closed late. Those at the play area invariably chose to return home via the nearby IND rather than the IRT or BMT.

Riders who chose the Independent were greeted by an an ultra-modern station with more attractive contours than its counterparts. Three spacious platforms serviced two tracks and each platform was adorned with new lighting fixtures. Just

East of the Plaza

Before the Astoria el came, Long Island City was undergoing a transformation from a rural hinterland to an industrial center. Jackson Avenue (Northern Boulevard) was serviced by a trolley line in this 1914 view of the landscape. The elevated line soon would change the vista forever. Billboards for Charles H. Fletcher's "Castoria" seemed to follow the subways and els in most boroughs.

The trolley tracks are undisturbed, but the rest of Second Avenue (now 31st Street) south of Broadway in Queens never would be the same, as foundations for the elevated pillars already are in place as far as the eye can see.

Construction progresses on the steel skeleton of the Astoria line at the junction of today's 31st Street and Northern Boulevard.

39th Avenue station witnesses a Ditmars Boulevard-bound set of Standards passing Type-D Triplexes stored on the center track of the BMT Astoria route. After the line's construction as a three-track run, it was determined that express service would not be practical because of the route's relatively short length. Therefore, the center track was used for layup or when one of the outer tracks was out of service for repair.

William Brennan

What came first, the chicken or the egg? In this case, neither. The Ditmars station and the approach viaduct to the Hell gate bridge were built simultaneously, as seen here on October 2, 1913.

Anticipating construction of the el over Queens Boulevard, realtors are advertising "small and large lots" for sale along the route. The once pastoral setting near the future Bliss Street station in 1913 would become an urban center by the start of the Roarin' Twenties.

Steam shovels and miniature steam locomotives were staples for construction of elevated lines. This scene, along Queens Boulevard, near Lowery, was commonplace in the summer of 1913. Note the almost lack of habitation in the background.

Forms for the massive elevated train viaduct take shape over a barren Sunnyside.

One of the most impressive el structures ever constructed belonged to the IRT's Times Square-Flushing line along Queens Boulevard. By June 1921, the art deco stations and viaducts would attract thousands of newcomers to the borough. As one can see through the el portals, homes still had not gone up at Bliss Avenue, but it would only be a matter of months before the building boom would take place.

Using the art deco Queens Boulevard el as a portal, it's possible to look straight across the land that would eventually become residential Sunnyside Gardens. Beyond are the buildings that would be the community of Astoria. In fact, the entire region was so open, it was possible to see all the way to the Hell Gate (railroad) Bridge at ground level. The open-ended gate cars on the trestle were waiting for commencement of el service.

A high view from the roof of the Packard Building of the IRT's brand-new concrete elevated line along Queens Boulevard. A three-car Second Avenue el train is approaching; while on the center track, a gate-car-powered work train is pocketed along with stored Steinway cars, in this 1917 photo.

Main Street in Flushing would become the IRT terminus in Eastern Queens. But, in June 1913, it looked more like a Main Street in Middle America, rather than part of New York's metropolis. The subway station would not be completed until 1927 because of a ten-year hiatus brought about by a conflict between the IRT and Army Corps of Engineers over what type of bridge should be built over Flushing Creek.

R-12 type cars make the scene at 111th Street station in Corona just prior to the opening of the 1964 World's Fair in Flushing Meadow.

William Brennan

William Brennan

below, a mural graced the lower level terminal façade, adding a modernistic touch, albeit without total critical acclaim.

Spread across the main marquee, at the top of the exit ramp, were huge letters—INDEPENDENT SUBWAY—followed by three change booths and a set of eighteen new turnstiles built by the respected Perry Manufacturing Company.

With the Fair targeted to open on Sunday morning, April 30, 1939, all three lines had to have their stations in order and ready to go before then. What's more, the spanking new IND tracks had to be fully tested and approved well before the first fairgoer put his nickel in a turnstile.

The transit race to the homestretch was close. Only eight days remained to the fairgrounds' opening before the IND ran its test operation over the new tracks. Only *one* day was left before the S-SPECIAL—as the IND World's Fair Train was called—went through a full schedule audition. Recently-built R-7 cars proved as reliable as the R-1, R-4 and R-6 which preceded it among the Independent's rolling stock.

IND schedule-makers had concluded that the spur should run at headways determined by the number of straphangers. Minimum headway would be a train every dozen minutes while maximum would be every three minutes.

Both the GG and E trains became the S. It was estimated that travel time to Pennsylvania Station in Manhattan averaged a half-hour from the World's Fair terminal; not bad for a nickel! It was less than fifty minutes to reach Fordham Road in the Bronx.

While the IND still was undergoing final tests, the IRT-BMT launched its center (third) track express service six days before the Fair's premiere. Mayor Fiorello LaGuardia took over the operator's cab for an endless series of photos that Monday, April 24, 1939. "The Little Flower," as the mayor was affectionately known, then accommodated the photographers by posing as a straphanger as well as a seated passenger.

The new IRT-BMT express service proved an instant hit, mostly because it shaved six minutes off the Queens Plaza-Main Street (Flushing) running time. An extra added attraction was the upgraded Willets Point Boulevard station, centered on 123rd Street, just west of the original Flushing Line local stop. It may not have had all the art deco trappings of the IND terminal, but it was as much as embattled IRT-BMT riders could have hoped for considering their many years of campaigning for express (third track) service to and from Manhattan.

Coincidence or not, the World's Fair officially opened its gates at 11 a.m. on Sunday, April 30, 1939, after clocks had been moved ahead one hour for the inauguration of Daylight Saving Time.

All the trains were operating on schedule, but not to the capacity originally anticipated.

Alas, the weatherman had not been included in opening day planning.

Had he been consulted, his advice would have been, "Forget about it!"

Rather than a bright, sunny spring day, the Fair was engulfed in gray and buffeted by wind. It certainly *looked* like rain in the hours up to the ribbon-cutting and, finally, *Jupe Pluvius* unfortunately obliged by the afternoon.

The combination of clouds, wind and rain proved a tough parlay for promoters to beat and it was reflected in less-than-anticipated crowds. For those concerned about which lines proved more attractive, the final statistics gave IRT-BMT the nod, (approximately) 40,000 to 28,629 for the rival IND. Clearly, the LIRR's ten-minutes-for-a-dime promotion worked—to the tune of (approximately) 35,000 Fair customers.

Undaunted by the elements, Fair dignitaries opened festivities with a typical Big Apple flair. Heading the impressive list was President Franklin Delano Roosevelt, who faced not only the Trylon and Perisphere but television cameras as well. While top-hatted dignitaries sat behind him, Roosevelt spoke into almost a dozen radio microphones on a dais with the World's Fair Trylon and Perisphere symbol affixed to the platform's front.

Radio was not the only communications vehicle used by the president. Opening day also marked the first regular American television broadcasts which were carried by the National Broadcasting Company.

"I hereby dedicate the New York World's Fair," Roosevelt intoned as only a New York-bred patrician could. He then continued, putting major emphasis on certain words. "The NEW YORK World's Fair of 1939. And I declare it open to all mankind!"

Many other notables were heard, among them New York Governor Herbert Lehman and Mayor Fiorello LaGuardia. "The Fair," said LaGuardia, "will be dedicated to the future of the American people and the glory of the country."

Everywhere, first-day visitors were greeted by the Fair's official theme, "Building the World of Tomorrow."

Author David Gelernter put it another way: "The Fair epitomized late-Thirties New York. It thrilled and enthralled the city."[8]

Rain or no rain.

Even with precipitation, there were enough indoor activities to keep fairgoers away from the drops. One could spend an hour examining The Ford Cycle of Production or General Motor's Futurama. The problem was that those exhibits—among many others—were so popular, it often required more than an hour waiting on line before actually gaining entrance to the exhibits.

Virtually every exhibit had a "biggest-ever" sense about it. The Parachute Jump was a "largest" and "first" in America. The sundial, designed by Paul Manship, was described as "the largest in the world." The railroad exhibit was unprecedented in size and scope.

Not surprisingly, the Trylon and Perisphere proved to be among the top attractions, from opening day onward. The longest escalators in the world (to that time) were built to carry visitors into the Perisphere. One tunneled through the Trylon and then exited on a concrete path futuristically dubbed the "Helicline." A curved promenade adjoined a pool which acted as a moat between the Trylon and Perisphere.

Opening day rain only put a temporary damper on proceedings. Once the sunshine returned it was accompanied by the kind of throngs anticipated by planners. By day five, the Fair recorded its 1,000,000th customer and the subways responded nobly.

Ironically, it was the IRT-BMT run—having set turnstile records over five days—which suddenly was braked by an unusual event. The powerful United Mine Workers union, headed by thick-browed John L. Lewis, had called a coal-workers strike which tangentially affected both the BMT and IRT lines, each of which depended on their own stockpiles of coal to generate electricity.

Fearing a lengthy strike with a severe

reduction in the city's coal supply, Mayor LaGuardia ordered a cutback of coal use, which resulted in both lines diminishing their service by up to twenty-five percent on some lines, including the World's Fair trains. The strike did not affect the Independent, which had an arrangement with the Consolidated Edison Company, which, in turn, had vast coal resources in which to dip.

Despite dire predictions, the strike was relatively short-lived, and, by May 17, LaGuardia rescinded the service cuts, enabling the IRT-BMT unit to capitalize on the Fair's popularity.

And it *was* popular.

A good example would be *Italia,* the Italian pavilion.

Despite the fact that Italy was headed by the Fascist dictator Benito Mussolini, the country was courted for participation in the Fair by Grover Whalen. The $5,000,000 exhibit not only impressed from the outside—a dazzling stepped waterfall which cascaded from a statue at the top down to the base—but also featured a second-floor restaurant which captured visitors' imagination. It had been designed as a *faux* dining room, ostensibly from a top-of-the-line Italian steamship company.

Waterfalls also lured visitors to the Electric Utilities building although it was less impressive than its Italian counterpart. However, the impressiveness of each was multiplied in the evening when an array of lights illuminated them as they did virtually every exhibit of significance.

"Among scientific features introduced by the Fair," said Whalen, "perhaps the most revolutionary was the use of light."

Less revolutionary, but no less fascinating—especially to rail fans—was the City's own tribute to its underground railroad. It wasn't big, and it certainly wasn't gaudy in the manner of the sprawling railroad exhibit.

In fact, the Board of Transportation's exhibit was thoroughly lacking the kind of fuss and fanfare normally associated with the Fair's exuberance. Its geography said it all. The tribute to the Independent System was nestled—virtually hidden—in a corner of the City Building.

This was unfortunate considering that, square foot for square foot, there was much to offer; especially to a New York City transit buff.

For example, there was a listing on one wall of pertinent transit facts; another explained how the growth of the subway system affected communities. In bold letters it announced: REAL ESTATE VALUES GROW—WITH THE MILES OF TRANSPORTATION.

On the wall diagonally opposite—almost from floor to ceiling—was a map of the four boroughs with subway and elevated lines. Every route, not simply the IND's, was laid out in full and further embellished to its right by a period-by-period history of New York's transit from horse-drawn vehicles to the brand-new World's Fair Subway.

The IND's R-9 cars, its pride and joy, were promoted with a mock-up, cutaway version, five seats in different arrangements as well as the porcelainized "straps" and overhead light bulbs. Instead of windows, a number of photos depicting subway construction was featured.

But to electric train fans, this was all small potatoes compared to the main course; a marvelous six-car scale model of an IND consist of R-9s.

Collectors of model trains—Lionel, American Flyer or otherwise—were accustomed to seeing models of steam locomotives such as the New York Central's *Hudson* or the Pennsylvania's ultra-modern *Torpedo*.

Whether it was O27, O Gauge or the huge Standard Gauge model train, both Lionel and American Flyer featured either freight or passenger cars of main line railroads. One was unaccustomed to seeing a Standard Gauge model of a *subway* car; which is why the Board of Transportation exhibit was so special.

Not only was the six-car train exquisitely accurate in detail, but also utilized a third rail, just as the real R-9s did. And to actually make it run, the Subway Division built a motorman's *controller* on a circular base enabling even small children to power the set.

Directly ahead of the controller was a standard IND signal—green, amber, red—with an identification number WF 1939. When the signal flashed either green or amber, a pull on the controller would move the six-car unit around the loop.

After a short run, the consist would automatically come to a stop and a red light would flash on the signal. All of this was meant to not only promote the IND but tout its virtues, safety among them.

Under the three-light signal, the Board of Transportation emphasized the point with the following message: THE AUTOMATIC BLOCK SIGNAL SYSTEM MAKES THE NEW YORK CITY SUBWAYS THE SAFEST IN THE WORLD.

Compared to the other exhibits such as Eastman Kodak, Dupont and General Electric, the Board of Transportation's alcove kept its bragging to a minimum. It did, however, provide a boost to two of its engineering wonders, the Fourth Avenue (Brooklyn) viaduct, which crosses the Gowanus Canal, and the thoroughly impressive Fourth Avenue station at Fourth Avenue and Tenth Street. They were featured in a diorama and a smaller scale model.

Far from being the hit of the fair, the subway exhibit nonetheless captured the fancy of train buffs; just as Railroads on Parade did on a much larger scale.

The 1939 Fair was a huge success—much less so financially—and it was held over for a 1940 version which was scaled down for both political and economic reasons.

On the political side, Josef Stalin's brief honeymoon with Adolph Hitler was enough of a turn-off for Fair officials to cause them to boot the Russians right out of Flushing Meadow. (Nazi Germany had never been represented.) Before the 1940 edition opened, the Soviet exhibition had been razed.

England, which had been at war with Germany since September 1939, took a hit at the Fair when on July 4, 1940 a bomb exploded at the British Empire Pavilion, killing two policemen.

Nevertheless, on closing day, October 26, 1940, the Fair hit its two-year, single-day attendance record with 550,962 going through its turnstiles.

Overall, the subway turnstiles spun as well as could be expected. The IRT-BMT operation was the preferred route for heading to the Fair, yet the IND registered some of its best numbers at night for those going home. According to one estimate, the IRT-BMT captured about 65 percent of the riders while the IND had the rest.

Some transit theorists have argued over the years that the IND spur could have been a major problem-solver for the city had it been made permanent and eventually extended to the brand-new LaGuardia Airport nearby. A direct subway-to-the-planes certainly was possible from an engineering viewpoint and would have been a terrific transportation asset today.

But such a transportation panacea was not in the cards and, like most of the Fair's structures, the IND terminal, tracks and other aspects of the spur began being eliminated on January 15, 1941.

Fortunately, the IRT-BMT Willets Point expanded station remained intact and proved to be a tremendous adjunct to Shea Stadium when the Mets ball park would open in 1964.

In a transit sense, it was one meaningful legacy of the "World of Tomorrow." Frederick A. Kramer so aptly remarked in his superb *Subway to the World's Fair*, "There is another legacy that should not be overlooked, the indelible memories etched in the minds of millions."[9]

Without question, the 1939-40 World's Fair at Flushing Meadow left a lasting, positive impression with New Yorkers as well as visitors from out-of-town.

As a result, those 1939-40 fairgoers who still were around in 1964, when yet another extravaganza was targeted at Flushing Meadow, experienced a surge of excitement when the first post-World War II exposition was announced.

But in every way, shape and form the 1964-65 Fair was a disaster.

For starters, there was no way the Trylon and Perisphere ever could be duplicated in an architectural sense. For 1964 a rather prosaic Unisphere was the designated symbol. Erected by U.S. Steel, it hardly stirred the senses. While eighty countries were represented, the collection of buildings lacked the creativity and inspiration of the pre-war version.

Construction delays and other complications caused by World's Fair Corporation President Robert Moses further dampened spirits before opening day, April 22, 1964.

From the subway viewpoint, there no longer was a direct IND connection as existed in 1939. The IRT obtained a new fleet which was lavishly painted and remained one of the most attractive aspects of the entire operation.

The absence of the IND link, as much as anything, symbolized the disappointment of the 1964-65 edition of the World's Fair.

One Man's Memories of What It Was Like To Take the Subway to the World's Fair

When I was seven years old, in 1939, it was possible for me to take one of three subway routes to Flushing Meadow.

1. I either went by subway with my mother; or,

2. If I stayed overnight in Forest Hills, I went by subway with my Aunt Lucie; or,

3. If I wanted to take the ultimate scenic route, I'd go with my mother and father on the one and only Flushing Line. This, I should add, was limited to one—and *only* one—time only.

In all cases, trips to the fair were monumental in every way, shape and form.

For starters, bear in mind that I had never been to a World's Fair before.

And, New York City had never had an exposition of this magnitude.

This was my personal, real-life Oz.

From our house in Brooklyn, the traditional—easy to use—trip consumed about

Queens Boulevard and the Trains to the Fair

What the IRT Flushing Line did for the western portion of Queens Boulevard, the IND would do for the eastern district. In October 1930, the area around Queens Boulevard and 75th Road hardly could be called populous. A trolley line gave life to a rural landscape that would dramatically change with construction of the IND's four-track main line to Jamaica. Surveyors are checking out the terrain in preparation for the big dig.

The most ambitious subway project in Queens began unfolding in the midst of the Great Depression. A four-track IND line would run under Queens Boulevard all the way to Forest Hills, Kew Gardens and Jamaica. This March 1930 photo shows the beginnings of Queens Boulevard's transformation with the relocation of the trolley tracks to the edge of the street, enabling surface transit to continue while rapid transit is being developed.

Here is the almost-completed approach and station of the IND at the 1939 Fair. The Fair's symbol, the Trylon and Perisphere, is on the left in the distance, and on the right is the Jewish cemetery that still exists. Today's Van Wyck Expressway uses the IND roadbed as its foundation.

We see the almost-finished terminal at Horace Harding Boulevard, on October 3, 1938. Three platforms surround the two tracks, allowing passengers to exit via the outside platforms while boarding passengers waited on the center platform.

A quiet moment at the World's Fair station just prior to the beginning of the Fair, with a typical four-car shuttle train ready for boarding. The S-Special World's Fair trains shuttled between the 71st and Continental Avenues station on Queens Boulevard and the Fair.

David Perlmutter

For the 1964 Fair, the Flushing Line IRT cars were given a special paint job, along with a selected number of rolling stock with state names. Seen here in Corona yard are the State of Vermont and the State of Kansas cars.

William Brennan

While there have been no more world's fairs in New York City, the area still plays host to events of international importance. Here we see samples of the latest rolling stock along with recently-retired Redbird-type cars in view of the tennis stadium, home of the U.S. Open.

forty minutes, depending on whether we got off the GG local at Queens Plaza and changed to the E or F express; or if we took the local all the way to the Fair grounds, via the new connecting spur.

The beautiful part of the trip in 1939 had everything to do with newness.

Our GG, Brooklyn-Queens Crosstown line, was only two- years-old and as fresh as a subway could be. And the Fair was brand-new!

So was the spur.

In fact, the new World's Fair Train held as much promise to me as the prospect of the Fair itself. I wasn't particularly interested in the run from our home Myrtle-Willoughby station to Roosevelt Avenue express stop in Jackson Heights, but I knew that once we got to the Continental Avenue-Forest Hills stop, the train-riding fun would really start.

With my head pressed hard against the big, front R-9 window, I gaped at the tunnel ahead as we switched off the main, four-track line and headed under the 75th Avenue local station. The train meandered to the left—for what was a J-shaped run—straightened out and, suddenly, a flash of light was visible about thirty yards up the tunnel.

For a train buff, emerging from a tunnel portal usually is the best part of a trip whether it happens *en route* to Yankee Stadium, Prospect Park or, in this case, the World's Fair. It signifies daylight; something good and exciting ahead; or to put it another way, it's all about the joy of railroading!

As we lumbered out of the portal, I instantly realized we were about to cross a trestle that bridged the relatively new Grand Central Parkway. As cars buzzed east and west below, the train *thunk-thunk-thunk-thunked* over a series of switches,

moving directly toward the Jamaica tower, repair shop and the Jamaica yards which, to this day, is a major maintenance facility for the Queens subway.

Once past the yard, the train briefly lurched left once more, rolling in the direction of Willow Lake. A few trees dotted the Queens "countryside," in the surrounding trackside area. As we approached Fountain Lake on the left, I was told that Mount Hebron Cemetery was coming up on the right.

My grandfather—dad's father—Joseph Fischler was buried there, and I recalled pop and I once taking an endlessly long Flushing Avenue trolley ride out to visit the burial plot at Mount Hebron, a few years earlier.

The train began decelerating as we passed the tombstones, and as I peered left, I knew why: ahead of us was a panoply of structures; some tall (the Trylon), some round (the Perisphere) and others inconspicuous. All in all, it was a breathtaking panorama that grew more and more impressive as the R-9 approached the terminal and skirted the Amusement Area with its Parachute Jump and assorted other rides; some of which I wouldn't try if you had paid me.

Slowly and surely, the motorman brought his train to a stop several feet before a bumper which signaled tracks-end at the northern portion of the terminal. A station sign with big white lettering announced WORLD'S FAIR.

We were here!

After the four sets of doors opened, Mom and I stepped on to the fresh, grey concrete platform, walked left to the exit, past the turnstiles and down the ramp tongue that stuck out of the terminal's mouth.

The first thing I noticed as we approached the ramp was the array of flags which lined the sidewalks; first Old Glory, followed by the City's official banner, and then those of nations represented at the pageant.

At ramp's end, we were overwhelmed by the possibilities ahead. The assortment of rides immediately tempted me, but Mom thought it would be rushing things. Instead, she pointed to an amphitheater ahead to the left, facing eastward on Fountain Lake.

"We're going to the Aquacade," Mother declared. "I want to see Eleanor Holm."

And that was that. There was no debating this issue. And why should there be? I was so tickled to be in the World's Fair, *any* event would have suited me just fine.

The name Eleanor Holm meant nothing to me, but Mom explained that she was married to a famous impresario named Billy Rose. Furthermore, it was Rose who produced the aquatic musical revue and Holm was its star.

No doubt about it, Billy Rose's Aquacade was as popular as any show in the amusement sector and the crowds attested to that. Fortunately, the amphitheater, magnificently set at the lake shore, held 10,000, which kept waiting on line to a minimum.

Cheap seats—which always was our priority—went for forty cents (adult) with a fifteen-cent program. Considering Holm's popularity—and beauty—photos in the program made it a must.

At age seven, I was more interested in the co-star, Johnny Weissmuller, who was a movie hero as Tarzan, and an Olympic swimmer as well. To me, the show was a knockout, especially the Aquacade's 260-foot-long, 40-foot-high "water curtain," which beautifully lit up at night.

Rose, who also ran a Broadway night club named The Diamond Horseshoe, didn't miss a trick—with a cast of 500 girls, comics, singers and plenty of music. I couldn't have enjoyed it more. Ditto for Mom.

My most memorable stop, but not for obvious reasons, was the Ford Exhibit; but I'll get to that in a moment.

Once we left the Aquacade, Mom and I crossed World's Fair Boulevard—merely a walkway on the grounds—and passed the General Electric, Westinghouse and Electrical Products exhibits. We hung a left at the Bridge of Wings which crossed over Grand Central Parkway. That took us directly to the Ford building's entrance.

Right next to it was the most-talked-about General Motors pageant, which many considered the best of all at the entire Fair, but we had first come to Ford; so GM would have to wait.

The Ford exhibit stunned me to the very core. Remember, after Aquacade, this was the first commercial pavilion I had seen and it was even better than anticipated. The enormity of what was billed as the "Ford Cycle of Production" just knocked me out. (Much later, I learned that some critics regarded it as the best of all at the Fair.) Essentially, it was, as the title suggested, the cycle of car-building from the digging for raw materials to the automobile itself.

After about a half-hour of viewing, we agreed that it was time to sit down—my mother was 39 years old at the time—and take a breather. While Mom walked to the ladies room, I pulled out my latest prize acquisition.

Having been an avid listener to the Tom Mix five-day-a-week radio show, I sent in Ralston (cereal) box tops every time Mix had a giveaway. That meant at any given time, I owned a silver Tom Mix spur pin, a secret decoder, or a special Tom Mix comic book unavailable at any candy store. But best of all, was my pearl-handle Tom Mix single-bladed knife, which had only arrived by mail a day earlier.

I had carefully stashed the knife in my left pocket and managed to grasp it tightly wherever we went, for fear that it might slip out and be annexed by some other Mix fan who happened by.

While mother was gone, I lifted the knife out of its "safe" and began ogling the absolutely gleaming white pearl handle with the red TOM MIX lettering. With my right thumb nail inserted into the blade head, I carefully lifted the silver cutting device to its open position and tested its sharpness by lightly rubbing it over the inside of my thumb.

Man, it *was* sharp.

Too sharp.

I began closing it by pushing the blade to its half-way position and then started the final move, snapping the blade shut. Somehow, I misjudged two things: 1. I didn't realize how strong the spring was on the knife; 2. I forgot to remove my left index finger which managed to be in harm's way.

Snap!

The knife closed on my unsuspecting finger and, before I could even pull the blade to its open position, blood began spurting from my finger. Reaching into my right pocket, I pulled out a white handkerchief and wound it tightly several times around the wound.

For a moment it stanched the bleeding; but only for a few seconds. This was major stuff, and soon the handkerchief had turned crimson. Mom arrived not a

moment too soon and, with uncanny mother's intuition, realized that this was no minor matter. She pulled out her own rather large hanky—my mother sneezed a lot—and wrapped it as tightly as possible.

I guess I was too stunned to cry but I was terribly upset at what I had done. Meanwhile, Mom hustled me over to a first-aid station where the mother of all bandages was applied after the nurse had finally stopped the bleeding.

Thankfully, the General Motors exhibit was right next door because I needed something major to distract me from the agonizingly sliced finger.

There were plenty of other distractions—mostly beautiful exhibits, such as the redwood-faced Contemporary Art Building and the Medicine and Public Health Building, which featured several murals by Hildreth Meire. However, none could compare with the General Motors Pavilion.

Mother wanted to see the GM pavilion as much as she had the Aquacade. Already, a number of people on our block had raved about it and come home with little buttons that said, "I Have Seen the Future."

The waiting line was long, but that made the sense of anticipation even more acute.

Just about everybody around us had assumed there would be a delay because of Futurama's popularity. After all, it had been promoted in virtually every prominent publication, including *Architectural Record*. According to *The Record*: "At General Motors, the crowd was decoratively the making of the building, giving life, brilliant color, and motion to the snaked ramps against the blank cliff-like wall." Of course, I was less interested in the architecture than actually getting into the building iself.

Despite the hot sun, we busied ourselves, taking in the sights around us and chatting with some out-of-towners in front of us on the endless line. If there was one sight we never tired of gaping at it was the Trylon and Perisphere. With all due respect to the Eiffel Tower, Taj Mahal and pyramids at Ghiza, the Trylon and Perisphere—they *must* be considered together, never separately—endlessly arrested my attention, impressed me with their beauty and, more than anything, emerged not only as symbols of the Fair, but also New York City.

Our patience on the General Motors' line was justified. Once inside we were entranced by "Futurama." This was the GM *chef d'oeuvre*, designed by a big name of the day, Norman Bel Geddes. It portrayed an America of the 1960s linked by vast ribbons of highways. Since we never owned a car, and rarely were driven in one, I found it hard to envision the kind of highway system GM was projecting for us, especially with the modernistic autos that bore no similarities to my Uncle Ben's 1937 Pontiac.

After leaving the GM Building, we had several options; including the nearby Chrysler Motors Building, which featured wing-like pylons that seemed to reach to the sky. In its own way it reminded me of the magnificent Chrysler skyscraper in Midtown Manhattan.

Much as I appreciated the GM, Ford and Chrysler shows, I was more anxious to see the trains—railroad trains and subway trains—which were nearby in what was an enormous transportation area.

If I was impressed by the GM pavilion, I was overwhelmed by the train show.

Virtually every aspect of railroading was evident, from models of the earliest steam engines such as the famous "General" built in 1853, the Ross Winans built in 1845, and the Daniel Nason built in 1844, to the newest streamliners such as the 140-foot, 526-ton Pennsylvania steam locomotive, the 6100. It was the largest ever built by the Pennsy's shops in Altoona, Pennsylvania. I felt like doing somersaults of joy when I came upon the gigantic Pennsylvania Railroad flagship locomotive that in some way resembled my Lionel model, Pennsy Torpedo. In addition to the steam engines, a host of state-of-the-art diesels—soon to put the steamers out of business—were featured. Much as I preferred the steam locomotives, I marveled at the sleek designs of the diesels in the same manner that I gawked over the new Ford model cars and GM's car-of-the-future.

Mom instinctively knew that we could have spent the entire day at the train exhibit—which featured a dynamite show called "Railroads On Parade"—and I would have been thoroughly satisfied. "Railroads on Parade" included a re-enactment of the famous Wedding of the Rails at Promontory Point, Utah in 1869.

She gave me plenty of time to take it all in—my mother also very graciously purchased a souvenir "Railroads On Parade" booklet which I retained for many, many years before it somehow disappeared from our house. Then, we moved on to yet another transit aspect I adored.

Frankly, I never anticipated that the World's Fair would even have room for trolley cars but, sure enough, we found one. Naturally, it had to have a futuristic element to it even though streetcars were on their way out in many American cities.

But there *was* an ultra-modern trolley already on the streets of many cities, including New York (Brooklyn). It was called the Presidents' Conference Car—

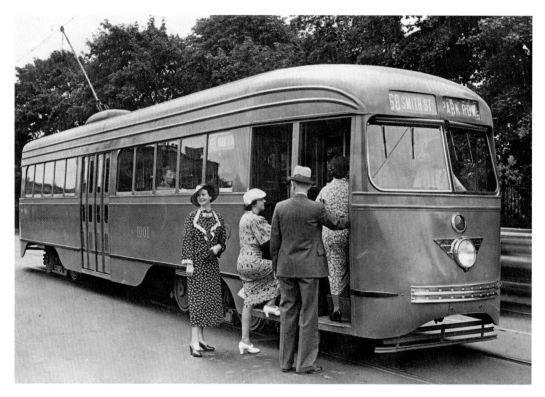

The PCC (Presidents' Conference Committee) Car was the most modern trolley to appear on Brooklyn streets. The quiet, speedy streamliners made their debut in 1936 and were so successful, much of their state of the art technology was used on subway cars built later.

PCC to transit *aficionados*—built by the St. Louis Car Company.

Loaded with many unusual features, including foot pedals instead of a hand controller and hand-operated brake, the PCC ran near our house on the Vanderbilt Avenue line. I had the pleasure of riding it a few times and was mesmerized by its speed, relative quiet and lyrical design.

To highlight the streetcar streamliner at the Fair, a large model PCC was set on a mini-stage with tracks running from end to end. A mock motorman's compartment—replete with all the PCC gee-gaws including foot pedals—sat facing the stage.

By sitting on the motorman's cushioned seat, you could maneuver the trolley by pressing the accelerator (right) pedal and bring it to a stop with the brake (left) pedal.

Of all the hands-on exhibits, *this* was

the one which excited me the most. By age seven, I had decided that I wanted to be either a subway or trolley car motorman and, here I was, getting my chance to "operate" a PCC!

Unfortunately, it wasn't to be.

The motorman's cab was designed for an adult operator. Once I took the seat, I realized that my little legs could hardly reach the foot pedals, let alone maneuver them. I stretched and stretched but the bottoms of my shoes just barely touched the brake and controller pedals.

Realizing it was a lost cause, I despondently pulled myself up and watched the cars go back and forth as taller and older folks ran the PCC. I hoped and prayed that by the end of the summer, I would have grown at least three inches for another run at the PCC.

A huge number of locomotives both old and new, as well as large and small, were on display at the 1939 World's Fair. One of my favorite aspects of the exhibit was the pageant, "Railroads on Parade." The staged show was written and produced by Edward Hungerford and featured classic steam locomotives. Some of the engines made the trip to the Fair under their own power; others towed in a convoy. Here, one of the older examples, the "William Crooks," traveled a long distance (from St. Paul, Minnesota) to the Fair under its own steam. At Binghamton, New York she comes at us at full bore.

No "Railroads On Parade" pageant would be complete without a re-enactment of the driving of the golden spike at Promontory, Utah in May 1869. Here a Chicago, Burlington and Quincy 4-4-0 was re-painted to resemble Union Pacific's Number 119, which had participated in the original event.

Among the varied locomotives featured as the 1939 World's Fair was the newly-built Norfolk and Western 2-6-6-4, flanked by a New York Central Mohawk, only partially seen on the left.

A Delaware, Lackawanna and Western Hudson-type locomotive with the words "Pocono Mountain Route" on its running board vies for attention with a Pennsylvania Railroad M1a Mountain-type locomotive.

The last—and in some ways best—rail exhibit we caught on the first day was the least impressive-looking from the outside of all.

Nestled in a corner of the New York City pavilion was the Board of Transportation's testimonial to its Independent Subway (as mentioned above). Oh, there was plenty to see in the City building, but my primary curiosity centered on whether or not justice would be done to the IND.

In all its simplicity, the IND alcove did right by me.

Seeing real signal lights up close was an adventure. Studying the New York transit time line on the wall was edifying, to say the least, and whetted my appetite for more subway history.

However, nothing about the Board of Transportation show moved me more than the six-car model of the R-9 IND trains.

Wow! Accustomed to my little O27 Lionels, I couldn't believe that I actually was looking at an electric train set of subways. (Neither Lionel nor American Flyer ever sold models of subway cars.) What's more, these were exquisitely drawn to scale right down to the CITY OF NEW YORK lettering on the side of the cars.

Better still, the cars didn't just sit there. They rolled for a long distance along a specially constructed "tunnel" that perfectly replicated the squarish IND structure which I had come accustomed to while riding the GG line. *And* to make the real-life aspect even better, the train set had a subway-type third rail! That was the capper.

"I guess I'm never gonna have a set like that in our house," I wondered out loud, "am I Mom?"

She wasted no time with her answer: "You're right."

No way could I complain about my first day at the Fair as we headed back to the Independent subway ramp. The walk brought us past the amusement area and the 250-foot parachute jump.

"Can I do some rides?" I asked my mother, knowing it was a long-shot.

She looked at the big Bulova clock to the right of the subway ramp.

"It's getting dark. By the time we get home, it'll be 'way past your bedtime. You'll be back again."

Frankly, I was too tired to complain. Plus, there was always Aunt Lucie and Uncle Ben, who lived right in the shadow of the Fair.

Among my family favorites, Lucie and Ben Friedman had only recently moved into the new Girard Apartments which were constructed right after the IND Queens Line opened. I could easily take the GG to Queens Boulevard and then the E or F express to Union Turnpike-Queens Boulevard. It was a short, pleasant walk to the Girard—I used to pretend that I was a BMT Standard car on that five-minute stroll—where Lucie and Ben treated me like visiting royalty.

One day in that summer of 1939 Aunt Lucie invited me over with the prospect of a World's Fair visit a good possibility.

On a bright, sunny Tuesday in July, Mom sent me off with plenty of nickels and a dollar to spend at the Fair. (I guess she figured that Aunt Lucie would handle the rest.)

Travelling the subway alone never was a problem even at age seven. I never hesitated about when to change from the local to express and which exit at Union Turnpike was closest to the Girard apartments. I even knew the "secret" side entrance to Aunt Lucie's building which took me past the laundry room right up to the elevator.

Lucie, one of my all-time favorites,

greeted me with a hug and almost instantly popped the question: "Would you like to go to the World's Fair?" I didn't even have to answer; just flashed a smile and she knew the answer. Lucie had the living room Philco radio on when I arrived. Martin Block, the *Make Believe Ballroom* disk jockey, was playing "Amapola," "Begin the Beguine," and "Moonlight Serenade." I loved the tunes and promised myself the 78 rpm record would be added to my collection which had started with Bob Crosby's rendition of "The Little Red Fox."

We took the E train to Continental Avenue station and then crossed over to the World's Fair Shuttle which whisked us right to the fairgrounds.

Aunt Lucie already had visited the Fair several times and made that happily clear to me. "It's your treat, Stanley," she insisted, "where shall we start?"

I didn't want to seem like a greedy, games-only kid, so I said, "Let's go to the Kodak place, then Heinz and, after that, I'd like to go to the rides."

Lucie had bought me a Kodak Baby Brownie *Special* camera for my seventh birthday, and I had it in hand for this special occasion. It was a squarish, black camera that sold for two dollars; much better than the plain Baby Brownie which went for a buck but lacked the stylish peephole of the *Special*.

What I liked most about visiting Kodak was its exhibit of color film which, at the time, seemed so advanced as to be unthinkable. The most memorable thing about Heinz—apart from the free samples—was the pickle-shaped souvenir pin everyone received at the exit. (I do believe that just about every kid in my Public School 54 class showed up in September with a Heinz pickle pinned to his or her outfit.)

Once we left the Heinz condiment show, Aunt Lucie wasted no time turning off toward Billy Rose's Aquacade and beyond to the amusement area.

There was virtually every Coney Island-type amusement and carnival event as well as a Merrie England area and then some in the Fair's vast entertainment section, including a miniature pyramid, Arctic Girl's Tomb of Ice, and Frank Buck's Jungleland.

Just about everyone who knew about the World's Fair understood that the automatic hit among the rides was the Parachute Jump sponsored by Life Savers candy. It was the amusement area's version of the Eiffel Tower and was based on the same type of device used by the Army Air Force to train its parachutists. Strand upon strand of steel stretched skyward, while strings of cables hung from the tower connecting to the white parachutes that dropped and climbed carrying the more intrepid fair-goers; none of whom ever fell out of their seats.

Of course, I had no intentions of testing my luck on that crazy ride. My type of ride was closer to *terra firma*. The merry-go-round was just fine. Bumping electric cars was just great, but the best of all was a ride I never thought I'd ever have the nerve to try.

Actually, the Bobsled seemed a lot tougher on the outside than it was inside. I mean, how bad can a Bobsled be? It's only "snow," right? And I loved snow.

Lucie gave me the required quarter and I got on line with a false sense of confidence. Unlike traditional roller coasters, which are solely outdoor rides, the Bobsled started on the inside.

Sleek and streamlined to give the feel of a true bobsled, the cars had deep, cush-

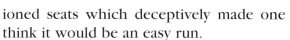

THE SECOND AVENUE SUBWAY—
THE LITTLE ENGINE THAT COULDN'T

One of the most popular riddles in the Big Apple involves Manhattan's underground. It goes like this:

QUESTION: What's the definition of a real New Yorker?

ANSWER: A real New Yorker is a person who knows (for sure) that the Second Avenue subway will never be built.

There never has been a project that has so constantly annoyed New York straphangers longer than proposals for an East Side subway linking Harlem to Lower Manhattan.

In 2004, the 100th anniversary of the subway was not the only underground event recognized.

Another, less honorable, milestone was the 75th birthday of the first proposal to build the Second Avenue subway.

Over and over and over again plans to build the 8.5 mile East Side line were advanced but never finalized.

Granted, some tunnels actually were built, and at one point it appeared that the Second Avenue project would be finished, but, in the end, money never was available for the project and it wound up back on the drawing board.

On December 23rd, 2003, a Newsday editorial zeroed in on the Second Avenue project once more and concluded: "It's time to find the money and build the public what it inarguably needs."

Funny, but those same words were being uttered on December 23rd, 1929.

Obviously, when it comes to the Second Avenue subway, nothing changes.

And nothing is finished!

ioned seats which deceptively made one think it would be an easy run.

It wasn't.

Once the Bobsled left its starting gate, it climbed a hill—just like a regular roller coaster—but once it began its downward plunge, it also began climbing a bobsled-like series of turns; more or less just like the real thing.

Its speed was much more than I had anticipated; and whenever the cars climbed the side of the run, there was always the feeling that they would go right up and over and that would be the end of all of us.

Well, it wasn't quite the end of me, but I had my doubts right through the last excrutiatingly dangerous turn until we finally straightened out and rushed down to the sharply-braked finish line.

After the Bobsled, I *was* finished.

"I think we can go home now," I implored Aunt Lucie, who immediately got the message.

My mom and dad rarely went together with me to the Fair. Usually, we'd go on weekdays—when it was less crowded—and that's when my father worked.

But we did go to the Fair on one memorable occasion because my folks granted my wish and agreed to take the IRT Flushing Line.

I wanted to go this route although it was far out of the way because the IRT had the newest cars on the system; newer, even, than the IND's R-9s.

Even though the R-9s were fresh off the assembly line, their design was the same as the R-1, which had made its debut almost a decade earlier.

However, the IRT departed from its usual frugal philosophy and invested in a totally different style car than the one which ran on its original 1904 Manhattan route. Manufactured by the St. Louis Car Company in 1938, the IRT's World's Fair cars in many ways matched the older IRT Low Vs but boasted more powerful motors as well as stylish lines that marked them as "modern."

These cars marked the first new equipment ordered by the IRT since 1925; which was enough reason to want to ride them.

We reached the IRT World's Fair cars by taking the IND to 42nd Street and then walking over to the IRT Times Square station. Once we reached the lower level where the Flushing line terminated, I spotted the new cars, which, despite a dark paint job, still were gleaming with newness.

Not only were the cars new to me, but the route was one I had never before experienced; mostly because we usually rode either the IND or the BMT.

As much as the Bobsled thrilled me in an amusement park fashion, the Flushing Line offered excitement like none other on the system. The run started eastward in Manhattan in mysterious-looking tunnels unlike anything I had experienced on the IND. I later learned that they were called the Steinway Tunnels, originally built for streetcars which would connect Manhattan with Long Island City and other parts of Queens. The tall, narrow tunnels had the feel of an amusement park fun house ride.

Curiously exciting, the IRT ride got even better as the World's Fair train—it had a convenient front window for watching—reached the other side of the East River. The first stop, Van Alst Avenue, still was underground, but the train soon climbed out to fresh air after 49th-Hunters Point Avenue and began a circuitous route above Long Island City in a manner that could only be described as roller-coaster-like.

Better still, the very audible *tkoo-tkoo-tkoo-tkoo* as the wheels crossed the elevated rail joints provided a variation on the Myrtle Avenue el rhythms, but distinctly more up-tempo.

Man, was I ever happy that my parents consented to this trip!

As we approached Queens Plaza el station, it got even better. This was the meeting place with the BMT Astoria Line which emerged from a tunnel and also climbed into the Queens Plaza station. And below was the Pennsylvania and Long Island Rail Road Sunnyside storage yards, which served Pennsylvania station and were filled with all manner of rolling stock. This was a rail fan's dream!

And the thrill went on.

After Queens Plaza, the World's Fair Train continued in a northeasterly direction until it reached a right-handed curve over Roosevelt Avenue, heading toward Queens Boulevard. At this point, we were riding on something that I hadn't seen anywhere before in my travels; a monstrous concrete viaduct which carried the three-track route for three stops to 46th Street-Bliss station.

Upon reaching Roosevelt Avenue in Woodside, the construction reverted back to the more traditional elevated trestle which—because of the steel rather than concrete—once again accentuated the wonderful rail sounds.

When we reached 61st Street station in Woodside, the trestle rose above the Long Island Rail Road's main line and its Woodside terminal. Below, I could see a

Two views of the 1964 World's Fair at Flushing Meadow—the Unisphere and the Chinese Pavilion.   Both photos, John Henderson

tuscan red LIRR train pulling away from the platform; its circular (ping-pong) windows almost staring me in the face.

The ride through Jackson Heights, and then Corona, offered one terrific view after another, until we finally could see the outline of the Trylon and Perisphere ahead of us. Within minutes, we had arrived at the rejuvenated Willets Point Boulevard station and the World's Fair.

For one—and only one—time I could say that the *ride* to the World's Fair was as exciting as being at the Fair itself!

The same hardly could be said about the 1964 World's Fair.

A quarter-century of my life had elapsed between Flushing Meadow expositions. At age 32, I hardly was as excited about going to see the dull, drab and lifeless Unisphere as I was about the Trylon and Perisphere.

When the 1964 Fair was being planned, I had been working as a reporter for Hearst's flagship evening newspaper, *The New York Journal-American*, and had followed the fair's evolution—political and otherwise—as a sometime City Hall newsman.

The Fair boss' Robert Moses—notorious for his anti-rapid transit stances over the years—had created a negative charisma quotient long before the pageant had even opened.

A sense hung over the city that there simply would be no way that the 1964 exhibition would capture the spirit and excitement of 1939.

It wasn't just the pall left by Moses' machinations that became a civic turn-off; nothing about the exhibits arrested attention as General Motors *Futurama* had done or the extravagant *Railroads on Parade*.

The 1964 amusement area, topped by the Parachute Jump in 1939, was a total bummer, and shows such as Billy Rose's *Aquacade* were sorely missing.

I remember subwaying to the 1964 Fair with a girlfriend via the Flushing Line. It was September 1964.

Only two things left me with positive feelings; the delicious Belgian Waffles and the new IRT cars.

The waffles proved to be a terrific discovery and the IRT never looked better—going and coming.

Perhaps it is significant that I never went back to that 1964 Fair again!

Bay Ridge was still awaiting its subway when this photo was taken in 1913 at 79th Street and Ridge Avenue.

CHAPTER SIX

GOING TO

Fort Hamilton, Bay Ridge, Bensonhurst and Dyker Heights

Over Hill, Over Dale,
As We Hit The Dusty Trail,
And The Caissons Go Rolling Along

Caissons were not an uncommon part of the Brooklyn landscape along the waterfront not far from the present Verrazano-Narrows Bridge.

Nor was there any shortage of cannons, bayonets and other military *materiel.*

This was Fort Hamilton, one of the oldest, continuously garrisoned federal posts in America.

It began as a home to the Nyack Indians; a magnificent tract, overlooking the entrance to the New York harbor with vistas extending to Staten Island on the west.

In 1652, the Indians sold the land to the Dutch West India Company. The governor of New Netherland had previously (1647) approved a deed for nearby New Utrecht to Anthony Jansen van Salee. Bay Ridge—along with New Utrecht—thus became one of the first six towns in Kings County.

For protection, the Dutch built a blockhouse overlooking the bay. Because of its strategic value, the land continued to be used for military purposes. During the War of 1812, American forces erected an earth and timber work which, according to historians, prevented a British assault on the county.

In time, the earth and timber work became obsolete and was replaced by the first granite fort in New York harbor. It was named for Alexander Hamilton and evolved into a major military installation.

The surrounding community originally was called Yellow Hook because of the ubiquitous yellowish clay which pervaded the earth. However, a yellow fever epidemic gripped the area in the late 1840s, inspiring locals to change the name.

Logic prevailed. Since the land was on a glacial ridge, overlooking the New York Bay, Yellow Hook became Bay Ridge; just as simple as that.

Major development of both Fort Hamilton and Bay Ridge began to take

"The U.S. Field Artillery March," music John Phillip Sousa, Carl Fischer, Inc., © 1918

Constructing Brooklyn's Fourth Avenue Subway

Bay Ridge had been home to upper-class New Yorkers until the Fourth Avenue subway arrived after World War I. This vista from 79th Street in 1913 looking north to the mansions along Shore Road would dramatically change once the BRT began tunneling under Fourth Avenue going south to Dyker Heights.

The Dual Contracts had just been approved, paving the way for a new Fourth Avenue Subway to run from Downtown Brooklyn through Bay Ridge. With the Brooklyn Academy of Music on the left, the intersection of Ashland Place and Lafayette Avenue is being prepared for the Big Dig. The Fifth Avenue-Culver el in the background should have been worried about the transit events about to take place. In time it was doomed to subway progress.

But for rare exceptions, the "cut-and-cover" subway construction technique was used for BRT building in Brooklyn. Some neighborhoods in Kings County already were well populated by the time digging for the underground had begun. Timber reinforcements can be seen on both sides of the four-track tunneling, which is well underway.

Before the Brooklyn Dodgers moved to Ebbets Field in 1913, their home stadium was Washington Park in the Red Hook-Gowanus section. After the Dodgers departed, Washington Park remained in use for Federal League games. By 1917, construction of the Fourth Avenue BRT subway was underway opposite the ballpark. This photo was taken in January 1917 at the corner of Fourth Avenue and Third Street.

OPPOSITE PAGE, TOP: As subway construction reached its height of intensity during the World War I years, the route of new lines often crossed those of elevated trains. In such cases, intricate and delicate provisions had to be made for the safety of existing trestles. The Fourth Avenue subway passes under the 36th Street connection between the Third Avenue and Fifth Avenue el lines. The Belt Parkway would eventually bring about the demise of the Third Avenue el.

By 1912, parts of downtown Brooklyn were littered with craters, which were filled as subway construction moved south from Fulton Street. As the photo of Pacific Street indicates, manual labor prevailed, abetted by horses and wagons. The elevated line is the Fifth Avenue-Culver route. On the right, under the el, is the Atlantic Avenue IRT station entrance, which is relatively new. Beyond the el to the right is the roof of the Long Island Rail Road's Flatbush Avenue terminal. While construction on Brooklyn's Fourth Avenue Subway was underway in the populous Downtown sector, it also was starting to take shape in Bay Ridge. By December 1913, contractors' equipment began dotting the corner of Fourth Avenue and Ridge Avenue.

When trench-digging began on a new subway route, steam equipment would be hauled into place both below and above ground. Sidewalk superintendents often would gather to observe the fascinating procedure at 50th Street and Fourth Avenue in Brooklyn.

OPPOSITE PAGE, TOP: As the Fourth Avenue subway extended toward South Brooklyn, temporary head-quarters were constructed along the route by the builders—Tidewater Building Co. and Thomas B. Bryson. Those were the days when kids wore knickers and horse-shoers could still make a decent living.

While construction on Brooklyn's Fourth Avenue subway was underway in the populous Downtown sector, it also was starting to take shape in Bay Ridge. By December 1913, contractors' equipment began dotting the corner of Fourth Avenue and 69th Street. The school in the distance is being built in anticipation of the rapid transit facility.

OPPOSITE PAGE, BOTTOM: In Brooklyn, the new Fourth Avenue Subway had competition from trolleys and the ever-growing number of automobiles. This 1923 Bay Ridge gas station is only a few feet away from the BRT tunnels.

shape after the Civil War during which the fort was both a regimental training ground as well as a prison for Confederate soldiers captured by Union forces.

Despite its expansion, the fortress never had a particularly negative affect on its neighboring towns and soon after the War, Bay Ridge was "discovered," so to speak, by New York City's blue bloods, across the bay.

One by one, Gotham's patricians became enamored of Bay Ridge's "suburban" qualities, and began building grand mansions—not unlike those dotting Riverside Drive in Manhattan—along the ridge overlooking Brooklyn's vast harbor.

During the late 19th Century, the rich, bay-side community was sprinkled with such power-broker palaces as the Crescent Athletic Club, a fortress of high society.

To a certain degree, the Bay Ridge-Fort Hamilton community was overlooked by transit interests. Steam railroads tended to bypass it in favor of more direct, down-the-middle routes to Coney Island, Brighton and Manhattan Beach on the Atlantic Ocean, although the Brooklyn, Bath and Coney Island Rail Road came close.

This situation would dramatically change after the turn of the century. When the subway finally arrived, the Silk Stocking sect moved out, and Bay Ridge would become more city than suburb.

Before the first subway to Fort Hamilton-Bay Ridge was conceived, only one significant rapid transit line came close to the military establishment: the Fifth Avenue Elevated.

Originally opened in November 1888, the Fifth Avenue el eventually stretched from Downtown Brooklyn to a terminal on 65th Street in Bay Ridge. It *was* heading in the right direction—mostly serving a rapid-

growing waterfront dock area—but it didn't go far enough insofar as slaking the rapid transit thirst of Bay Ridge residents who lived farther south.

Not until the original (1904) Interborough Rapid Transit (IRT) subway proved to be a success was Bay Ridge-Fort Hamilton given a tumble for future route extensions.

Instead of Fifth Avenue, the Bay Ridge subway would tunnel under Fourth Avenue, eventually terminating at 95th Street, Fort Hamilton.

According to blueprints, trains would cross the newly-built Manhattan Bridge—it provided for two separate two-track sets on the north and south sides of the span—where it would connect with other Brooklyn Rapid Transit lines at DeKalb Avenue junction.

After DeKalb, it would branch to what would be a handsome subway starting at a Pacific Street express stop and continuing south. Express stops also would be at 36th Street, 59th Street and 95th, the last of which was added in 1925. For six stops, the new subway would run directly parallel to the old Fifth Avenue el.

Once it was official that construction of the Fourth Avenue subway would take place, real estate interests immediately zeroed in on the once-quiet residential community. Although the line had not been fully completed, by 1915 the transformation of Bay Ridge was well underway.

The same could be said for the nearby communities of Bensonhurst and Borough Park, each of which underwent a metamorphosis because of the Sea Beach and West End BMT lines—and before them the steam trains that traversed what then was often barren acreage in the heart of Brooklyn.

One of the county's best-known and stable communities, Bensonhurst—once a division of New Utrecht—was nothing but farmland before the trains came in the 1870s. At the time, one of the most important landowners was the Benson family whose property was being eyed by a prescient promoter named James Lynch.

Like so many other 19th Century Brooklyn developers, Lynch's prime catalyst for building was the commuter transit provided by the Sea Beach and West End steam trains as well as the prospects for even greater transport possibilities now that elevated lines were sprouting in Manhattan and parts of northern Brooklyn, and the Fifth Avenue (Brooklyn) el was being projected to head in the general direction of Benson's turf.

If the West End and Sea Beach Rail Roads could carry thousands of people to distant Coney Island, Lynch figured, they certainly could do it even more easily to the Benson land for those who lived in what now is Brooklyn Heights, Clinton Hill and Fort Greene; a mere six miles away.

After negotiating with the Bensons, Lynch obtained enough land adjoining what now is Borough Park, Coney Island and Bay Ridge to establish a suburb for those wishing to escape the crowding of Lower Manhattan, as well as what now is the Downtown section of Brooklyn.

Respectful of those from whom he purchased the 350 acres, Lynch dubbed his self-created community Bensonhurst-by-the-sea. Using contemporary streets as a guide, the original tract was bounded by 23rd Avenue, Gravesend Bay, 20th Avenue and 78th Street.

Lynch didn't miss a trick when it came to beautifying his project. For additional arboreal splendor, he had 5,000 shade trees planted and, according to the *Encyclopedia of New York City,* "designed villas for a thousand families."

That he calculated correctly, soon became evident as middle-class families were attracted by Bensonhursts-by-the-sea's appealing rural aura, while being within an easy train commute to the bustling city.

The wealthy took full advantage of the aquatic possibilities of Gravesend Bay, establishing the Atlantic Yacht Club as well as the Bensonhurst Yacht Club.

In 1894, Bensonhurst-by-the-sea was incorporated into the City of Brooklyn. Only a year earlier (November 10, 1893), the West End line had become electrified. And three years after Bensonhurst had been annexed by Brooklyn, the Sea Beach run also replaced steam with electric power.

These developments—as well as electrification of the Culver Line—all combined to change the entire fabric of Fort Hamilton, Bay Ridge, Bensonhurst, Borough Park and New Utrecht. The Culver line's final steam run was on November 21, 1899.

A major component in the urbanization of Southwest Brooklyn was creation of the soon-to-be transit monolith Brooklyn Rapid Transit Company, which was organized on January 18, 1896.

The BRT took over the Sea Beach Railway a year later, and then the West End and Culver, both in 1899. Constantly expanding, the BRT would become the primary reason for a golden age of construction on either side of its surface lines, els and, ultimately, the underground routes, Fourth Avenue's subway being the most essential of all.

To understand how the Fourth Avenue

SPEEDY SKIP STOPS

By definition, an express is a train which bypasses local stops as in the A Express bypassing the Spring Street Station. However, the Transit Authority also runs locals posing as expresses. These locals—Numbers One and Nine—perform a "skip-stop" service. Between 137th Street and 242nd Street Stations, the locals alternately skip certain local stops during rush hours. By doing so, POOF! The locals become expresses. The same routine holds for the J and Z Trains on the Jamaica Line.

would intertwine with the Sea Beach, Culver and West End, it is first useful to envision what the BRT components in that sector of Brooklyn were between the turn of the century and 1910.

The West End Line originated at the 39th Street Ferry along the Narrows shore. It intersected with the Fifth Avenue el, continuing on to Bath Beach, Ulmer Park and finally the West End Depot in Coney Island.

Much shorter in length, the Sea Beach line began at 62nd Street and New Utrecht Avenue, branching off from the West End, and continuing south to Kings Highway and Avenue U before uniting with the West End at Coney Island's West End Terminal.

Paralleling the Sea Beach line for much of its run, the Culver emanated from a Ninth Avenue Terminal, crossed Fort Hamilton Avenue and continued south to stops at Avenue N, Kings Highway, the Gravesend Race Track, among others, before concluding its run at the famed Culver Depot in Coney Island.

Because of the still-rural nature of Brooklyn, the West End, Sea Beach and Culver lines all had operated along surface routes, just as they had during the original steam era.

When steam was replaced by electricity, trolley wire was utilized before third rails eventually replaced the overhead juice on el structures or in open cut.

As the population of Brooklyn exploded, the BRT understood that it had to keep pace with the transit times, or it would be left far behind by its Manhattan competitor, the Interborough Rapid Transit. And when the IRT gained Contract I to build the first subway up from City Hall to Washington Heights, the BRT was left at the post.

Even more threatening to BRT interests was the IRT's gaining of subway Contract II which enabled the Interborough to bring its subway right into the heart of BRT territory—Brooklyn.

Awakened to the invasion and potentially long-term threat, the BRT rushed to get into the act and succeeded when it became a major player by getting operating rights for a subway that would be integrated with its Sea Beach, West End and Culver routes—the Fourth Avenue subway.

On January 10, 1911, the BRT submitted a proposal requesting the Fourth Avenue route. Eventually it led to the historic meeting on March 19, 1913, which led to the most extraordinary transit program in the city's history; otherwise known as the Dual Contracts.

Out of this rapid transit package, the BRT not only gained the Fourth Avenue subway, but vast and dramatic changes to its Sea Beach, West End and Culver lines.

After the dust had cleared years later, Bensonhurst, Borough Park, Fort Hamilton and Bay Ridge were never the same.

While the Fourth Avenue subway may have seemed to be the most ambitious of the projects, the others were impressive in their own right.

Perhaps the West End was the least impressive, because it was transformed from a street level route to an elevated one to Coney Island. The same held for the Culver line which was converted to elevated. Interestingly, in each case the new projects measured 16 miles to the sea.

The most dramatic change would happen on the Sea Beach. Like parts of the Brighton line rejuvenation, the Sea Beach surface lines would be replaced by a four-track open cut from its run under Fourth Avenue to Coney Island.

While the open cut may have had certain disadvantages—especially in winter when there was no protection from snow—it was infinitely cheaper to build, while also having a certain suburban railroad quality to it.

Tastefully constructed, the Sea Beach open cut was virtually identical in design to its Brighton counterpart; the difference being that the Brighton cut ended in mid-Flatbush at Newkirk Avenue station, whereas the Sea Beach cut continued almost to the edge of Coney Island, terminating at the West End Depot.

In 1919, the BRT would amalgamate all its ocean-bound lines at a new eight-track, four-platform southern terminal called Stillwell Avenue depot. The poured-concrete elevated structure would welcome not only the West End, Sea Beach and Culver lines, but the Brighton as well.

One by one, a series of improvements continued to add to the transportation quality of life in Southwest Brooklyn. When completed in 1915, the Sea Beach open cut was viewed as an esthetic triumph as well as a practical one.

In terms of rolling stock, the new lines were complemented by the BMT Standard, which actually "auditioned" on the Sea Beach open cut before being put into use. Dramatically different from the old cars as well as the newer IRT subway trains, the Standards were regarded as limousine trains to the straphangers from Bensonhurst and neighboring communities. With a dark brown paint job—black on the roof—the Standards became synonymous with the BRT's advanced thinking and provided yet another enticement for New Yorkers to move to Southern Brooklyn.

Sure enough, the movement accelerated in the immediate post-war years and into the Roarin' Twenties. The landscape of Bensonhurst rapidly changed from the days of James Lynch. Following the tracks, developers built a mixture of housing; from six-story, elevator apartments to brick houses for two to three families.

The exodus from Manhattan's Lower East Side included an ethnic blend of mostly Italians and Jews. In Bay Ridge there was similar construction, but the population varied with Scandinavians and Italians predominating with fewer Jews.

Fort Hamilton itself remained a military base, replacing its armament with the times. By the time the subways had been built, long-range guns had replaced the Civil War fortifications but these, too, would be scrapped for more modern weaponry.

Another neighborhood which benefited from the Fourth Avenue subway was Dyker Heights, which abuts Bay Ridge. One of the last rural sections of Brooklyn, Dyker Heights had its face permanently lifted by the time the Fourth Avenue line added its last stop at 95th Street, near Dyker Beach Park, in 1925.

Seizing the opportunity, builders covered the land with one and two-family houses—some of them rather substantial in size—putting Dyker Heights in the same league as its neighbors to the north and east.

The bright, well-tended communities would obtain one other attractive transit amenity only two years after the Fourth Avenue subway's 95th Street station would open; another marvelous piece of passenger car equipment from the (former BRT) now Brooklyn Manhattan Transit (BMT)—the Triplex.

Conceived by BMT equipment superintendent William Gove, the Triplex—also called Type D—train was to be an improvement on the Standard, if such a feat were possible.

The primary difference between the Triplex and the Standard was in the car arrangement. While the Standard consist comprised a series of single cars with no ease of passenger movement from car to car, the Type D included three units which were linked by a steel diaphragm passageway connecting all three sections.

Similar to the Standard, it featured an front window—larger than the Standard's—which could be opened so that a passenger could stand at the head of the car for a full view of the tracks while enjoying the full subway breezes once the train gained speed.

Originally built by the Pressed Steel Car Company, the Triplex was a winner.

Transit expert and author, Brian J. Cudahy enthused about the Triplex in his definitive work, *Under The Sidewalks of New York.*

"The Triplex was a comfortable, quiet and pleasant subway unit that did yeoman service on the BMT's Southern Division for forty years," wrote Cudahy. "Some devotees of the Triplex will claim in the face of all opposition that it is the finest piece of railway rolling stock *ever* produced."[10]

Many riders delighted in its "extra added attractions," unavailable on other equipage and improvements continued to be made on newer D units after the first bunch was delivered on May 19, 1927.

Among the innovations were side destination signs that had both the destination and the route illuminated. By means of well-lit front signage, passengers were informed whether it was a (Manhattan) bridge (green sign) or tunnel (white sign) train.

The ability for riders to move from car to car via a safe, articulated passageway was regarded as one of the outstanding Triplex improvements. Its seating units, though different, provided just as comfortable a ride as those on the Standards. All in all, Type D got a Grade A from just about every straphanger in Bensonhurst and points south.

How effective were the new Brooklyn subways heading south?

In a nutshell, they transformed a large section of the borough from a rural to an urban community. What's more, each of the lines—although their original name designations have changed—is successfully operating and well serving their riders.

What It Was Like To Ride the Subways to Bay Ridge, Fort Hamilton, Dyker Heights and Bensonhurst

No subway line intrigued me more than what I called "The Fourth Avenue Group."

Smith 9th Street, the Top of the IND Line

RIGHT: A GG local crosses over to return to Queens at Brooklyn's Fourth Avenue station. Car number 475 is classified as an R-2. The Fourth Avenue station was considered a model of modern el construction.

BELOW: IND R-1 – R-9 types descend the curve leading north from the Smith-9th Street elevated station, a rarity on the Independent System.

Both photos, William Brennan

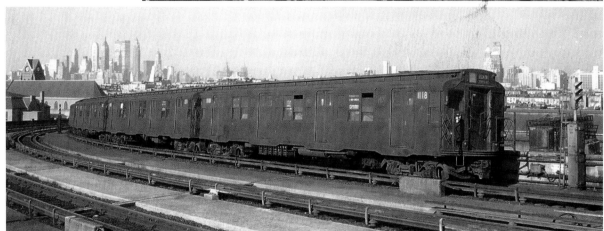

David Perlmutter

A recent view of one of the most-photographed sections of track on the entire New York City system is in Brooklyn's Red Hook section. The G (Brooklyn-Queens Crosstown Local) takes the long, winding, climb southward from the Carroll Street station toward Smith-9th Street, trestle-terminal, the highest spot on the entire system. The Downtown Manhattan skyline looms in the distance. Once the line was called GG, but the Transit Authority in its wisdom circumcised one of the Gs, with the result being a slightly shortened local name.

That included the Sea Beach, West End and Culver lines, primarily, although the Fourth Avenue run to Fort Hamilton held a different kind of curiosity value.

Several aspects of these routes made me want to ride them often but, since I lived far from these subways, it required special reasons to visit such distant venues as Bensonhurst or Bay Ridge. In fact, I was well past my 65th birthday before I even got to Dyker Heights.

My first ride under Fourth Avenue made me a fan forever.

It was 1942—I was ten—and my mother had to visit a friend in Bensonhurst. Her name was Irene Tick—husband was Joe and son, Stanley—and she lived on the Sea Beach Line.

By that time, I had been a veteran IND rider by virtue of its proximity to our house and also had done quite a bit of train work on the BMT's Myrtle Avenue and Broadway elevateds, as well as the Brighton line to Coney Island.

But Bensonhurst, Bay Ridge and environs were lumped into the *yenevelt,* otherworldly category, also shared by equally distant Canarsie.

As far as we could determine, there were no Jews in Bay Ridge, Fort Hamilton or Dyker Heights, therefore there was no reason to go to any of those communities.

Bensonhurst was something else.

It had plenty of Jews as well as one of the finest YMHA-YWHA-type centers called the Jewish Community House.

But we had all that in Williamsburg, so there had to be more reason to visit Bensonhurst; either to see relatives, friends or go to work.

Irene Tick was my mother's reason. She hustled me along because it was summertime, I was back from Camp Pythian and she wanted me to meet Stanley Tick, at least two years older, but still a possible companion for the day.

To get there, we started out with the reliable GG, right on the corner, and took the local to Hoyt-Schermerhorn Street.

After five years of riding the Brooklyn-Queens Crosstown local, my front-window-viewing had become a bit "sophisticated." I now studied the tunnel formation carefully; considered theories as to why there was a center (third) track at Bedford-Nostrand station; and whether the *screech* of wheels against rails on the 90-degree turn between Myrtle-Willoughby and Bedford-Nostrand stations could be avoided.

At Hoyt-Schermerhorn, we climbed the stairs to Fulton Street, walked over to DeKalb and one block east to Flatbush Avenue Extension, which had been re-built shortly after the opening of the Manhattan Bridge in 1909, when the vast and very complicated DeKalb Avenue station interchange was completed.

DeKalb Avenue was one of the looniest operations on the system because all Brooklyn-bound BMT trains coming from Manhattan had to be funneled through the junction. Thus, DeKalb depot had to handle the Sea Beach, Brighton, West End, Culver and Fourth Avenue subway. Trains not only were squeezed into DeKalb from the Manhattan Bridge but the Montague Street tunnel as well.

As a result, Brooklynites had come to regard the DeKalb junction as some kind of underground house of transit horrors. (It wasn't until 1967 that significant relief came in the form of the Chrystie Street tunnel in Manhattan, which enabled the integration of the BMT and IND and changes at DeKalb.)

Of course, as a keen train-watcher, I had no problem waiting around at DeKalb. With me, it was a case of the more trains, the better, although Mom was anxious to get to Bensonhurst and see her friend Irene.

At last, the Sea Beach Express could be seen crossing over a switch and peeking its head through the station portal. Never having been on the D-Type before, I was all agape when I got a good look at the front car and realized this would be my first Triplex ride.

Instantly, I noticed a close frontal resemblance to my "hometown" GG local. Like the R-1 through R-9 series IND cars, the Triplex featured big, illuminated signs up at the brow of the first car. The overall silhouette also bore a distinct similarity to the GG as did the interior.

There were numerous double seats with rattan covering and similar large fans hanging from the ceiling. Interior route signs were well-lit, clear and rather big compared with the IRT's metallic plates which were hand-changed by the conductors.

Even though the D-types were fifteen years old when I took that ride, there was a feeling of newness about them, mostly because of a feature unique to the entire subway system; the articulated cars which enabled passengers to easily move from one section to another without opening and closing any sliding doors.

Many a time, Mom, Dad and I would wander from one GG car to another—usually for me to get the front window—and have to open and close the doors while the train was in motion. It was often a scary process because we were in "open" air, bombarded with the train noise, and with not a lot of protection to prevent us from falling between the cars.

The Triplex eliminated that hazard. There were no doors to bother with; just a nice, big opening leading from car to car, with handles on each side of the steel curtain that protected us from the tracks below.

For me, the best feature was the front window—which opened—larger even than my favorite on the BMT Standards. I was all set for my first ride on the Sea Beach Line.

Once we cleared DeKalb station, our next stop was Pacific Street, another express station. Even on that short run, I could tell that I would like the Triplex—although never as much as the Standard. Its motor was relatively quiet and it had a commanding feel about it; something that never seemed a part of the IND R-1 to R-9 personality.

As we picked up speed, leaving Pacific Street in the distance, the Sea Beach Express really came into its own. Bounding down the southbound center track, it approached Union Street local stop at about 35 miles per hour. However, the tunnel configuration made it feel a lot faster than that.

On the IND, I had become accustomed to local platforms being visible from the front window of expresses like the A train or E or F. But the Fourth Avenue subway tunnel was built differently. The local stops were barely visible except for periodic openings to the right which—ever-so-briefly—allowed me to actually see the station. The openings flitted by *so* fast that the speed-experience was almost doubled; making the ride that much more thrilling to me.

We bypassed 9th Street local stop, then—at highest speed—Prospect Avenue and 25th Street. To that point in time, the

I knew this station—and line—well from my dating days. The line came into being with the advent of the 1920s. It was then that Brooklyn's elevated stations began to take on a more modern look. The BRT did an excellent cosmetic job, covering the steel with handsome concrete at Bay Parkway in Borough Park. The photo was taken in 1921.

run was *the* most exciting I had ever experienced underground, although not quite in a class with the Brighton Express speeding through the open cut and then up to the embankment.

New Utrecht Avenue express stop was our changing point over to the West End Line; which meant a climb to the el and a short run to Bensonhurst.

Riding the West End was like being on the Broadway-Brooklyn el. It featured the BMT Standards with the same el sounds whether it was a *squeek* from the trucks or *thum-thum-thum-thum* as wheels passed over rail joints.

By no means was the West End a downer, but it couldn't compare with a first trip on the Sea Beach with its eye-arresting Triplex cars.

I believe we got off at Bay Parkway station. This was an impressive street which I had only heard about in passing, when my parents and grandparents would talk about visits to Bensonhurst. Much later, I learned that it originally had been 22nd Avenue, but the City of Brooklyn decided late in the 19th Century to turn the street into a major, tree-lined boulevard of sorts from New York Bay to Ocean Parkway.

When we arrived at Irene Tick's, I was taken by the six-story apartment building. This, too, was new to me, since our Williamsburg neighborhood only had apartments that were four to five stories high; and none of them featured elevators. To me, elevators in apartment houses were big stuff!

Irene—a very funny lady who invariably sent my Mom into gales of laughter with her quips—was one of my favorite people, as was her husband, Joe. Their son, Stanley, was a bit of an enigma to me.

I liked him right off the bat because we had the same name. After that, our friendship was questionable.

He was a couple of years older than I, which was a slight problem to me, and he seemed a bit condescending because of that. On the other hand, he was an involved hockey fan and very kindly showed me his collection of Rangers photos and clippings.

At that time the Rangers had one of the best teams in the National Hockey League with a number of high scorers. Stanley Tick's favorite was Bryan Hextall, a right wing who had scored the Stanley Cup-winning goal for New York in the 1940 playoff finals. There was a big color picture of Hextall thumb-tacked on Stanley's wall. I was impressed.

But that really was as far as our friendship went, and when Mom said it was time to leave the Tick residence and take the subway home, I was rather relieved.

The West End and Sea Beach rides back were as good as the first-half of the trip; so much so that the last run—on our GG local—was quite a downer. Hey, you can't have everything!

My rides, over the years, on the Culver, Fourth Avenue, Sea Beach and West End Lines were preciously infrequent.

Once, during my SportsChannel television broadcasting years, I had to do a "shoot" at the Coney Island Aquarium. I decided to take the West End all the way from Times Square to Stillwell Avenue.

As it happened, there was a lot of construction work going on that summer, and we were constantly being slowed down by either signals or workmen. I didn't mind.

Any trip starting at Times Square was fun, if only because of the complexity of the junction. It was the meeting place of all kinds of lines, including the West Side IRT, the BMT's various routes that ran under Broadway and, of course, the legendary Times Square-Grand Central Station Shuttle.

Newcomers invariably were confused as to which line was where and, through the years, attempts were made to simplify the transfer of millions.

When I was a kid, the BMT and IRT had placed a series of colored bulbs on the ceilings of some corridors. If you followed the red bulbs, they would lead you to the Shuttle. If you followed the greens, they took you to the IRT West Side trains, and if you wanted the BMT Broadway Line, you just looked for the yellow lights.

I hopped on the front car of the West End and was lucky enough to find a car that still had a front window view; by this time window access was being limited by the Transit Authority.

Heading downtown, the BMT express was lacking some of the long-run express thrills of, say, the IND from 125th Street to Columbus Circle, but that was not a problem. You see, the best part of any BMT Manhattan-to-Brooklyn ride was *The Bridge.*

In New York City there are precious few spans which carry subways. The IRT has one over Spuyten Duyvil near the northern tip of Manhattan and there's one on the Flushing Line over Flushing Creek—between Willet's Boulevard and Main Street, Flushing. The IND reaches the highest point on the system when its F train crosses over Gowanus Canal; and that's a splendid experience.

But none of those can match the

breathtaking runs over either the Williamsburg (Broadway-Brooklyn line) Bridge or the Manhattan Bridge which connects with Flatbush Avenue Extension in Downtown Brooklyn.

The Sea Beach, Brighton and West End Line all shared the two sets of tracks on the Manhattan Bridge as opposed to only one set on its Williamsburg counterpart.

My focus was on the bridge crossing; and I wasn't let down by any stretch of the imagination. Any time a train breaks out of any tunnel into daylight, it's special, but this climb was extra special; the reason being the length of the Manhattan Bridge—6,855 feet.

After leaving Canal Street station, the train crept under the Bowery and found its light in the shadows of Chinatown. The first thing I could see out the window was the steel latticework, reminding me of a giant *Erector* set. Then, we climbed to roadway level and there was an endless stream of automobiles passing us by almost twice as fast as we were lumbering. Suddenly a flash of lights appeared down the track and there was a Manhattan-bound train, already braking for the red and amber signals designed to limit its speed.

Before we were a quarter of the way over, I made sure to look straight down so that I could detect the precise spot where the bridge passes from the shoreline to arching directly over the East River. In my mind that was a moment of truth; if only because of the long-nurtured fantasy that—some day—the bridge will grow tired of the train load and simply collapse into the river from fatigue.

With that in mind, it was always a relief when we reached land again on the Brooklyn side, rolling underground and past the abandoned Myrtle Avenue (and Flatbush Avenue Extension) station into DeKalb Avenue junction.

The speed that I had remembered from earlier West End rides was not there on this day. Our train ran so slowly at times that I actually could *see* the local stations through the columned apertures. While the sight was novel, it also was disappointing because I wanted *speed*, not the view of local platforms.

Nevertheless the ride did have its kicks. Easily, the best part was our emergence from the tunnel at 36th Street, turning left into the 38th Street cut, then 9th Avenue Station, on the last leg of the run to Stillwell Avenue in Coney Island.

Riding the Brighton Line so often, I had become accustomed to approaching Stillwell Terminal from an easterly direction. But now we were coming in from the north and a whole galaxy of track work appeared that made the train's slowness a pleasure.

I was able to pick out all sorts of switches, diamonds and signals which eased the various trains into the sprawling station. And since our train had to lurch left through two sets of switches, the *thunk-thunk-th-th-thunk thunks* were even more pleasurable to the ear.

It was a long but worthwhile trip, topped by the salt water scents of Coney; not to mention the whiff of hot dogs, french fries and boiled corn at Nathan's Famous diagonally across the street from our depot.

The Aquarium shoot was just as memorable as the trip. I was working with play-by-play ace Mike (Doc) Emrick. One of our routines involved having a (tamed) seal between us as we did our dialogue. For some reason, the seal kept wanting to plant a kiss on Mike's left cheek. The seal failed, but not for lack of trying!

THE TUNNEL THAT SHOULD HAVE BEEN—BUT NEVER WAS

Once the original subway had proven to be a hit early in the 20th century, city planners agreed that it would be worthwhile to extend the tracks from Manhattan to the other four boroughs.

Reaching Brooklyn, Queens and the Bronx was not considered an insurmountable problem, but Staten Island was an engineering challenge because it meant tunneling under New York Bay.

Nevertheless, a tube from Bay Ridge, Brooklyn to Staten Island—near where the Verrazano-Narrows Bridge terminates—was deemed a project that could be completed.

Blueprints called for it to link the BRT with its Richmond counterpart, the Staten Island Rapid Transit. Borings for the tunnel began at Owl's Head Park, not far from the current Bay Ridge Avenue station on the Fourth Avenue subway.

The proposed connection loomed as a splendid mass transit advance for the city, but soon political obstacles intervened.

During the immediate post-World War I years, New York's primary power broker was Democratic mayor John Hylan. Because of past differences with transit interests, Hylan was less than enthused about a cross-bay tunnel and created enough red tape detours to have it scuttled.

Vestiges of the tunnel, which would have been more than one mile long, remain in Owl's Head Park. Actually, more than 100 feet of tunnel actually had been built before Hylan intervened.

Work was halted, but after Hylan left office plans were revived for the Staten Island connection; this time as a portion of the newly-built, city-owned IND system. However, the Great Depression intervened, and funds were unavailable for such an expensive project.

Still another opportunity for a Staten Island tunnel arose when the Verrazano Bridge was being conceived. This time, another power broker—Robert Moses—who was notoriously anti-subway, turned thumbs-down on the project.

The tunnel to Staten Island, which was a rapid transit necessity, remains to this day on the drawing board—and nowhere else.

My most recent trips on what the BMT once called its Southern Division involved one ride on the Sea Beach and another on the Fourth Avenue Subway.

The Sea Beach Line took me to a hockey book-signing event during the winter of 2000. It was at a sporting goods store in Bensonhurst on a nasty, wintry afternoon. The station stop was Kings Highway, and before I departed, I found a photo of the station which was taken on June 11, 1915, less than two weeks before service began from Coney Island to Chambers Street, using the Fourth Avenue subway and the Manhattan Bridge.

This gave me a good opportunity to compare how one of the most ambitious Dual Contract projects looked some eight decades after the public hailed its completion in the summer of 1915.

The photo featured immaculately empty—and very lengthy—concrete station platforms with four tracks separating them. A viaduct, carrying Kings Highway over the tracks, was in the distance with four short tunnels under which the trains would go.

A solitary single Standard sat alone at the Coney Island-bound platform. It had a trolley pole on top which indicated that the third rail had not yet been installed and overhead power was being utilized.

Building the Sea Beach Line in Brooklyn

Four months before the outbreak of World War I, Brooklyn was growing too fast for its transit system. The BRT's lines at New Utrecht Avenue still were operating at ground level in April 1914, although work on the new Sea Beach Line is evident at the left, where piles of dirt and contractors are digging the open cut. When the West End and Sea Beach lines operated at ground level—and there was no Fourth Avenue subway—the West End and Sea Beach merged, here to the right, and connected with the Fifth Avenue el at 36th Street. The tracks going straight ahead went down to the Sea Beach dock and provided the route for the Sea Beach Line to the Fourth Avenue subway when the cut was eventually constructed.

By January 1917, the New Utrecht Avenue station on the BRT's Sea Beach Line not only is complete but features billboards touting Bessie Love and William Desmond at the Triangle Theater. The inscription over the express tunnels, 1914, advises when the station edifice was built. With the West End el looming over the background, we are at the same location as the flat ground junction in the previous photograph.

Before the Sea Beach Line could be deemed ready for operation, track tests had to be made. Instead of using a third rail—not yet installed—trolley wires (at far left track) were used.

By June 1915, the Sea Beach Line began looking like it almost was ready for action. Looking south from the Seventh Avenue station building, one can see the third-rail protective coverings all in place, even though the station roofs have not yet covered the new platforms.   In the distance, a new Brooklyn Rapid Transit Standard car sits on the southbound express track.

Cars for the new IND subway started arriving before the original city subway line was completed. Thus, the city loaned out its new R-types to the BMT for testing in service on the Sea Beach Line.

Lined up above the station was mute testament that the builders followed the subway. A series of eight, two and three-story homes had just been completed to coincide with the subway opening. And what a location, directly above the Kings Highway station!

Now, 85 years later, the scene was almost the same, although quite a bit faded.

No question, the once-gleaming open cut's concrete abutments looked like they needed a sand-blasting and the stations had lost some of their charm—along with the shiny, red Pulver chewing gum machines, but all in all, the Sea Beach had matured gracefully.

Perhaps the only downer for me was the fact that the train which braked to a stop was not one of my favorite Triplex units, but a stainless steel set of modern cars which now had become a staple of the Transit Authority's rolling stock.

My ride on the Fourth Avenue Subway was occasioned by a visit to good friend and co-author of *Metro Ice,* Tom Sarro.

Tommy lived in one of those sprawling one-family brick houses that adorn Dyker Heights. Unless I had planned to go by auto, the best way to reach his home was via the Fourth Avenue Subway to 77th Street, followed by a very aerobic ten-block walk to his villa.

Riding the Fourth Avenue these days is a lot more interesting than it is pulsating. My primary interest was seeing what the last, great BMT subway project in Southern Brooklyn looked like and how well it ran.

Since the Transit Authority had long ago succeeded in erasing the distinctions between West End, Sea Beach, et. al., the variety of trains entering and exiting the stations was far different than I had been accustomed to in my youthful days.

Now the lines were limited to numbers (on the IRT) and letters on what has become of the BMT and IND.

No longer was I greeted by a West End Express but rather the B and M lines.

Hey, it's the 21st Century—what are you going to do? William S. Menden wasn't running the privately-owned BMT any-more—as he was in 1940 when the Board of Transportation swallowed up the IRT and BMT private lines and merged them with the IND—it was a whole new ball game.

Still, there *was* a structural magnifi-cence about the Fourth Avenue Subway. And when we headed south from 59th Street station and rolled toward Bay Ridge Avenue, I felt the best because, at last, we had shorn ourselves of the Sea Beach and now operated purely on the extended route which terminated at 95th Street.

As a train buff, I felt that this little, southern stub was roughly equivalent to the last four stations on my old GG line going to the terminal in Forest Hills.

But I did get a kick walking along the street under which the Fourth Avenue Subway completed its route in Dyker. I did a visual flashback in my mind to the Dutch era and when this part of the colony was a section of the town of New Utrecht. I remembered reading that the Dutch had built dikes here because the now thoroughly built-up community was—four centuries ago—pockmarked with marshes.

Now it was a neighborhood with apart-ment houses and large one- and two-family homes. I enjoyed the long walk to Tom's house, had a wonderful visit, and then retraced my steps back to the subway.

The stations oozed class; which was the way it was meant to be when the line was conceived early in the 20th Century. Clearly, the Fourth Avenue Subway has done well by Bay Ridge, Dyker Heights and all the neighborhoods it has served.

However, when it comes to savoring a genuine old-timer, nothing can top a journey along what once was called the Culver Line, and prior to that, the Prospect Park and Coney Island Railroad.

For some reason—or reasons—the Southern Division line that totally fascinated me was the Culver. Unlike the Brighton, Sea Beach, West End or Fourth Avenue routes, or any others for that matter, it was the *only* line named after a person rather than a place.

The mere sound of the line had a music to it. Culver is sweet to the ears; at least it was to me. Maybe it was because it sounded so much like my favorite chewing gum from yesteryear, Pulver.

Another reason why I fell in love with the line is its history. Granted it's not *that* much different from the West End or Sea Beach but it *is* different enough.

The Culver's history made me want to ride the line for some of the same reasons I once was determined to ride the old Great Northern Railroad. The GNRR had a special train from Chicago to Seattle called *The Empire Builder.* It was classy.

In a Brooklyn sense, the Culver line had a certain class about it because of Mister Andrew R. Culver, himself.

To better understand my feelings about the line, let me explain a few things about Culver himself and his railroad.

It was 1869 when lawyer Culver perceived the possibilities of constructing a steam railway to Coney Island and then exploiting its virtues with a pier and observatory. His original plans called for a route along McDonald Avenue in Brooklyn from Ninth Avenue and 20th Street in Park Slope to Gravesend.

But that was just for starters. He needed more access and began a sequence of deals which ultimately would bring the rails not only to the central part of Coney Island, but also the most easterly portion of the island, known as Norton's Point (Sea Gate).

His first moves were the leasing of Gravesend Road and the purchase of the Coney Island Bridge Company. In order to connect his railroad to Downtown Brooklyn in 1871 Culver cleverly annexed a Vanderbilt Avenue horsecar line.

By 1875, Culver had all systems going. On a good summer Sunday, his PPCIRR registered more than 19,000 riders. As much as anyone, Culver was responsible for the one-day Coney Island expedition and did well by his planning; so well that he double-tracked his railroad in 1878.

But he didn't stop there. Culver wanted to capitalize on the Norton's Point steamboat pier, which carried passengers from Manhattan to the eastern tip of Sea Gate. A year after double-tracking his main line, Culver built the New York and Coney Island Railroad, which connected the Norton's Point steamboat pier with his Culver Depot in Coney Island.

As the PPCIRR became more popular, Culver added such amenities as high-class parlor car service and a further connection—thanks to a deal with the Long Island Rail Road—to the 65th Street ferry terminal.

What Grand Central Station meant to the New York Central, Culver's Coney Island depot was to the steam lines that called Coney Island their destination. Depending on your esthetic scale, it either was gaudy or grandiose; but it certainly

Brooklyn's Beloved Culver Line

Before the Culver Line was grade-separated, it featured trolley-poled el trains. This photo was taken at the 13th Avenue station in Brooklyn. Riders have just gotten off the train. This was taken in September 1916 before the new el trestle had been installed.

Thirty-one years later, at the same location, we see locomotive Number Nine pulling a train of newly-delivered R-12 IRT cars, while a B-type Culver local passes overhead on BMT tracks.

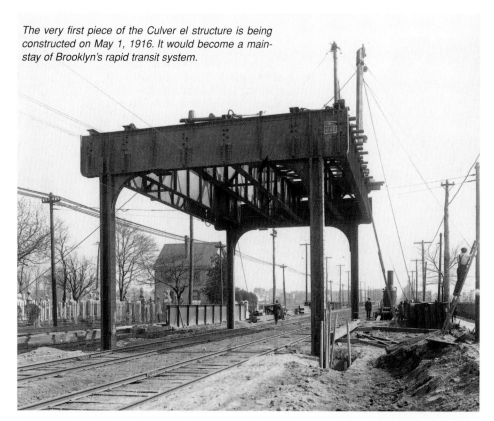

The very first piece of the Culver el structure is being constructed on May 1, 1916. It would become a mainstay of Brooklyn's rapid transit system.

Just south of Ditmas Avenue, the Culver el structure goes up over the street-level route which shared operations with the South Brooklyn line. Notable is the fact that trolley lines and freight lines shared the same tracks in the early years of the 20th century.

A year later—north of Ditmas Avenue—we see a trolley car preparing to take the loop reversing direction underneath the newly-completed Culver el skeleton.

Here at Kensington junction, the el follows the Culver route to the Ninth Avenue station and the Fourth Avenue subway. The line going straight ahead, into the distance, was the original route of the Prospect Park and Coney Island (steam) Railroad. It had become a streetcar line when this 1917 photo was taken.

THE UNUSUAL ROOSEVELT ISLAND STATION

One of the most curious aspects of the city is Roosevelt Island, located in the East River between Manhattan's Upper East Side and Long Island City in Queens.

Originally called Blackwell's Island, the 1.75 mile island—later renamed Welfare Island—was transformed, starting in 1971, into a residential community.

Renamed Roosevelt Island, the urban renewal area featured high-rise modern apartments, and a tramway which provided access from Manhattan.

However, the community lacked a subway station until a new tunnel was built, and the Roosevelt station opened on the island in 1989. The island is serviced by the 63rd Street (Manhattan) tunnel, which links with 41st Avenue in Long Island City. The F train is the line of choice for anyone wishing to see the most interesting island that is also a part of Manhattan Island.

wasn't boring! How could it be with the world's first roller coaster right next to the PPCIRR tracks and Cable's Hotel on the other side!

Culver's last steam run was on November 21, 1899, immediately followed by electrification.

Once the steam era had passed, the Culver terminal—adjoining a Coney roller coaster-type ride, Ben Hur Racer—lost none of its popularity nor opulence. It was a magnet not only for the Culver elevated railway as well as other lines, including the Brighton, as well as a web of trolley routes.

The Culver depot included a large, multi-track yard lined overhead with innumerable trolley wires. Before the Brighton el was built over Brighton Beach Avenue, Brighton trains used the Culver terminal starting in 1903. To reach the depot, the trains—using overhead trolley wires—reached the depot via a back-alley right-of-way.

Sandwiched between the West End Terminal at Stillwell Avenue and West 5th Street, Culver's terminal was an ornate, three-story building adorned with a marquee explaining the various train services from Coney Island north.

As the Southern tier of Brooklyn became populated around its steam lines, demands were made by the adjoining communities to get the trains out of the way.

In those early years of the 20th Century, the best way to do it in many parts of Brooklyn was to put the tracks on a steel elevated structure, and that's precisely how the Culver line became known. The el generally followed the earlier route, from 9th Avenue and 39th Street via Gravesend Avenue to the new Stillwell Avenue terminal in Coney Island.

By the time the Transit Authority got into the act, a major addition was made to the Culver Line. On October 30, 1954, a connection was made with the IND at McDonald Avenue, south of Church, where the subway climbed on to the Culver el tracks and proceeded on to Coney.

The connection made it possible to ride all the way from the Bronx to the Atlantic Ocean, via the venerable Culver Line. And that is the trip I took to sustain memories of Andrew Culver.

For nostalgia purposes, I launched the trip at Bergen Street where my Aunt Helen once worked at a goggles factory during

World War II. I often would visit her—the plant was on Bergen Street—and get off at the Bergen Street stop.

From there I rode the F train southward. It no longer was called the Culver Line because the Transit Authority essentially has erased all the glorious names from the past. But the F *was* the Culver.

First it climbed out of the tunnel at Carroll Street station and launched its wonderful semi-circular climb above the Gowanus Canal. As the train turned left, I could see right down to the Bay and beyond. A view of the Statue of Liberty was possible.

Smith-9th Street station is the highest (88 feet) on the line and still an impressive stop as is its subsequent station, Seventh Avenue, the one featured at the World's Fair in 1939.

After leaving Seventh Avenue, the F dipped back into the tunnel and remained there through the Church and McDonald Avenue station, once the last stop on the line.

But now I would experience the subway-el connection that was made in 1954, the year of my graduation from Brooklyn College, just a few miles away. Again, we ascended from the tunnel; only this time we climbed on to an Erector set-type of el, far different from the art deco Smith Street-Seventh Avenue concrete structure.

From Ditmas Avenue station and on south, it was old-time el riding at its best; the sounds crisp and sharp; the views of McDonald Avenue below just vintage Brooklyn, including the former site of the Gold's Horseradish Factory. It was a slow, meandering ride, but since I was in no hurry, I could have cared less that the F just loped along.

I kept visualizing the way it might have looked in Andrew Culver's days and thereafter. By the time we reached the Coney Island storage yards, I felt that *this* was the oldest el of all; at least the oldest remaining in Brooklyn service.

At long last the Parachute Jump, Wonder Wheel and the ocean came into view, along with the double-decked West 8th Street station.

The rickety structure somehow held up—although I wasn't so sure how— and carried the train around a 90 degree turn into the lower level of West 8th. From there it was one stop to Stillwell and my ride down memory lane on the Culver was over.

As I walked down the ramp toward Nathan's it suddenly struck me that a statue of Andrew Culver should have been erected in front of the terminal; but there was nothing there except a pop corn and jelly apple shop.

Andrew Culver deserved better!

The West End Elevated Line in Brooklyn

Construction for the lower level of the Culver Line's Ninth Avenue station was underway before the West End and Sea Beach lines—seen merging on the far left—were grade-separated.

New Utrecht Avenue is a good example of a dirt road that would first accommodate railroad tracks and, in 1915, see an elevated train structure be built over the original steam line. The aerial photo indicates the point-counterpoint between meadowland on one side of the viaduct and newly-constructed three-story brick apartments on the other. The 76th Street station over New Utrecht Avenue can be seen in the distance in its skeletal stage.

CHAPTER SEVEN

GOING TO

Babe Ruth's Broadway Home, Van Cortlandt Park and Other Uptown Sites

East Side, West Side
All Around The Town,
The Cops Play Ring-A-Rosie,
London Bridge Is Falling Down.

William Earle Dodge Stokes was an extremely prescient man at the end of the 1890s when the idea came to him to build a hotel on Broadway and 73rd Street that would look like a baroque palace and would attract the world's most renowned characters.

Dodge, one of the wealthiest men in town, also wanted his edifice to be easily available to anyone who lived in Manhattan.

He was aware that the Ninth Avenue elevated line was a short walk away from his projected site, but he had more than the el in mind.

Was Stokes basing his blueprints for the *Ansonia* on public knowledge that New York's City fathers were considering construction of the world's greatest subway?

And if the proposed grand underground railway would have a major express-local station at the corner of Broadway and 72nd Street, wouldn't it be wise to build on available land fronting Broadway, between 73rd and 74th Streets?

It certainly would.

That, of course, at least partially explains why Stokes ultimately built what he believed would be "the world's grandest hotel," the *Ansonia.*

Or, as some New Yorkers alluded to it, "The Waldorf-Astoria of the Upper West Side."

Whatever it was called, Stokes certainly could afford such a gamble; even if the subway never came through as planned.

One of several heirs to the $11,000,000 Phelps-Dodge copper and manufacturing fortune, Stokes was loaded with dough. When he finally gave the "Go!" signal, his group bought the frontage of what had been the New York Orphan Asylum, and imported French architect Paul E. M. Duboy to create his dream hostelry.

"The Sidewalks of New York," words and music Charles B. Lawlor, James W. Blake, Howley, Haviland & Co., © 1894

Not so coincidentally, digging for what someday would be described by author Saul Bellow as "the neighborhood's great landmark" took place precisely when the finishing touches were being applied on Manhattan's subway plans.

And speaking of coincidences, the *Ansonia* opened its doors in precisely the same year that the Interborough Rapid Transit's maiden line made its debut on Broadway as well.

"The hotel looked like one of the great Beaux Arts hostelries of Paris or the Riviera," said historian Peter Salwen, author of *Upper West Side Story,* "only bigger: a rich, startling mass of scrolls, brackets, balconies and cornices.

"The apartments were sumptuous, many with oval or circular rooms giving panoramic views over the city…and the world's largest indoor swimming pool."[11]

Underneath it was a brand-new subway and diagonally across the street—in the middle of Broadway—sat a majestic IRT edifice which led to the 72nd Street station below.

The handsome entry building was only one of three—the others being at 116th Street and 103rd Street—on the system at the time.

Since August Belmont's IRT was designed in part to lure the upper crust, it was not uncommon for the wealthy set to ride to the hotel by subway during the early years of the Ansonia.

In terms of the hotel's clientele, there was every reason for New Yorkers to take the IRT to 72nd Street.

Hardly a week went by when some notable from the world of stage, films or sports didn't check in, and that included impresarios such as Florenz Ziegfeld—of Ziegfeld Follies fame—his actress-wife

Billie Burke, and famed operatic tenor Enrico Caruso.

But a nickel subway ride to 72nd Street would just as often transport a sports fan driven to get a look at—or an autograph from—a noted athlete.

Among the most notable were New York Yankees slugger Babe Ruth and heavyweight boxing champion Jack Dempsey.

It was not uncommon to see professional baseball players riding the IRT to 72nd Street station for no other reason than that they were camping at the *Ansonia.* Many members of the Yankees called the hotel their base as well as visiting teams including the notorious 1919 edition of the Chicago White Sox; later to be known more infamously as the Black Sox.

More than likely the *New York American's* Gene Fowler came to the *Ansonia* on the IRT's uptown express when he interviewed Dempsey prior to the Manassa Mauler's defeating Jess Willard for the heavyweight championship right after World War I.

On that day, Fowler induced Dempsey to deliver one of the most definitive lines ever uttered by a boxer when the reporter wondered "what was the best way for a boxer to get out of a corner?"

To that, Dempsey declared, "One way is to quit and the other is to fight your way out!"

As it happened, the *Ansonia* would figure in more than a few notable sporting events. Author Jim Reisler (*Babe Ruth Slept Here*) noted, "Who would figure this landmark hotel with its Beaux-Arts style decorations, rounded-corner towers, and healthy supply of gargoyles, would play a prominent role in Black Sox (baseball) Scandal?"[12]

One of the more arresting characters who frequented the *Ansonia* was Arnold

Rothstein, gambler extraordinaire, bootlegger and organized crime figure.

Not surprisingly, the *Ansonia* was deemed the most appropriate meeting place—on September 21, 1919—when some of the White Sox players agreed to orchestrate a "dumping" of the 1919 World Series with the Cincinnati Reds.

According to author Eliot Asinof, who chronicled the Black Sox scandal in his book, *Eight Men Out,* "In the history of American sport, it would be difficult to find another meeting that led to events so shattering."[13]

Rothstein—known affectionately as "A.R."—agreed to bankroll the fix to the tune of $100,000. One of the fixers was White Sox pitching ace Eddie Cicotte who was to signal that the dump was in motion by hitting the first Cincinnati batter, Morrie Rath in Game One of the Series.

Instead of going to the game, Rothstein chose to listen to reports which were posted in a room at the *Ansonia.* The moment it was revealed that Rath had indeed been struck by Cicotte's pitch between the shoulder blades, Rothstein had all the information he needed.

"And with that," commented Reisler, "Rothstein walked outside the *Ansonia* into the rain and caught a cab for one of his gambling dens."

A.R. obviously was too rich for the IRT below him!

A year after the Black Sox had left, Babe Ruth moved into the *Ansonia* and remained there as a semi-regular guest for a decade.

"The hotel became a sort of imperial court," said Peter Salwen, "with the regal Babe, in a red dressing gown, puffing an expensive cigar as a parade of friends and strangers came to pay homage."[14]

The Yankees capitalized on the IRT's move up Broadway before Ruth ever donned the pinstripes.

Their original stadium—not designated Yankee Stadium—sat on a hill overlooking the Hudson River in Washington Heights. Quite naturally, it was called Hilltop Park and the Yankees were then called the Highlanders. Their field was well-situated for rapid transit since the original IRT line to the Heights was only a year away from opening when the Highlanders started playing at Hilltop in 1903.

However, the deep 168th Street-Broadway station, closest to the ball park, didn't open until the start of the 1906 baseball season; which meant that the Yankees had six years of IRT use until the franchise moved out of the Heights following the 1912 season.

One of the Broadway Line's more famous straphangers at the start of the 1920s was Babe Ruth's future teammate, Lou Gehrig. A Manhattanite, Gehrig was born at 1994 Second Avenue—under the el—on June 19, 1903. He went to elementary school in Washington Heights before attending the High School of Commerce (near where Lincoln Center now is located) and then Columbia University. Its main entrance is at Broadway and 116th Street, precisely where the IRT's 116th station sits. South Field, the college ball park, was just a short walk—home run-hitting distance—from the subway entrance.

During Gehrig's campus life, South Field was situated on a grassy expanse across from 116th Street and facing Low Library to the north. The diamond—on campus—actually was nestled between several Columbia buildings and not far from Amsterdam Avenue on the east and Broadway on the west.

Fifteen Minutes to Harlem

More than a year before trains would begin thundering under Columbus Circle, the 59th Street station essentially is complete in March 1903. The local platforms could accommodate only four-car trains in those days. Completed at this time was art work (engravings of the Santa Maria, Columbus' ship), lighting fixtures and ceiling ornamentation. A ticket booth and entrance piping appeared four months before the grand opening in October 1904.

The Ansonia Hotel at Broadway between 73rd and 74th Streets overlooks the IRT's handsome 72nd Street subway entrance. Both the hotel and the entrance still are in place along with the church (center) and residence on the right. However, Broadway trolleys long ago were replaced by buses.

One of the most arresting aspects of the original IRT was the manner in which engineers mastered the unusual geography-geology of Morningside Heights and the Manhattan Valley area of the Upper West Side. Until 120th Street, the subway remained underground. However, because the terrain sharply dipped from 120th to 125th Streets, the tracks were brought out of a portal at 120th Street and on to a steel viaduct which crested at the 125th Street elevated station. The tracks then returned to a tunnel at 135th Street. This photo, taken in May 1901, shows the early work already done on the hill dipping at 134th Street, with the makings of an uptown portal just ahead. Broadway, which eventually would be lined with huge apartment buildings, was sprinkled only with farmhouses.

With Grant's Tomb on Riverside Drive peeking through the trees at the right, completion of the elevated viaduct over 125th Street (then called Manhattan Street) is not far off in an area that later would be known as "The Athens of North America" for its preponderance of universities in a very small area.

In 1966, the Broadway IRT still featured an express rolling along the center track at 125th Street station over Broadway in Upper Manhattan. The Low V rolling stock eventually would be replaced by stainless steel cars. Expresses no longer use the center track, but high-speed local service—the number one and number nine lines—provide plenty of trains.

William Brennan

An aerial view of a southbound local leaving 125th Street station on the same day in 1966. William Brennan

A pair of Number One IRT locals pass each other over Manhattan Valley in the year 2000.

John Henderson

It has been said that when the Iron Horse was scouted as a member of the Lions' varsity, he often walloped home runs over 116th Street that reached the steps of Low Library. Another round-tripper was said to have landed just yards from Broadway, actually coming to a stop close to the thoroughfare at 116th Street.

A few more feet and it might have rolled right down the IRT steps and into the subway!

When Columbia decided to expand its athletic facilities at the northern tip of Manhattan, the university's sports moguls simply followed the IRT tracks to 215th Street and Tenth Avenue.

Only three blocks away, the university established a more elaborate facility which had been bankrolled by George F. Baker, a prominent banker. Baker's bucks became Baker Field at 218th Street and the west side of Broadway. It sits at the edge of Spuyten Duyvil—a narrow, tidal strait, separating Manhattan from the Bronx and connecting the Hudson River to the west with the Harlem River on the east.

By 1925, Baker Field—capacity of its wooden stands was 32,000—was home to both Columbia's baseball and football teams.

The IRT's Broadway line was then—and continues to be—the only rapid transit link to Baker Field; now known as Lawrence A. Wien Stadium at Baker Field.

Apart from innumerable outstanding football and baseball matches, Baker Field's claim to fame in the electronic era is that it hosted the first baseball game ever televised, on May 17, 1939. Princeton beat Columbia, 2-1, and Bill Stern did the play-by-play.

It's hard to believe that this area—as well as Washington Heights all the way south to 155th Street—once was a war-torn chunk of turf.

That was more than 225 years ago, when a major Revolutionary War battle was fought between the British and Continental armies. The revolutionaries erected Fort Washington on a tract that now is Fort Washington Avenue, between 181st and 186th Streets. While the British won the battle, Washington's troops eventually won the war and, in time, what once had been No Man's Land turned into farmland, albeit poor.

By mid-19th Century, the Heights became appreciated by the wealthy class for its panoramic beauty. One by one, estates of the rich began sprouting along the Hudson. The homes were large enough to permit continued farming until the turn of the century, when a subway named IRT changed the face of upper Manhattan forever.

Although the original Broadway line extended only as far north as 145th Street in 1904, everyone in Washington Heights knew that construction would continue toward the Bronx and that the day of grand riverview estates was over.

Early in 1907 the IRT's Broadway line invaded the Bronx and the signal was loud and clear that an upheaval in development would soon be underway.

And it was!

Seemingly endless rows of six-story apartment buildings sprouted on what once were estates and farmland. But, unlike construction in Brooklyn and Queens, the subway also inspired even taller structures. Classic, well-sculpted high-rise apartment buildings—similar to those on West End Avenue—also followed the Broadway Line as did other notable edifices.

At Audubon Terrace, George Gustav

Haye founded the Museum of the American Indian near the 157th Street-Broadway station. It opened in 1916 along with other museums along the route.

Arguably the most impressive major complex was developed on land where Hilltop Park once dominated the Heights.

Columbia-Presbyterian Medical Center opened in 1928 over the IRT 168th Street station and a short distance from where digging was taking place for the IND's original Eighth Avenue subway.

Once the Independent station opened, the medical center—one of the most prestigious in the world—was serviced by some of the world's best rapid transit—and still is to this day.

Perhaps the only drawback is the fact that 168th Street station is so deep (120 feet, equivalent to 8 to 10 stories deep) that access to the hospital is available only by a bank of elevators. Until recently, the lifts were among the nation's slowest and most undependable. A rebuilding job late in the 1990s resulted in better service and increased speed.

Proximity to the new subways always was a factor in construction of everything from ice skating rinks (Kelton's Bronx Riverdale Rink under the Broadway IRT el) to Irish football stadiums.

One of the most unlikely athletic units to exploit the subway was located in one of the most anomalous neighborhoods in New York—Marble Hill.

What makes Marble Hill unusual is that the neighborhood—located on a bluff looking down on the Harlem River—actually is situated on turf that comprises the Bronx, though legally it is part of Manhattan (New York County).

This curious state of affairs came about because during the latter part of the 17th Century, Marble Hill had been part of Manhattan Island and remained so even after a marble quarry was developed in the early 1800s. But when the Harlem River Ship Canal was dug in 1895, Marble Hill became detached from Manhattan. Now it was an island with the canal on one side and Spuyten Duyvil Creek on the other.

The canal's life was rather abrupt, and early in the 20th century it was filled in, at which point Marble Hill wound up part of the mainland. It was hardly populated until the Broadway subway bridge was completed early in 1907. Once the Interborough line crossed Spuyten Duyvil, a Marble Hill IRT station was opened on January 27, 1907.

Once a rather forlorn part of town, Marble Hill took on a new personality immediately after the subway arrived. Apartment buildings shot up in no time at all, as well as what would become a new magnet for sports enthusiasts.

Despite the fact that it was situated immediately next to the IRT, Marble Hill (225th Street) station *in Manhattan,* the 23,000-seat stadium, which was completed in 1920, was labeled the Bronx Velodrome. (However, in a concession, no doubt, to geographers, it also was known to some as the New York Velodrome.)

Whatever the name, the Velodrome's proximity to rapid transit made it an athletic hot spot, especially for those fans who favored bicycle and motorcycle races as well as the fights.

According to New York sports historian Lawrence S. Ritter, *the* singular Velodrome event was a boxing match between Benny Leonard and Jack Britton.

"The bout created considerable excitement," wrote Ritter in *East Side, West Side—Tales of New York Sporting Life,*

The IRT's Uptown World

Lenox Avenue and 142nd Street has a distinctly suburban, arboreal look in March 1903 before the IRT's Lenox Avenue line was open for business. The brick structure on the right will become the subway's maintenance and storage yard.

Cut-and-cover was the construction technique of choice as the IRT's Broadway Line made its way north along Broadway. Here, at 145th Street and Broadway, the cutting has taken place as well as substantial steel covering over what will be a three-track line. Note the new apartments sprouting along the subway route that still was more than a year-and-a-half from completion. Manhattan's sub-surface has always been suitable for construction of skyscrapers but, conversely, it made it difficult for subway excavators.

The other magnificent stop on the original Broadway Line is at 181st Street under St. Nicholas Avenue. In March 1906, workmen were finishing installation of ceiling lamp fixtures, inspiring some straphangers to call it a "Chandelier Station."

1910-1960, "because the rivals were both current world champions."

So intense was interest in the fight, that by the time all box offices had closed, the Veledrome bulged with more than 2,000 fans over its capacity.

Favored by 3-1 to win the fight, Leonard fell behind until the thirteenth round. The popular Jewish boxer looked like a goner until he flattened Britton with a mighty left to the body.

Inexplicably, Benny didn't wait for the referee to reach the ten-count. Leonard left his corner and walloped Britton before he could get up. As a result, Benny lost the fight and nearly 26,000 fans left the Velodrome wondering what the heck had happened.

Leonard came back to fight and win, but the Velodrome only lasted eight more years. While Marble Hill grew into a substantial middle-class community—largely because of the subway—the Velodrome disappeared amid a conflagration during the summer of 1930. Arson was believed to be the cause.

Like the Velodrome promoters, other sportsmen followed the el tracks, hoping to make a modest fortune and deliver some athletic fun.

Well after the Broadway IRT line was completed to 242nd Street, two members of the Gaelic Athletic Association of Greater New York discovered a hospitable chunk of acreage in the shadow of the el.

It looked good enough to host Irish football, hurling and similar Gaelic sporting events. In 1926 they bought the land, thereby creating Gaelic Park. In no time at all it became a hub for Irish sports matches as well as social events, thanks to a bar and ballroom in addition to its playing field and stadium.

IRT riders can clearly view the ball park as the train passes 240th Street and Broadway. Ironically, after the original owners went bankrupt, the land was taken over by the city and title wound up—of all places—in the hands of the Metropolitan Transit Authority!

Just a few blocks from Gaelic Park there's another spread of greenery which benefited immensely when the Broadway line finally reached its last stop in the construction process at 242nd Street on August 1, 1908.

This park hardly was in a class with the Gaelic version.

Van Cortlandt Park covered 1122 acres in northwestern Bronx and remains one of New York's most attractive centers of arboreal splendor, albeit different from its original state during the Dutch occupation of the area.

In its pre-Revolutionary War life, the land was part of an estate belonging to the Philipse family. The name Van Cortlandt entered the lexicon when Frederick Philipse I's daughter, Eva, married Jacobus Van Cortlandt. To hail the wedding, Philipse I gifted Jacobus with the land in 1691.

From then on various Van Cortlandts peopled the property and graced it with several significant structures, one of which is exceptionally close to the IRT terminal at 242nd Street.

In 1748, Frederick Van Cortlandt built a sturdy, handsome stone mansion that later became a Revolutionary War headquarters for both Generals George Washington and William Howe.

Once hostilities ended, the Van Cortlandts resumed their pre-war lives and retained it as a family center through most of the 19th Century.

New York City assumed control of it in

1889 when the Van Cortlandt family bequeathed both the mansion and surrounding acreage as a public facility. Several features were added over the years to make the park even more inviting.

The first, in 1889, was a golf course, unique at the time because it was the original municipal golf course in America. It is not uncommon to see duffers lugging their golf bags on the IRT *en route* to the course.

A stadium, playground and swimming pool were among the later additions complementing Van Cortlandt's bird sanctuary, nature walkways and the foremost cross-country track in the United States; and all of it serviced by the Broadway local!

One suspects that had he glanced at the land 300 years after he had built his home there, Jacobus Van Cortlandt would have been proud.

What It Was Like
To Take the Subway
to Uptown Sites

My first trip to the Ansonia by subway was not a pleasant one—far from it.

During the summer of 1994, I had injured my right Achilles tendon slipping on the deck of our country house in the Catskills.

It was suggested by my orthopedist that recovery would be accelerated if I checked in with a physical therapist. As luck would have it, her gym was located in the Ansonia.

To get there, I got on the IRT Downtown local at 110th and Broadway, my home station, which also goes by the name Cathedral Parkway. You have a choice here, but it all comes out the same when you get out.

This, of course, was an original 1904 stop, changed only by the fact that it was enlarged in the 1950s to allow ten-car trains to fit the platforms, whereas the 1904 version could accommodate only four cars.

There are two exciting ways to board the Broadway local at 110th Street. You either: (a) Turn right after clearing the turnstile and walk all the way to the front of the platform; or (b) Turn left and meander down to the tail end of the station.

Part (a) enables you to watch the Number 1 or Number 9 local blast down the hill from 116th Street station until it comes to a stop within inches of the platform's end. It also enables you to "capture" the front window, if it is available. Also, there's a better chance of getting a seat— should that be your aim—than at any other spot on the platform. The other advantage is that you have an excellent view of the uptown local after it emerges from 103rd Street station and rounds the curve that follows the Broadway route as it merges with West End Avenue up above. One hears the uptown local before one sees it and that invariably heightens the excitement, which peaks once the train pulls into full view.

Part (b) is for one who enjoys the thunderous approach of a train barreling down an incline from only six city blocks away. You can see the headlights appear as the local pulls up at 116th Street.

But once the train begins its descent, you move to the back wall and train your eyes on the platform's edge, carefully watching to see when the first of the ten silver cars *whooshes* by until the last car clears the tunnel and doors open.

THE GREATEST ARCH

The Manhattan Valley Viaduct at 125th Street on the IRT West Side (Number Nine and Number One) Local has a total length of 2,174 feet. Its most important feature is a two-hinged arch of 168.5 foot span. Opened in 1904, the handsome trestle ranks among the finest examples of railroad architecture in the East.

My preference always is the front car and every so often it still is possible to find one that actually enables you to peer out the front window.

On this day, I got the window and had my eyes up against the glass as our operator pulled on the controller.

Safety limitations prevent the local from hitting full speed as it bears left before reaching 103rd Street, which makes the first leg of the ride somewhat dull.

Interest picks up, however, as the local accelerates out of 103rd Street. Just ahead are two express tracks used by the Number Two and Number Three lines.

These are interesting tracks because they symbolize the foresight of New York's subway planners.

Rather than terminate *all* express service at 96th Street—rather far north for Manhattan in 1900—designers chose to extend the four tracks in two directions. One segment would head north under Broadway, while the other (center) pair would head eastward.

Hence, the Number Two and Number Three trains begin *their* alternate run by dipping down an incline north of 96th Street station and then curving right (east) under 104th Street before continuing east under the northern tier of Central Park until it curves left (north) into the 110th Street station under Lenox Avenue.

This was a remarkable stretch at the time because the tracks ultimately would tunnel under the Harlem River and terminate at what then was considered by many New Yorkers to be the wilderness—Bronx Park!

With those elements in mind, I always would fix my eyes on the point to the left, where the Bronx express tracks below suddenly became visible. Invariably, I would flash back to 1904 and try to imagine what the original Interborough cars looked—and sounded—like as they climbed the underground hill to meet the local at 96th Street.

The hope of every subway buff is to be able to *see* the roof of the express as it groans up the incline and finally levels off at the switch a few yards north of the station platform.

For decades, the 96th Street station has captured my imagination because of its design. The original four-track local platform remains in its original 1904 form and size on the uptown side. It reminds me of a museum model on display every day, showing us exactly what it was like for local riders a century ago.

Another fascinating feature of 96th Street is the open grating—you can see right up to Broadway above—over the express tracks. It's not a peek-a-boo grating either; there's plenty of room for the rain to splash down on the ties below. And, in winter, there's sometimes enough white stuff on the tracks to build a little snowman!

From the 96th Street platform, one can look beyond the angled steel supports—a distinctive feature of the early IRT construction—and almost see the cars, trucks and buses bustling along Broadway above. (One could see streetcars, including the sleek "Huffliners," until 1947.)

When I look up in that direction and consider how close all the heavy traffic is to the subway roof, I am constantly astonished to think that *never* has this 100-year-old underground structure ever collapsed under the weight of all those vehicles and pedestrians.

To me *that* is one of the most meaningful testimonials to the ability of those who designed and built the Interborough system.

On this day there is no express to meet and greet. My Number One lurches right as it bounces through the switches and comes to a stop at the very end of the platform. Whoever projected a half-century ago that the local platforms had to be more than doubled in size to accommodate ten-car trains had an effective crystal ball. During rush hours it often seems as if 15-car trains would be more appropriate!

Heading southward from 96th Street, Number One stops at the esthetically spiffy 86th Street local station. This is an excellent example of the Transit Authority maintaining—in some ways—the philosophy of original owner August Belmont. It was the aristocratic Belmont's wish to have as artistic a look as possible throughout his IRT; and he was not chintzy about paying for it.

This line of thinking was spelled out in the original 1904 booklet, *The New York Subway,* produced by Belmont's Interborough cohorts. In the section dealing with the artistic look of the stations, it explains:

The ceilings are separated into panels by wide ornamental mouldings, and the panels are decorated with narrower mouldings and rosettes. The bases of the walls are buff Norman brick.

Above this is glass tile or glazed tile, and above the tile is a faience or terra-cotta cornice. Ceramic mosaic is used for decorative panels, friezes, pilasters, and name tablets.

A different decorative treatment is used at each station, including a distinctive color scheme. At some stations the number of the intersecting street or intial letter of the street name is shown on conspicuous plaques, at other stations the number or letter is in the panel.

At some stations, artistic emblems have been used in the scheme of decoration, as at Astor Place, the beaver; at Columbus Circle, the great navigator's Caravel; at 116th Street, the seal of Columbia University.

The walls above the cornice and the ceilings are finished in white Keene cement.

Just about everything mentioned in italics above holds for such stations as Columbus Circle, 116th Street and 110th Street. But at 86th Street an entirely modern motif greets the straphangers. It is tasteful—but nowhere like the original.

I like riding the Number One. Even though it has a local's drawbacks, it rapidly gathers speed and maintains a good pace even into the next station. It has the personality of an express even though it is a local.

When we pull into 72nd Street, there is a crowd on the platform. This is no surprise; when the station opened in 1904 as an express-local stop, the narrow platforms could handle its customers. Over the years, however, apartment houses grew skyward and the population soared accordingly. As a result, the Metropolitan Transit Authority

OPPOSITE PAGE, TOP: Note the inscription at Dyckman Street station—FORT GEORGE, 1776-1905—honoring a pair of historic events, one from the Revolutionary War and the other from completion of a subway tunnel to North Manhattan. Here, one of the elevated railroad steam engines services as a stationary power source for the project.

It's November 1910, and the effect on the community of the subway at Dyckman Street already is seen in the distance. The shells of apartment buildings signify the area's growth. Workmen utilizing the crane are constructing the bellmouth and the tunnel portal for the IRT's Broadway Line. Car 3342, here serving as a pay car, was an experiment in steel subway car design. This piece of rolling stock was built in Altoona, Pennsylvania at the Pennsylvania Railroad shops, with the cooperation of the IRT. What was learned from its construction led to both the all-steel Gibbs Car and the MP 54 coach used by both the Long Island and Pennsylvania Railroads.

OPPOSITE PAGE, BOTTOM: This under-construction station at 225th Street in Marble Hill, Manhattan provided an ideal interchange between the West Side subway and the Marble Hill station of the New York Central and Hudson River Railroad. Originally located just east of Broadway, the depot's location was moved by Metro North a few hundred feet to the west of Broadway.

finally acknowledged the problem and ordered an expansion of the station.

But when I get out, the thin stairways have difficulty funneling the crowd, and when I reach the change booth level, I am immersed in one of the busiest blockhouses of a station imaginable, with riders dashing through or out of the turnstile at record—for the IRT—speed.

Finally, I burst through the wooden doors facing southward to the intersection where Broadway and Amsterdam Avenue intersect. The station is on an island in the middle of the street, and it is necessary to be extra vigilant when making the move to the sidewalk on the west side of Broadway.

Now I'm heading north, and as I reach Broadway between 72nd and 73rd Streets, the *Ansonia* looms; looking more like a cartoon caricature of a 19th century New York castle.

Or, as Peter Salwen described it, "with leering satyrs over the doorways and domed corner towers topped with huge open lanterns."

Even to those accustomed to seeing it every day, the *Ansonia* has the ability to cause a temporary form of lockjaw among its admirers.

I visited the landmark many times in the course of my physical therapy and never ceased to find some aspect of the architecture worthy of study, and plain old-fashioned sightseer gaping.

One of the best aspects of an *Ansonia* visit was its aftermath. I generally walked south on Broadway to Columbus Circle IRT station just for the exercise *and* the sights.

Right across from the *Ansonia*—at 2120 Broadway—is the Hotel Kimberly, which was home to actress Lucille Ball in the late 1920s when she was an aspiring star and model. (It has since been renamed the Fitzgerald and turned into a condominium.)

I walk west one block to West End Avenue and then head north. I remember when Yankee fan friends of mine would take the IRT up to 79th and Broadway and then walk over to 400 West End Avenue and 83rd Street. Fans of the Bombers knew that their hero, the Yankee Clipper, Joe DiMaggio, lived at 400 after he married the actress Dorothy Arnold late in 1939. When I got to 91st Street, I was at the spot where another Yankee hero, Lefty Gomez and his actress wife June O'Dea lived.

Heading back downtown, I cross over the Broadway line, stopping at West 85th Street where New York Giants baseball heroes Christy Matthewson and John McGraw used to live.

I go back to Broadway and follow the IRT south to 66th Street, where Broadway and Columbus are about to intersect. High-rise apartments and office buildings now stand where St. Nicholas Arena once thrived from 1896 until it was razed in 1962 and replaced by the ABC-TV studio office building.

When I reach 62nd Street and Broadway, I look for the 1883 Broadway address. Once upon a time, vaudeville was the most popular form of stage entertainment in the Big Apple, and at the corner of 62nd and Broadway, the Colonial Theater ranked among the top vaude houses in town.

Among those featured at the Colonial were Charlie Chaplin—he made his American debut there—and George Burns with his sidekick Gracie Allen. It's been said that the Charleston dance was launched at the Colonial in a play called "Running Wild," on October 29, 1910.

At Columbus Circle, I make a point of

checking out Christopher's statue. New Yorkers were doing that a century ago but for a different reason; when the IRT was being built, the subway was dug *directly* under the Columbus memorial.

Italians had donated it to the city and it was unveiled ten years before serious work had begun on the subway. Despite fears among many citizens that the considerable underground digging would undermine the statue designed by Gaetano Russo, it survived the opening of Columbus Circle station and the constant rumblings of the IRT ever since!

Normally, my subway trips from our home (110th Street) station take me downtown. However, there was a period in my life when I depended on the IRT for regular runs to Columbia-Presbyterian Hospital (168th Street-Broadway station).

This was in 1993, the year that my then 15-year-old son, Simon, was stricken with *cardiomyopathy,* a debilitating heart disease.

Simon had been a student at Northwood Academy in Lake Placid, New York, when his body apparently was attacked with a virus that reached his heart. He was in a doctor's office one afternoon late in June, 1993, with my wife, Shirley, when Simon collapsed and was taken to St. Vincent's Hospital. After two days of diagnosis, the serious nature of his illness caused doctors to remove him to Columbia-Presbyterian, which specializes in heart disease treatment among many other things.

Almost immediately, we were told that Simon would require a heart transplant if he was to survive. However, there was no telling when a suitable heart would be found; nor was there any guarantee that Simon would live until that heart arrived.

Once my wife and I learned all the facts, we established a routine for staying at the hospital with Simon.

Shirley would generally start her stint at about three in the afternoon and remain overnight, sleeping in the room with our son.

I would take care of business at home in the evening, walk our *Airedale,* Cleopatra, and go to bed. In the morning, I would walk Cleo, occasionally stop at our neighborhood synagogue, *Ramath Ora,* for prayers and then head for the hospital to relieve Shirley.

This was a routine that lasted for almost the entire summer of 1993.

And it was dependent on the Number One local, morning, noon and night!

For some reason, during those depressing weeks, the subway ride provided some comfort to me.

After spending a day at the hospital, I would take a left turn on Broadway and walk the half-block to the IRT entrance. In those pre-Metrocard days, I made sure that I had a token handy, because the booth lines always seemed to be too long.

Then came the almost endless elevator ride down to the deep station. Always—even at off-hours—the elevator was crowded and the operator seemed displeased.

The moment the elevator doors opened down below, there was a rush in the hopes that a train was about to arrive. If so, I'd take any car but, as usually was the case, I most often would make a right turn on the platform and walk to the very end of the station.

Mostly, I liked being there because no one was around. Being alone with my thoughts—and prayers!—was what I needed. The southern tip of the platform gave me that respite.

Also, there was an endless water leak

from the tunnel ceiling. It was relentless; and when the water hit the platform edge, a twelve-inch circular pool of drippings remained.

This *drip, drip, drip, drip* must have gone on for a long, long time because rust had shaped on the outside of the pool and beyond.

To some more sensitive souls this may have seemed like a disgusting scene but I found it relaxing; the *drip, drip, drip, drip* had a hypnotic effect. And if there was anything I needed at that time, it was relief from the outside world.

Every so often, I would peer left down the tracks to see if a train was coming. It was particularly easy to do in this station, thanks to the concrete arch construction of the tunnel.

Because of Manhattan's mixed geology, the section of track from 157th Street and Fort George—under Broadway—required digging through rock. That particular segment was the second-longest double-track tunnel in the country, immediately behind the Hoosac Tunnel in North Adams, Massachusetts.

Since the tunnel arch was so big and the tracks so straight, it was easy to see all the way to 181st Street station and even beyond. When the bright, white lights came into view, I followed the downtown train all the way to the front of my platform and then hoped for a window view.

Riding through a double-track rock tunnel is a rather unusual experience on the New York subways although there are more than a couple to experience. I found it interesting to see how the operators would react to oncoming trains. More than occasionally, they would flash their front lights or pull a couple of times on their whistle-horns.

At 145th Street a third (center) track is added to the line. There's a neat downhill from 145th into the City College (137th Street) station and at each side of the main line there are several sets of lay-over tracks where the rush-hour trains are held until use.

One of the most pleasant interludes on the homeward run came as we left 137th Street on the way to 125th.

Because Manhattan Valley (125th Street) dips so precipitously, engineers decided it would be more prudent—and cheaper—to take the train out of the subway and run it on a viaduct from 133rd Street up to the elevated (125th) station and then down to street level and, finally, underground at 120th Street.

Since this was the only remaining elevated line in Manhattan, it had become a curio of sorts, and I found it very refreshing, from time to time, to get off at 125th Street and merely imbibe the fresh air while enjoying a view of the Hudson River and New Jersey.

But there were no such respites during that summer of 1993. My distraction rather was listening to the sound changes underneath as the Number One moved from its dirt-ballast base to the steel of the el. Abruptly, the softer sound gave way to the pronounced, almost sensuous *tsk-de-tsk-de-tsk-de-tsk-de* as the ten-car train pulled into 125th.

The tracks re-enter the tunnel at the 120th Street portal, but before Number One gets that far, it reaches street level a block earlier for what sometimes is a fun-run alongside Broadway's vehicular traffic before we both disappear.

By the time I would arrive at 110th, I would be relieved just thinking trains. But once outside, the challenging world around me was all too apparent.

For the most part, Number One IRT was good to me that summer; but it did have its unpleasant moments; two in particular.

One morning, I was hospital-bound on the uptown local at about 11 a.m. For some reason—I'm not sure what—Shirley wanted to leave the hospital a little earlier than usual. Getting there on time was important that day and I felt quite good when I left a half-hour before my usual departure time and caught a train at 110th.

I took my usual place at the window, eyeing the tracks ahead as we rolled toward the Columbia platform. Sometimes, when we reach a station, I gaze around at aspects such as a newsstand or a waiting passenger. This time my eyes were fixed on the tracks.

As usual, the operator took Number One at speed right into the station and then began braking. We must have traveled about twenty yards inside 116th when I *thought* I saw an object on the track.

Before I could even *think* about what it might have been there was a deafening *BOOM!* It was followed by an abnormal flash of electricity-generated light, a rush of air-braking and the sound *CHOW!*

The emergency brakes brought us to a fightening halt with the front car about half-way down the platform. Two thoughts came to mind: 1. What the hell happened? 2. Will I get to the hospital on time?

To this day I don't know what had happened. None of the transit people informed us—they were too busy trying to figure it out as well—and I never read about the incident in the papers.

We were holed up in the train for about fifteen minutes before the conductor explained that arrangements were being made for a safe exit. Doors eventually

THE MISSING 2nd AVENUE SUBWAY

Because the Third Avenue Elevated Line never was replaced by the promised-and partially-begun-but-never-completed Second Avenue Subway, the East Side of Manhattan is serviced by only one North-South route, the Lexington Avenue Line. The West Side roster includes the Eighth Avenue, Seventh Avenue, Sixth Avenue as well as PATH under Sixth Avenue. As a result, the worst overcrowding takes place on the Lexington Avenue line.

opened and I made my way to the street, hailed a cab and reached the hospital only a few minutes later than expected.

As Simon's condition worsened through July, the train trips became equally depressing and yet some balm as well.

Once, late at night, I caught the Number One just as it was arriving at 168th Street station. It was late July, we had no word on a new heart arriving and I was as low as I could be. On top of that, we had been hit by a heat wave and, even with air conditioning, my Number One was uncomfortable.

The moment I got aboard, I plastered myself against the opposite (closed) door and let it hold me up. From time to time, I peered out the window, getting relief from the train sounds and sights as we rolled from station to station.

I felt so lousy that I couldn't wait to get home, walk the dog and plop into bed. What I had forgotten was that construction along the line had caused some disruptions. New ties set in concrete were replacing the old ones on ballast in several places and one of them was on the run from

116th Street and beyond 110th Street station.

When the conductor announced that the train would bypass 110th Street station, I nearly put my head through the window!

The train did stop at 103rd Street. As I struggled up the stairs I heard someone call my name. I wheeled and saw an old friend, Terry Foley, who once lived at 515 West 110th Street, diagonally across the street from us.

Engaging, intelligent and funny, Foley was my kind of guy.

But not on this night.

I desperately wanted to get home, but he asked the question that had to be answered: "How are things?"

"Shitty," I responded—and then explained the reasons why.

Sometimes these ventilating moments are a balm to a depressed mind but this was not one of them. After detailing the problem, I quickly bade Terry good-bye and walked up hot, humid Broadway to 110th Street and then made a right turn to the apartment house.

I may even have cursed the Broadway local.

On August 5th, Simon's situation had become desperate. On my ride to the hospital, I wondered how much longer he could hold on, and the events that day were hardly encouraging.

But, late in the afternoon, while I was sitting in the parents' waiting room, Dr. Marianne Kichuk of the transplant team walked in and told me that it appeared that a heart was on the way. Shirley soon arrived and I gave her the good news; then arranged to head back home to walk the dog. She and I agreed that we would stay at the hospital that night to see the entire procedure through.

This time, when I walked on to the 168th Street platform, I felt a lightheadedness that had eluded me for months. I understood there still were pitfalls ahead but now, for the first time since the end of June, some hope was on the horizon.

It was one of the most enjoyable rides on the Number One that I can remember. On the way back, an hour later, the ride was one mixed with expectation and anguish. I tried to think positively.

Simon got his new heart on the morning of August 6, 1993, and there were many IRT rides for me thereafter. The first days after the transplant were as nerve-wracking in some ways as those preceding, but with a different feel. Now it was a matter of the new heart being accepted, the medicines working to achieve that goal and a dozen other matters that piqued the mind.

It wasn't easy. It never is! Simon had a relapse a couple of years later while a freshman at Brooklyn College. These were new and different problems which were no less frightening than the original. But, after a few weeks of treatment, he was back home with us again, although he had to take a medical leave of absence from the university. His recuperation was slow but relentless. In time he moved to California, working for two years in the film industry. He later decided to move to Israel where he became a citizen of the Jewish State. Ever since his hospitalization, Simon has been on a strict, daily regimen of pill intake. Since 2002, he has worked in the city of Rehovot, where he teaches English to Israelis. His health generally has been good and he enjoys a normal life.

In retrospect, I believe that the subway rides had a calming effect on me through the whole, ugly mess and I continued to enjoy riding on the uptown stretch; sometimes for fun and other times for historic reasons.

From time to time, I get off the Broadway local at 168th Street and walk to that isolated spot at the front of the downtown platform. I reflect for a few moments on those doleful days and nights in 1993 and never hesitate to be thankful for Simon's recovery.

Apart from those hospital visits, the Broadway local has provided many other interesting adventures for me. Every so often I would lead a tour in conjunction with the Madison Square Garden "Cheering For Children" foundation. Fans would bid a certain amount of dollars for my tours, and the winning bidders would be taken for a ride up to Van Cortlandt Park station.

The trips would take us past many of the sites mentioned earlier and a few others that always had sentimental value for me. One, in particular, was Dyckman Street, which followed 190th Street station going north.

During the late 1930s, my parents—who never owned a car—enjoyed hiking along New Jersey's Palisades. Since we didn't have an auto, the only way we could get across the Hudson River was by taking the Dyckman Street ferry that connected the tip of Dyckman Street in Manhattan's Inwood section to Fort Lee in New Jersey.

Any ferry ride was a kick to me but the Dyckman Street boat had a charm all its own because—unlike its Downtown counterparts that moved between industrial sections—it cruised westward directly toward the Palisades. The rock outcropping was an awesome sight to see; embellished even more by the ferry's proximity to it.

Although my folks preferred taking the Independent's A train to Dyckman Street—

it was closer to the ferry—I liked the IRT version because of its historic significance.

After all, Dyckman station on the Interborough was the first outdoor depot not built on a steel-supported viaduct like the 125th Street station nor like the ones further north.

Dyckman was just a few yards north of the tunnel portal with a concrete-based platform. At the time of construction in the early 1900s, Dyckman Street was virtually undeveloped, as was the rest of Inwood right up to Spuyten Duyvil.

On my tours, I liked to point out that the *original* Dyckman was Jan Dyckman who emigrated to New Amsterdam from Westphalia in 1661. Jan's grandson, William Dyckman, built a fieldstone, brick and white clapboard house in the late 1780s at what now is 204th Street and Broadway.

During the World War I years, the Dyckman family restored the house and bequeathed it to New York City. Ironically, the Dyckman Street ferry is gone—too much competition from the nearby George Washington Bridge—but Dyckman House remains a Big Apple landmark as the last remaining farmhouse in Manhattan.

Following the Dyckman stop, my tour continued northward as Number One turned right, toward 207th Street, surrounded on the left and right by six-story apartment houses.

It is difficult to imagine that this northern section of Manhattan supposedly is the place where Peter Minuit bought Manhattan from the Indians for the equivalent of $24; roughly a week's worth of subway rides today!

A photo showing the land in 1910 reveals how the subway entirely regenerated Inwood (see page 238). Taken from above the Dyckman Street station, the picture shows undeveloped property—trees, bushes, etc.—stretching as far as the eye can see. In the distance, however, the shells of new apartment houses can be seen. Now it is totally populated from the Hudson to the Harlem River.

My favorite aspect of the final, four-station run from Marble Hill (225th Street) to the Van Cortlandt Park terminal is the old-time, elevated train *feel* of the ride.

Granted, the trains are comprised of the most modern rolling stock—usually built by Bombardier—yet no matter how state-of-the-art the cars may be, they still produce the *sounds* of an old-fashioned el.

Embellishing this feel is the Transit Authority's decision to retain the old "coupled" rail units rather than replace them with smoother welded rail which is a feature of other parts of the Broadway line.

The combination of venerable trackage with plenty of rail gaps on a steel viaduct produces some of the best throwback subway sounds available on the entire system.

Toss in some exciting curves once past the Harlem River and the ancient 242 Street station with its bumpers, and you have a train buff's delight.

My only regret is that Bronx Velodrome isn't there any more in Marble Hill.

I would have loved to have taken the IRT to see the fights!

———————————

CHAPTER EIGHT

GOING TO

The Greenery and the Animals—Bronx Park, Central Park, Prospect Park and the Botanic Garden

*New York, New York,
It's A Wonderful Town;
The Bronx Is Up
And The Battery's Down!*

At one time, the Bronx was so far *up*—at least in the eyes of sophisticated Manhattanites—it was considered "the country."

Before rapid transit crossed the Harlem River from Manhattan, some New Yorkers regarded the Bronx as an eastern version of Montana.

Its undulating hills and valleys originally attracted Henry Hudson's eyes after he sought cover from a storm for his ship, the *Halve Maen,* in Spuyten Duyvil Creek. That was in 1609, when only the *Weckquasgeeks* Indians enjoyed the only section of New York City that belongs to the continental mainland.

And its virtues certainly attracted the Swedish sea captain, Jonas Bronck, who came from Holland and set up a farm in the vicinity of what now is Lincoln Avenue and 132nd Street.

Thanks to Jonas Bronck, the Bronx got its name.

Just three years after his arrival, Bronck and a flock of Danish, German and Dutch who had accompanied him, had established themselves, after which a peace pact was signed between the *Weckquasgeeks* and the Dutch.

The armistice was signed on a desk in Bronck's home.

Armistice was unknown to the Bronx during Revolutionary times when numerous skirmishes between the British and Continental Army erupted over the landscape. The English had the upper hand and occupied most of what now is the borough until 1783.

The second American conflict, the War of 1812, impinged on the Bronx in another more positive way: a series of factories opened in the West Farms sections, mostly devoted to bleaching, pottery, paint and

*"On the Town," words and music Leonard Bernstein and Roger Edens,
M. Witmark and Sons, and Warner Brothers, Inc., © 1949*

Westchester Avenue in 1916. From this vantage point, it may as well be Iowa.

A tiny steam engine does the cutting for the soon-to-be Pelham IRT subway in the Bronx.

The IRT Pelham line's elevated structure in July 1919 is climbing over tracks below that belong to both the New Haven's Harlem Branch as well as the New York, Westchester and Boston Railroad. Despite the intricate steelwork taking place, trolley operation (see streetcar on the far left) still is possible. The photo was taken between the Elder and Whitlock stations.

Here's what an elevated line looked like before the stations were completed. This is the IRT Pelham line's Westchester Square stop.

glass. Most of the remainder of the 42 square miles were devoted to farming.

To a certain extent the Bronx became the breadbasket of Manhattan, with farmers shipping an assortment of fruits, vegetables and milk products across the Harlem River to the city's population center.

In terms of growth, West Farms had a geographic advantage over other Bronx farm communities; it was located on the Bronx River, which flowed into the East River. Shortly after mid-19th Century, West Farms developed port facilities, and in the latter part of that century it became the natural target for railroad planners.

The need to connect trains from Manhattan to the Bronx became even more acute in 1874, when New York City acquired West Farms which, by then, was a bustling river port.

Clearly, the Bronx needed trains, and the challenge was met by an outfit called the Suburban Rapid Transit Company. SRTC was specifically created to bridge the Manhattan-Bronx railroad gap, and it did so by erecting a bridge over the Harlem River.

From its southern terminal at the end of Manhattan's Second Avenue elevated line at 127th Street, construction began in 1883 and three years later the first steam engine belched over the span to 143rd Street in the Bronx. Thanks to a deal swung by SRTC moguls, the line could also link with the New York, New Haven and Hartford Railroad depot in the South Bronx at 133rd Street and Willis Avenue.

Slowly yet relentlessly, SRTC extended its domain north. Stations were built at 133rd Street, 138th Street, 143rd Street, 149th Street, 156th Street, 161st Street, 166th Street, Wendover Avenue, 174th Street—into West Farms—Tremont Avenue, 183rd Street, Pelham Avenue and, finally, 200th Street-Bronx Park in 1902.

This was perfect timing, because Bronx Park—blueprinted during the 1880s—was designated as a combined site for zoological as well as botanical gardens precisely when the railroad was headed in that direction. Only three years after the zoo had officially opened, the first train serving Bronx Park was in business.

This would be the first line in the Bronx to begin operation with electricity rather than steam power. It all began on July 1, 1902. There was one unique aspect about the operation. Trains that were to be stored were transferred to the yard by an elevator. It carried the cars from the el tracks to a surface yard under the structure where they were kept until needed again.

No question, establishment of SCTC service to Bronx Park was a major advance in the borough's development although the Bronx didn't officially become a county until January 1914.

Meanwhile, the trains transformed the borough.

Immigrants who had come to the Bronx to work on the original el remained. Factories in the Melrose and Belmont sections lured thousands of Italian immigrants, some of whom were hired to develop Bronx Park and the Botanical Garden. Construction of the Jerome Avenue Reservoir required a work force of its own, drawn in part from European emigrants.

As the el snaked its way toward the Bronx Zoo, attractive apartments followed. Thousands of Jews from Eastern and Central Europe, who originally had settled in Lower East Side (Manhattan) tenements chose to follow the train—with its inexpensive fare—to the better quality of life in the Bronx.

But the bigger boost was to come with the city's first subway from City Hall to Van Cortlandt Park. While this section, justifiably, receives most of the attention, a branch of the Contract I and II Interborough construction deserves as much play simply because of its positive effect on the Bronx.

This section is the one that splits from the four-track station at 96th and Broadway and then proceeds to Lenox Avenue under the northern tip of Central Park. The Lenox Avenue run ends at 145th Street.

One train concludes its run there, adjacent to the cars and shops at 147th Street.

However, the Bronx-bound trains switch to the right to comprise what was called the West Farms Line. These trains then would enter a tunnel under the Harlem River. First stop in the Bronx would be Mott Avenue, followed by Third Avenue, Jackson Avenue, Prospect Avenue, Simpson Street, Freeman Street, 174th Street, 177th Street and finally Bronx Park, 180th Street.

The first Bronx Park train made that run on January 10, 1908; which meant that for a nickel one could ride all the way from Brooklyn Borough Hall to Bronx Park through the city's most populated areas.

Development of the Bronx now became irresistible. In addition to the Jewish move from the Lower East Side, groups of Armenians, Yugoslavians and other European immigrants leaped at the opportunity to live in the new part of town.

To satisfy this demand, a spate of feeder trolley lines were established, and these, too, were increased as more subway-el construction continued in the borough.

For the Bronx Park, it was a bonanza in terms of boosting attendance. No sooner had it become obvious that the West Farms Line was a hit, extensions were planned that would carry it farther north.

But more importantly to the future of both the Zoo and Botanical Garden was the Dual Contracts of 1913, which provided for even more subway service to the Bronx, and specifically, right to the zoo.

To do so, the Interborough would build a Lexington Avenue line, continuing the original City Hall to Grand Central portion and extending it north from Grand Central to 125th Street in Manhattan. It would then veer off under a new tunnel to the Bronx.

The White Plains Road Line would consist of three tracks from the Contract I project. From 177th Street it would curl around Bronx Park, and head north on White Plains Road to 241st Street, just short of the County line. This would be the most northerly penetration of the subway-el system. To this day, Wakefield-241st is the closest that any line reaches toward Westchester.

Had Bronx Park planners designed it themselves, they could not have produced a subway with closer proximity to the zoo. Stations such as East 180th Street, Bronx Park East, Pelham Parkway and Allerton Avenue were positioned as close to the zoological gardens as possible. (An original scheme to run the trains directly *through* the zoo was rebuffed by wild animal experts as threatening to the well-being of the beasts.)

The Botanical Garden also was a beneficiary of the subway-el expansion. Actually, the tracks which came—and still do under Metro North—closest to it belonged originally to the New York Central Railroad's Harlem Division. (The

Putnam Division bisects Van Cortlandt Park.)

If the Botanical Garden needed an "Extra Added Attraction," transit-wise, it was provided by yet another subway line, although this one arrived quite a bit later than its Interborough counterparts.

Long after the IRT had conquered the Bronx, the city's own subway moved on from its Manhattan digs in the early 1930s.

While the IND's original A Train would reach Inwood (207th Street) by heading north from 145th Street in Harlem, the Independent also would turn right (east) toward the Bronx, thanks to a lower level at the same 145th Street terminal.

A Harlem River tunnel would carry the newest IND line to the Bronx after it cleared 155th Street (Polo Grounds) station in Manhattan. First stop in the Bronx would be 161st (Yankee Stadium), after which it would extend to its northern depot at 205th Street-Norwood, just a short walk to the Botanical Garden.

In a sense Brooklyn's counterpart—interestingly named *Botanic* Garden instead of *Botanical*—received just as much subway support as its Bronx cousin; with one key difference. The Brooklyn version actually had a subway station named after it.

In Brooklyn, the intertwining between botanic gardens and railroad was tight. Before the Brooklyn Institute of Arts and Sciences even laid out the gardens, a train line ran right through the site which had been used as an ash dump by the Parks Department.

What was to become the Brighton Line—Brooklyn, Flatbush and Coney Island Railroad—ran from its Bedford Station point of origin, south to Dean Street and Sterling Place stations, the latter of which was just north of the future Botanic Garden site.

When the system had become electrified in the early 20th Century, the Brighton Line started its run at Franklin Avenue-Fulton Street, followed by Dean Street and Park Place. The next station, Consumers Park, was adjacent to the future gardens.

The rough meadow land just south of Eastern Parkway—precisely where the last Ice Age glacier stopped its southerly movement—was selected for the horticultural center. In 1910 the Brooklyn Botanic Garden opened for business and almost overnight became a borough favorite.

According to the *Encyclopedia of New York City,* the Botanic Garden "became known for its emphasis on plant physiology and genetics and for its efforts in public education."[15]

Brooklyn school kids certainly could vouch for that. Each spring, in virtually every elementary school, the Botanic Garden would distribute seeds for assorted plants and vegetables, which children could buy for a penny or two. (Bulbs also were a big hit.) The seeds would arrive in plain brown wrappers and, according to an informal poll of students (conducted by the author), would flower about five per cent of the time!

The BBG's first director, C. Stuart Gager, orchestrated a splendiferous Japanese hill-and-pond garden designed by Takeo Shiota in 1915, that, along with the Cranford Memorial Rose Garden and Japanese cherry trees, were major attractions.

Once the Botanic Garden took shape, it could best be reached by not one but two BMT lines (Broadway-Manhattan, via the Manhattan Bridge and the Franklin Line from Fulton Street). But it was only the Franklin route which officially had designated a "Botanic Garden" station, just north-west of Ebbets Field.

Through the years, BBG continued to expand its exhibits as well as its legendary status in the borough. It wasn't merely such additions as the Steinhardt Conservatory and the Trail of Evolution that commanded attention, but the more mystical as well; namely, *The Fox.*

For decades and decades, the Botanic Garden has been notorious for its version of the much-discussed-but-never-seen Loch Ness Monster.

The BBG *fox*—and its heirs—supposedly has roamed the Garden in secret while keeping the grounds rodent-free. And for decades BBG officials insisted that no such fox existed.

However, the fox-sighters offer "proof" of sorts; asserting that they have actually seen its tracks in the garden and, occasionally, across Flatbush Avenue in Prospect Park. They further assert that the fox tracks were seen in snow, among other places.

"Others say they have seen its tracks, perhaps crossing the park's rose garden with its round pools and then moving on down the hill to the Vale of Cashmere," wrote David W. McCullogh in his book, *Brooklyn—And How It Got That Way,* *"where the thin, twisting pond is frozen over, and on through a pass where a concrete post once held a bronze marker decorated with a patriotic eagle commemorating a white oak that had been chopped down on an August morning in 1776."*

As popular as the Botanic Garden was—and is—it always has played second fiddle to its sister 526-acre green to the west, Prospect Park.

In many ways more beauteous than its Manhattan counterpart, Central Park, Prospect Park was designed by Calvert Vaux, who also was involved with the Manhattan greenery, along with Frederick Law Olmsted.

Construction began—nearly 2,000 earth-moving workers were required—immediately after the Civil War so that a grand opening could be held in 1868.

If ever a park was a hit with its citizens, Prospect Park was it. Almost 2,000,000 Brooklynites visited it in 1868, and that was even before the first railroad serviced the green.

With its popularity growing with such features as band concerts, sailing on the lake and sports, it was vital to provide a rapid transit link in some form, and the Brighton, Flatbush and Coney Island Railroad obliged by establishing two stations—one called Prospect Park and the other Flatbush Station—adjoining the park.

Eventually, Prospect Park would benefit from subway-el electrification as well as the Brooklyn Rapid Transit Company's vision in improving the junction at Flatbush Avenue, Empire Boulevard and Parkside Avenue, where station improvements greatly aided passengers coming from Manhattan on the Manhattan Bridge (Broadway) Line as well as trains heading south from Fulton and Franklin Avenues.

The first major improvement took place shortly after the turn of the century when the Brighton Line, operating over the Fulton Street el to Franklin Avenue (from Fulton Street), was changed from a surface to an elevated line starting at Franklin Avenue and Fulton Street.

After Park Place station, the el described a steady decline until depressing into an open cut at Prospect Park. At the time BRT rolling stock consisted of wooden cars, many of which had previously

The White Plains Road Line

It's still the time of the trolley on White Plains Road, near East 223rd Street in the Bronx. The date is April 3, 1914, with the time of the subway not far off, as the IRT already was wending its way northward through the borough both underground and on elevated tracks.

Ten blocks north, at 233rd Street, a station is under construction. Realtors followed the subway and el as building progressed north. The real estate shack at the right is typical of the kind that could be found under the new el lines.

A new era in transit: Even as the new IRT el superstructure is going up in the Bronx, a trolley is able to make its way under the hauled-steel. So fresh is the installation that piles of dirt still surround the base of the pillars. The photo was taken on August 14, 1915.

A Westchester Electric Railroad streetcar is heading to its 177th Street terminal along White Plains Road. Meanwhile, a steam crane works atop the elevated trestle to complete the IRT White Plains line. Not an automobile is in sight on May 19, 1915.

As the IRT grew in popularity, additions were made to the original lines. Here, the newer Lexington Avenue line connects to the first IRT segment in the Bronx. Piles of timber, cables and other construction implements, such as the ladder sitting between the rails on the left, indicate that the work at Mott Avenue, Grand Concourse and 149th Street is far from finished.

At the 177th Street IRT station, a northbound express of Low Vs passes a northbound local, braking for the stop in this 1962 scene. William Brennan

From the other direction, a set of Steinway IRT cars curves into the same station; also in 1962.

William Brennan

been in use during the steam locomotive era.

However, once the BRT began running trains over the Manhattan Bridge, it was planned—part of the famed Dual Contracts—that there would be yet another improvement at Prospect Park station.

The key to the BRT upgrading involved moving the Manhattan Bridge train traffic through the new DeKalb Avenue junction and then stations at Atlantic Avenue and Seventh Avenue, before reaching Prospect Park.

Meanwhile, the Franklin Avenue Line would blend with the new subway in an intricate tunnel coupling under what then was called Malbone Street but long ago was changed to Empire Boulevard. (The appellation alteration came about following a disaster on November 1, 1918 in which 97 BRT riders were killed in the just-completed tunnel leading to Prospect Park.)

Park of the embellished Prospect Park station involved a new tunnel bringing southbound trains on the relatively steep incline into the portal directly under Malbone Street.

Only a few yards prior to entering the tunnel, tracks begin curving right toward a 90-degree right hand curve and then left into the new, four-track Prospect Park Station. Trains from Franklin Avenue wind up on the Brighton Beach-bound local track while those from Manhattan Bridge arrive on the center, express track.

As part of the station restructuring, northbound Franklin Avenue trains leave Prospect Park on the local track while those heading for Manhattan depart on the center northbound track.

What made the unified station so interesting, from a train buff's viewpoint, was the point-counterpoint of construction. Trains *en route* to Coney Island enter Prospect Park depot in a tunnel but as soon as the first car reaches the platform, it emerges to daylight, courtesy of an *open cut* which insulates the trains from street traffic while allowing them to travel in a relatively inexpensive-to-build setting.

The *open cut,* which then was unique to the BRT, later was applied to the line's Sea Beach division which opened June 22, 1915, with equal success.

Despite the horror—and lasting trauma—inflicted by the Malbone Street wreck, Prospect Park station emerged as a successful amalgamation of lines, as well as the perfect feeder for both the park and Botanic Garden.

Park-bound riders climbed a stairway leading to the change booths and then another set of stairs that deposited them on bustling Flatbush Avenue near the intersection of Empire Boulevard (Malbone) and Parkside Avenue.

To reach the park, one merely had to cross Parkside, and there it was! For the garden, two crossings were required—first Flatbush and then Empire Boulevard. The Botanic Garden's southernmost gates sit right on the corner of Flatbush and Empire.

The BBG equally benefited from the Interborough's New Lots Avenue subway which had a station at Eastern Parkway near the garden's northern entrance.

Another beneficiary was the Brooklyn realty industry. Both the completion of Prospect Park, and then the Botanic Gardens, lent an aura of class to a section of the borough which would become Kings County's version of the fashionable Upper East Side of Manhattan—but with a kicker.

Whereas the Upper East Side offered a normal grid of city streets—with the notable exception of Park Avenue—Olmsted and Vaux saw to it that two major park-thoroughfares fed directly into Prospect Park and each of them would be the envy of any European boulevard.

Influenced by Berlin's and Paris' grand avenues, Vaux and Olmsted designed a six-mile thoroughfare running from the southeastern edge of Coney Island to Prospect Park. Unlike Manhattan's Park Avenue—separated by a thin mall—Ocean Parkway not only had a width of 210 feet but featured two malls, two side roads, two sidewalks, a bicycle path and a central roadway.

Festooned with trees and shrubbery, Ocean Parkway became a magnet for the affluent, who built impressive houses along the route, especially near Prospect Park.

The same was true of Eastern Parkway, designed in 1866 by Olmsted and Vaux.

An avenue *par excellence,* Eastern Parkway differed from Ocean Parkway in a few notable ways; including the fact that a subway never tunneled under the latter, whereas the IRT's New Lots Avenue and Nostrand Avenue routes run under Eastern Parkway.

The world's first six-lane parkway, Eastern Parkway started at Ralph Avenue at the edge of Crown Heights and Brownsville and concluded at Prospect Park's Grand Army Plaza.

Once again it was the genius of Olmsted and Vaux which was responsible for the grandeur of this approach to Prospect Park. Constructed in 1870, Grand Army Plaza features an 80-foot triumphal arch—adorned with a four-horse bronze chariot group and sculptures—designed by John H. Duncan.

The classiness of Eastern Parkway became a lure to the wealthy, who, in the latter portion of the 19th century, erected majestic house after majestic house.

Likewise, Park Slope, on the western border of Prospect Park, lent itself to similar upper class development. Among the more affluent avenues was Prospect Park West, a portion of which—from Grand Army Plaza to First Street—was dubbed "Brooklyn's Gold Coast." One of the most arresting buildings, the Montauk Club, is located near the park on Eighth Avenue at Lincoln Place and Plaza Place.

The Montauk. a blue blood social club, was designed by Francis H. Kimball. He was said to have been inspired by the Gothic palaces of Venice; hence one of the most distinctive edifices of its kind in the city.

And if the Wall Street tycoons wanted to reach their brokerage houses in a hurry, they need only stroll to the Grand Army Plaza station of the Interborough for a speedy ride to Manhattan's financial district.

Yet with all its charm and elegance, neither Prospect Park nor Brooklyn Botanic Garden could measure up to its Manhattan rival in terms of sheer popularity and geographic centricity to the subways and city population as a whole.

From the get-go, Central Park was the king and has remained so to this day.

"Of all the city's wonders," wrote Henry Hope Reed, "Central Park ranks first in the affection of New Yorkers."

Central Park's first curator, Reed will not find many New Yorkers to challenge his point. As he so aptly noted, "Hundreds of thousands think of it as 'their park.' It is many things to many people."[16]

To Vaux and Olmsted, it would be their *magnum opus.*

THE GREATEST RIDE
BETWEEN STATIONS

The Howard Beach/JFK Airport stop in Queens is in an area that could pass for Peoria, Council Bluffs or some other part of middle America. From there, the A Train highballs to Broad Channel station. Apart from being naturally scenic, that 3.5 mile stretch happens to be the longest run between stations on the entire system.

In 1858, they designed what ultimately would be a totally man-made park.

"Every foot of the park's surface, every tree and bush, as well as every arch, roadway and walk," commented Olmsted, "has been fixed where it is with a purpose."

Or, as Reed added, "Central Park is a giant public garden, a supreme American work of art."

Prior to the completion of Central Park, New Yorkers would take the ferry to Hoboken, New Jersey, where the Elysian Fields—part of the John Stevens estate—provided a dollop of greenery.

But wouldn't it be so much better—and easier—if rapid transit could carry millions of Manhattanites to an even grander common in the very center of the island?

It certainly would and, in time, the elevateds and later the subway would dramatically change the social *ambience* of Central Park.

However, in the beginning, its 843 acres were not designed for the common folk. Quite the contrary.

Affluent businessmen and property-owners, who had returned from Europe, enthralled by grand parks in its major cities, envisioned a similar greenbelt some-

where in an undeveloped section of Manhattan.

The wealthy had their carriages, but they did not have the kind of park that would enable them to take lengthy carriage drives. Central Park would be the answer for the mobile rich.

Nathaniel P. Willis, long ago an observer of the New York society scene, put it bluntly: "As a metropolis of wealth and fashion, New York has one great deficiency—that of a driving park. Rome has its Pincian Hill, Florence its Cascine, Paris its Bois de Boulogne, and London its Hyde Park. Such a place is not considered indispensable in New York because it has never been enjoyed."

The carriage drives did come along with rolling meadows, cliffs, lakes, ponds and just about everything the designers could hope for—with some necessary amendments.

Not that everyone in the Big Apple was enthused about it.

Since it was one of the city's grandest projects, both in its geographical grandeur as well its symmetry, enormous changes were wrought on the land with marked displacement of pre-park residents.

Irish pig farmers, German gardeners and shantytown inhabitants all were evicted along with a community of African-Americans who resided in the vicinity of Eighth Avenue and 82nd Street. Including a school and three churches, Seneca Village was razed by some of the 20,000 workers required to build the park, which was completed just prior to the Civil War.

Unfortunately, it was difficult for the average New Yorker to get there unless he or she lived within walking distance, since transit facilities were limited.

Most of those who partook of the facilities were bluebloods who came in carriages and even engaged in carriage parades around the well-manicured grounds.

However, it would not be long before the trains came and, in the eyes of some notable New Yorkers, not a moment too soon for Central Park, the Upper West Side and some of its precious attributes, including the American Museum of Natural History.

Created in the 1860s by the scientist Albert Bickmore, the museum opened across from the park—between 77th and 81st Streets—when Central Park was in its infancy. As remote as the park was to most New Yorkers, the American Museum required precisely what the greensward needed, mass transit.

"We could only wait and hope that the elevated train company would soon extend its lines north to 77th Street," said Bickmore.

The museum founder was referring to the New York Elevated Railroad Company's Ninth Avenue el. This was an outgrowth of Charles Harvey's original line over Greenwich Street and Ninth Avenue. That landmark rapid transit route began operation in 1870. It was designed to extend to the New York Central's early terminal, which had almost a dozen tracks and four platforms.

However, the single-track, cable-operated route—it had no intermediate stops between Dey and 29th Street—was not up to the task either mechanically or fiscally.

A reorganization which resulted in the New York Elevated Railroad Company, put the line on a more solid footing, and by 1877 it was running between South Ferry and 59th Street, including several stations in between.

That left the Ninth Avenue el just a mile from the Museum and not far from the park. What's more, it's success guaranteed that it would be pushed farther and farther north in Manhattan.

On the morning of June 9, 1879, the *chug, chug, chug, chug* of a steam engine could be heard for the first time from the grounds of Central Park and the halls of the American Museum of Natural History.

It huffed and puffed its way up Ninth Avenue—long since renamed Columbus Avenue—paralleling Central Park all the way to 110th Street. At that point, the exceptionally high elevated tracks turned sharply to the right (east) and rolled over 110th Street (Cathedral Parkway) for two blocks before completing the S-curve with a left turn on Eighth Avenue—across from Central Park—where it continued northward to 145th Street and the Harlem River.

Ninth Avenue el riders could easily reach Central Park from any one of seven stations—59th Street, 66th Street, 72nd Street, 81st Street (American Museum of Natural History), 93rd Street, 104th Street and 110th Street.

And they could do so with more comfort than one might imagine.

"The el was opulent," wrote Peter Salwen in *Upper West Side Story. "It had to be, to lure fashionable folk out to the hinterland. The steam locomotives were painted pea green; the carriages were variants on the Pullman Palace Car, a dainty light green outside, with oak and mahogany woodwork, plate glass windows with adjustable blinds, Morocco leather seats, and Axminster carpeting.*

"Stations, designed by a popular landscape artist, Jaspar Cropsey, resembled little Alpine chateaux, with pavilion roofs and wrought-iron crestings and finials."[17]

Manhattan Els

At 34th Street on the Third Avenue el, there was a spur to the Long Island Rail Road's 34th Street ferry that connected to its terminal in Long Island City. Opened in 1880, this spur operated for 50 years until its closing in 1930. This branch's popularity declined after the LIRR commenced using Pennsylvania Station in 1910 and subway service through the Steinway Tunnels began in 1917. After these events, ferry service was abandoned. In this view looking east from Third Avenue, the connecting track to the Third Avenue line is in the foreground. The track on the other side of the platform ended in a bumper. In the distance, the tracks widen out for a center island platform that connected to the Second Avenue el. Further in the distance there was a third station at the waterfront ferry dock.

A Third Avenue el station was built at Houston Street along the Bowery. The original stations were three cars in length and completely under canopy. In later years, canopy-less extensions were made at each end of the platforms to accommodate five-car trains.

Here's what the Ninth Avenue el looked like in 1914 along Greenwich Street in Downtown Manhattan. Now fully double-tracked and electrified, the el, while still occupying the sidewalk edge, is much more substantial than it was originally (see photo on page 467).

ABOVE: The Ninth Avenue elevated was still popular enough in 1915 to have a center (third) track installed for added business. While a train hovers in the distance, workmen adjust the express track steel-work, which will extend over the local tracks on both sides below. As a result of the Dual Contracts, the Ninth, Sixth and Third Avenue lines were all triple-tracked. Because at 53rd Street, the Sixth Avenue el had a flat junction with the Ninth, the center track had to be raised so it could vault over the intersection. There were plenty of trackside superintendents checking out the operation.

LEFT: Elevated stations were heated by coal stoves. Seen here is typical of what was found on el mezzanines throughout the city. They generated a lot more warmth on cold, wintry nights than one can imagine!

West Broadway, serviced by the Sixth Avenue elevated, saw both kinds of el construction. In the distance, the el is over the street's center; and here, between the Grand and Franklin Street stations, it fans out to the sidewalk edge. Parking was, obviously, not a problem in March 1927.

This is the second of the famous "S" curves on the Ninth Avenue el. It carried the line north along Columbus Avenue and then east (right turn) at 110th Street (Cathedral Parkway) and almost immediately left (north again) at Eighth Avenue. The July 1925 scene here, looking north up Eighth Avenue at 110th, shows the 90-degree turn which was known as "Suicide Curve." A station, served by an elevator, was just west of the downtown-heading train on the left. The northbound open gate cars are being passed by MUDC (Multiple Unit Door Control) former gate cars which had been converted to more modern operation.

A remarkable Manhattan street scene in May 1912 at 103rd Street and Lexington Avenue. Not one but two elevated lines—the Third Avenue el in the foreground, the Second Avenue in the background—are seen; each with trains simultaneously crossing 103rd Street in Harlem. The corner on which the couple stands eventually will be excavated to make way for the IRT Lexington Avenue subway, which will proceed north from 42nd Street and Grand Central Station. Horses-and-wagons predominated among the merchandise-carriers. In 1912 there was more rapid transit servicing the East Side of Manhattan than there is now!

The IRT City Hall station had two levels. The top was for the Second Avenue Line and the lower for the Third Avenue el. Notice the stairway under construction at the right.

The lower level platforms and ticket booth of the Third Avenue el's City Hall station.

So popular was the Ninth Avenue el that it began running no less than forty trains daily and soon found itself with competition from another el that also would benefit Central Park.

Dr. Rufus B. Gilbert, a Civil War physician, was given the civic green light to build an elevated railroad along Sixth Avenue, and by 1878, it was in service from a southern depot at Morris Street all the way to 58th Street, just one block shy of the park.

"More luxurious than its competition," wrote Joseph Cunningham and Leonard De Hart in *The Manhattan Els and the I.R.T.*, *"it featured fine woods in cars, carpeting, a two-tone green paint scheme, chandeliers, separate waiting rooms for men and women, and compressed paper wheels. The last feature was designed to mollify residents who raved about the noise.*

"Cartoons appeared, some to the effect that anyone living near the road would shortly be carted off to the insane asylum having cracked from the noise."[18]

Well, not quite.

The Sixth Avenue line built a westerly extension along 53rd Street to Ninth Avenue, where it merged with the Ninth Avenue line, sharing its trackage through the Upper West Side and, finally, Harlem.

As the el construction crews pushed the massive steel structure up Ninth Avenue, building gangs followed close by, erecting houses where desolate lots once filled the landscape. More often than not, the homes were three stories high and sometimes four- and five-story walk-ups.

A few high-rise apartments, starting with the Dakota at 72nd Street and Central Park West—just a block from the Ninth Avenue el—and later the Majestic (across from the Dakota and San Remo (74th Street) followed. In time Central Park West would be a canyon of luxury apartments.

That rapid transit was a catalyst for their development was recognized by the daily press.

Precursor to the *New York Herald-Tribune*, the *Herald* unequivocally endorsed the role of trains:

"Steam transit has accomplished in a year what a decade would have failed to do without it. The admirable service on the elevated roads has shown what comfort and facility a home in this vicinity can be reached."

Homeowners were not the only beneficiaries of mass transit on the Upper West Side. Soon after the Sixth and Ninth Avenue elevateds had reached their peak, an arena grew across the avenue from the Ninth Avenue el on the northeast corner of 66th Street.

At first, the St. Nicholas Palace—opened in 1896—featured ice skating—but two years after the Interborough opened its 66th Street station, it began to headline professional boxing as well as wrestling, dog shows, public roller skating and even—when there was a demand—funerals.

St. Nick's Arena, as it became known, housed New York's first truly famous hockey club, named after the rink. Featuring Princeton collegiate hockey star, Hobey Baker, the rink's 4,000 seats often were filled to capacity; especially when touring Canadian teams came to town.

But the red brick building would become most famous for the fights. (Many local boxers lived in nearby rooming houses and got in shape running and jumping rope in Central Park.) Such world-renowned boxers as Jess Willard and Jack Johnson were featured on St. Nick's cards over the years.

Perhaps the biggest business the el—before closing—and Broadway IRT did for a fight on the Upper West Side was on the night of February 20, 1939 when the largest audience in St. Nick's 43-year life came to see a pair of Jewish boxers from Brooklyn settle a Brownsville rivalry.

In one corner was Al Davis, nicknamed "Bummy," and in the other, Mickey Farber. (Bummy, by the way, was short for his Hebrew name, *Avrum,* which, around Brownsville candy stores, became altered to *Vunny* and, eventually, *Bummy.*) A brawling, unscientific fighter, Davis was a crowd favorite, drawing more than 5,000 fans that night, many of whom rode all the way from Brownsville on the IRT's New Lots line to St. Nick's.

The Sixth and Ninth Avenue elevated lines did well by Central Park, the American Museum and the Upper West Side in general for about two decades; or until the noise and—in the eyes of some critics—unsightliness became a turn-off for civic groups and homeowners who preferred a more modern means of transport.

August Belmont's Interborough Rapid Transit helped solve that problem, except that the Broadway line, when it opened on October 27, 1904, was farther from the park than its Ninth (Columbus) Avenue counterpart.

The IRT's rival, Brooklyn Rapid Transit, also got a piece of the Central Park subway action as a result of the Dual Contracts of 1913.

One improvement designated for the BRT was officially called "Broadway-Seventh Avenue-59th Street." While it offered many meaningful sections of trackage—especially a tunnel to Brooklyn and another to Queens—its most vital tube would be a four-track segment running under the spine of Manhattan.

Essentially, it would operate from City Hall—adjacent to the original Interborough Brooklyn Bridge station—up four tracks heading north under Broadway to Times Square.

From 42nd Street, it would continue north under Seventh Avenue—at this point the IRT is running north under Broadway—with stations at 49th Street, 57th Street—just two blocks shy of Central Park—with another serving the park at Fifth Avenue.

As part of the Dual Contracts deal, BRT trains were permitted to run on tracks of the Interborough's elevated lines in Queens. However, the advent of the ten-foot wide BRT steel Standard cars made them incompatible with the smaller-width IRT rolling stock; which meant that adjustments had to be made.

In order to successfully meld the joint services, the Queensborough Plaza depot's northerly section was given over to the BRT while the IRT's skinnier cars utilized another part of the complex terminal.

Once the BRT's Queens-Broadway addition began operating, it enabled residents of Astoria, Woodside, Jackson Heights, Elmhurst and Flushing, among other communities, to have easy access to Central Park via the BRT connection at Queens Plaza, with the two stations within easy walking distance to the southern park entrances at Central Park South and Seventh Avenue as well as Fifth Avenue and Central Park South.

This was particularly useful to parents and children visiting the Central Park Zoo and the park's pony rides which were located near Fifth Avenue.

By the time the BRT Broadway-Queens

line was up and running, Central Park was being serviced by two elevated lines (Ninth Avenue and Sixth Avenue) and one underground unit.

Still, in terms of giving the park *total* subway access, something was missing.

What was lacking—if it could be called a *need*—was a rapid transit system which covered the entire length of the park, from 59th Street (Central Park South) to 110th Street (Cathedral Parkway) at the northern end.

This gift of total transit finally came about in the mid-1920s when the city went into competition with the privately-held BRT (now BMT) and the IRT. With the blessings of Mayor John Hylan and his successor, Jimmy Walker, the city's last major subway construction undertaking would be underway—and Central Park would be one of the fortunate beneficiaries.

In the midst of the Roarin' Twenties, when Manhattan was booming and swinging as it never had before, Central Park finally got a subway it could call its own, the Independent System's Eighth Avenue line.

According to its designers, both expresses and locals would barrel alongside Central Park for sixty-one city blocks.

Stations directly serving the park would be located at Columbus Circle, 72nd Street, 81st Street, 86th Street, 96th Street, 103rd Street and 110th Street.

The IND got into business in a serious way on March 14, 1925 when Mayor Hylan jabbed a spade into the dirt at West 123rd Street and St. Nicholas Avenue, launching the impressive Eighth Avenue subway project.

It required seven years before the first leg of the Independent linked Chambers Street (Hudson Terminal) and 207th Street

in Washington Heights, by which time Central Park had markedly changed from the years when it was serviced only by the Ninth and Sixth Avenue els.

During the Eighth Avenue subway's digging year of 1927, philanthropist August Heckscher funded Central Park's first equipped playground (on the southeastern meadow) and, later, the Great Lawn was laid out.

Shortly after the IND's opening, the Parks Department built almost two-dozen playgrounds around the border, and the zoo was reconstructed and improved. In the post-World War II era of development, the Wollman Ice Skating Rink in the park's southern tier became a major focus of park-goers, many of whom used the subway to reach the facility.

If any special interest group in the vicinity of Central Park benefited from completion of the Eighth Avenue Subway, it was the real estate industry.

While Central Park West boasted a number of impressive pre-20th Century highrise apartments, construction of the Independent System spawned a whole new generation of upscale buildings from Columbus Circle north to 96th Street.

Some architecture critics assert that the best structures of the era during which the IND was completed were built on Central Park West.

These include the San Remo, the Beresford, and Majestic, each of which was famous for more than its engineering.

For example, Bruno Richard Hauptmann, tried and executed for the kidnapping and death of the baby son of Charles Lindbergh, was a carpenter who worked on construction of the Majestic Apartments at 115 Central Park West. (A quarter century later, gangster Frank

The First City-Owned Line —
The Eighth Avenue Subway

OPPOSITE PAGE, TOP: Central Park West, just south of the American Museum of Natural History, was a tranquil, tree-lined neighborhood in 1925 before digging began for the first city-owned Independent Subway. The not-so-rapid transit along the avenue was provided by streetcars which took their power from below ground rather than overhead trolley wires. The New York Historical Society is at the far left, with the Museum buildings to its right on the next block. The distant apartment house is at 81st Street.

Central Park West already had been a well-developed—and high-priced—thoroughfare before the mid-1920s when the street was surgically torn asunder to make way for a new IND Eighth Avenue line operating to Washington Heights. Once the subway was completed, the trolleys would disappear. The hoist to the left was used to lift the dirt up from below. A line of trolleys appears to be held up by the construction vehicles.

OPPOSITE PAGE, BOTTOM: A Mack truck, nicknamed Baby Alice, makes its way up a wood-planked embankment along Central Park in the West 70s. Construction of the original IND line proceeded adjacent to Central Park while normal streetcar and automotive-truck traffic kept moving along Central Park West. Note that wood-planking extends from one side of the street to the other.

A Central Park West scene before the IND Eighth Avenue line began operation. A trolley's roof can be seen at the right, behind the parked auto, while a bus belonging to the New York Department of Plant and Structures tools west along West 86th Street.

The tune "Take the A Train" had not yet been composed but once the digging here at St. Nicholas Avenue and 125th Street in Harlem was completed, there would be inspiration for Billy Strayhorn to write the song. The A-Express would be the Eighth Avenue Subway's flagship route from Downtown Manhattan through Harlem to Washington Heights. The photo was taken in July 1927 at what would become the area's major express station.

As the contractor's sign in the distance indicates, the northern portion of the original IND line was called the Washington Heights Subway. Morante and Raymond, the builders, had set up shop at 173rd Street and Broadway in the midst of the Roarin' Twenties. The original Interborough Rapid Transit line had long been in use when this photo was taken. Five- and six-story apartment houses along Broadway paralleled much of the IRT run.

The first order of subway cars arrive for the soon-to-be-opened Independent Subway System.

Two weeks before the opening of the 8th Avenue subway, a practice run of an uptown express stops at 42nd Street, carrying someone who couldn't wait for the service to begin!

Costello was shot in the lobby by a gang hit man, yet lived to tell the tale until the age of eighty.)

The Beresford, 211 Central Park West, had a predecessor at the same address, which was a hotel. One of its claims to fame was that President Franklin Delano Roosevelt's Treasury Secretary, Henry Morgenthau, Jr. was born there on May 11, 1891. The current Beresford apartment skyscraper has had many prominent tenants among whom was anthropologist Margaret Mead from 1966 to 1968. Mead used the 81st Street IND local station situated right at her corner.

No architect took more advantage of the subway-real estate boom than Emery Roth, who was responsible for eight major structures along the Independent route. Regarded by West Side historian Peter Salwen as the "patriarch of a New York architectural dynasty," the Hungarian-born Roth is best-remembered for the San Remo.

Inimitable is the best way to describe what was New York's first twin-towered high-rise apartment. When completed, it spanned the Central Park West block, from 74th to 75th Streets, looking down on the IND subway grating along the sidewalk.

Reaching 27 stories above the Upper West Side, the San Remo—and the Independent System—inspired still more construction up and down the avenue.

Salwen: "By 1931 three more twin-towered buildings—the Chanin organization's Century and Majestic and Margon & Holder's El Dorado (for which Roth was the associate architect)—had joined the San Remo to give Central Park West a dramatic new skyline." And more customers for the AA local, which stopped nearby.

While the subways were able to draw the theater district north from 14th Street to 34th Street (Herald Square) and, ultimately, Times Square, they never were able to push Manhattan's entertainment center beyond Columbus Circle (59th Street), the northern border of Times Square, although it wasn't for lack of trying.

A number of movie-vaudeville houses were built right over the Broadway IRT line, and some future film stars—who would be seen on the screens—grew up within a nickel's throw of the subway or, in the case of Warner Brothers beauty, Lauren Bacall, who lived *under* the el at Columbus and 86th Street.

Ironically, the one movie house designed to match the best of Times Square was Samuel (Roxy) Rothafel's Beacon Theater, just two blocks from the IRT's 72nd Street express station.

Filled with the same trappings that gilded his Roxy Theater, the Beacon still exists today; only now when straphangers walk from the 72nd Street station, they're heading for an *off*-Broadway theater, not a movie palace!

What It Was Like
To Take the Subway
to the Greenery
and to the Zoos
in Brooklyn, Bronx
and Manhattan

No doubt about it, the Bronx Zoo was to the city's zoological gardens what the New York Yankees have been to Big Apple baseball: top of the line.

There was only one problem for me—a big one—it was so darn far away!

From Williamsburg to *anywhere* in the Bronx was a difficult enough trip—but the zoo was up there—beyond Yankee Stadium, beyond Morrisania, even beyond West Farms.

Translated into transit terms, it meant that riding a minimum of *three* different subway lines was required before reaching the lions, tigers, elephants and other exhibits of truly fabulous fauna which *only* could be found at Bronx Park.

Oh, there were some neat animals at nearby Prospect Park Zoo and a few good exhibits—actually only one, the seals—at its Central Park counterpart.

But I always felt that when I was visiting either Central Park or Prospect Park zoos, I was observing a minor league menagerie.

On the other hand, those relatives—also Mom and Dad—kind enough to take me to the zoo preferred staying closer to home; meaning Prospect Park.

Getting there actually was easiest by Lorimer Street trolley because it went directly from the corner of Vernon and Nostrand Avenues all the way to the park, as well as to the Botanic Garden.

The bad news is that the trolley—as my mother would say—"creeped along"—and my family was not much for creeping.

There *was* a not-that-rapid compromise of sorts. We could ride the Myrtle Avenue el to Bridge Street station and then walk over to DeKalb Avenue where we would take the Brighton Line to Prospect Park station.

It wasn't much shorter a ride than the trolley; it just *seemed* that way. On the other hand, it was a lot more fun. *Any* trip on the Myrtle Avenue el was fun, especially heading downtown toward Fulton Street.

A couple of aspects of the ride enthralled me the most. One was what I called "The Forgotten Spur."

It was a section of steelwork—which once obviously carried tracks—that veered off to the right from the main line, and then, inexplicably, stopped dead in front of a tenement house on Myrtle Avenue.

"How," I wondered, "could they have built a switch off the regular route that curved directly into a house wall?"

It was an unsolved mystery for me that lasted a half-century, or until I researched the early Brooklyn els.

Late in the 19th Century, when the first Brooklyn elevated line was built, part of the original main line *did* curve to the right north of Grand and Myrtle Avenues. But in 1890 it was abandoned and eventually razed. What I had been seeing on those rides downtown was the last vestige of that curve leading to the old main line.

I considered that a *major* personal discovery which I have carefully kept to myself ever since!

A second source of fascination was the intersection of the Lexington Avenue el with the Myrtle. Here we had two of the oldest rapid transit routes in New York melding at Grand Avenue and Myrtle.

As I stood at the front window, I could see the Lexington tracks coming off from the south and curving left over Myrtle Avenue. Sometimes, our train would encounter a red light, causing us to stop, allowing the Lex to take the curve, switch on to the Myrtle tracks and then roll on to the Brooklyn Bridge ahead of us.

Railroad switches have always fascinated me but those on the elevated lines had an even stronger attraction.

First of all, I could *see* them whereas in the subway, switches usually were hidden in the dark of the tunnel.

One of my favorite vantage points on Brooklyn's Myrtle Avenue el was at Grand Avenue station in Clinton Hill. It was there that the Lexington Avenue el branched off in a southerly direction from the eastbound Myrtle Avenue tracks. This view—northwest from the north end of the eastbound platform— shows the curving Lex tracks as well as the tower and el junction. The photo was taken immediately after World War II, when both lines still operated.

Secondly, there was the mind game: I could not fix it into my brain precisely how train wheels on a straight track could roll over the curved rail that crossed *directly* in front of it. Or, to put it another way: I always wondered why the train did not derail while crossing the switches. That particular fascination remains to this day.

Finally, there was the *sound;* a drumbeat with overtones of the late, great, jazz drummer, Gene Krupa, doing his solo behind Benny Goodman's classic *"Sing, Sing, Sing."*[19]

Once the Lexington Avenue local—by the way there were no expresses on the Lex or Myrtle Avenue lines—cleared the switch and headed toward the bridge, I fixed my eyes on the red (stop) signal, awaiting its turn to amber (proceed slowly and with caution). But first, the switch had to move from its curved position to the straightway and that was always fun to watch—and hear—because of its crisp movement and *ker-thunk* sound.

With the switch in proper formation and the Lexington train far in the distance,

our Myrtle Avenue consist lurched forward and into the Washington Avenue station.

Since our destination, Bridge Street, was coming up, we prepared for our exit by walking to the open platform where the first and second cars were coupled.

Like all the ancient els, Myrtle Avenue's edition employed a conductor who worked the iron gates that had to be opened at each stop. He would stand between the cars with his left leg at the edge of the first car and his right at the edge of the second car.

Each hand would encase an iron handle on which he would pull once the train had come to a stop. The handles would activate a primitive—yet effective—mechanism that would open each gate, first inward and then to the side, allowing the passengers to alight.

Once all the riders who were getting off had cleared the exit, the conductor then would push forward on the handles, thereby closing the gates. Finally, he would wait for his fellow conductors to clear their platforms and pull twice, activating a

The IRT Moves to Brooklyn

A subway is being dug under Flatbush Avenue, while the el already is in business overhead. A trolley is seen far in the distance under the elevated tracks, while primary store deliveries in 1905 are being made by horse-and-wagon. Not a single automobile is visible in this photo. Note the primitive steelwork on the el structure; yet there is no evidence that any ever collapsed. The entire two-track el structure would be razed in time and completely re-built.

An excellent example of the "cut-and-cover" subway-building technique in Brooklyn. In the background, one can see the area of tunnel that was dug—and then covered over—while in the foreground, the subway right-of-way has been cut but not yet covered in 1905.

Everything is new at the IRT's Nevins Street station in November 1908, less than a year after it officially opened in January of the same year. This was part of the Interborough's first venture into Brooklyn. Note the one-cent chewing gum machine and the glass ceilings above the local tracks, which allowed natural sunlight to pour into the station.

Both in Manhattan and Brooklyn, the early two-track elevated lines proved so popular that it was necessary that changes be made to accommodate the demand. The most common improvement was the addition of one or two tracks, depending upon how much room the street below would allow. In this case, at Nostrand Avenue (Brooklyn), the widening will allow for both express and local tracks. The Dual Contracts called for removal of the two-track Fulton Street structure and replacement with full-length platforms to accommodate longer trains. The wooden extension platform bridges seen here enabled the line to maintain service while all the work was being done.

Simultaneous with the widening of the Fulton Street el was the extension of the IRT deeper into Brooklyn, as seen here on Eastern Parkway. It was one of Brooklyn's most majestic thoroughfares before the IRT New Lots Avenue and Flatbush Avenue subways were constructed. By the end of 1915, the roadway had been ripped asunder and flatcars lined the embankment. Remarkably, the Parkway was restored to its pre-excavation beauty once the underground construction was finished.

bell. Once our conductor heard his bell ring twice, he would reach upward, grabbing a loop of cord, and—with a sharp tug—pull twice.

The double-ring in the motorman's cab signalled that all was clear and the time had come to move forward. Pulling on his controller, the motorman moved it into first position. The *groan* of the ancient electric motor—located in the car's truck below—signalled our movement and coincided with a swaying of the car as the couplers strained with the motion.

Holding tightly to the iron gate, I would look directly down at the couplers and wonder what kept them from coming apart, allowing the train to split into thirds. (Of course, this never happened.)

As we gained speed, I now fixed my sights on the final portion of the Myrtle ride and one last interesting view; the viaduct carrying our local over Flatbush Avenue Extension.

For decades I also had wondered about this particular phenomenon of the expedition. Unlike any other aspect of the Myrtle superstructure, the viaduct over Flatbush Avenue Extension had a long, lyrical—and almost modernistic—look to it. To my eyes, it was totally out of synch with an elevated railroad that had been built late in the 19th Century.

Eventually, I learned that there *was* a reason for the architectural disparity.

It all had to do with Flatbush Avenue in the early 1890s, when Brooklyn was a city unto itself, separate from New York.

At the time, Flatbush Avenue, heading north, ended at Fulton Street, home to yet another venerable elevated line. Since Fulton Street was the only direct avenue connecting with the Brooklyn Bridge, congestion often developed between the

Brooklyn Bridge, Fulton Ferry and the Fulton Street shopping center.

Demands to relieve the horse-drawn-inspired gridlock became so intense that, finally, Brooklyn Mayor Charles Schieren sought a solution.

His transit committee originally suggested that Flatbush Avenue be linked straightaway to Fulton Ferry. However, this plan was altered when blueprints for the new, 6,855-foot-long Manhattan Bridge were formulated.

In its final form, Flatbush Avenue was extended from Fulton Street in a northerly direction to where the bridge exit reached *terra firma*.

Separated by a pair of trolley tracks bisecting the boulevard, Flatbush Avenue Extension was a handsome, double-lane addition to Brooklyn's downtown street grid.

However, to reach the bridge site, construction crews had to dig under the already-aging Myrtle Avenue el structure. And since Flatbush Avenue Extension would be uncharacteristically wide, the elevated's steelwork required an alteration. Hence, the viaduct spanning the street.

When work finally was completed in 1915, the four-lane roadway was appropriately named Flatbush Avenue *Extension.*

After getting off at Bridge Street, we walked to Flatbush Extension—Brooklynites invariably omitted the *Avenue* part—and then proceeded south to the DeKalb Avenue BMT station. Although we could have entered the subway at the Myrtle Avenue BMT local station (since eliminated), I always insisted on walking along Flatbush Avenue.

The Extension was an exciting street to me because it was the easterly gateway to

The Creation of Flatbush Avenue Extension

When the BRT subway was extended over the Manhattan Bridge into downtown Brooklyn, provisions had to be made to accommodate tunneling in the area of Myrtle Avenue. An addition to Flatbush Avenue was built to link the bridge with the original Flatbush Avenue. This photo shows the extension in its early stages with the bridge towers in the background. What this indicates is the cleared right-of-way for Flatbush Extension in 1912.

Some of the most attractive streets in Brooklyn Heights were affected by subway construction. When the IRT reached Brooklyn, Hicks and Joralemon Streets would be uprooted as the subway headed toward the Atlantic Avenue terminal.

Flatbush Avenue Extension after its completion. The Myrtle Avenue el is in the background, while horses and wagons dot the new thoroughfare. Myrtle Avenue el pillars would eventually prove to be an impediment to smooth traffic flow on the busy avenue. They would be removed and a new trestle support system would vault the el over the thoroughfare.

Downtown Brooklyn's entertainment and shopping district.

Most prominent of the structures was the Brooklyn Paramount Theater, with a monstrous marquee that extended from Flatbush Avenue Extension all the way around to DeKalb Avenue. The size allowed exceptionally long details about the feature films, performers and sometmes even the selected short subjects.

It often appeared as if the Paramount Theater marquee read like *"War and Peace."*

We crossed DeKalb Avenue to the BMT subway entrance, which was snuggled in between a hot dog emporium and a bar, and then stepped down the stairs.

DeKalb station's charm was its superficial simplicity yet internal complexity. It had six tracks, four platforms and two bypass tracks.

A variety of lines—Brighton, Sea Beach, et. al.—converged on DeKalb from both the Manhattan Bridge and tunnel. So, naturally, one of the fun things to do was guess which train was arriving as its lights came into view through the tunnel.

Even with a long wait, it was interesting because of car-watching possibilities. Sea Beach then had the Triplex trains, which I rarely rode, while the Brighton and tunnel cars were Standards.

Once our train arrived, it was a short run to Prospect Park. *Speedy* would be the better description of the 7th Avenue to Empire Boulevard segment because of the straightaway between stations.

The Standard finally slowed down as natural light, pouring through the Prospect Park station open cut, could be seen on the upgrade leading toward the platform.

We pulled in on the center (express) track, got off at the front of the station and walked back to the exit at Flatbush Avenue near Empire Boulevard.

Immediately after we had climbed to street level, our nostrils were graced with a blend of edible scents. First there was the smell of fresh baked goods from the Bond Bread bakery across Flatbush Avenue. It combined with the whiff of hot dogs and fresh, roasted peanuts, emanating from the stands on Empire Boulevard leading to Ebbets Field.

If nothing else, it made me want to eat *something* right away.

Instead, Mom yanked me across the intersection to the park side of Flatbush Avenue, stepping lively to avoid being struck by a Franklin Avenue trolley on the left coming up from Parkside Avenue.

Before getting to the zoo, one had to walk a path that led zoo-goers past one of the more appealing—for a kid—park features; the pony ride.

This always was a "must," which was endorsed by my parents—if not the pony—because it was so safe. With the handler's help, I mounted the animal which then was led by leather strap around a dirt-covered oval.

Every so often, I'd be fortunate enough to encounter a funny, talkative handler who made the ride all the more enjoyable. But even with the dull ones, I didn't mind. Being in the saddle, even if it only was a pony, enabled me to pretend I was Tom Mix, Gene Autry or Roy Rogers; at least for five minutes, although at a slower pace than either *Tony, Champion* or *Trigger* ever managed.

Before reaching the zoo, we could see and appreciate some of the creations of architects Olmsted and Vaux, not to mention historic sites which had—and still have—special meaning to Brooklynites like me.

One of them was Litchfield Mansion, for which there were numerous park signs pointing it out for the pure and simple reason that Litchfield is to Prospect Park what the Belvedere Castle means to Central Park.

Prospect Park's Litchfield was built by well-heeled businessman, Edwin C. Litchfield, who in the mid-1850s chose to locate his new villa in the middle of Brooklyn.

He selected designer Alexander Jackson Davis to create the mansion—named Grace Hill Estate—which was ready for occupancy in 1857.

As handsome as any mansion in the city, Litchfield, unfortunately, was built in the wrong place at the wrong time.

Only two years after its owner moved in, the New York State Legislature authorized the City of Brooklyn to purchase property to be used as a public park.

This was not what Edwin C. Litchfield had in mind when he decided to build his villa but he had no choice. Central Park already was a big hit in Manhattan and that inspired passage of the act creating Prospect Park.

With Central Park's design already under their belts, Olmsted and Vaux vowed to make their new creation even better and bigger. The problem, for Litchfield, was that the final design map of the proposed greenery included his mansion and its acreage.

To their credit, Olmsted and Vaux had the good sense to preserve, rather than demolish, the mansion which ultimately was turned into administrative offices for the Parks Department.

Approaching the zoo, it was apparent to us what Olmsted and Vaux had in mind. Apart from the zoological gardens, there was a lake, forests, a bridle path, rock for-mations statues and bridges the equal of Central Park's in their design and beauty.

Clearly, Grace Glueck and Paul Gardner had it right in their book, *Brooklyn—People and Places, Past and Present* when they called Prospect Park, "a stirring sweep of greenery that refreshed the cityscape with natural beauty."[20]

As zoos go, Prospect Park's lacked the depth, breadth and scope of its Bronx counterpart, but for a five-year-old like myself, who didn't know better, it was just fine. At that age, I wasn't thinking how cruel it was to pen a lion in a cage that would have seemed claustrophobic to an ant; nor did I quibble over the fact that the zoo lacked a reptile exhibit. In fact, when the original Prospect Park Zoo was designed by Olmsted and Vaux, its first exhibits included bears, deer, peafowl and sheep.

That wasn't enough to suit me. I liked what I *liked;* namely the elephants and the seals.

By contrast to most of the other animal exhibits, the elephant house was sizeable and included an outdoor pavilion where the pachyderms could enjoy a little stroll. Sometimes they would *galumph* in the direction of the metal barriers behind which we would observe them.

However, the zoo designers had included a rather deep moat separating the animals from the spectators. No dummies, the elephants knew that one step too far would land them horizontally into the moat, so they treaded carefully when inching forward to nab the inevitable peanuts that were hurled their way.

As much as I enjoyed watching—and, occasionally, feeding—the elephants, I got a bigger kick out of the seals.

Of all the exhibits, the seal pool did the

most justice to its inhabitants. There was plenty of water in which to exercise, and a seal "house" where the sleek, barking fellows could enjoy some shade. Plus, one or two of them usually could be found copping a few z's on the roof of their home.

I could easily spend an hour watching the seals because I never could predict what they would do from one dive to the next; from one squawk to the other. But there always were the monkeys to check out—invariably a few laughs there—and a few exotic birds.

If the weather was warm enough, as it was that day, we would exit the zoo and walk toward Prospect Park Lake. My mother, who was a wise woman despite the lack of a college education, liked to fill me in on history wherever she could; and Prospect Park was rich in history.

She pointed out the Lefferts Homestead, reminding me that there was a Lefferts Avenue nearby. Built in 1783, the estate in the park originally belonged to Lieutenant Peter Lefferts and was given to Brooklyn by his descendants. Dutch Colonial in design, the homestead was turned into a museum featuring period furniture.

"It recalls to life the early eighteenth century with such authenticity," wrote Glueck and Gardiner, "that you would not be surprised to find a dimpled Dutch Colonist preparing pumpkin soup in the kitchen."[21]

Equally notable was the Boathouse which was built in 1905 and looked like something that would be at home along the Grand Canal in Venice. It lent a sense of grace and grandeur to the waters around it and underlined the point made by its designers that Prospect Park was more than a place for getting fresh air and exercise.

"The main object of Prospect Park," said Olmsted, "is to produce a certain influence in the minds of people and through this to make life in the city healthier and happier."

So many parts of the park's turf oozed history. Not far from the zoo and lake was an area called Battle Pass. During the Revolutionary War, a critical confrontation took place between George Washington's troops and the British. On a rise near the Boathouse stands the Maryland Monument, designed in 1895 by Stanford White. Atop Lookout Hill, the highest point in the park, Continental troops from the Maryland Regiment outfoxed the British, enabling Washington's soldiers to conduct an orderly retreat to safety.

When time permitted—as it did this day—we left the park along Flatbush Avenue at a point midway between Empire Boulevard and Grand Army Plaza. This was a favorite spot of mine because of the manner in which Flatbush Avenue crests before descending south toward the Bond Bread building.

There was a "Trolley Station" about twenty yards from the crest, and, quite often, the streetcar coming from Downtown Brooklyn would brake to a halt picking up park passengers.

I always was enthralled with trolleys but the Flatbush version had a special look to it. Unlike our more traditional double-ended Nostrand, Tompkins and DeKalb Avenue streetcars, the Flatbush Avenue tram not only was single-ended, but also had a slight, streamlined look to it that marked this particular early 1930s model special.

As a result, I always encouraged my mother to wait five or so minutes until one came along, and she usually obliged.

Once we crossed Flatbush Avenue, our

trip continued with a visit to the Botanic Garden, one of Mom's favorite spots in which to relax.

Dubbed "Shangri-la in Brooklyn," the Botanic Garden also has been called "an urban miracle."

Call it what you will, I always found it more interesting than captivating; more fantasyland than fun.

To me, the *mélange* of cedars, evergeens, spruce and other samples of *flora* seemed as if they had come from another world. After all, we had no trees on Marcy Avenue and, as far as I can remember, only one tree around the corner on Vernon Avenue; and that one got in the way of our punchball games!

Where else could a kid come across no less than four thousand rose bushes or seven hundred varieties? As Gerald Green observed in his best-seller, *The Last Angry Man,* "Luckily, the opportunity to enjoy trees and flowers, lawns and gardens is still one of the great boons that Brooklyn has to offer. I refer, of course, to the Brooklyn Botanic Garden, that island of peace and beauty in the heart of my favorite borough."

No question, I shared Green's sentiments, although not nearly with the same intensity as my Mom did, because, after all, she adored flowers and plants a lot more than trolley cars!

Another striking feature was the greenhouse which included the Desert Pavilion. It always surprised me with its extraordinary warmth in comparison to the outside air.

After our Botanic Garden visit, we had a pair of options upon leaving: we could head back to the Flatbush Avenue-Empire Boulevard exit and take the Lorimer Street trolley home; or we could head in the other (northerly) direction where the new main branch of the Brooklyn Public Library was being completed.

New buildings never failed to interest me, and the Public Library was high on the list—if only because it took so long to complete. Long before I was born—in fact before my father entered the U.S. Navy during World War I—the Central Library was designed as a Victorian-style building.

As often happened, construction was halted because of the war effort and later due to a lack of funds during the Great Depression. Finally, in the late 1930s it was decided to shelve the original design and create an ultra-modern, art deco library salvaging the skeleton of the never-fully-completed original.

And what a change it was!

Designed by Alfred Morton Githing and Francis Keally, the revised Central Library at the northern tip of the Botanic Garden is a handsome structure with an especially striking entrance, enhanced by gilded reliefs by C. Paul Jennewein and screen by Thomas H. Jones. To my eyes, it was breathtaking and well worth the long walk; because we still had to stroll along Eastern Parkway to Nostrand Avenue for our trolley ride home.

Walking along Eastern Parkway gave every Brooklynite a special pride. Its expanse and tree-lined beauty made us feel that we had streets the equal of any of the world's best. In fact, Eastern Parkway has, over the years, been compared with the Parisian's beloved *Champs Elysees* or Berlin's *Unter den Linden.*

En route to Nostrand, we passed another borough classic, the Brooklyn Museum, built in 1897 and our answer to the Metropolitan Museum of Art on Fifth Avenue.

A director of the Brooklyn Museum,

Robert Buck, once observed, "If we were anywhere else in the country, we'd be recognized for what we are—one of the best museums in world."

We in Brooklyn never claimed that our museum was *the* best nor that our zoo had reached the top of the charts. For the best museums, we took the train to Manhattan and for the best zoo—arguably tops in the whole world—there was the IRT to take to the Bronx.

Easy, it was not; especially for a Williamsburger.

That explains why my visits, as a youth, were few and far between.

The complication—prior to 1940, when the IRT, BMT and IND were unified into one system—involved transferring from our home IND line, and later to the IRT.

Granted, the fare was only a nickel; but in those days of the Great Depression, the difference between five and ten cents was *huge*. In order to get to Bronx Zoo, we had to change from the IND near City Hall and switch to the IRT. That meant ten cents instead of five and that was not at all appealing to my folks.

Of course, kid that I was, I couldn't have cared less. Riding the crazy, old IRT was an event in and of itself and just *had* to be done.

So, we did it!

The first leg of the trip—from Myrtle-Willoughby on the GG to Hoyt-Schermerhorn and the A train—was prosaic to me compared to what was ahead.

At Broadway-Nassau Street station on the A, we left the Independent System and walked up to the streets of Downtown Manhattan.

In those days, each of the three subway systems displayed distinctly inimitable colored globes to identify each line.

By far the most intricate was the BMT's green-and-white, leaded fixture that seemed to weigh a ton and appeared to be a second-cousin to the Statue of Liberty. It was in no uncertain terms, a beauty! By the way the letters S-U-B-W-A-Y were emblazoned on a white side panel, should anyone have any doubts about what was below.

Likewise, the IRT's counterpart was magnificent in its simplicity; a perfect globe with a distinctive dark blue hue that told every New Yorker that this was the Interborough.

The Subway-Come-Lately Independent opted for a square, bevelled fixture in two separate colors; light (very attractive) green and white.

Each station entrance—unless it happened to be an old IRT kiosk—usually carried four such fixtures, one at each corner.

Since my father knew the subway system inside-out, it didn't take very long for him to spot the IRT's blue globe.

Down the stairs we went into what for me, then, was a whole new and different subway world.

Bear in mind that the IRT was the oldest system and the one most foreign to me and the first "foreign" aspect that I noticed was the aroma.

The IRT not only looked different, it smelled different; more acrid, more used, far stranger than the BMT.

How strange?

To begin with, the turnstiles were borderline intimidating.

They were bigger and more complicated than the relatively simple operation on the new IND. When you entered the turnstile at Myrtle-Willoughby, it swallowed the nickel with no particular reaction.

But on the IRT, the second the five-cent

piece entered its receptacle, a very harsh *thunk* was heard, as if the turnstile were clearing its metallic throat.

Then there were the wooden, swinging gates themselves—beat-up, almost to the point of having splinters—which required a hefty push to get them moving. And once you completed the turn and passed through them, there was a sort-of aftershock, as if to emphasize that the sale was complete!

Once on the Fulton Street station platform, we walked up to the front—naturally—and awaited the Bronx-bound train.

In those days, many IRT stations had a distinctive feature. Local station platforms had only enough room for four or five cars, whereas express trains could carry as many as eight cars. (This would change following a platform-lengthening program in the 1950s.)

Another distinctive IRT mechanism was the signal light. Three-tiered like the ones on the IND and BMT, the IRT signals had a noticeably larger face on the red, amber and green and visors for each one that looked like the tip of a baseball cap.

I immediately fell in love with the Interborough!

The trains were something else.

Except for the World's Fair cars, introduced on the Flushing Line in 1939, the IRT rolling stock reflected a company that had been in bankruptcy for years. The car's exterior was a deep, dark brown, caked with years of accumulated steel dust. Its motors generated a groaning sound that seemed to wail on straightaways and inclines.

Even the single doors appeared tired.

They were wider than the ones on the IND or BMT and only slid in one direction, to the left, to open and the other, to the

TURNING OLD INTO NEW

The subway's 100th birthday in October 2004 coincides with Columbia University's 250th anniversary that same month. The coincidental celebrations inspired the Metropolitan Transportation Authority to restore three Upper West Side stations. The $60 million renovations to the 103rd, 110th and 116th Street stations began as an MTA project, but Columbia University quickly signed on, contributing $1 million to the renovations that began in February 2003 to the three stops which were part of the original IRT system.

right to close. They had large rubber "bumpers" to cushion the closings and were remarkably easy to hold open for other passengers.

These were the Low V (as in voltage) cars for which the IRT had been famous—or, notorious, as the case may be.

Not that I was complaining.

Once inside the car, I found plenty to like.

First of all, the front vestibule of the car was an area of its own, distinct from the seating part of the passenger compartment. Not only did it have a primary window in the center, but a secondary one to the left, from which one could easily view the tracks had the main window been occupied by another subway buff.

I was lucky. I had the entire front window to myself, my right hand gripping the door handle. Precisely when the motorman yanked on his heavy controller to move the train, I pulled to the left on the brass handle, pretending to operate the Low V by myself.

My enthusiasm for the IRT grew as our

express began passing the local stops—Canal, Bleecker, Astor Place—and we reached top speed. I would imagine the train was rumbling along at thirty-five to forty miles per hour, but it seemed much faster because of the IRT tunnel configuration.

Unlike the squarish IND to which I had become accustomed, the IRT tunnel was supported by thousands upon thousands of steel trusses that angled off the primary beams and attached to the roof.

Staring ahead at them from a speeding subway, I felt that the passing trusses had a hallucinatory effect, especially when the express passed through the lighted local stations.

But this was only one feature of the IRT that arrested my attention. Smaller than their IND or BMT counterparts, the Low-Vs had a cozy feel about them, especially since the seats all were lined up along the sides of the car, forcing passengers to face each other, unless, of course, they were standing.

Then, there was the antique quality of these trains—the last of them to be built dated to the mid 1920s—including metallic destination signs which were manually changed by conductors at the end of each trip.

Another unique feature was the curved platform we encountered at 14th Street-Union Square. Because of the angle, dangerous gaps developed between the platform edge and the car door. To alleviate the possibility of passengers falling through the hole and down to the tracks, the IRT devised a movable grate which fitted into position once the train came to a stop.

Before the doors opened, passengers were assured that the gap had been removed, and they simply walked over the grate and into the car. To me, that invention seemed equal to Thomas Edison developing the electric light bulb.

Once the train reached Grand Central Station, we had completed our ride on what had been the original 1904 subway. From 42nd Street north to the Bronx, we were on the newer portion of the IRT built as part of the Dual Contracts.

After the initial success of the subway had been established with completion of the original IRT, several other massive projects were blueprinted. For the East Side IRT, the scheme was to extend the line past Grand Central under Lexington Avenue over four tracks all the way to 125th Street.

At that point, the line was tunneled to the Bronx at 135th Street and proceeded north for yet another fun part of the ride which was the outdoor sprint toward the park.

Climbing out of the tunnel to daylight always is a kick, but when it's on a new line in a borough that had been thoroughly foreign to me, it was even more of an adventure.

Here we were, tooling over Westchester Avenue and then Southern Boulevard while I took in so many Bronx sights that my eyes could hardly contain themselves. There were theaters and shops, and not far from the East 174th Street station, an arena which featured wrestling, boxing, bicycle races and, at one time, an ice hockey team called the Bronx Tigers.

In later years I learned that the oval-roofed structure at 1100 East 177th Street was called the Bronx Coliseum and next to it was the Bronx version of Coney Island—dubbed Starlight Park. With a roller coaster of its own as well as a giant outdoor swimming pool and other amusements, Starlight

Park also offered midget auto races and soccer matches during the summer.

But the Coliseum had a more intriguing past because it started its life in—of all places—Philadelphia.

Oddly enough, in 1926 the Philadelphia Sesquicentennial International Exposition building was dismantled and, piece by piece, dispatched to the acreage at East 177th Street, East Tremont Avenue, Bronx River Avenue and Devoe Avenue.

There in the Bronx it was rebuilt into an imposing structure which could seat more than 16,000 spectators.

Occasionally the Coliseum would bulge when major fighters—among them Tami Mauriello, Fritzi Zivic and Barney Ross—would appear. But the most popular of all was the Raging Bull himself, Jake LaMotta, a Bronx boy who made good in the ring.

In the early 1930s, the Coliseum was home to the Bronx Tigers, a franchise in the Eastern Amateur Hockey League. Bronx hockey fans got to see teams from Baltimore, Atlantic City, Hershey, Brooklyn and two Manhattan clubs, the St. Nicholas Athletic Club and the New York Athletic Club.

The Coliseum stayed in business a little more than a dozen years, finally yielding to our armed forces which annexed the building in 1942 for use as a training and storage facility. After the war—and before its closing and demolition in 1997—the venerable structure became a bus maintenance and repair shop.

Unlike the Coliseum, Bronx Park has enjoyed a history of growth and development unsurpassed in the borough. What impressed me most as our train bobbed and weaved over Southern Boulevard toward East 180th Street was that the Bronx had a park the equivalent in size, if not beauty, to our Prospect Park.

Not only that, it had something Prospect Park couldn't offer, a river of its own.

Bronx River is spanned by the el and actually begins its southerly run as far north as the hills of Westchester (Kenisco), flowing through the Bronx before reaching the East River. I was to later experience its beauty when we ambled through the Bronx Botanical Gardens, where the Bronx River Gorge gives the visitor an impression that he's somewhere far away from one of New York's most populous places.

For me, however, beauty would take a backseat to the simple fun of seeing the animals in a setting other than my hometown Prospect Zoo.

A few more stirring twists and turns on the IRT finally got us to East 180th Street station and the zoo. I skipped down the stairs then followed my folks to the entrance.

From the outside, I could tell that this was something special; bigger even than I had imagined and with all kinds of exhibits not available in Brooklyn.

The first thing to catch my eye was the reptile house, not far from the entrance and off the path to the right. Up until that point I had only read about alligators, crocodiles and snakes in books and had seen them in movies.

Up front and in living color, it was another story; rather pleasant, I'll admit, since there was nothing truly ferocious in any of their movements. I marveled at how still the alligators were; almost to the point of seeming to be dead.

A bit more scary were the snakes, particularly the Anaconda, but it, too, had little of the aggressiveness that one exhibited in

THE SUBWAY
IN THE CEMETERY

When the Independent Subway was being built in the late 1920s, storage repair yards were to be built in the Inwood section of Manhattan. Excavators soon discovered that they were digging on the site of a former Revolutionary War cemetery. Before proceeding with the work, the diggers exhumed the corpses and reburied them at Woodlawn Cemetery, north of the repair site.

a movie I had seen not that long before our visit to the zoo. The film snake artfully trapped a chicken and a pig before devouring each. It was a creepy scene that led me to wonder how the Bronx Zoo's Anaconda might have handled the situation.

Gorillas, monkeys, elephants all were more impressive than their Brooklyn cousins, but the one truly enchanting display was an enormous outdoor aquatic bird house which was constructed so that visitors actually could walk through the part inhabited by the various specimens.

Apparently unconcerned by the onlookers, birds were swooping to an fro while I stood transfixed by their machinations. "Mom," I said at one point, "I could stand in this corner for the whole day just watching these guys."

She agreed that it all was very enthralling but—c'mon!—there were other things to see.

After the birds, my second favorite turned out to be the polar bear pavilion which was off to the right with plenty of rocks on which they could meander and a large pool in which to swim.

On this day the bears were frisky and put on quite a show; diving in and out of the water and doing other polar bear things that amused me no end.

At one point I turned to my dad and said, "Is this the way Carmichael behaves?"

I was referring to a running Jack Benny Radio Show skit of the late 1930s in which the comedian kept a pet polar bear named Carmichael in his bathtub.

"I don't think so," my father replied.

We finished the visit with trips to the lion and elephant houses, each of which kept me on my toes. As zoos go, this *was* major league, and I knew then and there that I would be back there many, many times before I was very old.

Naturally, I didn't want to leave, because there still were many animals to see, but my mother delivered one of her favorite lines which she saved for moments like this: "You can't dance at all the *hassanas.*" Meaning, you can't dance at *all* weddings at once. Or, Stanley, there are just so many animals to view in one visit to Bronx Park.

I later came to realize how extensive Bronx Zoo was after finally going to Central Park for the first time in my life. The Manhattan version was tiny by comparison.

The subway system was particularly kind to those wishing to visit Central Park. In our case, we could have taken the IND's Eighth Avenue Subway to Columbus Circle or the IRT's Broadway Line to the same destination.

But I wanted something new, and in 1940, when I was eight years old, the city's newest subway, the IND Sixth Avenue Line, had just been completed.

Anything like riding a brand-new subway, was going to be a treat, so I prevailed upon my parents to give me a break and take me to Central Park on the Sixth Avenue Line.

Even though it would have been easier on the Eighth Avenue, we started our trip—at Myrtle-Willoughby station, of course—on the GG Line, changing for the A train at Hoyt-Schermerhorn Street.

We only rode the A for one station, alighting now at Jay Street-Borough Hall stop so that we could now switch to the Sixth Avenue Line for the first time in my life.

Wow!

Normally, when we would depart Jay Street on the A, our train would make one last stop in Brooklyn at High Street-Brooklyn Bridge station, but the D would be totally new and different.

Instead of leaving Jay Street for High, the Sixth Avenue Line headed farther north and stopped at a station which was totally new to me, York Street. What it did have in common with High Street station was that its tunnel configuration had been rounded out from the typical box-like structure, indicating that we soon would enter the East River tubes.

Now I was officially on the Sixth Avenue run and rather excited about it.

Not that there was anything that special about the York Street station. As a matter of fact, it looked exactly like High Street on the A except that the station signs were different.

Nor was the new rolling stock any change from the Eighth Avenue line. Like all Independent trains, the new Sixth Avenue line employed the same style 60-foot-long pieces of equipment that ran on the very first A train.

It still looked exactly like the R-1, except that now some years of modifications had brought the style number to R-9,

but from a distance you wouldn't know an R-1 from an R-9.

Still, there was a nifty newness about the R-9s, of which 153 had been delivered for the Sixth Avenue service, and the city was quick to celebrate their arrival with appropriate fanfare.

New Yorkers, headed by Mayor Fiorello LaGuardia, were suitably proud of the new line—costing $59,000,000—because several engineering feats had to be accomplished to get the route finished.

Tunneling under the East River was one, and as the train left York Street station, I took due notice of the freshly completed concrete work; the placing of signals; and the speed with which the R-9s climbed the incline from river-center toward the first stop in Manhattan, East Broadway.

The first thing I realized was that East Broadway bore no resemblance whatsoever to the first Manhattan stop on the Eighth Avenue, Nassau Street, which was a rounded exact version of High Street and York Street stations.

By contrast, East Broadway had the squarish look of most IND non-river-tunnel-entrance depots. That puzzled me as the D continued up to Delancey-Essex Street, Second Avenue and Broadway-Lafayette.

These all were local stops and I was disappointed that what purported to be an express was making like a local at every station. Finally, we pulled into West 4th Street station, connecting with the Eighth Avenue and Houston Street lines.

Most curious to me was the location of the D (Sixth Avenue) platform in relation to the A and its local sidekicks, the CC and AA. They were on an upper level while we were directly below. It got me wondering just how difficult an engineering job that must have been, linking the two lines after one already had been in operation.

No less complicated was the design and construction at 14th Street where the IND Sixth Avenue route had to cross the long-operational BMT 14th Street Canarsie Line.

That, however, was small potatoes compared with the engineering complications when the Sixth Avenue Subway reached 34th Street. Not only did it have to contend with the BMT's Broadway Line, which crossed Sixth Avenue at Herald Square, but also the Hudson Tubes (now known as PATH) of the Hudson and Manhattan Railroad.

Similar problems had to be licked at 42nd Street, where the IRT's Flushing Line ran from West to East at Bryant Park, as well as at 59th Street-Columbus Circle, where the Eighth Avenue and its kid-cousin railroad met once again.

My focus, until we reached Central Park, remained fixed on the new stations' shiny tiles, big signage, terrifically long platforms—especially compared with the tiny IRT local stations—and the smooth manner in which the R-9s operated.

Riding as far as possible on the D, we got off at Columbus Circle and climbed out of the station within listening reach of the IRT. In the distance, I could distinctly hear the plaintive wail of a Low-V making its way out of 59th Street station.

Being at the southern tip of Central Park, we entered through the Merchant's Gate, adorned by a monument to those sailors killed when the battleship Maine blew up prior to the start of the Spanish-American War.

Ironically, a community west of Columbus Circle once was known as San Juan Hill (as in the Spanish-American War battle), but the Manhattan San Juan Hill was more notorious for its night clubs including Reisenweber's Café, once home to the Original Dixieland Jazz Band, which premiered at the club at about the time America entered World War I.

Heading in a northeasterly direction, we crossed the bridle path (no horses at the time!), the bird sanctuary, and Capstow Bridge, which leads directly to the zoo.

Unbeknownst to me, Central Park actually had the city's very first zoo, if you could call it that.

According to legend, workers who were completing park projects during the early days of the Civl War, were given a live bear and other animals as a present in addition to payment for their services.

In no time at all, a menagerie of sorts had developed at the park, and soon funds were set aside to develop it into a zoological garden.

Despite the fact that large numbers of visitors came to Central Park to see this original zoo, its conditions were considered deplorable enough for several civic leaders to press for its abolition.

The critics were heard but no firm action was taken until 1934, when then Parks Commissioner Robert Moses had the old menagerie razed and replaced in the midst of the Great Depression by a more modern, attractive version.

That was the one I saw when we entered the zoological garden grounds from the south and proceeded to the attractive red, brick buildings neatly arranged in a semi-circle around the seal pool. To me, it was like Prospect Park all over again except that they had better ice cream in Central Park.

It didn't take very long for me to discover that there was a lot more to Central Park than its zoo.

The lake, for instance.

It was wonderful for rowing and, when *really* cold weather permitted, a splendid place for ice skating. I can truthfully say that two of my favorite days ever spent at Central Park took place on the frozen lake.

Of course, I had to take the subway to get there.

The first splendid Central Park ice skating day took place during the winter of 1947-48. Although we didn't have the coveted White Christmas every New Yorker always hoped for in those days, the snow started to come down hard on Christmas Day, and it kept coming and coming and coming!

My Aunt Lucie had taken me and my cousin Joan (her daughter) to Radio City Music Hall that afternoon of the snowfall and by the time we had left the theater it was evident that this was more than a storm; it was a *blizzard.*

The IND's AA, A and, finally, GG got us back to Brooklyn right on time, but the snow continued on into the next day until it was being compared to the Blizzard of 1888!

As much as I loved snow, this was a concern to me because I had been playing on an organized roller hockey team called the Woodside Whippets and we had a game to play that Saturday.

Normally, I would take my skates, stick and puck on to the GG, ride it to Roosevelt Avenue in Woodside; then clamp, and strap on my *Chicagos* and skate over to our rink in a neighborhood park. (Sometimes, I'd spend a half-hour in the empty mezzanine at Roosevelt Avenue station, shooting the puck off the wall in an attempt to improve my shot.)

On Friday I got a phone call from our captain, Jim Hernon, advising that the snow-covered outdoor rink had turned to ice and there was no way we could play our game. Instead, the Whippets were heading for Central Park to play ice hockey on the frozen lake.

This sounded like a phenomenal idea.

I never had played ice hockey before and relished the idea. For some reason, I decided to play goal, although my regular position was defense. Now, in order to play goal, one needs goalie pads to protect one's leg from being destroyed by the six-ounce hunk of vulcanized rubber known as the puck.

Not having a regular set of goalie pads, I decided to improvise. When my grandmother was not looking, I discreetly lifted two plastic seat cushions from the kitchen chairs. With the help of some white adhesive tape, the cushions would become the goalie pads; for better or worse. (As it happened, it would be the latter!)

Fully armed with skates, stick and—most important—Grandma's plastic seat cushions—I boarded the GG, taking it to Hoyt-Schermerhorn where I changed for the ever reliable A.

What I loved about Hoyt-Schermerhorn was its size.

Most express stations on the New York system carry four sets of tracks, two for the locals and two for the expresses. Hoyt-Schermerhorn went two better. It had two for the GG, two for the A and another pair—located at the far ends of the depot—for what had been the ill-fated HH; the Court Street Shuttle. *Vast* would be an understatement in describing this terminal.

When the A arrived, I was in business as usual; up at the front, parking my equipment snugly against the front door so that I still could lean forward and "pilot" the train.

The run to Columbus Circle took less

DESIGNER SUBWAY CARS

For sheer, drawing-board creativity, the Raymond Loewy-designed R-40s were the best looking. They were the only cars with a distinctly slanted nose that gave the trains a truly futuristic look. The problem was that the cars had built-in safety flaws that eventually were addressed. But as good as they looked, the R-40s were otherwise bad. The R-42 followed as an R-40 without the slanted nose and marked the last of the 60-foot IND cars. They were introduced in 1969-70. Another unusual car was the R-44-46, which, when introduced in 1971-73, became the longest pieces of rolling stock on the system. Measuring 75 feet, these stainless steel cars became part of the Staten Island Railway as well. However, they could not run on either the J, M, Z or L lines of the BMT Eastern Division because of their size.

than half an hour, which was not bad considering the distance. I left the station at 59th Street and walked east along the southern fringe of Central Park South past the Essex House—where my Uncle Ben and Aunt Lucie were married—the Hampshire House and New York Athletic Club at Seventh Avenue.

That's where I entered the park, finding Jim and the boys skating on a pond in the shadow of the skyscrapers.

I'd like to say that the afternoon was a resounding success; and it *was* for about ten minutes. Or, from the time I had strapped on Grandma's cushions to my legs with the not-so-sticky adhesive tape, to the moment of disaster.

For the first nine minutes or so, I was having a ball in the makeshift goal. Pretending to be like my National Hockey League hero, goalie Turk Broda of the Toronto Maple Leafs, I guarded the six-foot space between snow piles with enormous intensity, blocking mostly-easy shots with *élan.*

But the longer I played, the less effective the tape which was supposed to keep the cushions wrapped around my legs, thereby protecting them from all manner of shots.

After nine minutes had elapsed, the tape was virtually useless and the once-wraparound-pads now had straightened out just as if they were sitting atop the kitchen chairs.

This would not have been a problem as long as the shooters kept the puck *on* the ice. But since there was no rule against *lifting,* I should not have expected any clemency from those firing the rubber at me.

Then *it* happened.

Our guys lost control of the puck, and it wound up on the stick of an opponent. He skated to within twenty feet of me and fired a moderately hard shot to my right.

I saw it coming all the way and, Broda-style, I shot my right leg out to the side in the hopes of kicking it harmlessly to one of my defensemen.

The idea was excellent; the adhesive tape was not!

As my right leg flared to its full limit, the tape became totally unglued, leaving the cushion hanging aimlessly to the side of my leg. A split-second later the puck *clunked* off the big bone to the left of my right knee.

Egad! I actually had made the save and the puck richocheted to Fred Meier, one of my defensemen, who carried it in the other direction.

Having gone down to make the save, I now had to rise again and resume my position for the next counterattack.

Unfortunately, nobody bothered to convey that message to my wounded knee and whatever spare body parts were necessary to render me vertical again.

I put pressure on my right leg to lift myself but nothing happened; I mean *absolutely* nothing. *Nada!*

It was the strangest, most alarming, body-experience I had experienced until that time. Total numbness in my right leg prevailed over ten, twenty and now thirty seconds.

Meanwhile, play had continued at the other end of our "rink"—which was fortunate for me—as I tried every which way to get upright.

Then, I got a break. We scored a goal at the other end, and, while the others hugged and cheered, I finally wiggled my body to the side to obtain some *feel* to my leg.

As the boys skated back to center for the post-goal face-off, Freddie noticed my unusual imitation of the *Indian Rubber Man* and innocently shouted, "Hey, Stan, get up, we're starting again."

Not saying a word—I could hardly talk, let alone move—I waved him over to me.

"I can't move, Fred, you gotta pull me over to the snowbank."

He realized that I was experiencing a strange kind of pain and—with Jim's help—lifted me so that I could rest my arms on their shoulders. Then, they sat me down on a rock where I spent about twenty minutes, non-stop, massaging my knee.

In time the feeling returned enough for me to limp over to the IND once the boys had completed their scrimmage; the others took the IRT Flushing Line home to Woodside.

I managed to haul myself from the A to the GG, and by the time I had reached Myrtle-Willoughby, I felt secure in the knowledge that I would walk normally again.

More importantly, I was even more secure in the knowledge that I never would play goal again wearing my grandmother's plastic seat cushions!

My second memorable subway-Central Park hockey experience happened in the winter of 1962-63 at a time when I still was playing quite a bit of amateur ice hockey.

My good friend—and world-acclaimed jazz critic—Ira Gitler lived a few blocks from the park on West End Avenue and 73rd Street.

Gitler was a hockey nut like me and someone who managed to find free time during the day. I had *plenty* of free time then because I worked at the *New York Journal-American* newspaper and we were in the midst of a 113-day strike which would last until the end of March.

I'm not sure how many days of subfreezing temperature cold we had that winter, but it must have been at least two weeks worth when Ira suggested that we play some hockey on Central Park Lake.

This would be on the *real* Central Park Lake, not the pond on which the Whippets skated. The hockey site would be within view of the Dakota landmark apartments, and when the idea was proposed by Gitler, I was reminded of a classic winter photo of the Dakota and the frozen lake.

The picture had been taken in the late 1880s, shortly after the building had been opened. It must have been an awfully cold winter because Central Park Lake was frozen solid and literally hundreds of skaters—including men in overcoats and bowler hats—were showing their stuff on the ice with the huge apartment looming like a fortress in the background.

Gitler and I agreed to meet at the 72nd Street-Central Park West subway entrance to the park at noon. I lived on East 19th Street between First and Second Avenue at the time; which meant that I had to haul my hockey stick and skates to First Avenue and 14th Street, where I caught the Canarsie Line heading to Eighth Avenue.

I then crossed over to the IND—free transfer—and hopped on the A train to 59th Street. Then, I crossed the platform and finished the trip to 72nd Street on the AA Local.

Ira was there right on time, which hardly surprised me.

This was the *perfect* day to bat around the puck on an outdoor "rink."

The temperature was hovering at about ten degrees above zero Fahrenheit with no intentions of climbing any higher. Rays of sun were glistening off the snow flakes that adorned the ice. Hardly anyone else was on the frozen lake and it appeared as if we would have this natural ice palace to ourselves for much of the afternoon.

We sat on a frozen mound of dirt near lake's edge and laced on our skates. Neither of us could contain our enthusiasm, for this truly was a *first* in both our lives.

For some reason, the cold hardly mattered. Perhaps it was the sun; perhaps it simply was our fervor for the game of hockey that distracted us from Jack Frost. Whatever it was, we instantly knew the moment we dug our skates into the frozen surface that we were experiencing the sort of athletic utopia which happens only a few times in one's life.

I pulled the black, rubber puck out of my pocket and tossed it a few yards ahead. Gitler, who had completed his skate-lacing before I did, smacked the disk with a *thwack* that could be heard all the way to the sailboat house on the other side of the park.

Now, I was on my skates and the workout was underway.

Every movement produced a *crunch, crunch, crunch* of steel skates digging into the hard ice. We didn't play a game—not much you can do with a one-on-one—but rather passed the puck back-and-forth, from one side of the frozen lake to the other.

The cold which turned our cheeks crimson bothered us not at all. We told stories, laughed and discussed the reasons why the Rangers would—or would not—win the Stanley Cup.

With no one around to bother us, there were no boundaries limiting our skating, so we glided endlessly—sometimes aimlessly—even doing imitations of hockey people we knew.

Ira cracked up when I did my impression of "Wild" Bill Ezinicki, a hero of mine from his days with the Maple Leafs. He also got a kick out of my skating mimicry of referee Frank Udvari.

The cold never got to us but hunger and thirst eventually did, and after about two hours of non-stop skating, chatter and imitations, we untied our skates and headed to the nearest luncheonette.

After a couple of hot chocolates, Ira walked me over to the IND at 72nd Street and bade me good-bye as I skidded down the steps with my skates, stick and thoroughly sweated-through shirt and pants.

Once the local arrived, I stretched out on a seat, musing over the wonderfully athletic-friendly afternoon it had been. At

Columbus Circle, I changed for the A and managed to doze off for a delightful snooze, interrupted only by a crowd of people entering at 34th Street, one of whom delivered a slight—and inadvertent—kick to my hockey stick.

That served as an alarm for me to stay awake and not miss the 14th Street stop, where I had to change for the Canarsie Line. When it finally carried me to First Avenue station, I was almost too tired to lug my equipment to 19th Street and First.

But I managed to get to 348 East 19th, *shlepped* up the three flights and plopped down on the couch for a long winter's nap.

The only thing I remember thinking before absolutely sacking out was that it was too bad there wasn't a subway stop on the corner of First and 19th, instead of five blocks away!

———————————

Grand Central Terminal on the eve of its completion in 1913. New exits from the original IRT station were being completed in the center of the photo at the corner of Vanderbilt Avenue and 42nd Street. Beware of the Hansom cab as you cross temporarily wood-planked Vanderbilt! The west end of the Third Avenue shuttle station is in the distance.

CHAPTER NINE

GOING TO

The Railroads—Grand Central Terminal, Pennsylvania Station, Long Island Rail Road Station and Hudson Terminal (PATH)

Waitin' For The Train
To Come In,
Waitin' For My Man
To Come Home.

New York City's subways and the railroads, both of which have serviced The Big Apple for a century, have been as closely related as pages in a book.

What better example than Manhattan's original underground, the Interborough Rapid Transit system, which started its run at the Brooklyn Bridge train junction and proceeded north, completing its East Side run at Grand Central Terminal, home of the New York Central Railroad.

Similarly, the IRT's first foray down Seventh Avenue—as part of the massive Dual Contracts—included Penn Station, flagship depot of the Pennsylvania Railroad, as its first major stop south of Times Square.

And when the IRT invaded Brooklyn for the first time, its designers ensured that a primary express-local station would be immediately adjacent to the Long Island Rail Road terminal at Atlantic and Flatbush Avenues.

The intertwining of New York's railroads and rapid transit can further be underlined by an unusual—if not surprising—fact, dating back to 1831.

On that date, more than a dozen businessmen requested that the New York State Legislature give the green light to the New York and Harlem Railroad Company, and allow it to build a Manhattan rapid transit system.

Thus, the city's first rapid transit—forerunner of our subway system—began as a railroad linking East 23rd Street and Madison Avenue (Madison Square Park) with the Harlem River.

Actually, there were two different stations on the same block; the New York and New Haven Line at 26th Street and the New York and Harlem at 27th Street and Fourth. The stations eventually were sold and—a roof was put over the structure—rebuilt into P.T. Barnum's Hippodrome.

"Waitin' for the Train to Come In," words and music Sunny Skylar, Martin Block,
Martin Block Music, © 1945

Where It All Began—
City Hall and Brooklyn Bridge

A key element of the Interborough's first tunnel was a track-loop built under City Hall. Taking shape in September 1901, it would result in a magnificent, vaulted City Hall station, which still was unfinished a year later, but completed by January 1904, ticket booth and all. In this photo, the cameraman is looking up one of the two staircases—note the daylight at the top-center—as workmen collect lumber to complete the project.

A year later, the City Hall station is advanced considerably but neither the track bed nor platform have been built. The vaulted ceiling's beauty already is discernable.

Nine months before the City Hall station opens for business, the platform and the station's unique tiling are finished and await the grand opening.

One kiosk (far left) is completed while another still is in its skeletal form two months before the official opening ceremonies at City Hall Station. The notorious Tweed Courthouse looms in the background, while streetcars roll among the steel and wood detritus of subway-building. The three-story structure in the center actually was cut in half in order to make room for construction of the City Hall IRT loop.

The northward expansion of Brooklyn Bridge IRT station called for the closing of the Worth Street station. Here we see it in September 1962, one week before its closing.

William Brennan

William Brennan

The new Brooklyn Bridge station is being served by both the new and the old as the venerable Low-Vs are in the process of gradual retirement. The photo was taken in April 1963.

When the unheated building proved unsuitable for the circus animals, Barnum decided to move his menagerie to a more suitable arena. Patrick Gilmore bought the building, made money on flower shows, and changed the building's name to Gilmore's Garden. It later became the city's first Madison Square Garden after the Vanderbilts purchased it. Thus, the old railroad station became New York's first Madison Square Garden.

Meanwhile, Commodore Cornelius Vanderbilt, already a multi-millionaire before the Civil War, purchased the New York and Harlem River line in addition to the New York Central and the Hudson River Railroad.

Now all he needed was a terminal.

Where to locate this depot? That was the question. In the years immediately following the Civil War, the area north from the Battery to 23rd Street was relatively well-populated, but acreage as far north as 42nd Street, where the New York and Harlem Railroad steam locomotive facilities were located, was still regarded as God's country. Streets were still unpaved and residents of the city considered 42nd Street as far, far from the maddening crowd; certainly no place to erect a comprehensive rail station. Yet that was precisely the location selected by the foresightful Commodore. "Everyone," wrote Oliver Jensen, "thought it was a great joke, building a station so far uptown. The newspapers christened it the 'End-of-the-World Station.'"

Forty-Second Street may have been a 45-minute horse car ride from City Hall at the time, but Vanderbilt realized that the relentless population surge inevitably would move the city's center farther and farther north. Besides, there were other practical reasons for selecting 42nd Street

as the depot site, not the least of which was a municipal ordinance forbidding steam engines south of 42nd Street.

The honor of designing the structure was bestowed upon Isaac C. Buckhout, Vanderbilt's trusty chief engineer for the Harlem Railroad. Buckhout and the Commodores son, William H. (Billy) Vanderbilt, were the chief overseers of the project. By the end of 1869, all red tape had been cleared, and on September 1, 1870, the initial foundation stone was set in place.

In every way, from scope of design to sheer physical immensity, the project was awesome. The train shed of the terminal, a gaping, cylindrical mouth of wrought-iron, rose 100 feet in the middle and 200 feet at track level. Running 600 feet in length, the shed was designed by engineer R.G. Hatfield and constructed by the Architectural Iron Works of New York, which also produced the elaborately detailed cast-iron girders. A total of 12 tracks were housed under the shed—patterned after San Pancreas Station in London—along with five platforms, each a step above track level. Two of the dozen tracks continued southward, through a pair of portals and down to the original station at Fourth Avenue and 27th Street.

No less impressive than the shed was the façade at the north end, from which the rolling stock emanated. Topped with huge lettering—"ERECTED 1871"—the façade comprised a curtain wall of glass and iron, and included a small cupola from which the railroad's dispatcher monitored the incoming and outgoing trains.

The 42nd Street, or southern end of the station, which contained three separate waiting rooms, ticket-selling and other necessary facilities, was designed by architect

John B. Snook and, in many ways, was the most impressive aspect of the entire $3,000,000 project. The L-shaped edifice continued from 42nd Street around to Vanderbilt Avenue, which was created for the station. Author William D. Middleton in his book, *Grand Central: The World's Greatest Railway Station*, describes the terminal's Second Empire façade as "finished in rich, red pressed brick with ornamental coins, cornices, and window frames of cast iron, painted white in imitation of marble. Five ornate mansard-roofed towers surmounted the 42nd Street and Vanderbilt Avenue facades."[22]

Commodore Vanderbilt's wisdom in building the depot at the 42nd Street location was borne out. The wide crosstown street soon was paved with cobblestones and, naturally, became the recipient of a new crosstown horsecar line.

Another seemingly vexing problem, which was quickly solved by the Commodore, involved a linkage between trackage heading north from the proposed depot and his Hudson River Railroad tracks, which heretofore continued along the western perimeter of Manhattan Island to St. John's Park and the line's freight house at Canal Street. What Vanderbilt needed was a linkage in northern Manhattan along Spuyten Duyvil and thence to the tracks which flowed along the east side of Manhattan down to 42nd Street. The Commodore unraveled the knotty problem with remarkable ease. He began in 1869 by forming the Spuyten Duyvil and Port Morris Railroad, which then laid seven miles of track from the Hudson River to the Harlem line's tracks at Mott Haven. From Mott Haven south to 42nd Street the three railroads utilized the Harlem's tracks into the city.

The vital connection was completed in 1871, just in time for the grand opening of Grand Central Depot, the official handle for Commodore Vanderbilt's opulent terminal. "It was a gaudy building," recalled author Oliver Jensen, "a cross between the Louvre and a cast-iron toy bank. Critics complained that it was wanton to slap a slate mansard roof onto a Renaissance building, but it is highly unlikely that the Commodore was disturbed by this sort of carping."

Why should Vanderbilt complain? He now was maestro of the foremost railway station in North America, one which served not one but three different lines—the New York Central and Hudson River, the Harlem and New Haven—and one which seemed imposing enough to last a century.

In fact, it wouldn't survive a half-century.

Grand Central Depot was obsolete the moment it opened, and this depressing fact was partly a function of the Commodore's vanity. When Vanderbilt inspected the two acres of glass on the station's roof, he became appalled at the prospect of the elaborate glass becoming defaced by the soot belching forth from his steam engines. How, then, could the passenger cars be delivered and dispatched from the train shed?

"This meant some very tricky railroading," wrote Jensen, *"when the trains came in. The floor of the shed was tilted so that departing trains had only to release their brakes and coast out to where the engines were waiting; but arriving trains had to be 'switched on the fly.' As the train approached the station, the engineer braked a little to give the brakeman some slack at the couplers. At a signal from the whistle, the brakeman pulled the pin,*

uncoupling the train from the engine, which darted over to an adjacent track.

"The open switch swung shut behind the engine, and the cars coasted up into the station. This maneuver was every bit as dangerous as it sounds, yet we are told that there was never an accident."

Despite its difficulties, Grand Central Depot was a rousing success in terms of ridership. Because of that, it was imperative that Manhattan commuters have easy rapid transit access to the terminal.

This equation was solved when the New York Elevated Company completed work on the Third Avenue el, which ran along Pearl Street, The Bowery, and then north along Third Avenue.

For the use of railroad patrons—and others interested in doing business along 42nd Street—the New York Elevated Company built its line north along Third Avenue in August 1878. Turning left (west) at Third Avenue and 42nd Street, the el's tracks continued westward over 42nd Street to a depot adjacent to Grand Central at 42nd Street and Park Avenue.

The Third Avenue's service to Grand Central Depot was the second such linkage between a New York rapid transit line and a major railroad terminal. This connection remained even after the depot was replaced in the next century by an even more majestic structure.

Such a change in terminal-building was deemed necessary because Grand Central Depot simply couldn't provide the kind of service for which it was built.

For example, the dozen tracks into Grand Central Depot were hardly enough to meet the demands of the three railroads. This problem defied solution through the turn of the 20th century. Yet another vexing issue was smoke.

Right from the start, smoke proved an annoyance to both Commodore Vanderbilt's passengers and New Yorkers who lived near the depot or plied the streets in the immediate vicinity of the train shed. The problem became aggravated in 1876, when an additional six terminal tracks were laid to accommodate the increase in traffic. By far the worst situation existed in the Park Avenue tunnel at the edge of the station. There, according to one report, "the smoke was frightful." There were a number of recorded incidents when engineers fainted from the coal gas. Accompanying firemen, to protect their lungs, stretched themselves along the bottom of the cab on the assumption that they could therefore avoid the worst of the smoke.

The black clouds gushing from the steam engines occasionally blotted out the engineer's view of the red and green signals near the terminal's entrance. This led to disaster in 1902. A commuter train operated by the New York, New Haven and Hartford Railroad was halted by a red signal. It was the morning rush-hour and another train, this one belonging to Vanderbilt's New York Central line, was approaching *on the same track.* Ordinarily it would have halted at its own red "Stop!" signal, but smoke had obscured the red light, and the New York Central express plowed into the rear of the commuter train. The disaster cost the lives of 17 passengers. It also inspired demands for the elimination of polluting steam engines in and about the depot area.

Grabbing hold of a good issue, New York's politicians developed a far-reaching law, ultimately approved by the state legislature, forbidding steam locomotives from entering Manhattan after July 1, 1910, on

Building the IRT Up To Grand Central

IRT officials proudly pose amidst the fresh concrete in the original subway tunnel under Houston and Elm Streets. The date is October 15, 1901 and considerable work still must be done. Evident along the four-track right-of-way are the angled supports that would be a trademark of the Interborough system.

Dig we must for a growing subway! Dynamiting was necessary throughout construction, as shown here. Manhattan's rock base was a constant challenge to builders of the Interborough. This photo was taken on Fourth Avenue, between 15th and 16th Streets in 1901.

Tunnel construction around New York's rock base required some of the most delicate operations imaginable. That the original work was masterfully done is confirmed by the fact that all of the tunneling from the early 1900s has held up for a century with no collapsing of any of its sections.

Eight years after the IRT's 1904 opening, Fourth Avenue was widened to become Park Avenue South. As a result, the relatively new kiosks, such as this one at 23rd Street station, found themselves out in the street and had to be removed.

In 1901, the original subway digging disturbed the trolley car barn on the right—between 33rd and 34th Streets. Notice in the far distance the tower of the original Grand Central Depot after its remodeling in 1900.

The original Grand Central Depot opened in 1871. It was a three-story structure in red brick and stone with mansard roofed towers. Because of a faulty design, it was a troubled building from the very beginning of its use. The three railroads using the terminal had separate waiting and baggage rooms. The latter were not internally connected to the waiting rooms. As a result, in 1900 the station was remodeled to one large waiting and baggage room. The head house was enlarged to six stories with a sandstone finish. It was rather ugly and acted as a stopgap until the current Grand Central Terminal was built a decade later in 1913.

The original temporary terminal—and later shuttle—of the Third Avenue el ended right at Grand Central Terminal, partially blocking the station's architectural beauty. Note the wood planking covering 42nd Street because the new Grand Central Terminal station of the uptown IRT was being built underneath.

Further east, work on the same project was ongoing, with additional support for the el structure in place during construction. The unsightly and underutilized el spur met its demise in 1924.

passenger service. Fortunately, the Vanderbilt family had chosen well when it appointed lieutenants. In this case, the job of revamping Grand Central to accommodate electrification fell on the shoulders of William J. Wilgus, the depot's chief engineer. Electrifying the station itself would be a monumental project but, in addition, Wilgus realized that the station would have to be expanded considerably to accommodate the relentless growth in both commuter and long-distance railroading.

Electrification seemed, off-hand, like the easier of the two projects. After all, electricity had already proven its usefulness on Manhattan's elevated lines and soon would be utilized on the subway lines to be built under the city streets. But finding more room was a more perplexing dilemma, since Grand Central's 48 acres could not be added to by more than a few feet.

Early in the planning the architects became aware that they desperately needed to increase the available space. By winning concessions from the city and purchasing nearby property, the railroad eventually was able to increase the total space available from 23 to more than 45 acres. More than a million cubic yards of earth and two million yards of granite were hauled away over a decade of excavation and construction. The result was a gaping hole in the middle of Manhattan which measured 40 feet deep, 770 feet wide and a mile and a half long. Given this space, the builders were to create a 32-track upper level for major trains such as the Twentieth Century Limited, that plied the New York-Chicago run, and a 17-track lower level for the commuter lines which rolled to Westchester County and Connecticut. Wilgus's original formula called for a rather

clever, and ultimately elaborate, link with the New York City Interborough Rapid Transit (IRT) subway, which had opened in 1904. The New York State Public Service Commission (PSC) had hoped to persuade a conventional railroad company, such as the New York Central, to take over the operating responsibility for the city subway system, but neither the New York Central nor any other railroad did so.

What did emerge was a plan for the expansion of the suburban Harlem and Hudson division commuter lines, and for these the railroad cleverly utilized razed iron and other debris as part of the refurbishing of the suburban routes.

"It was planned," wrote Wilgus, "that the yard excavation should be made in three successive 'bites,' each to be completed before the other was undertaken, working westward from Lexington Avenue, so that the traffic of the three railroads using the terminal...might continue without hindrance."

The first "bite" included the additions to the property that had been purchased at a time when it was deemed necessary to add to the existing acreage. This "bite" included a portion along Lexington Avenue and the east side of the site. A number of buildings along Park and Lexington avenues had to be demolished to get this project in motion. After nine years it was still unfinished, although some 750,000 pounds of dynamite were detonated to pave way for construction.

One of the major elements in the redesign of Grand Central was expansion of existing trackage to accommodate the ever-increasing number of trains. Trains approached the station over the four-track mainline until they reached 57th Street, where they were now routed to a ten-track arrangement, of which six moved onto the upper level and four dropped to the commuter-oriented lower level. The tracks for the commuter lines were placed directly on the rock floor of the excavation.

Electrification of the New York Central commuter lines to White Plains was finished in 1907—utilizing the newly designed Sprague-Wilgus under-riding 3rd rail, which is still in use today—under the stewardship of Wilgus. Ironically, it was to play a part in his departure from the scene several years before he planned to leave. The problem developed three days after the electric commuter lines went into service.

On February 16, 1907, an electrified commuter train heading for White Plains left Grand Central pulling five wooden cars. It moved north through Harlem and thence into the Bronx. As the train speeded around a curve near 205th Street, it jumped the tracks, causing four of the five cars to somersault into splintered wreckage. Twenty-three passengers perished.

The disaster prompted an immediate investigation, including the testing of the relatively new electric locomotives. But the intensive probe proved futile in terms of a definitive reason for the wreck.

During the post-wreck controversy, Wilgus and the Central's vice-president and general manager, A.H. Smith, collided in public over the issue of responsibility for the accident. Shortly thereafter, Wilgus handed in his resignation. His was followed by that of George A. Harwood, chief engineer of electric zone improvements.

The construction of Grand Central itself was not without its tragedy. In December 1910 a switching operation—which involved moving a train onto a yard track near 50th Street so that its car-lighting gas supply could be renewed—caused

more trouble. In those days, most of the rolling stock used Pintsch gas rather than electricity to illuminate the inside of cars. As the train was being backed into position, it accidentally was pushed past a bumping post, severing a gas line. The leaking gas wafted its way into an adjoining power substation used for the New York Central's electrification. The ensuing explosion leveled the substation, flattened a trolley operating on a nearby street and shattered $25,000 worth of plate glass in nearby buildings. A total of ten people were killed and 100 seriously injured, which hastened the discontinuance of Pintsch gas and its replacement with electricity on the New York Central.

Meanwhile, the widely discussed new depot was rapidly emerging from the enormous cavities around Park Avenue, 50th Street and Lexington Avenue. One of the most talked about features of the main structure was the Grand Concourse and its curved ceiling. A French artist, Paul Helleu, won the honor of painting a mural for the ceiling, and he produced the zodiac in blue and gold and the middle region of the sky. The ceiling was graced with 2,500 stars in gold leaf on a field of cerulean blue. When the ceiling was displayed to the public, it was discovered that Helleu had mistakenly painted the galaxy in reverse; West being where East should have been! The faux pas gained wide publicity, much to the dismay of the New York Central.

"The ceiling," countered the Central's public relations department, "is purely 'decorative'; it was never intended that a mariner should set his course by the stars at Grand Central."

When the terminal finally was opened to a select group of 2,000 guests on February 1, 1913, the raves far overwhelmed any

Building the New Uptown Grand Central Terminal

The most ubiquitous element of outdoor IRT subway architecture ever since the line's earliest days was the kiosk. Neither the BMT nor IND ever matched the unique entrance roof and lyrical lines. Often, the kiosk had the company of a news stand as evidenced in this Manhattan scene during the late 1920s. The news stand is featuring upper-class women's magazines as well as the plethora of New York City daily newspapers.

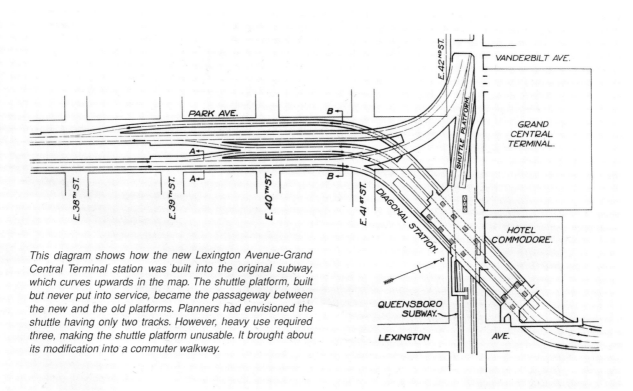

This diagram shows how the new Lexington Avenue-Grand Central Terminal station was built into the original subway, which curves upwards in the map. The shuttle platform, built but never put into service, became the passageway between the new and the old platforms. Planners had envisioned the shuttle having only two tracks. However, heavy use required three, making the shuttle platform unusable. It brought about its modification into a commuter walkway.

The sharp curve of the original line from Fourth Avenue to 42nd Street necessitated digging right up to, and through part of, the foundation of the Belmont Hotel.

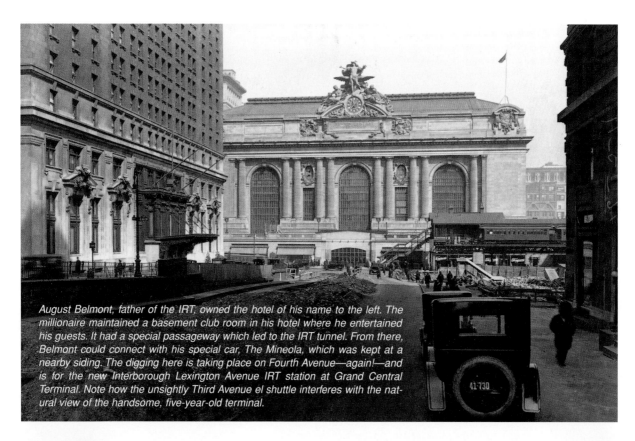

August Belmont, father of the IRT, owned the hotel of his name to the left. The millionaire maintained a basement club room in his hotel where he entertained his guests. It had a special passageway which led to the IRT tunnel. From there, Belmont could connect with his special car, The Mineola, which was kept at a nearby siding. The digging here is taking place on Fourth Avenue—again!—and is for the new Interborough Lexington Avenue IRT station at Grand Central Terminal. Note how the unsightly Third Avenue el shuttle interferes with the natural view of the handsome, five-year-old terminal.

In this scene, south of 42nd Street, the IRT station construction requires extensive support of the Third Avenue shuttle which sits above 42nd Street. Note how an artificial, wood-planking support system was necessary to keep the el and the avenue from collapsing. This was in December 1915.

North of 42nd Street we see the roof and support columns of the subway station-to-be, four months after the previous vista, in the hole that was dug. Once the work is completed, a new Hotel Commodore—adjoining Grand Central Terminal—will be built right over the subway digs.

Here in 1920, we see the almost filled-in hole as well as a passageway. Looming over the scene is the new Commodore Hotel, which was one of New York City's finest. In recent years it was replaced by a totally new hostelry.

nitpicking about the geography of the ceiling. More than 60 years later, writing in *Railroads In America*, Oliver Jensen observed, "Grand Central was and is one of the most successful stations ever built...beyond all that fine functionalism, the station is beautiful."

So was the IRT's own Grand Central station—albeit on a much smaller scale—on the original subway. However, when the station was completed, the IRT in those days had only one line, which serviced the railroad terminal before heading west to Times Square.

Meanwhile, the Third Avenue el continued to deliver passengers on its shuttle-stub line which rubbed shoulders with the viaduct leading directly to Grand Central Terminal.

On the other side of town, competition for the New York Central and Grand Central Terminal had come from the railroad's rival, the Pennsylvania Railroad.

The PRR chose to build its elaborate terminal close to rapid transit as well. Long before Penn Station was built, not one but two elevated lines were close enough to provide easy access.

The closest was the Ninth Avenue el with stations at West 30th Street and West 34th Street. Not far away, the Sixth Avenue el offered a station at West 33rd Street. Both would be vital conduits for New York commuters using the Pennsylvania Railroad.

The elevateds were well into operation when on December 23, 1902, New York City's Board of Aldermen passed a resolution approving a franchise for extending the Pennsylvania Railway under the Hudson River to a passenger station located in Manhattan and thence under the East River to a connection with the Long Island Rail Road.

Integrally linked with the Pennsy project was a spate of improvements on the Long Island Rail Road, including the electrification of the commuter line within city limits; construction of freight stations on the line from Bay Ridge, Brooklyn, to East New York; and, most significantly, rejuvenation of the Atlantic Avenue Division, a bustling passenger carrier running at street level across Brooklyn. Homeowners across the route wanted the trains taken off the streets and put either in the air (on an elevated structure) or underground. The LIRR did both. It erected a handsome new terminal at Flatbush and Atlantic Avenues in downtown Brooklyn in 1906 and constructed tunnels under Atlantic Avenue eastward to Bedford Avenue, where the tracks climbed out to the first "el" station at Nostrand Avenue. The elevated double-track then proceeded east above Atlantic Avenue until it re-entered a tunnel at Eastern Parkway and Atlantic Avenue.

The Pennsy's engineers completed their plans and presented them for approval. Among the essential projects was an offshoot of the mainline of the Pennsylvania Railroad near Newark. The new spur would cross Hackensack Meadows, burrow through Bergen Hill and thence under the Hudson.

From the new station, four tubes would tunnel under the East River, linking with the Long Island Rail Road in Queens, and a new passenger train yard in Sunnyside, Queens. James Kip Finch, an engineering historian, described the venture as "one of the boldest and most courageous undertakings ever conceived by the creative imagination of man."

Construction work began in 1904. From the public's viewpoint—since sidewalk superintendents could view the work—the most impressive project was the development of the colossal Pennsylvania Station on eight acres of land bounded by 31st and 33rd Streets and Seventh and Eighth Avenues on the west side of Manhattan.

The distinguished architectural firm of McKim, Mead and White conceived the depot. Designed in the Roman Doric style, the terminal, when completed in 1910, was the Pennsy's pride and joy.

Of all the aspects of the new Pennsylvania Station, none was more awesome than the main waiting room, a huge vaulted hall considered a reasonable facsimile of the Baths of Caracalla in Rome. Upon its completion, the waiting room was the largest of its kind in the world, with a floor area of more than 300,000 square feet and a ceiling 150 feet above street level. Passengers crossing this huge area, intent on locating signage as to track assignment of their train, would be softly greeted by a basso-profundo announcer, whose voice would fully inform while reaching them from a different dimension.

In a commentary published by the Isaac H. Blanchard Company after Penn Station was completed, William Couper observed: "*As we enter, the daring color treatment is at once apparent. The pleasing effect of the travertine, of which the interior is constructed and which has since the days of Roman ascendancy been a favorite building material abroad, pervades the atmosphere and adds a thrill which is tempered only by the silence—the awesome silence when we realize that there is no audible evidence of the hastening throngs seen all around us.*

"The most salient feature of the station is the main waiting room: so large is it that many of the best known hostelries in the country could be placed in this one room. Spaced about the lofty travertine walls are enormous Corinthian columns, standing on pedestals, which support the coffered vaulted ceiling. At the north and south ends of the room there are colonnades of Ionic columns and immediately below the six large lunette windows which surround the room are panels on which have been painted conventionalized maps in colors blending with the beautiful, warm, sunny color of the travertine."

As attractive and intriguing the new addition to Manhattan's magnificent architecture was—ditto for Grand Central Terminal—the practical side dictated that Pennsylvania Station also required easy rapid transit access.

Designers and backers of Penn Station always had rapid transit—subway style—in mind, despite the presence of nearby el stations on Ninth Avenue and Sixth Avenue. The PRR immediately began promoting the idea of the IRT extending its service south from its Times Square-42nd Street local station to 33rd Street and Seventh Avenue, in front of the new depot.

Once it had been evident that the original Interborough subway was a resounding success, the possibility of a PRR-IRT linkage became real. Finally, on December 5, 1910, the Interborough revealed that it had blueprinted a major expansion costing $128,000,000—of which the city would pay half—which would extend the IRT Broadway Line.

According to the plan, a new West Side branch would tunnel south from Times Square, have a four-track express-local stop at Penn Station and continue under Seventh Avenue to South Ferry and eventually Brooklyn.

The original plans began jelling a year

New Seventh Avenue Subway Construction
Below Times Square

Sometimes—on the rarest of occasions—"cut-and-cover" failed to precisely follow the blueprints. Here, the cutting had been done, but before the covering could take place, the makeshift street caved in, taking a trolley car and tons of wood planking with it. This happened in September 1915 along Seventh Avenue in Manhattan between 22nd and 23rd Streets where the IRT's Seventh Avenue Line was being extended south from Times Square.

Uniting the old and the new in June 1915. The curve of the original subway route is to the left, and the near-completed 7th Avenue extension is on the right. The Times Square local station, now used by the shuttle, can be seen in the distance.

The western end of Penn Station abuts Eighth Avenue, directly across from the Farley Post Office, both of which were designed by the same architectural firm, McKim, Mead and White. To regain some of the splendor lost in the razing of the station, the post office is being redesigned to serve in the future as part of Amtrak's new Penn Station.

Despite the rubble from IRT Seventh Avenue subway excavation piled up in front of it in June 1914, Pennsylvania Station loses none of its majesty. The 34th Street subway station would directly link with the railroad depot, which was four years old at the time. Penn Station was North America's most majestic edifice. Its demise—and Jacqueline Kennedy's influence—inspired creation of a New York City Landmarks Preservation Commission, which has helped prevent the further raping of the city's venerated landmarks; most notably Grand Central Terminal.

Turnstiles were not a part of the subway scene in 1905. As this photo of the South Ferry IRT station indicates, a ticket-chopper was operated by an attendant opposite the ticket booth. The glass-lined ceiling allowed for natural light to pour through and partially illuminate the station.

An IRT train rolls under the East River.

later when the Dual (IRT-BMT) Contracts began taking shape. Most importantly, the existing—and original—IRT track layout from the East Side, swinging left (west) at 42nd Street and then right (north) at Times Square, would be altered to develop what amounted to an H formation.

In other words, the East Side IRT would be extended north under Lexington Avenue to the Bronx, while the West Side IRT would follow the original blueprint, leading both locals and expresses to Penn Station, on to South Ferry and then through a new tunnel to Brooklyn.

To complete the H formation in the center, a Shuttle service would run over the original IRT tracks connecting Grand Central Terminal with Times Square.

Establishing subway service to Penn Station would be a major asset to the PRR as well as New York straphangers, but completion of the project did not happen overnight. It was a slow, deliberate process, bedeviled by many engineering challenges; not the least of which was construction under the skyscrapers that already had been built in the area. Nevertheless, enough progress had been made by early 1915 that some suitable Big Apple-style fuss and fanfare was in order.

One such offbeat fete took place on February 20, 1915, after completion of a section of tunnel leading to the IRT's 34th Street station. A formal dinner was held *inside* the tunnel itself between 37th and 38th Streets. According to one report, the party not only featured a full-course meal but music and even boxing matches!

Another celebration was held on August 1, 1918, at the Hotel Astor, situated directly above the IRT Broadway Line at 45th Street. This observance commemorating the official completion of the H plan.

After Mayor John Hylan toured the line on a ten-car train from South Ferry to Times Square, his entourage then marched—with the IRT Band leading the way—to the hotel for speeches and toasts.

Meanwhile, finishing touches were put on switches, tracks and signals, and the connection between the IRT and Pennsylvania Station finally was in operation.

Completion of the H meant wonders for commuters on both sides of town. On the East side, Grand Central Terminal–users now had a handsome, new four-track express-local station at 42nd Street and Park Avenue with direct access to the Bronx as well as the East-West shuttle service to Times Square.

On the West side, a brand-new four-track station was opened at Times Square with direct access to Penn Station, South Ferry and Brooklyn as well as the Shuttle to the East side.

As an added fillip, the IND later installed a 34th Street station with direct access to Penn Station when the system's Eighth Avenue Subway was completed in 1932.

While Grand Central Terminal and Pennsylvania Station clearly were head-and-shoulders over all other railroad depots in New York, there were others which were impressive in their own way, but on a more modest scale. And each of them required a subway connection to succeed.

In Brooklyn, the Long Island Rail Road had been a going concern since pre-Civil War days and in the latter part of the 19th Century had been running trains from the Downtown center, eastward along Atlantic Avenue to Jamaica and all points of Long Island, terminating at Greenport on the North Fork.

Like the New York Central and Pennsylvania railroads, the LIRR required an up-to-date Brooklyn terminal to complement the fact that the Pennsylvania Railroad—which in 1900 had bought the majority of the LIRR stock—had electrified the Long Island track along Atlantic Avenue in 1905.

The Long Island Rail Road's miniscule counterpart to Penn Station was completed in 1905 at the corner of Atlantic and Flatbush Avenues on the fringe of the borough's Downtown shopping center.

This was at a time when the LIRR was approaching its boom years and, of course, it had to be serviced by more than the Fifth Avenue (Brooklyn) elevated line or adjacent trolleys.

It was the IRT which supplied the solution when it tunneled under the East River as part of its original line and connected Bowling Green in Manhattan with Brooklyn Borough Hall on January 10, 1908.

Less than four months later—May 1, 1908, to be exact—the IRT opened its Long Island Rail Road connecting station at Atlantic Avenue. The station's debut was hailed as a momentous occasion in the borough, and even brought Mayor George B. McClellan from Manhattan, who celebrated the debut along with more than 500 spectators.

At the time, some subway visionaries believed that it would be possible to run the IRT trains on LIRR tracks out to Nassau County. To accomplish the connection, a rail link was actually built at Atlantic Avenue station. However, such an integration of the lines never materialized. (Speculation had it that August Belmont did run a few "specials" to his race track in Elmont.)

Like the LIRR, the Hudson and Manhattan Railroad—otherwise known as the Hudson Tubes—was a heavily-used commuter line with a rich history.

The Tubes' godfather was a Southerner—and quite a character—William Gibbs McAdoo. As he projected it, McAdoo's trans-Hudson commuter subway would link not merely the Jersey shore with Manhattan, but also would have an assortment of tentacles throughout New Jersey, including a main line running to the metropolis of Newark.

McAdoo soon obtained the necessary financial support, and an attempt was made to link New York and New Jersey under the river.

McAdoo chose wisely when he named Charles M. Jacobs his chief engineer. A number of successful innovations were introduced during construction, not the least of which was the baking of watery silt over the shield into hard clay by means of hot torches brought into the tunnel.

Working from the New Jersey side, Jacobs' sandhogs burrowed toward the New York shore. Exactly 404 days after work begun, the linkage was accomplished.

In anticipation of the triumph, Jacobs had rigged a temporary telephone from the tunnel to McAdoo's office. When the final burrowing was completed, the chief engineer invited his boss down for a look-see. When McAdoo arrived, Jacobs took him in hand and they clambered through a door in the shield. From there, they explored the 5,650-foot tube from end to end, an experience which later moved McAdoo to exult, "For the first time in the history of mankind, men had walked on land from New Jersey to New York."

McAdoo next invited a horde of jour-

Covering 14.3 miles—all of it out-of-doors except for the St. George Terminal in Richmond—the New York City Transit-managed Staten Island Railway is as un-Big Apple-like as possible. Its run through the arboreal outer-borough is more reminiscent of an interurban trolley ride of the 1920s than a comtemporary rapid transit run. Still, it carries more than five million passengers a year.

nalists. To the surprise of some who had earlier expressed open skepticism, the trip was completed without catastrophe. They realized that there would be no holding back completion of the comprehensive Hudson and Manhattan Railroad. Construction already was underway on the Manhattan spur of the H and M. It would link the downtown (New York) terminus at Christopher Street in Greenwich Village with a new station at East 19th Street and Sixth Avenue. Across the river, the line was stretched north to the Hoboken terminal of the Delaware, Lackawanna and Western Railroad.

The vigorous McAdoo pushed forward construction of a second pair of trans-Hudson tunnels even before the first pair had been completed. Rather than connecting with Greenwich Village, the newer tunnel would speed the electric trains to a new station to be located at the base of a skyscraper called Hudson Terminal, within shouting distance of New York's City Hall. Equally ambitious were plans for the Jersey side of the new tunnel. Couplings would be made with the Pennsylvania Railroad's Exchange Place station, with the sizeable terminal of the Erie Railroad, and there

would be a connection with the Hudson and Manhattan's own pair of tubes—the originals—at Hoboken.

While all this was going on, workmen forged ahead, completing the original tunnel in preparation for the operation of the new trains.

In December 1907, the line began running cars filled with sandbags instead of passengers through the Hudson tunnels. Within a month the time had come to test the trains with people instead of sandbags. D-Day was set for January 15, 1908. On that occasion, McAdoo led an entourage down the stairs of the station at Sixth Avenue and 14th Street, where an eight-car, freshly-painted steel train awaited them. When all dignitaries had taken their seats, the company's superintendent, E.M. Hedley, pulled the heavy steel controller handle in the motorman's cab and the train rolled slowly toward the tunnel, easily negotiating the curves that eventually brought it to the straightaway and the dip down under the Hudson. The excursion reached Hoboken without mishap and then returned to Manhattan, where McAdoo was toasted as the man who had mastered the underwater crossing of the Hudson River.

Connecting Hoboken, New Jersey with Christopher Street in Greenwich Village, the Tubes opened to the riding public on February 25, 1908 and delivered yet another subway to Manhattan, although not in the same category as the IRT.

But the H&M did claim considerable mileage in the city, running its subway tracks straight up Sixth Avenue all the way to Herald Square (33rd Street), a point reached in 1910. The original H&M plan was to extend its tunnel northeast to Grand Central Terminal with its final stop designated to be at Lexington Avenue and 42nd Street, but the idea never was realized.

From an architectural viewpoint, the most impressive aspect of the Hudson and Manhattan Railroad was its primary terminal in downtown Manhattan. With twin towers, the Hudson Terminal melded a skyscraper with the H&M's primary depot in Manhattan.

Located at Cortlandt and Church Streets, Hudson Terminal was close enough to the Wall Street financial district that it drew many New Jersey-bound commuters daily; not to mention other New Yorkers who either had relatives or business across the river.

As such, a subway connection was as much a must as for the LIRR, NYC or PRR.

This hardly was a problem, because by the time The Tubes were in business, there were useful rapid transit connections. At Herald Square, for example, the Sixth Avenue el crossed directly over the H&M's last northerly station in the borough.

Meanwhile, the original Interborough subway line to Brooklyn first had to pass through Downtown Manhattan in Tubes' country, with IRT stops conveniently located near Hudson Terminal at City Hall, Fulton Street and Wall Street.

But the Hudson Terminal had to wait until 1918—when the Seventh Avenue IRT was extended south as part of the Dual Contracts—before a right-next-door connection was made. This was the Interborough's Cortlandt Street station, enabling easy access to the Tubes.

Likewise, the Brooklyn Rapid Transit's Broadway (Manhattan) Subway also had a nearby Cortlandt Street stop which doubled the commuter possibilities for the H&M and the subways. This was completed in 1918.

And if that wasn't enough, the Independent System chipped in with a Hudson Terminal station of its own at Chambers Street when the original IND Eighth Avenue Subway was finished in 1932.

Easily the strangest subway-railroad connection in the city's history took place in the Bronx, although it actually was supposed to be situated—according to original plans—at Grand Central Terminal.

The saga involved what was to be a state of the art commuter railroad known as the New York, Westchester and Boston.

Backed by some of the nation's wealthiest men—among them J. P. Morgan and William Rockefeller—the NYW&B was targeted to operate between Grand Central and a terminal in Boston. The operative word here is *supposed.*

But before any shovels dug any dirt or any ties were laid, the NYW&B leadership decided to bypass Grand Central—already overtaxed with rail traffic in 1909—and find a site farther north in the city. Finally, the Bronx was decided upon for what, then, seemed to be good reasons.

And those reasons all had to do with the subways.

The NYW&B's rationale was that the city's population center was continually moving north and soon the Bronx would be as much a hub as the Grand Central area. More importantly, by terminating the new railroad in the Bronx, its depot would be immediately adjacent to the new IRT subway in the borough.

From the Bronx NYW&B terminal, commuters then could easily switch to the IRT and ride the rest of the way to midtown Manhattan on the new underground.

Although the line was being built during the golden age of steam, it was in the

The Other Manhattan Subway—
The Hudson Tubes

The Hudson "Tubes" had two terminals in Manhattan. Seen here is the mezzanine level of the uptown terminal at 33rd Street, Herald Square. Notice the stairways going down to the platforms. Unlike the current 33rd Street station, in this one the mezzanine was completely over the track level.

This 33rd station on the Hudson Tubes, seen here at platform-level, lasted until 1935, when it was demolished to make room for the new Sixth Avenue IND subway station. The track arrangement was the same as it is now in the current station.

William Brennan

We are approaching the current 33rd Street station, actually located two blocks south at 31st Street. PATH took over operation of the Tubes three years prior to this photo, but the black Tube cars still were in service on the onetime Hudson and Manhattan Railroad, which was the proper name for the Tubes.

William Brennan

Looking back toward the ramp and mezzanine at 33rd Street H&M station—familiar to all current PATH riders—we see a close-up of the cars that made the Tubes the standard trans-Hudson subway.

William Brennan

Interior view of a Hudson and Manhattan (Tubes) black car. Notice that the seating arrange-ment is similar to the original—and present—IRT trains.

William Brennan

This PATH train at 14th Street station is nestled between the local tracks of the Sixth Avenue IND line, whose 14th Street depot is located just outside these walls. The express tracks are directly underneath.

The original downtown terminal of the Hudson Tubes—seen at the left—was called Hudson Terminal. The pair of buildings just beyond the Jersey Central Railroad ferry slip represent one of the more noteworthy exhibits of lower Manhattan architecture. Hudson Terminal was sacrificed to make way for the World Trade Center's twin towers.

The landmark Hudson Terminal clock beckoned passengers to their trains; hopefully on time! It was one of the items that gave the depot its unique quality.

Platform-level at Hudson Terminal. This aspect of the station was visible from trains arriving at the World Trade Center station. One quick solution to repairing the destruction of the WTC station was to re-open the original Hudson Terminal facility. This, however, was a plan that ultimately was rejected.

area designated exclusively for electric power.

Since Grand Central Station had already been ruled out, the planners decided on the Bronx. They wanted the Westchester's terminus to link directly with the Interborough Rapid Transit (IRT) for the cheap connection to the city's subway. They searched for a prime location and finally found one at East 132nd Street and Willis Avenue.

The site was chosen for several reasons, not merely for the link with the IRT. It was deep in the South Bronx adjacent to the New Haven's Harlem River freight yards and passenger station. This enabled the Westchester to share the trackage of the New Haven's Harlem River Branch until West Farms junction, where the Westchester turned off to its own route.

At the Willis Avenue-East 132nd Street terminal, the Westchester connected directly to the IRT's shuttle elevated trains that ran to 129th Street, Manhattan (the Third Avenue el). Given a choice between Grand Central and a higher fare or the Bronx terminal and a lower fare, passengers by the thousands were expected to switch to the Westchester.

From Willis Avenue-East 132nd Street, the Westchester snaked up the Bronx. The second stop would be Port Morris (East 135th Street), followed by Casanova (Legget Avenue), Hunt's Point (Hunt's Point Avenue), Westchester Avenue, 180th Street, Morris Park, Pelham Parkway, Gun Hill Road, Baychester Avenue, and Dyre Avenue. From there the route drifted over the city line north into Westchester County.

Not to be overlooked was the cosmetic touch. Stations would get the grand architectural treatment. They would be, as one observer put it, "monuments, constructed of concrete in renaissance, mission or classic style."

Structures built within the New York City limits—and now a part of the IRT system—were of the modified Mission type. Wherever possible, trees, shrubs, and hedges were planted around the stations. Terrazo facing was used in all station interiors, including the ticket booths. The respected *Electric Railway Journal* commented in June 1912:

"The passenger stations and signal towers may be said to constitute the most attractive group of way structures possessed by any electric or steam railroad in the United States. The result was made possible by the progressive attitude of the company, which was ambitious to erect buildings which would add to rather than detract from the expected high-class suburban development of this territory.... Many of the stations have cafes, haberdasheries and other stores in addition to the usual magazine and candy stands. Some stations have a room for baggage handling. At certain places the station building is being utilized as a natural headquarters for the local real estate development."

On May 29, 1912, the elephantine—at the time nobody dared called it a white elephant—project made its official debut. It ran from East 180th Street and Morris Park Avenue, near West Farms Square in the Bronx, to North Avenue, New Rochelle, Westchester. Much station and track work still remained to be done, but nobody noticed that. What caught the eye were the majestic stations, the broad, smooth right-of-way, and the splendidly speedy trains. The Boston & Westchester had purchased thirty steel cars, seventy feet long, which were equipped to draw current through the overhead pantographs.

The big green rolling stock, each of which could seat seventy-eight passengers, was equipped with powerful Westinghouse motors that could move the trains at speeds of sixty mph. Everything else about the car's appointments was first-rate, from the electric lamps to white enameled ceilings, shaded windows, and roomy seats. From every aspect the Westchester's cars were a 1912 commuter's dream-come-true.

Yet, the NYWB failed because of a geographic *faux pas.*

The mistake was placing the terminal in the Bronx and misjudging the usefulness of the railroad-subway connection uptown rather than at Grand Central. Some limited attempts were made to extend NYWB service southward via the stronger structure of the Second Avenue el, but narrow platform clearances and three blocks to the east didn't help.

"Passengers," wrote rail analyst Bernard Linder, "given a choice between Grand Central and a higher fare, or the Bronx terminal and a lower fare, chose the former. They hollered louder when fares went up, but that's all—they paid rather than change in the Bronx. The building boom came to Westchester, all right; apartment buildings sprouted on pastures and in woods, but not many of them elected to locate along the swift, low-priced line, which made a change in the Bronx necessary."

Placing the terminal in the Bronx proved to be a tricky business, although the NYWB planners could not be faulted for their thinking at the time. In their grand vision, the Bronx eventually would turn into the city's Mecca. Everything would be concentrated in the northernmost borough.

However, it was Cornelius Vanderbilt who had the best idea. As boss of the New York & Harlem (later the New York Central) Railroad, Vanderbilt wanted a terminal that not only would serve his line but also the New York, New Haven & Hartford and the Hudson River Railroad.

At that time, the area around 42nd Street was coveted, on the theory that New York City inevitably must expand northward. "Some day in the not-too-distant future," Commodore Vanderbilt predicted, "Grand Central Station will be in the center of the city."

Vanderbilt's "folly" soon turned into Vanderbilt's gold mine. If Grand Central Terminal was the center of the business district in 1920 and expansion continued in the direction of Westchester, it was reasonable to assume that by 1930 the business and commercial district would extend to the South Bronx.

But this theory was doomed with the city's first zoning law, written into the books in 1916 at a time when the Westchester was still hoping to have the Harlem River freight yards someday surrounded by tall office buildings. The new law limited Manhattan's commercial area to the precincts *south* of Central Park's southerly (59th Street) boundary. "Westchester's planners," wrote historian Roger Arcara, "could not reasonably be expected to foresee this development; to them it seemed, and rightly so at the time, that New York's business district was destined to go on expanding northward on Manhattan Island until, perhaps by the middle of the 20th Century, it would cover most of the island, with its northern portion somewhere around 125th Street, right across the river from the New York, Westchester & Boston Railway."

Once the zoning law was approved, the

The Curiously Refreshing Dyre Avenue Line

There are precious few remnants of the New York, Westchester and Boston Railroad—predecessor of the IRT Dyre Avenue Line—in evidence today. But shortly after the city took over the defunct four-track, high-speed commuter railroad at the start of the 1940s, many of the NYWB appurtenances were evident. In this photo, at Baychester, the two-car el train is framed by the NYWB's catenary steel-work. The two inner express tracks are still intact along with the overhead wires which had been used by the high-speed line. In this photo, third-rail operation is only available for the Dyre Avenue locals. All that remains of the NYWB today are original station structures sprinkled along the Bronx route. El trains were long ago replaced by contemporary rolling stock. When the city assumed control of the line, it supplied el cars because the NYWB had no physical connection to the rest of the subway system.

The IRT's Dyre Avenue Line runs in part on the original right-of-way designed by the New York, Westchester and Boston Railroad at the turn of the century. The four-track, high-speed line never made it to Boston, but it did boast handsome stations and mainline railroad-type trappings. This 1944 view, taken at the Pelham Parkway station, shows the two-car gate trains in use during World War II. While the Dyre Avenue Line was separated from the rest of the system and a new service to the Board of Transportation, IND motormen operated the trains. This changed in the 1950s when fly-overs were constructed to allow through IRT service to Manhattan. Also, fares were collected on the train as there were no ticket agents in the stations.

When through trains started service, the el cars were replaced on the Dyre Avenue line by regular IRT equipment. Here we see a set of Steinways on the center tracks just south of the Dyre Avenue station. A small portion of the express tracks were retained as a lay-up yard. William Brennan

On the same day in 1962, a set of Low Vs slows for the Gun Hill Road station. The greenery was abundant on this run, giving the line a most rural character. William Brennan

William Brennan

Passengers about to board the southbound train at Gun Hill Road station. Note the absence of center tracks, which had been a major asset of the original high-speed route.

Westchester's directors realized that the NYWB's plan was obsolete and new thinking was necessary. The natural solution was to extend the line from its Harlem River freight yard depot into Manhattan and south down to the midtown commercial district. All the Westchester needed to accomplish this was money. Therefore, the solution at once was no longer simple.

Ideally, the Manhattan extension could be built from the line's profits and thereby build still more profits. But no matter how the Westchester's accountants juggled the books, there simply was never a profit with which to work; therefore, no extension could or would be built. Thus the Westchester's depot remained in the Bronx, and the line continued to operate only by grace of its parent, the New York, New Haven & Hartford.

Patience and money simultaneously ran out on the New Haven in 1935 when the line reorganized and began to liquidate its unprofitable holdings. New Haven officials claimed they spent $50 million on the Westchester in a futile effort to put it in the black. Hence the NYW&B was the first to go.

In a last, desperate attempt to revive the line, the Westchester was put by court order under the trusteeship of Clinton L. Bardo, an efficient railroad man who had been general manager of the New Haven. Bardo had some sound ideas for saving the Westchester, but his reorganization plans required money. There was no cash available, and on April 15, 1937, the line was declared irrevocably insolvent. Less than four months later, Bardo died. The railroad itself enjoyed its last *clickety-clack* at about midnight, December 31, 1937 when some fifty passengers, most of whom were railfans, rode the final run.

In the end, the collapse of the NYW&B proved William Shakespeare to be on target when he wrote, "Sweet are the uses of adversity."

What was a bust in the railroad sense turned into a bargain for the New York City subway system.

Having united the BMT, IND, and IRT, New York City now owned the greatest rapid transit system of any municipality in the world. Mayor Fiorello LaGuardia and his constituents were appropriately proud of their subways and looked to further expansion. One such possibility was an extension of the IND Bronx division past its 205th Street terminal farther eastward in the borough. This could be done for an estimated $2,500,000 and would probably have been done had it not been learned that the existing NYW&B tracks within the Bronx from East 174th Street to the Mount Vernon (Westchester) border could be obtained for only $1,783,577. LaGuardia was persuaded that it would be more practical to buy the Westchester than plunge ahead with an extension of the IND.

The 205th Street extension was shelved, and New York City instead took over the Bronx portion of the NYW&B, installed a third rail, and assigned twenty Third Avenue elevated cars to the run. To make the adjustment, several mechanical alterations had to be applied to the Westchester's right-of-way. Unused BMT signals were hooked up on the Westchester route; clearances were adjusted for the wooden, open-platform elevated cars—a terrible comedown from the high-speed NYW&B trains—and finally, the name of the line itself was changed to Dyre Avenue.

And now the Dyre Avenue Line is an integral part of the subway system where once it was a railroad.

Over the past century, the importance of New York's subways to the railroad and commuter-trains servicing the city has remained evident.

Both Grand Central Terminal and Pennsylvania Station have changed in their functions since World War II, but they still are intensively used, along with the Tubes—now called PATH—and Long Island Rail Road.

Without the subway connections, they simply couldn't do their jobs as efficiently.

What It Was Like To Take the Subway to the Railroads

I was a railroad-rider almost as early in my life as I was a subway-rider.

As far as I can recall, the very first train ride I ever had the pleasure of taking—and it *was* great fun—happened in 1940, when I was eight years old.

It was a year after our home station—Myrtle-Willoughby on the GG line—had opened; when the Independent (IND) System still was brand-new compared to its IRT and BMT counterparts.

My destination was Amenia, a resort town in Upstate New York's Dutchess County.

The circumstances around which the trip was taken are somewhat fuzzy. I say this because I made the railroad journey with my father, not my mother. She already *was* at the hotel we were visiting, and I can only guess that she had gone ahead because—I believe—she was recovering from an unspecified ailment.

Whatever the case, Dad and I were to take the New York Central Railroad to our destination, and that alone made me certain that this would be an adventure of a lifetime.

Reaching our starting point, Grand Central Station, was not that simple in those days.

We took the GG to Hoyt-Schermerhorn; switched to the A Train, and then got off at Broadway-Nassau. We walked over to the nearby IRT Fulton Street station and took the Uptown Express to Grand Central.

The moment we got off the IRT Express, I knew I had arrived in a special place.

Lining the walls of the IRT's local tracks were mosaics of a kind I had never dreamed of seeing in a subway station.

They depicted the front view of a New York Central steam locomotive from the World War I era, with its cowcatcher and smokestack very vivid to the eyes.

To me it was a splendid prelude to my upcoming journey to Amenia.

Dad and I climbed the stairs and entered the ramp leading from the subway to the railroad station.

Left and right, there was shop after shop: a book store, locksmith, shoemaker, bakery. You name it, Grand Central had it.

We finally turned a corner, and there ahead of us, was the main hall.

Just the sight of it left me gasping. Between the information booth—with its distinctive four-faced clock—to the remarkable ceiling, I didn't know what to gape at first.

Meanwhile, Dad led me over to the ticket counter where he placed a few bills on the ivory counter and bought a pair of tickets to Amenia.

We then determined that Amenia was on the NYC's Harlem Division and that, at a certain point going north, up the line, the

WHEN YOU GET CLAUSTROPHOBIC ON THE IRT

Although the New York subway system is unified, its cars are not. The IRT cars, originally designed for owner August Belmont, were deliberately ordered thinner by him so that wider cars could not use his tunnels. The BMT and IND rolling stock, which followed, was longer and wider. Consequently, neither BMT nor IND cars can fit in IRT tunnels. However, IRT cars use BMT/IND tracks when in need of repairs at the Coney Island Shops. There are four connections between the A (IRT) and B (INT-BMT) Division tracks: 1. The 207th Street Yard links with A Division Number One Line and the B Division Eighth Avenue Line; 2. The A Division Number Seven connects on the upper level of Queensborough Plaza with the B Division N at a diamond crossover. Interestingly, this is the only place where the Flushing Line mixes with the the rest of the system; 3. The A Division Number Three connects (one track) with the B Division L near Junius Street Station. This provides access for the Linden Yard which employs diesel-powered work trains; 4. In the Bronx, the B Division Concourse Subway connects with the Number Four Line at the yard near Kingsbridge Road Station and 205th Street.

electric locomotive would be changed and we would revert to a genuine steam engine, of the kind I loved reading about in my train books.

Dad checked the various white-on-black signs that filled the terminal and finally located the one for our train.

We walked down a long ramp, leading to our platform. There were big—compared to the subway—cars on both sides of us. They looked exactly like the ones I had seen in my train books, except there were sounds and sights that I never heard before. One car was hissing; another was dripping water. A third car (the smoking car) had a distinctly different look to it.

All in all I was dazzled by the total train picture!

A conductor, with his round, peaked hat, was beckoning people on to the train.

I felt that walking on to my first railroad train, I had instantly grown up by one year, at least. Following my father, I walked through the opening between the cars, peering down at the intertwined steel plates that enabled us to safely cross into the next coach.

A pair of leather "softy" diaphragms were hooked to the ends of each car to further insure that no one could fall into the opening and, as I passed them, I couldn't help admiring the inventor who had come up with that brilliant idea.

Once we entered the second coach, I noticed that it had many empty seats. Dad led me to the middle of the car and then put our valise on the rack above us and pointed to the window, indicating that I could have the choice position while he would sit on the aisle.

My father may not have realized how important a decision he had made in my favor, especially since we were occupying a railroad car that dated back to the early 1920's. In those days of all-steam travel, coaches were equipped with windows which not only could be manually opened, but also provided enough open space to allow a youth to occasionally stick his head out as the train reached a curve.

Since we were on the right-hand side of the train, it meant that on a decent curve I could get a good look at the chugging locomotive. In train-watchers' terms, that's about as good as it gets.

I couldn't wait until the local finally began moving away from its Grand Central platform. Finally, there was a slight *lurch* as the couplers strained under the forward pressure, and the station platform began fading in the distance. We were off!

One aspect of a railway journey's beginning that always is entrancing takes place upon leaving the depot, especially one as complex as Grand Central.

In order to exit the terminal, our train—like most others—had to criss-cross over innumerable switches before reaching our proper track.

I knew we were on a real railroad and not the subway as soon as I heard the heavier-sounding *clunkety-clunk-clunk* of the New York Central's Harlem Division car-wheels finding their way through the maze of tracks. This kind of railroad sound made its subway counterpart seem like toy trains.

We cleared the complex switches and picked up speed under the Park Avenue tunnel. By 90th Street, the darkness began clearing as we mounted the incline toward the 96th Street portal and the viaduct ahead.

After a brief stop at 125th Street station the train rolled north to a junction at North White Plains where all the electric locomotives on that division gave way to their steam counterparts.

It was a well-oiled transfer of motive power climaxed by a sharply defined *ker-chunk* as the steam locomotive and its tender backed into the passenger car for the coupling.

That done, we were off and running for the North Country, ultimately switching off the main (Hudson River) line and into Harlem Line turf.

This was the kind of railroading of which I had often dreamed, the locomotive belching smoke from its stack, the engineer periodically blowing his whistle as we approached the ubiquitous railroad crossing gates, always accompanied by the *clang-clang-clang* of warning bells.

Since it was a hot, mid-summer day, my father had no compunctions about allowing me to have the window wide open, nor did he admonish me when I stuck my head out to catch the breezes and gape at the passing countryside.

Unquestionably, the high-point of the entire trip was reached during a long slow curve to the right.

There, about six cars ahead of us, was the locomotive, puffing hard up the incline. The Pacific-type engine looked a lot like one featured in my Lionel toy electric train catalogue.

I remember doubting very much if it were possible for me to be much happier.

We arrived at Amenia, met my mom and had an enjoyable three-day weekend. Yet all I remember about the trip is the train part. First, the wonderful journey, which began with the subway trip to Grand Central, and then, the New York Central extravaganza—electric and steam locomotives on one ticket—to the resort.

I couldn't tell you one thing about the hotel except that it sat on a hill overlooking a valley. During late afternoons and in the early evenings, I would sit on the hilltop waiting patiently and then, hearing the *chug-chug-chug* in the distance, I would contently smile as the locomotive rounded the bend and rolled into view. Obviously from that very early age, trains were in my blood.

This theory was reinforced not long after the New York Central experience, when I took the subway to yet another railroad; and this time it would mark my first *solo* ride on a major railroad.

My destination would be Philadelphia; I was eight years old, and heading to the City of Brotherly Love to visit my Aunt Hattie, Uncle Paul and just-born cousin Ira Sheier.

Since Philadelphia is on the Pennsylvania Railroad's main line, I would be riding the Pennsy—for the first time—from Manhattan's Pennsylvania Station at 33rd Street and Seventh Avenue.

By subway it was a relatively simple one-switch operation. With Mom accompanying me, we boarded reliable GG—now all of three years old and still looking new—at Myrtle-Willoughby for the ride to Hoyt-Schermerhorn. There we awaited the A Express.

Whenever we arrived at Hoyt-Schermerhorn, I was puzzled by the track formation.

Normally, at an express-local stop, the local tracks are located at the far sides of the station—either far left or far right.

But at Hoyt-Schermerhorn, the GG tracks ran right down the center pair of the six-track depot. To me, the formation seemed to confer a special status on the GG in relation to the A, whose tracks were at the outside of the GG's.

From Hoyt, we journeyed to Manhattan on the fairly-pleasant express run. The express part of the A was evident only twice; once at Spring Street and the other at 23rd. Those were the only local stations we would bypass, thereby demonstrating the A had true *express* powers.

Pulling into the 34th Street platform, the train revealed another weird IND Station layout; yet different from the strange one at Hoyt-Schermerhorn. At 34th Street, instead of having the uptown express and local platforms on one center

island, servicing both trains, it was distinctly different.

The Uptown Express platform was shared with the Downtown Express. Meanwhile, each local platform was at the respective far sides; which meant that an express passenger could not simply walk across the platform and board a local or vice versa. I never figured out why it was done this way.

Penn Station was ideally situated for subway connections. East of the station, at Seventh Avenue, the IRT Broadway Line had its express-local station—with, by the way, the identical odd ball platforms configuration—while at the West End at Eighth Avenue was the IND stop.

Mom and I merely had to walk up a flight of stairs and we were deposited at the entrance to Pennsylvania Station.

At first glance, Penn Station struck me as a museum; maybe the largest museum in the world. The tall columns outside impressed me no end, but it wasn't until we actually walked the stairs into the great hall that my jaw dropped in utter amazement.

To an eight-year-old, Penn Station was beyond big. Describing the great hall as "cavernous" would be the understatement of the half-century.

The confluence of glass, steel and stone masonry left me gaping. But, when all was said and done, it was not so much the architectural triumph that most dazzled me about Penn Station but rather a somewhat innocuous invention.

Certainly it won't qualify in a class with the internal combustion engine or radio, but the electric eye—automatic doors—which I never knew existed then—just knocked me for a loop.

I discovered the automatic doors as we

THE SUBWAY HOLE THAT NEVER WAS FILLED

Ever since the early part of the 20th century, there has been talk of building a Second Avenue subway, and, in fact, a tunnel was built but never completed.

Early in 2004, the Metropolitan Transit Authority blueprinted plans for a smaller version of the original Second Avenue idea. The miniline would run from 96th to 72nd Streets and then shoot over to Broadway to bring passengers downtown.

New stations would be built along Second Avenue at 96th, 86th and 72nd Streets. The line would then curve west—stopping at the 63rd Street and Lexington Avenue F line station, then run downtown along the existing Broadway tunnel.

walked to the main waiting room. As we approached them, I noticed what appeared to be two lit flashlights sticking out of a railing in front of the doors.

Later, I was told that the facing lights represented an "electric eye." When my body came between the lights, it set in motion an electrical mechanism which automatically opened the door.

So taken was I by this strange—to me—device that I importuned my mother to allow me to go back and forth through the door three more times. And since we had plenty of time, she agreed.

Eventually we made our way down the stairs to track level and awaited the train to Philadelphia. Mom repeated her mantra. "Listen to the Conductor! When he says 'Philadelphia,' you get ready to get off.

"Your Aunt Hattie will be waiting for you on the platform."

For some strange reason, I was not afraid to travel solo at age eight, although adults I knew were amazed at my undertaking.

I was more attentive to the streamline electric (GG-1) locomotive that pulled the Tuscan red coaches into the station. I had seen photos of the GG-1, but it was nothing like viewing the sleek, black engine topped by the catenary power from wire above.

Mom kissed me good-bye, insisting that I not let the ticket leave my hand. I gripped it firmly and waved good-bye.

GG-1 or not, the ride to Philly just wasn't in a class with my trip to Amenia. Mostly it was because the electric engine made no noise, emitted no smell, and was just plain streamlined and efficient.

Not that I didn't enjoy the speed and the fact that this was big-time railroading. I loved it, and when the conductor shouted "NEXT STOP PHILADELPHIA!" I was sorry that the journey had ended so soon.

Sure enough, Aunt Hattie was there as billed, and after a hug and kiss, she whisked me away in her 1937 Plymouth, two-door, black sedan.

"Don't you have a subway in Philadelphia?" I asked.

Aunt Hattie smiled. "Yes, we do," she said, wondering why I would ask that question. Then she gave what appeared to her to be the logical postscript: "But the Plymouth takes me where I want to go!"

On my return from a delightful two weeks with Aunt Hattie, Uncle Paul and Cousin Ira, I was deposited back on the Pennsy for the return to Manhattan.

Dad was there to meet me, and when he wondered about the success of the trip I quickly replied that it was "swell" and then asked him about something unusual I had seen as we pulled into Newark's Penn Station on the way back to New York.

"Dad," I inquired, "when we were in Newark Station, I looked across the platform and saw what looked like a subway on the other track. What was that?"

My father pointed out that while Newark had what it called a "City Subway," it really was a trolley car that ran underground.

"What you saw," Dad went on, "and thought was a subway train actually was the Hudson Tubes."

"Does it go to New York?" I wondered.

"Sure does," my father asserted. "We can take it sometime to visit Rose and Joe Honig who live in Newark."

And that is how I came to take the subway to another railroad, although this was more like taking the subway *to* the subway.

The Tubes—as we came to call them—still operate, only now under the sobriquet PATH (Port Authority Trans Hudson). But, when Dad took me to Newark, it was the Hudson and Manhattan Railroad, partly owned by the Pennsylvania Railroad.

Like the New York Central and Pennsylvania Railroads, the H and M had its own depot in Manhattan.

But unlike the other stations located uptown, the Hudson Terminal was situated near Wall Street and City Hall, close to the site of the island's original Dutch settlement.

And much in the manner of the PRR and NYC, Hudson Terminal's location was chosen because of its proximity to rapid transit.

The IRT's City Hall station had been open for several years before construction began on Hudson Terminal. In addition,

the H and M *major domo*, William Gibbs McAdoo, knew that the city soon would be extending the IRT right down to Cortlandt Street with an entrance directly into Hudson Terminal.

But when Dad and I took the subway to The Tubes, we chose a line that would connect with Hudson Terminal two decades later.

That would be the Eighth Avenue Subway which, when it made its debut, extended from Washington Heights, in the northern end of Manhattan, to Chambers Street in the southern sphere of the city.

Since the A train stopped at Chambers, we took the usual GG ride to Hoyt Street Station, and then boarded the A train to Manhattan. We arrived at Chambers Street station in no time at all. When we debarked from the R-1 car, my eyes caught two different aspects of the depot. First, there was the signage CHAMBERS STREET—HUDSON TERMINAL. For some reason, I never had noticed the Hudson Terminal part before.

Secondly, there was the odd design of Chambers Street Station.

It was like two different stations in one; with the uptown platform nowhere opposite the downtown counterpart. The way it was on just about every other station to which I was acquainted, the uptown and downtown platforms faced each other.

We easily followed the signs and found our way to Hudson Terminal, which was totally unlike either Grand Central or Penn Station.

The latter pair were artfully designed to be nothing more than flagship terminals; no more, no less.

By contrast, Hudson Terminal encompassed a massive—and very impressive—office building that sat directly on top of the station.

THE CURIOUS APARTMENT
ABOVE THE IRT'S GRAND CENTRAL STATION

IRT passengers who exit from Grand Central Terminal frequently pass one of the most curious spaces on the island of Manhattan.

It is the area of the terminal once called the Campbell Apartment and is named after the onetime Chairman of the Board of the Credit Clearing House, John W. Campbell.

When Grand Central Terminal originally was built, the depot was supposed to include a 20-story office tower above the station and the IRT subway.

The plans never materialized, but instead the New York Central Railroad provided other offices to outside businesses.

One such office was situated just off the West Balcony at the Southwest corner of Grand Central Terminal.

When Campbell rented it in 1923, he transformed it into what was described as a 13th century Florentine palace.

One reviewer called it, "The most remarkable office New York has ever seen."

After business hours, Campbell and his wife would hold lavish parties in the office, which housed beautiful, precious objets d'arte.

It was typical of sumptuous private offices of the period except that it was at street level in Grand Central Terminal instead of at the top of a commercial skyscraper, said the New York Times.

The office was abandoned by the 1960s, after Campbell's death. It later was used as a Metro North commuter railroad police storage room until it was renovated in the late 1990s.

It now houses a restaurant.

This hardly detracted from my absorption with the enterprise. For Hudson Terminal offered so many surprises of its own, that I quickly overlooked its non-railroad trappings.

Instead, I noticed several subway type characteristics: H and M trains looked very much like the IRT subway cars, but the tunnels were different.

Instead of smooth walls, the H and M featured the basic skeletal steel without any concrete cosmetic covering. It reminded me of an oversized *Erector* set and, frankly, gave me the creeps.

Any fear I harbored that the Trans-Hudson Tunnels might collapse was dissipated by my concern that the Tubes trains would merely stay *on* the tracks.

Before dipping under the Hudson, our train wormed around a series of curves that would have tested the nerves of any roller coaster inspector.

If the series of S curves weren't thrilling enough, the straightaway sprint under the Hudson was a pulsating revelation, enhanced by the curious "Erector" tunnel formation. With a big, easy-to-see-out-of front window, the Tubes' lead car was as perfect as could be for a young subway buff like me.

And, make no mistake, I still believed that I was in a New York subway car because the H and M rolling stock had the same length, width and a similar rapid transit seating arrangement.

The difference was in speed.

Tube train motors were more powerful than anything on the IND, BMT or IRT

Taking the Hudson Tubes to Newark

William Brennan

RIGHT: The service between Hudson Terminal and Newark on the Hudson Tubes was a joint operation between the H&M and the Pennsylvania Railroad. Both companies provided equipment for the route. Here we see one of the newer MP-52, Pennsy-supplied cars eastbound at Grove Street station in Jersey City.

BELOW: Hellbent for Newark, a Hudson Tubes F-class Black Car has cleared the Trans-Hudson tunnel and speeds through the rock cut at Waldo Tower, approaching Jersey City station. When I would ride these trains, I found them to be among the most exciting of any in the Greater New York area.

William Brennan

A two-car H&M set at the Journal Square, Jersey City station.

William Brennan

William Brennan

In the small yard just west of the Journal Square station, a Pennsylvania Railroad (Gibbs Car) MP 38 waits its turn for the next run. Prior to PATH, Pennsylvania Railroad conductors handled the trains between Journal Square and Newark. This portion of the line had separate ticketing for the H&M east of Journal Square.

After leaving Jersey City, the Tubes trains accelerate to speeds of up to 60 miles per hour. This photo was taken at the Kearny Meadows. For myself, this was the absolute highlight of the speedy trip and was far faster—and much more exciting—than anything on the city subway system. The only drawback—if one can call it a debit— was the fact that that Tubes' front windows didn't open as they did on the BMT Standards. Note the Pennsylvania-type signal that governed this portion of the line.

William Brennan

William Brennan

Newark, we are here! The Tubes' MP-52s have completed their run from Manhattan, arriving at the handsome Penn Station in Downtown Newark. The station is shared by Amtrak as well as New Jersey Transit trains.

lines. Consequently, our H and M train emerged from the portal adjacent to the New Jersey Meadowlands swamps in a great big hurry.

Almost simultaneously with the train busting into morning brightness, the motorman pushed his controller to its highest notch and we were off and running faster than I had ever imagined a subway could roll.

Actually, I didn't believe that we were rolling; flying was more like it! This was the straightaway of straightaways; on the left, Jersey industry; on the right, millions and millions of swamp weeds.

I kept trying to get used to the galloping H and M, but I was mesmerized right up to the moment our train crossed the Passaic River railroad bridge and decelerated into Newark's Penn Station.

As we walked to the Lyons Avenue bus, I tried to find words to fit my feelings about the Tubes trip. All I could manage was, "Dad, that was terrific."

In fact, it was so terrific that when we returned home and boarded the A Train at Chambers Street, I felt I had experienced the ultimate build-up (H and M) to a letdown (IND).

It took me about three weeks after riding the Hudson Tubes that memorable day to appreciate our subway again!

———————————

CHAPTER TEN

GOING TO

Riis Park, The Rockaways, Staten Island, Parkchester, East New York and Other Distant Places

We'll Take Manhattan,
The Bronx
And Staten Island, Too…

Were it not for the ever-growing New York subway system, some of the most distant—and enjoyable—regions of the city never would have been available to the average, non-automobile-driving Big Apple resident.

What better examples than Rockaway Beach and its westerly cousin, Jacob Riis Park.

The excellent virtues of the beach originally were enjoyed by its first inhabitants, the Canarsee Indians. According to Canarsee tongue, *Reckouacky*, supposedly connotes "place of our people."

From *Reckouacky*, we get Rockaway which, in time, would become the place of other peoples.

The ethnic transformation began in 1685 when the Canarsees sold the land to a John Palmer who, apparently, was not fully aware of its possibilities. However,

one Richard Cornell—he lived in Flushing—thought otherwise and purchased it in 1687 from Palmer.

The Rockaway peninsula—consisting of a four-mile-long barrier beach—located in Queens borough, got its first taste of modern civilization in 1809 when the land was divvied up into forty-six sections.

Less than three decades later, Rockaway—as a beach paradise—had been discovered. It was another case of a sweet use of adversity.

Early in the decade of the 1830s, a cholera epidemic threatened New York City, compelling many residents to escape for less inhabited locales. One of them was Rockaway.

To accommodate the escapees, the Marine Pavilion Hotel opened, thus becoming Rockaway's first such hostelry, but certainly not its last. Remaining in business for a little more than three decades, the Marine Pavilion had no shortage of notable guests; among them author Washington Irving and poet Henry Wadsworth Longfellow.

"Manhattan Serenade," words Harold Adamson, music Louis Alter, Robbins Music Corp., © 1928

The Marine Pavilion's popularity became a catalyst for more hotel-building, and it was only a matter of time before railroad interests would choose to exploit the seaside potential.

In 1860, the South Side Railroad Company of Long Island was incorporated. Its directors had their eyes on Rockaway, and nine years later tracks linked the mainland to the beach. The Long Island Rail Road followed suit in 1872 and the rush to development was on, although not in the rapid manner some had envisioned.

Like Atlantic City, which essentially had been a sandy peninsula separated from New Jersey's population centers, Rockaway Beach was poised for a major leap forward as a resort area in the post- Civil war era.

While the railroad turned Atlantic City into one of the nation's premier hotel-resorts, trains never quite lifted the Rockaways to such an exalted level. Nevertheless, those hopes were nurtured as mainlanders increasingly sought easily accessible summer retreats.

Still more trains filled the transportation gap in 1880 when the New York, Woodhaven and Rockaway Railroad (NYWRR) reached the beaches. The line—soon to be part of the complex LIRR empire along with the South Side Railroad—like its Coney Island counterparts would inspire hotel-building, although on a smaller scale.

Before that could happen, meaningful improvements in the Rockaway terrain were necessary. Nine years after the NYWRR began carrying New Yorkers to the Atlantic paradise, Long Island Rail Road president Austin Corbin conjured up a grand plan for turning Rockaway from a minor league resort to a major league destination.

The key was beachfront property, and Corbin obtained more than enough—300 acres with a half-mile along the shore—to erect an exclusive residential community.

That was the good news.

The bad news was that hotel development failed to match the grandiose scale of either Coney Island, Brighton Beach or Atlantic City.

One such Rockaway venture, the Hotel Imperial, was erected at a cost of $1 million—and bombed faster than anything like it in Brighton or Coney.

Undaunted, Rockaway promoters greeted the new (20th) century with yet another grand plan—and half-a-million dollars to support it—that would give the beachfront more allure to tourists.

More than 20 acres of the bay were filled in so that an oceanfront boulevard as well as a twelve-block boardwalk could be erected. In addition, more than a dozen streets were blueprinted along with appropriate amenities such as electricity and sewage treatment.

The similarity to Coney Island was reinforced at the turn of the (20th) century, when the first major playground, Rockaway Beach Amusement Park, began spinning its turnstiles in 1901. What the Sea Beach, Brighton, Culver and West End lines were doing for Coney, the Long Island Rail Road began doing for Rockaway.

Fun-seekers filled the LIRR trains during the pre- and post-World War I days in increasing numbers after a second significant amusement park, Rockaway Playland, opened nearby.

In contrast to Coney Island—including Brighton Beach—Rockaway never was to host more than one railroad once the LIRR obtained a monopoly on rapid transit in Nassau and Suffolk counties as well as the Rockaways.

Specifically, the difference came to this: After electrification late in the 19th century and early in the 20th century, the various lines (Sea Beach, West End, et. al.) reaching Coney Island came under the aegis of the Brooklyn Rapid Transit (BRT).

As a New York City supervised subway, the BRT's fare required a static ten cents; later to be reduced to a nickel. Brooklyn's much-heralded beach made Coney affordable for *everybody*, but especially the City's poor who ordinarily never would have ventured across the city line—or even to Rockaway—for vacation pleasure. They simply could not afford the travel costs.

But a twenty cent round-tripper (later to be only a dime) to Surf Avenue and West 8th Street was within almost anyone's budget. Better still, it would remain at this low price right through the World War II years.

Not so for the Rockaways.

While the BRT was consolidating its quartet of Coney-bound subways, the Long Island Rail Road become the sole train operator to Rockaway. The prime route—and one which essentially has remained intact until today—dates back to 1892.

It was then that the LIRR drove 50,000 piles deep into the mud and sand of Jamaica Bay and built a new line across the slightly more than four miles of shallow water. The LIRR then began running trains across this short route to the Rockaways, simultaneously wishing it had never got involved with the idea of bridging Jamaica Bay.

Ironically, fire—over the waterway—became the most common hazard. The trestle, only a few feet above water most of the way, was particularly vulnerable. The hot sun dried out the wooden ties; cigarettes popped out of open windows to land on dry, creosoted wood, where they smoldered for five or six hours and then burst into flame, fanned by drafts through the open lattice of the ties.

Unfortunately, the LIRR had no alternative but to extinguish the fires and hope for the best. Certainly, there was no thought of abandoning the line, because Rockaway's popularity was reaching new heights. In fact, the allure of the beaches had reached such a high level that in 1898 the Brooklyn Elevated Railway Company (BERC) got into the act.

BERC moguls made a deal with the LIRR to rent the track and run summer excursion trains over the trestle to the Rockaways. To do so, the BERC had to build a special ramp at Chestnut Street and Atlantic Avenue in the East New York section of Brooklyn so that its trains could switch directly on to the LIRR tracks heading for the shore.

Ridership to the Rockaways was not dramatically different from that of the BRT which serviced Brooklyn's beaches. As at the Brighton beachfront, Rockaway saw a rush of bungalow-building near the ocean, and, by the end of World War I, the summer trade in Rockaway was similar to that of the beaches to the west.

The primary difference was that it cost more to get to Rockaway—50 cents for a round trip—than it did to ride the subway.

The LIRR's rationale—or at least one of them—for the higher fare was equated with miles: especially after the Long Island's East River tunnels were completed in 1910.

Once the LIRR began operating trains from Pennsylvania Station—under the East River—and then through the Queens heartland before rolling over Jamaica Bay,

Rolling to the Rockaways

The Long Island Rail Road realized the possibilities of a train to the Rockaways as far back as the late 1800s. A two-track trestle eventually was built and later the line was electrified. One stop along the route, at Goose Creek, offered a hotel, rented fishing boats with plenty of Jamaica Bay available to land a good catch. The photo was taken in August 1914, after the LIRR run had become electrified.

A decade after the turn of the (20th) century, Rockaway Beach and environs began taking shape as a popular summer resort. This 1911 scene from the Rockaways shows the at-street-level, pre-electrification Long Island Rail Road tracks which serviced the beach-goers. Beyond the road, in the background, is the Atlantic Ocean.

Another street in Rockaway Beach with more elaborate properties. Imagine the traffic problems if the Rockaway subway line still was on the ground today, with the present population and motor vehicle density!

the run consumed 11.3 miles, a bit longer than the BRT's four shore-bound lines.

If there was a difference—and there was—in the type of crowds drawn by Rockaway in relation to Coney, it could be measured along ethnic lines. While the bungalow colony inhabitants of Brighton and Coney Island summer conclaves were predominantly Jewish refugees from Manhattan's Lower East Side, Brooklyn's Williamsburg and Flatbush neighborhoods, Rockaway Beach attracted a mostly Gentile audience, with the Irish and Italians most evident.

Many of the riders came from Brooklyn, and in good time the politicians began eyeing the Rockaway tracks for possible inclusion in the city transit system. Meanwhile, the LIRR began suffering through serious fiscal problems which would peak in the years immediately following World War II.

Easily the most calamitous event had nothing to do with money—yet, conversely, would in the long run. In 1950, someone flicked a burning cigarette out the window of a LIRR coach, causing a fire that burned out 1,800 feet of trestle.

With virtually no money to spare, LIRR bosses decided that the line simply would not repair the damaged trestle to Rockaway. It petitioned for abandonment of Rockaway service and, in the meantime, sought potential purchasers.

This was—as sportscasters love to say—"a golden opportunity" for New York's subway operators, who wasted no time making an offer. The LIRR accepted the $8,500,000 put on the table and—*poof!*—just like that, the city owned yet another railroad that went to the sea; only this one went to Rockaway—but not so fast!

Damage had been so extensive that an additional $47,500,000 was required to fix the trestle and modernize the line so that it was operational. Even at that price, it was considered a bargain. Much of the money spent was used to build a fireproof bridge across Jamaica Bay.

This was accomplished by constructing two man-made islands, spanning most of the four-mile stretch across water. The ties were buried in ballast and sand, flush to their tops, so that no drafts could seep from underneath to fan into a destructive blaze started by a dying cigarette resting on a tie made flammable with creosote oil.

Among the more intense battles during reconstruction was a daily clash between transit men and squadrons of dive-bombing gulls that arrived from the nearby Jamaica Bay Bird Sanctuary, which the Transit Authority had built as part of the new Rockaway Line project.

The gulls overflowed the sanctuary and began homesteading on the new railroad bed. When TA men approached the nests, the gulls attacked. "The damn things dive-bombed us," one of the field crew complained. "They knocked off hats and glasses in a wink!"

The birds enjoyed the side benefits of the Rockaway trestle work. During the months that thousands of tons of sand were being pumped up to create the new islands, clams and fish also were pumped up, creating a cornucopia of gull goodies.

By construction standards, the Rockaway line was a topsy-turvy job. "It always had been a considerable problem disposing of fill," said Francis V. Haynes, division engineer of the project. "But for the Rockaway job we needed two million cubic yards to *fill*."

To get it, the contractors dug to the bottom of Jamaica Bay. Because the United

States Defense Department wanted a ship channel, nearly one million yards of sand were pumped up, and this formed what became known as Sand Island. The birds almost immediately took possession of this island. The longer of the TA-created islands was given the appellation The Embankment. It ran for more than two miles across the bay.

To ensure that the new islands would not erode into the sea, the TA planted grass on a voluminous scale. More than 100 acres of the new land were planted virtually foot by foot with beach grass, about the only vegetation that could thrive in the salty sand, to anchor the islands.

Before the modernized Rockaway line was completed, it had scored several "firsts" for rapid transit. One was the dispatching of a field engineer, Victor Lefkowitz, to the scene for the sole purpose of formulating a battle plan against mussels; creatures that could destroy trestles as easily as cigarette butts had the LIRR span.

Camping in a pile crack, the mussels increase the size of the opening, permitting other marine life to get inside with them where they gorge themselves on tasty pile innards not protected by creosote. Piles used on the old LIRR trestle were found completely hollow inside the creosoted shell. Some 500 had to be replaced and these, together with the old ones, form the skeletons of the two man-made islands over which the line hops Jamaica Bay.

To outdo the destructive mussels, the TA engineers produced a concrete foundation. Another "first" was a floating concrete factory that was towed along the line. The factory precast thirty-ton slabs of concrete which were lifted by a fifty-ton crane. It then dropped them on the concrete trestle foundations, forming a virtu-

ally finished roadbed. "Shovels and wheelbarrows were practically unknown," said a TA engineer.

Building the new extension was a remarkable accomplishment in itself, but completing it on time—considering the major obstacles—was the most outstanding feat of construction.

Studies of the old trestle and the surrounding terrain had been conducted by TA engineers as early as 1950. When the actual heavy work began in 1955, the target date for completion was set at June 28, 1956. Wisely, the TA wanted its subway-to-the-beach to debut in time for the heavy July 4th crowds.

Construction moved smoothly until the Westinghouse Electric Corporation went on strike in October 1955. Westinghouse had the contract to provide the power equipment for the line, and as the strike dragged on, the deadline for completion seemed unlikely to be met.

The strike lasted for 156 days and, when it was finally settled, Westinghouse informed the TA that equipment would not be ready until October, four months after the deadline.

But the Authority's determined chairman, Charles Patterson, would have none of that. He announced on January 26, 1956 that the June 28 deadline *would* be met! And he meant it.

Nevertheless, workers at Jamaica Bay scoffed when they heard what Patterson had said. "With this strike," one said, "how the hell does he expect us to open on time? What are we going to do for power equipment if Westinghouse can't deliver until the fall?"

Patterson had the answer.

He ordered his men to borrow some equipment from the IRT's Dyre Avenue line, and the Aqueduct substation was skeletonized. Arrangements were made to buy other power.

By spring, a few optimists at TA headquarters began thinking they just might pull off the impossible. During a meeting with trestle builders, one contractor told Patterson: "You know, I wouldn't be surprised if we are ready to run on June 28th."

"Ready?" Patterson shot back. "We *will* be running then!"

Despite strikes, dive-bombing gulls, and a horde of skeptics, the Transit Authority's trains rolled to Rockaway on June 28, 1956 just as Charlie Patterson had vowed.

And what a line it was; arguably the most scenic on the entire system.

After heading south from Howard Beach station, the train begins its run over Jamaica Bay with the Wildlife refuge visible from the windows. After a stop at Broad Channel, the consist reaches Rockaway where the main line splits in half.

One section heads south to its terminal at Rockaway Park-Beach 116 Street station. The other rolls north to the Far Rockaway-Mott Avenue depot.

It is noteworthy that integrating the Rockaway Line into the city's subway system required more than work on the trestle as well as along the beachfront. Considerable construction had to be done in Brooklyn itself where the IND's A Line originally terminated at Euclid Avenue, which was not that close to the original LIRR Rockaway route.

(A color photo of the Rockaway "Subway to the Sea" Line can be found on page 494.)

How to bridge the gap? That was the question.

A ramp was built enabling the A train to climb past Euclid Avenue and up to the Fulton Street elevated line. The trains then proceeded to a connection on a ramp to the former LIRR Rockaway tracks at Liberty Avenue near Woodhaven Boulevard.

Completion of the Rockaway Line improvement had tremendous impact not only on the beach community but satellite areas as well. One of them was Aqueduct Race Track, which was the first street-level stop after Rockaway Boulevard station, the latter of which was on the Fulton Street el structure.

With the Rockaway Line in operation, the TA began running Aqueduct Special trains for racing fans. One of them was Bing Crosby, horse-lover and star of screen, radio and just about everything else. The subway system received a terrific public relations boost one day when a New York *Daily News* photographer happened to notice *Der Bingle* nonchalantly holding on to a subway pole, studying the racing form on his way to the track on the Aqueduct Special.

When the picture appeared on page one the following day it moved New York straphangers to think, "Hey, if Bing Crosby rides our subway instead of taking a cab, the A train can't be all bad."

In a similar fashion—and over the same route—the Transit Authority thought it was on to a good thing when it chose to utilize its subway-to-the-Rockaways as cheap transportation to and from Kennedy International Airport situated within a short bus-ride from the "new" subway line.

Until this time New York City residents never enjoyed the convenience of an inexpensive airport commute. To change this state of affairs the TA came up with an innovative "Train To The Plane" (TTTP).

Properly operated, TTTP would have

successfully competed with Manhattan-airport bus services such as Carey and the Grey Line—at considerably lower fares.

Theoretically, TTTP was an excellent concept, but in reality it egregiously failed to fulfill its potential.

Primarily, the failing was rooted in geography and lexicography.

Its very slogan—The Train To The Plane (TTTP)—suggested that the subway indeed connected Manhattan with Kennedy Airport. Unfortunately, it missed by about a mile. And that mile-or-so meant every difference in the world in terms of TTTP's success or failure.

Actually, TTTP more accurately should have been dubbed The Train Almost To The Plane, simply because the A train's station adjoining the airport terminal was Howard Beach. From there, airport-bound passengers were required to board a city bus that commuted directly to the airport.

This somewhat minor transfer ordinarily would not trouble the average workday New Yorker but for baggage-burdened air travelers, it *was* a bit much!

TTTP lasted for 12 years before the Transit Authority abandoned it amid relatively mild protests.

Unfortunately, New York's subway history is sprinkled with abandoned projects which would have worked wonders for the city's development had they moved along through the blueprint stage to actual building.

One such project predated TTTP by more than four decades and could have been called the Subway to South Brooklyn, otherwise known as Marine Park. The pity of it all is that part of this subway *was* built and begged for completion.

If the IRT's Nostrand Avenue Line had been a piece of human body sculpture, it would have been completed from the head to the knees with nothing farther down.

What could have been an immense transit improvement began with the widespread and enthusiastically received Dual Contracts, which granted the BRT and IRT considerable construction routes in Brooklyn.

Previously, the IRT's Brooklyn rails extended as far as the Atlantic Avenue-Long Island Rail Road station. This was a portion of the original IRT Contract which included the City Hall to the Bronx route.

Once that proved a hit, the IRT belatedly lobbied for a cut of the Brooklyn pie and finally won a couple of slices before its BRT rival would snatch many of the borough's rapid transit lines for its own.

The Interborough's twin triumphs grew out of an extension of its Atlantic Avenue LIRR terminal.

After the Atlantic Avenue terminal, the IRT trains would roll southeast to stops at Bergen Street followed by Grand Army Plaza (Botanic Garden) station. At that juncture, the subway would turn left (east), speeding under beauteous Eastern Parkway with its next stop, the Brooklyn Museum.

IRT planners devised two routes growing out of the Eastern Parkway run: 1. the Nostrand Avenue Line; 2. East New York service, which would terminate at New Lots Avenue after climbing out of the tunnel to an elevated structure. After sharing tracks with the New Lots Line until Nostrand Avenue, the Flatbush-bound IRT would take a right (south) turn at Nostrand and continue for seven stations, finishing its run at the intersection of Flatbush and Nostrand Avenues. This portion of the IRT's Dual Contract project was completed in August, 1920.

Like the IRT's Bronx venture, the

Flatbush route wrought major development in an area that had considerable building potential. While Manhattan had been building north from Columbus Circle, Brooklyn was building south from Eastern Parkway, and the Nostrand Avenue IRT line merely accelerated that growth.

Apartment houses of assorted sizes—some only four stories high, others up to six floors—grew on formerly empty lots, and a major shopping area emerged at the Flatbush-Nostrand hub, locally known as "the junction." Even the Ringling Brothers and Barnum and Bailey Circus chose a site near the IRT Flatbush Avenue depot to pitch its big top for its annual appearance in mid-Brooklyn, on Nostrand Avenue near Avenue H.

One of the most notable city institutions, Brooklyn College, had its main campus located on a former golf course in Flatbush. The state's Board of Higher Education chose that site precisely because it was adjacent to the IRT's Flatbush-Nostrand terminal. The subway would provide easy access to the campus on Avenue H for students from all points in the borough. The neo-Georgian campus opened in 1937 and to this day is best serviced by the IRT.

It had been hoped that continued Brooklyn home building in the areas of Flatlands, Sheepshead Bay and Marine Park would move subway planners to extend the IRT south from Flatbush Avenue under Nostrand Avenue all the way to a terminal at Avenue U and Nostrand.

Such an extension made all the sense in the world—and still does—particularly since that southeastern part of the borough is totally bereft of rapid transit.

Hopes that such an addition would be built were raised in 1951 when voters passed a $500 million transit bond.

Although most of the monies—about $446 million—were earmarked for a brand-new, badly-needed Second Avenue subway, a Nostrand Avenue extension also was part of the package.

Sadly, neither the Second Avenue Subway nor the IRT's Nostrand Avenue Extension ever materialized. Instead, the funds were diverted to improvements on existing lines, including platform extensions for IRT locals which had been limited to four-car trains but would soon be able to run ten-car consists.

Ironically, the aborted Nostrand Avenue IRT proved a boon to summertime oceangoers after the city's Parks Department completed its magnificent Jacob Riis Park beach complex and pavilion in the midst of the Great Depression.

Although Riis Park featured an enormous automobile parking area, few people could afford cars during those difficult years. To reach the bathing paradise, Brooklynites relied on the IRT. After riding the Nostrand Avenue Line to its last stop, the beach crowd would board the Green Bus Lines' vehicles at the Flatbush-Nostrand hub for a non-stop run past Floyd Bennett Field—the first municipal airport in New York City, built in 1930—over the Marine Parkway Bridge and thence to Riis Park.

Without the IRT-Green Bus Lines connection, millions of New Yorkers never would have been able to enjoy the city's newest and best pre-World War II beach and ball fields.

A similar situation developed in terms of rapid transportation to Staten Island; that is, the failure to extend a subway to its logical terminus and, instead, employ another mode of transit to make the linkage.

During the golden age of subway construction in the Roarin' Twenties, just

JOHN JACOB ASTOR
IN THE SUBWAY

The Bas-relief of the beaver at Astor Place local station on the original (1904) IRT Line not only symbolizes builder August Belmont's accent on platform esthetics but also honors John Jacob Astor, who originally made his fame in the beaver trade.

about any subway construction anywhere in the city seemed possible—Staten Island included.

In fact, an attempt to tunnel under the Narrows, from Bay Ridge, Brooklyn, to Richmond County was begun near the present 59th Street station on the BMT's Fourth Avenue line.

According to the concept, BRT—later to be BMT—trains would link with the Staten Island Rapid Transit's surface electric railway line. What seemed like a natural project never materialized, although the SIRT invested in a fleet of 67-foot rolling stock built by the Standard Steel Car Company. The SIRT cars were precisely the size of the BRT's Standards although there were differences in design.

Based on the similarities, it was assumed that in time the SIRT's trains would be operating in the BMT tunnels, but for an assortment of reasons it was not to be.

Those who wanted to reach Staten Island by subway had to rely—as commuters still do—on IRT service to South Ferry terminal for a ferry connection across Upper New York Bay to St. George where SIRT service originates.

Such mistakes in transit planning were on the minds of Metropolitan Life Insurance Company executives when they were laying out an enormous housing complex in the Bronx.

Parkchester, when it was completed, would become one of the largest housing developments in America and Met Life wanted to be certain that it was nestled close to rapid transit; in this case, the IRT's Pelham Bay Park Line.

Long before Parkchester was built, the neighborhood in the eastern Bronx was occupied by the New York Protectory under the Christian Brothers' aegis. The Protectory combined a farm and trade school for male delinquents.

In 1948, the Met Life builders began constructing its Parkchester project. When completed in 1942 it would occupy 129 acres with 12,273 units in apartment houses ranging from seven to thirteen story buildings.

Long before the nation became saturated with shopping malls, Parkchester planners designed a shopping area unlike any other in New York City. It featured more than one hundred stores including the first Macy's department store that was not located in Manhattan.

Parkchester became a model community of its kind, partly because of its superb rapid transit access. For example, the IRT's Pelham Bay route—now the Number Six line—runs all the way to Brooklyn Bridge (City Hall) station.

By the time the last major subway line was completed in 1932, it could be said that the fingers of New York's rapid transit system touched virtually every important facet of the city's life.

Most of the links were done purposefully, as in the case of City College of New York. Its campus was located next to the IRT's original subway station at 137th Street and Broadway, completed only three years after the Broadway line began operating in 1904.

Other connections were accidental, but convenient for New Yorkers nonetheless. A good example—on the cultural front—is the Cloisters situated in Fort Tryon Park, which is about as far north as one can go on the isle of Manhattan, short of Inwood Hill Park; which extends to Spuyten Duyvil and the Harlem River.

A cultural haven on a bluff overlooking the Hudson River, the Cloisters is an unusual museum housing medieval art and architecture.

It originally was called the Barnard Cloisters, named after sculptor George Grey Barnard, who was responsible for assembling the first exhibits in Europe.

But, as a city landmark, the Cloisters—as it is now known—didn't come into its own until 1925, when the Metropolitan Museum of Art—boosted by a generous contribution by John D. Rockefeller, Jr.—bought the Cloisters.

With Rockefeller's aggressive support, the Cloisters image was boosted both literally and figuratively, thanks to his many donations. But it was the Metropolitan which really put the medieval museum on the map with a number of meaningful moves; among them a top-to-bottom remodeling of the original Barnard premises as well as expansion of the grounds.

When the "new" Cloisters re-opened—under Metropolitan's auspices—in 1938, it marked a major advance for the city's cultural community and a truly unique museum because of its treasures.

No less than five French monasteries contributed architectural monuments to the Cloisters. "Its chapels and exhibition halls contain fine works of Romanesque and Gothic art," noted Elliot S. Meadows in

The Encyclopedia of New York City, "the most notable of which are the Unicorn Tapestries."[23]

The fanfare that greeted the Cloisters' remodeling and re-opening caught the fancy of the Big Apple's art community, not to mention lay New Yorkers anxious to visit a new museum.

Cab fare to the upper reaches of Manhattan was expensive for anyone below 110th Street, but the Independent Subway still was charging only a nickel in 1938 and the IND proved to be *the* way to go in 1938.

As luck would have it, the original Eighth Avenue Subway's next-to-last stop happened to be Dyckman Street adjoining Fort Tryon Park and the Cloisters.

Thanks to the IND, the Cloisters became one of the most appreciated visiting spots in the entire city; a place for musing, museum-ing, and meditation; with a speedy underground ride thrown in for good measure!

One might wonder, while strolling through the Cloisters terraced gardens, where would New York—and New Yorkers—have been without its subway?

What It Was Like
To Ride the Subway
to Rockaway, Staten Island
and the Cloisters

Taking the train to Rockaway Beach was not a high priority in our household.

To a Williamsburger, Rockaway was a faraway place with a strange-sounding name; far away over Jamaica Bay.

When we wanted to beach it, the choices were many, varied—and closer.

Brighton Beach and Coney Island were favorites because they were a nickel subway ride away but also—once swimming was over—there were the extra, added attractions such as the Cyclone, Wonder Wheel, Bobsled and *Tirza* with her "wine bath," which was nothing more than a poor man's stripper working under a shower of grape juice.

When we wanted a cleaner beach with such amenities as outdoor showers, bath houses and a grade-A softball game thrown in, we'd head for Jacob Riis Park, even though it meant spending an extra dime each way to ride the Green Bus Lines from the subway station at Flatbush and Nostrand Avenues.

Rockaway—like Palisades Amusement Park in New Jersey—always seemed out of reach; and therein was its allure.

Every so often, I would read about Rockaway, or see a poster heralding its amusement park called Playland. I always would wonder how Playland stacked up against Coney's counterparts—Steeplechase, The Funny Place or Luna Park, which still was going strong in 1943, when I was eleven years old.

Merely out of curiosity, I wanted to visit Rockaway to see what it was all about and in the summer of 1938, I got my wish.

Those were the days when the only rapid transit across Jamaica Bay to Rockaway's peninsula belonged to the Long Island Rail Road. And like Rockaway, the LIRR was only something I had *heard* about but never had experienced first-hand.

I knew the Long Island Rail Road existed because whenever we would take the Lorimer Street trolley to see the Brooklyn Dodgers play at Ebbets Field, the streetcar would pass under the LIRR elevated structure at Atlantic and Nostrand Avenues.

On my lucky days, the trolley would stop at Atlantic just after a Long Island train had stopped at the overhead Nostrand Avenue station. To me, this was an *event*.

Why? Because LIRR rolling stock was unique to me. The cars were like subway trains in the sense that they took their power from a third rail. Long Island's cars were only slightly bigger than their IND or BMT counterparts, yet a trifle smaller than those on such *real* railways as the New York Central or the Pennsylvania systems.

Perhaps the most intriguing element of the LIRR car design—at least in the late 1930s—were the front windows. I had never seen *round* windows on any of our subway cars but there they were on the Long Island! (I later learned that because of the ball-like window design, the cars were called *Ping Pongs*.) The Tuscan red color scheme—borrowed from the parent PRR—also marked them as distinctly different from what I had seen on the subways.

Still, I had no idea what it was like to actually *ride* a Long Island train until Mom took me on the trip to Rockaway.

By subway, the closest LIRR station for us was its depot at Atlantic Avenue and Flatbush Avenue near the towering Williamsburg Savings Bank skyscraper. It was easy enough to reach now that the IND's GG line had been operating for a year right under our house on Marcy Avenue.

We got on at good, old (actually young!) Myrtle-Willoughby station, heading toward Downtown Brooklyn, but instead of getting off at Hoyt-Schermerhorn, we alighted one stop earlier, Fulton Street.

This marked the first time I had ever

YOGI BERRA, PROFESSIONAL ATHLETES, AND THE SUBWAY

Baseball players, and their counterparts in football, basketball and hockey, have frequently used the subway to get to their respective ball parks or arenas.

When the Brooklyn Dodgers played their home games at Ebbets Field in Flatbush (Brooklyn), some of them lived at the Hotel New Yorker on Eighth Avenue and 34th Street in Manhattan.

To reach the stadium, they would walk a few blocks to Herald Square (34th and Sixth Avenue) where they would ride the Brighton (BMT) Express to Prospect Park station, which was a short distance from Ebbets Field.

When Yogi Berra was a rookie with the New York Yankees in 1946, the Bronx Bombers played an exhibition game against the Dodgers at Ebbets Field.

"I took the subway from the Bronx," says Berra, "and I got lost. I had never been on the subway before. Luckily, I made it to the ball park just in time.

"The next day I left an hour early 'cause I didn't want to get lost again!"

Many of the Dodgers, who lived in Brooklyn, rode the BMT from their home station to Prospect Park.

In his rookie year (1947), the Dodgers famed rookie, Jackie Robinson, was photographed by a New York Daily Mirror cameraman while riding the BMT to work one afternoon.

The photo later was used by the Metropolitan Transit Authority for one of its MetroCard promotions.

exited the GG at any station other than Myrtle-Willoughby or Hoyt-Schermerhorn, so I was already feeling excited about the trip.

Once we reached daylight at Lafayette and Fulton Streets, Mom directed me toward Hanson Place and the Williamsburg Savings Bank tower.

The bank skyscraper meant to Brooklynites what the Empire State Building was to Manhattan. It was an architectural version of the Brooklyn Dodgers; extremely likeable and attractive, if not exactly a champion in its class.

I thought the building was just terrific when I viewed it up close in 1938, because of the four-faced clock which was the largest in the world.

Our skyscraper—the tallest in Brooklyn—was only nine years old when I ogled it for the first time that day and it still offered an air of newness right up to the gilded dome at the top. I remember thinking how great it felt to be a Brooklynite as opposed to those poor saps who lived in the other four boroughs.

En route to the LIRR we also passed the Brooklyn Academy of Music, Kings County's answer to the Metropolitan Opera House.

This, too, was a classic structure, erected in 1908—the year my father, Ben, graduated from Public School 149 in East New York—and featured not only an opera house but also a playhouse and ballroom. The first time I visited the place was to see a Punch and Judy puppet show a year earlier.

At Flatbush Avenue we turned left, and there before us was Brooklyn's version of a railroad terminal—economy sized. Had it been in Peoria or Dubuque, the LIRR depot might have been more impressive, but since I was comparing it with Grand Central and Penn Stations, it was somewhat to the left of awesome.

Riding the Rapid in Staten Island

The Staten Island Rapid Transit is in a class by itself. Shortly after leaving St. George Terminal, the line passes through its only short tunnel. In non-rush-hours, the trains were almost always of two cars. The photo was taken in 1968.

This line was electrified in 1925 with BMT Standard-style cars, because there was serious talk of building a tunnel from Brooklyn to Staten Island, thereby linking the Richmond line with the BMT. Here the train approaches its Tompkinsville station.

William Brennan

Clifton, on Staten Island, was the site where the South Beach Line diverged from the Tottenville Line on the Rapid. The South Beach branch was abandoned in 1953. The tower that controlled this junction is visible behind the train.

William Brennan

The Staten Island Rapid cars looked more like railroad cars than New York subway rolling stock for three reasons: (a) There was a headlight over the center end door; (b) A small cowcatcher hung at the ends; (c) Two of the automatic side doors were located at the very ends of the car, forming cab-vestibules. This small station at Old Town was lengthened when the line was completely grade-separated from cross streets.

William Brennan

About to stop at Dongan Hills, this example of the Staten Island Rapid reveals front windows that open, as well as screening which covered all windows on the cars.

384 THE SUBWAY AND THE CITY

William Brennan

Before its annexation into the city system, the Staten Island Rapid was owned by the Baltimore and Ohio Railroad. In that era, the Rapid operated under B&O signaling and its book of rules. Even after the city takeover, the line continued for a time to operate under B&O regulations. As one can see, the New Dorp station has more the feel of a rural railroad depot than that of a rapid transit stop.

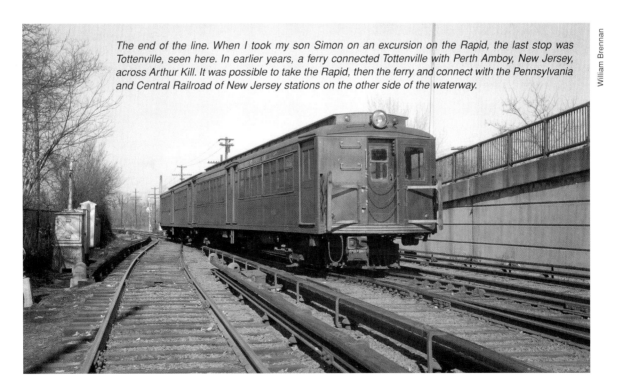

The end of the line. When I took my son Simon on an excursion on the Rapid, the last stop was Tottenville, seen here. In earlier years, a ferry connected Tottenville with Perth Amboy, New Jersey, across Arthur Kill. It was possible to take the Rapid, then the ferry and connect with the Pennsylvania and Central Railroad of New Jersey stations on the other side of the waterway.

William Brennan

That, of course, didn't detract from my excitement over riding the LIRR for the first time. I followed Mom down the steps to the platform where our train was waiting. I was tempted to pet the outside of the car but my mother was tugging hard, not wanting to have the doors close in our faces.

We took our seats on the right hand side of the car where—to my amazement—the window already had been opened all the way to the top. (Those were the simpler days when railroads worried less about passengers sticking their fool heads out of the windows.) I didn't exactly thrust my cranium through the opening, but I sure was tickled that the possibility existed!

While looking over the car, I instantly realized that it was nothing like the subway. All seats were railroad-style, facing forward in pairs; there were no ceiling fans nor center doors, but there were overhead racks for luggage.

Heading east, the train rolled through a tunnel under Atlantic Avenue until it reached Bedford Avenue, where it climbed out of the portal, arriving at the Nostrand Avenue station, which I had previously viewed from trolleys below.

Once we accelerated out of Nostrand, I was taken by the fact that—unlike our traditional New York City els—there were no rails nor walkways on the right side of the tracks. In fact, there was *nothing*.

Nothing but the street below.

As I peered out the window and looked down, I couldn't see a stitch of the elevated structure and suddenly got nervous about the possibility of our speeding LIRR train tilting over and falling down to Atlantic Avenue below.

And when I say "speeding," I mean *speeding!*

This was a gallop, the likes of which I never had experienced on any subway. Atlantic Avenue was becoming one big blur, and I was feeling the kind of exhiliration-fear blend that I would experience years later on the Cyclone roller coaster. This was the *big* league of rapid transit.

The train finally slowed down for a stop at East New York junction before moving on east to Jamaica. From this point on, the ride offered a different brand of excitement as we turned south, with Jamaica Bay in our sights.

All this time I was positively overwhelmed by the rush of wind through the open window—the distinct *clickety-clack-clickety-clack* of wheels over rail joints—all with much greater force than I had experienced on the Brighton, GG or even the very-fast A express.

Never during any subway or el trip prior to this one had I known what it was like to ride a rapid transit vehicle so close to the water.

Taking the Broadway (Brooklyn) BMT over the Williamsburg Bridge—or the Brighton BMT over the Manhattan Bridge—meant we *were* over water (East River), but the river was so far below the tracks, it was virtually invisible.

On the other hand, once our Long Island Rail Road train reached the wooden trestle leading to Rockaway, I felt that I could reach down and actually *touch* the water; it was that close.

There was no speeding over this rickety-looking, fragile-sounding span. The wooden structure reminded me of a trestle I had recently seen in the Paramount Pictures film, *Union Pacific*. It didn't seem capable of bearing the weight of LIRR's steel cars without buckling, but somehow it did, and we reached Rockaway in one piece; although my heartbeat was very audible throughout the ride.

I remember less about Rockaway than I do about the train ride to the beachfront, other than the fact that the surf was intense; wavy in the Riis Park manner. Playland's roller coaster was smaller than the Cyclone, the frozen custard (vanilla) excellent and the train ride back was better than anything!

As Mom and I walked out of the Long Island terminal on Atlantic Avenue, I wondered how I would react to the GG local after the lightning-fast LIRR experience.

Just as I had feared, the ride from Fulton Street to Myrtle-Willoughby was a huge letdown, especially when I realized that the windows on our Brooklyn-Queens Crosstown Local didn't even open from the bottom. Hence, I couldn't even look out of them had I wanted to—not that I did!

It only took a couple of weeks to get over my LIRR love affair because I knew in my heart of hearts that it would be a long time before I'd be back on those very-fast trains again.

The frustration of riding a local like the GG was matched in boredom by the IRT's Nostrand Avenue Line, which was an express in Manhattan, but turned local coming off Eastern Parkway for its seven-station, southerly spin to Flatbush and Nostrand, where we would transfer to the Green Bus Lines bouncing to the glories of Riis Park.

For me, the frustration had less to do with the creeping crawl under Nostrand from President Street to Sterling to Winthrop to Church to Beverly and Newkirk before grinding to a halt at the Brooklyn College terminal.

Even as a ten-year-old, I sensed that there was something very wrong about the IRT coming to a final halt before a track bumper only half-way across Brooklyn.

"Why," I wondered, "would the IRT—whose trains went to the very northern edge of the Bronx—not extend itself to the southern tip of Brooklyn?"

What I really wanted was for the train to continue past the Flatbush-Nostrand hub, turn left (South) on to Flatbush and roll all the way to Marine Parkway Bridge and right up to the Riis Park bathing pavilion.

That's what I wanted. And I figured that if the BMT could extend itself all the way to Stillwell and Surf Avenues in Coney Island—just one block from the beach—the IRT should have been able to do likewise *vis-à-vis* Riis Park.

Well, I could dream, couldn't I? And I did; but the extension of the Nostrand Avenue IRT never happened, although it made all the sense in the world; the same held for a subway to Staten Island.

As a Brooklynite, I viewed Richmond County, across the Bay, as the exact equivalent of New Jersey; with the exception of Hoboken or Newark, which could easily be reached via the Hudson Tubes.

Why in the world—at least that was our thinking—would anyone from Brooklyn want to go to Staten Island?

Well, there were three possible reasons: (A) To see relatives who lived there; (B) To visit the Staten Island Zoo or Clove Lakes Park; or (C) Just to ride the Staten Island Ferry for the fun of it, which included sailing right past the Statue of Liberty.

In my case, "A" was out since we had no uncles, aunts or cousins on the island.

"B" was a possibility except that the Staten Island Zoo was no bigger or better than the Prospect Park Zoo, which was much, much closer.

When all was said and done, we went to Staten Island only to turn around and go right back to Manhattan.

We went to Staten Island only to gaze at the Statue of Liberty, to wonder what the heck was doing on Governor's Island and to have a peek at Ellis Island.

My most memorable trip to Staten Island as an adult was because of "C" plus some curiosity about the place.

I had decided that my younger son, Simon, should see as much of the city as possible, and since Richmond County was as legitimate a part of the city as Kings County, Queens County or New York County, he deserved a look at the place.

Since we lived on West 110th Street in the Upper West Side—some would call it Morningside Heights—our subway of proximity and choice was the original IRT Broadway Line.

This was in the early 1980s, when the Transit Authority still had the good sense to operate subway cars with clear front windows, out of which train nuts such as myself could view the tracks ahead.

Whenever I would take either of my sons—Simon or his older brother, Ben—for a subway ride, I invariably would carry one of them on my shoulders, stand at the front window and both of us would observe the passing parade of stations, trains and tracks.

Ever since my wife, Shirley, and I moved to the Upper West Side in 1968, my affection for the IRT—little when I was a youth—had grown by yards and yards. My appreciation of the Broadway Line had to do with its history and its configuration.

This was a living, speeding, working landmark.

This was the first of its kind and, essentially, was performing as well as it had on opening day in 1904. Not many transit lines could make that statement!

Plus, it was a fun line to ride.

From 96th Street station, all the way down to Chambers Street (City Hall), the Interborough ran as both express and local. But it was the former which produced the genuine excitement.

Both the Wakefield (2) and 148th Street (3) expresses barged through the tunnels with an exuberance that made you believe that they were champion track stars on wheels.

Those were the days when the IRT still utilized rolling stock which featured front windows that opened, just like the old BMT Standards. With my son, Ben—later it was Simon—perched on my shoulder, I would bend my knees just enough so that the lad could see through the window and savor the subway wind.

The breeze was particularly powerful on the southbound express sprint from 34th Street to 14th Street and then, again, from 14th to Chambers. Sometimes I had to back up away from the window, because the breeze felt like a hurricane-force wind to the youngster.

At Chambers Street station, we would cross the platform and complete our trip on the local for three more stops before our train noisily crawled left around the curve, screeching like a banshee before coming to a stop in one of the stranger terminals on the entire system.

The South Ferry stop dated back to 1905, when the Broadway-Seventh Avenue local comprised only four cars. In fact, the station's curved configuration was very similar to that of the original IRT City Hall station, from where the very first Interborough train made its way uptown in 1904.

Because the platform at South Ferry could now hold only five cars, passengers in the last five cars had to make their way to the first five in order to debark.

My kids never seemed to mind walking between cars, whether the train was at a full stop or whether it was going at high speed. Since I had been a walker-between-cars all my life, I worried not a bit about myself but was extra careful with the boys.

The Staten Island ferry ride, as always, was wonderful, especially since the day was clear and we could almost look Lady Liberty right in the eyes.

As we approached Staten Island, I did my best to explain to my son how a fifth borough, which was much closer to New Jersey, actually was legally part of New York City. (The lads never really believed the tale that a sailboat race between representatives of each state actually resulted in a New York win and thus Richmond became part of the Empire State.)

After walking off the ferry ramp, we made a right turn and followed signs leading to the *very* unusual Staten Island Rapid Transit line (SIRT).

I was very excited; probably more so than my son; and for good reason. After all, I had been riding subways all of my life and yet never once had stepped aboard an SIRT train, although I knew all about the line's history.

Naturally, I was hoping we could ride one of the ancient 67-foot BMT-style cars with the big headlight in front, but as soon as we reached the SIRT platform, I saw that the rolling stock had been upgraded to modern, stainless steel types like those on the mainland.

Once we departed the St. George (ferry) terminal on the way to Tompkinsville, we both realized that this was going to be like no train ride we had ever taken; for both better and worse.

The bad news was that, compared to the high-speed IRT, the SIRT moved at something just above a crawl. The good news was that we were experiencing more of a railroad *ambience* than anything on the mainland.

I explained to my son that the reason why the SIRT had a railroad feel to it was simply because it once *was* a railroad. And for that we could look back in history to the mid-19th Century and thank entrepreneur Cornelius Vanderbilt, who already had made a mint in the ferry business.

Vanderbilt helped bankroll what was to be the original Staten Island Railroad, and in 1860 the line that eventually would become part of the New York City transit system opened for business. It connected the towns of Vanderbilt's Landing (now Clifton) and Eltingville, seven and one-half miles south.

The railroad was a source of conversation even before its official opening. Its unique iron locomotive, the Albert Journea, named for the president of the railroad, caused quite a stir, as reported in the March 21,1860 edition of the *Staten Island Gazette*:

"The locomotive has been indulging itself, since its arrival by making pleasant little trips on the railroad as far as New Dorp, and has been quite useful in conveying materials…where required for use. Each day it is the subject of renewed comment and admiration by those who reside along the line transversed….One old man among the number had never seen a locomotive. He said he lived between 'Iron Spring' and 'Skunk's Misery,' and has walked five miles to take a look. As 'She' advanced with a shriek, he

jumped about a foot, and exclaimed 'I swear,' but as he was dumb thereafter, we cannot say what he thought of it."

A second locomotive was added in May 1860 and service extended to Annadale. A month later the line moved on to Tottenville and the dream of a quarter-century was realized. Staten Island had its railroad. But it wasn't a very pleasant dream right from the start. Revenue was slower in coming than the line's locomotives and, less than a year after it had opened, the railroad was threatened with foreclosure by the New Jersey Locomotive Works for failure to pay the bills on the two steam engines. An SOS was sent out to Commodore Vanderbilt, who responded by dispatching his son to Staten Island as the line's receiver and making some adjustments with ferry operators to synchronize their arrivals and departures with the railroad.

But good fortune never would smile on the Staten Island line, and one of a long list of tragedies occurred on July 30, 1871 when the ferryboat *Westfield*, co-operated by the railroad, blew up at the Whitehall Street pier in lower Manhattan, killing sixty-six passengers. It also killed the railroad for a number of years.

The line made a comeback in 1883 when Robert Garrett, president of the Baltimore & Ohio Railroad, was approached as a backer of a revived Staten Island Railway. Garrett realized that the Baltimore & Ohio needed a railhead in New York City and immediately supported the plan. The new company was called the Staten Island Rapid Transit Railroad Company, becoming the first to apply the words "rapid transit" to a railroad. Thus, the country's oldest railroad to become a rapid transit operation merged with the Baltimore & Ohio, America's oldest railroad.

On July 31, 1884, thirteen years and a day after the old line had ceased to operate, the SIRT began service between Clifton and Tompkinsville. New lines were added, and by the early 1890s it appeared that boom years were just ahead. But they never materialized. Trolley cars were introduced to the island before the turn of the century and they began cutting into the SIRT patronage. By 1899 the railroad was in big trouble again. It went bankrupt and, this time, was bought outright by the Baltimore & Ohio for the "upset price" of $2 million at an auction.

Although ridership was less than encouraging in the early years of the twentieth century, the Baltimore & Ohio bosses saw some hope in the possibility of a connection with Brooklyn across the bay. Engineers for the Brooklyn Rapid Transit Company (later the BMT) suggested that as part of the Fourth Avenue (Brooklyn) subway project, a connecting subway tunnel be bored under the Narrows (lower New York Bay) to St. George in Staten Island.

The idea was well received and likely would have been pushed to fruition were it not for a freakish turn of fate involving the BRT's Brighton Line at Malbone Street in Brooklyn which killed ninety-seven passengers and bankrupted the line. For the moment, at least, tunneling to Staten Island was out of the question.

Meanwhile, revenues took an upward turn for the SIRT in the early twenties as the island's population grew. In 1921, more than 13 million people rode the Baltimore & Ohio's rapid transit route compared to only 2,460,000 in 1907. Tunnel talk was stirring again, and this time it appeared to be so much a certainty that realtors began speaking of a Staten Island land boom to follow the new sub-

MYSTERIES OF GRAND CENTRAL—I

The subway area around Grand Central Terminal has been sprinkled with peculiar tunnels, passage-ways and lay-up tracks ever since the IRT's founder, August Belmont, had a secret entrance to his orig-inal Interborough line built in the basement of the Hotel Belmont.

After dining in his sumptuous subterranean club room, Belmont would escort his friends to the secret entrance where they then would board his private subway car, Mineola, for a ride along the IRT tracks.

A similar connection at Grand Central was provided for President Franklin Delano Roosevelt in the 1930s but for a less frivolous reason.

Because the Chief Executive suffered from polio, his advisors felt that it would be politically pru-dent to conceal that fact from the electorate for public relations and morale purposes.

On the occasions when FDR visited New York, he would stay at the Waldorf-Astoria Hotel. His entourage would come to the city on the New York Central Raiilroad via the system's Park Avenue viaduct. The train would then tunnel under the thoroughfare from 96th Street to its destination, Grand Central Terminal.

In order to shield the president from the public, a secret underground platform—not far from the IRT East Side subway along Lexington Avenue—was utilized.

Adjacent to Track 61, the platform connected to a six-foot-wide freight elevator and also to the Waldorf.

The presidential train would prematurely stop before reaching the depot, allowing FDR to leave by the concealed exit under the hotel at 49th Street and Park Avenue.

Once off the train, Roosevelt would be whisked through the Waldorf's garage and—surrounded by Secret Service agents—up to his private suite.

way tunnel. In 1925, headings for the tunnel were begun and an elaborate track connection in which the SIRT would link with the BMT Sea Beach line in the Fourth Avenue tunnel had been worked out. Unfortunately, the planners never cleared it with the politicians.

New York's Mayor John Hylan had been an enemy of the BRT since 1907, when he had been working as a motorman on the line and his alleged carelessness had almost killed a towerman. He was fired and bore a grudge against the line, and its suc-cessor, the BMT, ever afterward. New York State's Governor Al Smith was, in 1925, owner of considerable Pennsylvania Rail-road stock. A link between the Baltimore & Ohio's Staten Island line and the BMT could, conceivably, have hurt the Pennsylvania Railroad.

Cynical New York City political pundits believe that neither Hylan nor Smith want-ed a Staten Island-Brooklyn rail tunnel to be realized. Work on the tunnel, which had begun in both boroughs, stopped abruptly soon after it had begun. Nobody is certain why it happened, but the project was never again resumed. Meanwhile, in antici-pation of a coupling with the BMT, the SIRT had electrified the system and pur-chased a fleet of BMT-type cars for use on its own lines.

Despite the tunnel setback, the SIRT continued to move forward.

Grade crossings were eliminated wher-ever possible, and by the early forties, the line was as healthy as it ever would be. But soon after World War II had ended, the city began consolidating transit facilities and, in 1948, the Board of Transportation annexed the Staten Island bus routes. It immediately reduced fares and, in so doing, sliced SIRT revenues by 60 percent.

The SIRT saw the handwriting on the wall and tried to unload the entire system on the city, but the answer for the moment was negative.

Once again there was hope of a rail link to Brooklyn—this time by bridge. The Triborough Bridge and Tunnel Authority was given approval to erect a huge bridge across the Narrows, and in 1964 the span was completed. Unfortunately, its most vocal supporter was Robert Moses, who had vast political clout at that time. Moses, who consistently vetoed rapid transit in favor of the private automobile, insisted that the SIRT and the BMT be kept off the bridge and, as usual, Moses triumphed.

Still the SIRT limped along, serving those Staten Islanders who appreciated a pleasant train ride to the New York ferries. When the Metropolitan Transportation Authority (MTA) annexed the Transit Authority in 1968, new life was pumped into the SIRT. A fleet of shiny silver commuter trains was installed, replacing the old BMT-type cars that had been in use since 1925, many of which were actually later used in BMT service.

Cosmetically, the SIRT was never in better shape, but its financial state was less attractive. The failure of the line to link directly by rail with Brooklyn was its most significant drawback and ridership remained disheartingly low.

This was evident as Simon and I checked out the platforms at stop after stop. From Clifton station to Grasmere;

from Old Town to Dongan Hills; the SIRT had more of a *Toonerville Trolley* feel to it than a major rapid transit arm of New York City.

Not that we weren't enjoying the ride. Even the odd-sounding station names were fun to read—GRANT CITY, NEW DORP, OAKWOOD HEIGHTS, BAY TERRACE, GREAT KILLS, ELTINGVILLE, ANNADALE, HUGUENOT, PRINCESS BAY.

By the time our train swung and swayed its way into the Pleasant Plains stop, I felt we were in some Upstate town like Warrensburg or New Paltz; the scene was so markedly different than anything on the IND, BMT or IRT lines.

Our final destination was Tottenville, which was finally reached after stops at Nassau and Atlantic stations.

Frankly, I didn't know what to expect at the SIRT's southern terminus but the result was even lower than my expectations. As depots go, Tottenville had very little to offer so, after exiting the SIRT, Simon and I took a walking tour of the community.

Since Tottenville directly faced Perth Amboy, New Jersey across the bay, I was hoping to find some nice waterfront park, a promenade or *something* that would afford us a spot to enjoy the nautical surroundings.

But there was nothing; I mean *nothing.* What waterfront there was consisted of shipyard relics, messy driftwood and assorted flotsam and jetsam that had one common denominator: they were ugly to the eye.

To say that Tottenville was a disappointment would be an enormous understatement. After a short stroll around the side streets, Simon and I couldn't return to the train fast enough. Before boarding, we did find one item of interest. Sitting at a siding, a lone SIRT 67-footer from the 1920s caught our eye.

It was in relatively good shape, but appeared to be abandoned and forlorn. We took a good look at it before getting back on the stainless steel car that had carried us to Tottenville and eagerly awaited our return trip to St. George and the ferry ride returning us to Manhattan's version of civilization.

All things considered, railroading through Staten Island was like a trip through time on a rural branch line. For that aspect alone, it was a pleasant adventure, although not one I would like to experience more than once a decade.

On the other hand, a subway trip to Rockaway—over the Transit Authority's rebuilt line—is one that I could enjoy every month. Granted, it's not as much fun as my first ride to Rockaway on the Long Island Rail Road was with my mother, a good six-decades-plus ago but, still, it had some enjoyable moments.

One afternoon, my friend—and professional photographer—Dave Perlmutter and I toured Rockaway via the A train and its country cousin, the Rockaway Park Shuttle.

What's so interesting about Rockaway's subway-el is the manner in which it branches into two distinct lines after leaving the Broad Channel stop in the middle of Jamaica Bay.

The "main" line for the A Train turns left (North) on the peninsula for five stops before terminating at Far Rockaway-Mott depot. Rockaway Park-Beach 116th Street, the Southern depot, is reached by the Shuttle which takes a right (South) turn before reaching Beach 90th Street station and two more—Beach 98th, Beach 105th—all within view of the Atlantic Ocean.

For starters, Dave and I rode the Rockaway Park Shuttle to Broad Channel, which was a joy in itself.

After paralleling the beachfront, the Shuttle turns left (north) where it meets the main line (Far Rockaway) in a nifty "Y" track formation and then rides over the waves on the first of two trestles rebuilt by the TA by realigning the railroad route and radically changing the islands in the bay. All of this was done before the Broad Channel IND station made its debut on June 28, 1956.

Riding a subway train while seagulls perched on the track signals ahead is something I don't experience very often. And that's one of several fascinating aspects of Rockaway Line commuting.

Getting off at Broad Channel is an experience in and of itself; much more so than even the visit to Staten Island's Tottenville. Anyone from the mainland who has visited Broad Channel knows that he or she is in New York City's *Outback*.

Anyone who has studied Broad Channel's history and geography understands why. To begin with it is *the only inhabited island in Jamaica Bay.*

Early in the 19th Century it merely was an uninhabited isle west of a waterway which happened also to be named Broad Channel. Accessible only by water, Broad Channel became a haven for fishermen who built a few hovels from which to stash their gear and accommodate themselves until they took their boats back to the city.

When the first railroad reached Rockaway, four fishing platforms embellished construction of the five-mile-long trestle. This was the prelude of Broad Channel becoming established as a full-fledged anglers paradise complete with a hotel and saloon.

With Jamaica Bay's nautical attractions

Long after the New York Central Railroad folded, Grand Central Terminal was converted into a depot exclusively for suburban commuter lines linking upstate New York and Connecticut with Manhattan.

In addition, an exclusive Metro-North train was provided for President George W. Bush— when he stayed at the Waldorf-Astoria Hotel—in case of an emergency.

The escape option, available in the event of a terrorist attack, involved an arrangement similar in some ways to the secret exit provided for President Franklin Delano Roosevelt when he visited New York City.

However, there was one significant difference. In the case of President Bush, the new, full-size train is always running and ready for instant exit should there be an emergency.

Publicized during the 2003 opening of the United Nations General Assembly session in September of that year, the emergency Metro-North consist was dubbed by the Media The Dubya Train.

It sat at Track 61 and was easily reached from the hotel via the Waldorf garage and freight elevator which links with the underground train platform.

The New York Post revealed in its September 26, 2003 edition: In the event of a security breach, Bush and other leaders could have boarded the train, which could then have sped off to a secure location.

The platform and adjacent tracks are normally used as a yard for out-of-sevice Metro-North trains and can be seen by commuters going in and out of Grand Central.

available for tourists—rowboats were available for rent—the hamlet was on its way to establishing a presence. This was clear in 1924 when Cross Bay Boulevard was extended through the community.

Long Island Rail Road service did little for Broad Channel in comparison to the IND which, for a much lower fare, provided direct service from as far north as 207th Street in Manhattan (Inwood) as well as many parts of Brooklyn.

Through it all, Broad Channel has militantly maintained its personality as a quiet, predominantly Irish village, priding itself on independence—not to mention distance—from mainlanders.

During our stop there, Dave and I could see the flag-draped streets, where a population of less than 3,000 minds its own business; and wishes that visitors would too, whether the A train runs through town or not.

And believe me, that A Train *does* run. From Broad Channel to its next stop, Howard Beach-JFK Airport, the seamless, welded rail provides a smooth, straightaway trackbed that seems to move the train to a gallop.

We were fortunate to ride on one of the older, stainless steel cars that still had the full-size front window out of which we could view both sides of the bay, not to mention Kennedy Airport in the distance to the right, beyond the water.

The stop at Howard Beach was *almost,* but not quite, as enthralling as Broad Channel. For here was another extraordinarily non-New York-type community within the Queens County boundary line.

Although it, too, is on the water, Howard Beach's roots are considerably different from Broad Channel's.

Rather than fishing being its attraction, goats provided a *raison d'etre* for the community because a glove-maker named William J. Howard needed skins for his mitts. What could be better for kid gloves than goat skins? On a 150-acre meadow, Howard operated his goat farm and thereby kept his company in business during the 1890s.

Not long afterward, Howard realized that his waterside acreage could be suitable for more than just goats. He purchased adjacent land, created even more by filling in the water and made a pitch for visitors by establishing a hotel alongside bungalows.

The moment he realized he was on to a good thing, Howard continued to expand the property which eventually came under the umbrella of the Howard Estates Development Company. This was the start of something really big, and by 1913, the Long Island Rail Road opened a station—originally called Ramblersville, later changed to Howard Beach—for the community.

Howard saw to it that his development featured all necessary amenities, including water and gas. He built homes that attracted city folk, and by the conclusion of World War I it had become a much-sought maritime village within the borough.

When we toured Howard Beach, it was evident how much it had grown with no less than four elementary schools among its many civic assets. To me, the most arresting aspects of Howard Beach were the homes—some of them on stilts—sitting on top of the water; or so it seemed. If ever New York had a truly *seaside* town of its own, Howard Beach was it.

And let's not forget that it also has regular subway service to and from the city.

Our city-bound train next stopped at Aqueduct-North Conduit Avenue station, the last of those on the ballast-bed track that had been a straightaway en route to Rockaway.

Once the A Train rolled north out of Aqueduct, the surroundings rapidly changed from rural to urban. We soon could see the ancient elevated line on Liberty Avenue where another version of the A moved east to a terminal at Lefferts Boulevard in Ozone Park.

The train slowed before taking a left-handed curve. This led to a cozy climb on center tracks between the pair of Ozone Park tracks.

As we reached the outer tracks, our consist lurched to the right, over the switch and screeched its way on to the elevated station. Here at Rockaway Boulevard, the fun part of our Rockaway excursion was over. That was obvious since there was no marine life in sight anymore.

Such elevated runs can be a treat if they follow a long trip underground. I always had that feeling when riding the IRT in Manhattan. It was most fun when the trains emerged from the tunnels and climbed to the elevated tracks where I could see the light of day; or night, as it were.

Of all such trips, the most memorable took place in the early 1950s when I was still single and dating girls who, for the most part, lived in Brooklyn or, on rare occasions, Manhattan.

We had an unwritten rule among the boys in Williamsburg that one never would travel as far as the Bronx on a date because it simply was *too* far. A blind date in the Bronx was simply out of the question.

Yet, one day a college buddy named Al Guskin told me that he had an aunt living in the Bronx whose daughter purportedly was a raving beauty. Out of the goodness of his heart, Guskin was offering me Lydia's phone number.

"But," I asked, "what about our unwritten rule? She lives in the Bronx."

"Rules," Guskin replied, "are made to be broken. And when you see Lydia, you'll understand why."

I hesitated but Pal Al was unrelenting in his salesmanship. He described her as a "Can't Miss Chick"—whatever that meant—and threw in a few other come-ons until my appetite had been sufficiently whet.

Plus, Guskin knew I was a subway nut and then tossed in the clincher: "Besides, you've never taken the train to Parkchester, have you?"

Parkchester? I didn't even know where it was. My only knowledge of Parkchester came in the form of newspaper ads for Macy's Department Store. At the bottom of the ad there always was a postscript that read, "*Also Available At Our Parkchester Store.*"

Ten minutes of Guskin's salesmanship wore me down. I took Lydia's phone number, returned home and called her.

She sounded pleasant enough; we chatted for a bit and then I asked her for a Friday night date.

No problem.

Lydia gave me her address and directions on the IRT. She lived on Theriot Avenue just a few blocks from Parkchester. (Talk about far away places with strange sounding names!) That meant I had to eventually take the Pelham Bay Line and get off at St. Lawrence Avenue station.

At that point in time I didn't even know that a St. Lawrence Avenue even existed.

My trek to Parkchester was greeted with great skepticism by the lads in my crowd. The obvious question was why *shlep* up to the Bronx when there were plenty of gorgeous datable girls in Brooklyn?

Never would I have let on to my buddies that the true reason for my making the trip was to see firsthand what the Pelham Bay Line was all about.

As expected, it was a *shlep*.

Make that a *shlep*-and-a-half.

I started with the GG; switched to the A at Hoyt-Schermerhorn and rode it to Times Square. At 42nd Street, I walked over to the IRT Shuttle running to Grand Central and then found the platform for the Pelham Bay Line.

By the time I had reached the Bronx, I had forgotten how long the trip was taking. I was too busy gaping at what for me was virgin territory; and that was no reflection on Lydia by any means.

In fact, I was so taken by such neighborhoods as Crotona Park East, Bronx River and Bruckner that I almost forgot to get off at St. Lawrence Avenue. I just made it through the closing doors.

As I skipped down the steps from the elevated's platform on that fateful Friday in February, it suddenly dawned on me that not only was it awfully cold in the Bronx but snow was falling at a rapid rate. A weatherman would have called it a blizzard.

Actually, tickled with the snow—I always loved a good snowstorm—I made my way to Lydia's apartment house, rode the elevator to the sixth floor and rather tentatively rang the bell.

I never trusted Guskin's build-up so I had fully prepared myself for a letdown.

Suddenly, the door opened and there in living color was the beauteous Lydia Cohen. Well, let me re-phrase it. She wasn't exactly Betty Grable—or Catherine Zeta-Jones, for that matter—but Lydia was damn good-looking. Quickly, I lifted my temporary curse on Guskin.

Not only was Lydia fetching, she was a good sport. When I asked her where she would like to go—movie, of course—she said, "How about roller skating?"

That's my kind of gal. Athletic, vivacious. A cheap date!

Hey, how much could it cost at the Fordham Rollerdrome? With soda and carfare; just a couple of bucks. I was so interested in Lydia that I have completely forgotten how we traveled from Theriot Avenue to Fordham Road. But we got there, blizzard and all, rented skates and then skate-danced the night away.

Lydia not only was pretty but she had a nice pair of legs—I've always been a legman—and since she had worn a skirt, the gams were evident all evening.

Also evident was the indisputable fact that Lydia wasn't quite as enamoured of me as I was with her. In plain English, the vice wasn't versa.

Gentleman to the end, I dutifully escorted my Bronx beauty back to her digs and even stole a kiss; but all I got was her left cheek and that was that.

Upon leaving Theriot Avenue, I trudged through the snowdrifts toward Westchester Avenue and the St. Lawrence Avenue station. By now the snow was blinding and piling up sufficiently in the streets to limit traffic to only an occasional vehicle.

I finally found the el, climbed to the change booth level and then to the platform.

Train nut that I am, I refused to warm myself around the pot-bellied stove near the change booth. Instead, I walked right out on to the platform and straight to the front where the lead car would stop.

As intense as the storm had become, I really didn't mind, although I was more than mildly depressed about the outcome of my short life with Lydia.

"What did I do wrong?" I asked in what evolved into a long dialogue with myself. "Would she ever go out with me again?" And so it went as the snow piled on the signals, covered the tracks and turned St. Lawrence Station into a replica of an Alaskan Railroad depot.

After considerable musing, it suddenly dawned on me that I had been standing at the IRT station for a long time. Not a train could be seen—in either direction—and now the cold was finding cracks in my overcoat while the snow drifted over my galoshes.

I wasn't exactly freezing to death but I *was* freezing. And now I was worrying.

Was it possible that the IRT had shut down because of the blizzard? Would I wind up as a semi-permanent snowman to be discovered the next morning when the snow finally stopped?

If I decided to leave the station, where in the world would I go to escape the Bronx and return to my beloved Brooklyn?

Over a forty-five minute period, I debated these and other frigid questions until, at last, I detected a faint, flickering light in the distance, near East 177th Street station. "Alas!" I muttered through my frozen lips, "the IRT rescue train was on its way. With or without St. Bernard dog, it would be most welcome."

As it rolled toward the platform's head, the train was an unusual study in white as windblown snow flew off the roof and on to the station. I prayed that it would not pass me by and my prayers were answered.

The curses I had bestowed on the IRT were gradually retracted in direct proportion to the growing warmth inside the coach. Not that it got *that* warm but it was all relative at that point in time.

I remember thinking, as the Pelham Bay local dove into the tunnel, out of snow's reach, that this was one of those rare times when I preferred being underground rather that outside on the el.

It wasn't until I finally delivered myself to the GG local that I felt any semblance of warmth. That R-9 car knew how to throw out the heat and by the time I emerged from Myrtle-Willoughby station—a good two-and-a-half hours after mounting the IRT el steps—I actually felt like a human being again.

Late the next day, I met Al Guskin at our local candy store.

"So how was Lydia?" he wondered.

"Al," I replied, "it was a toss-up who was colder for me, Lydia or the IRT!"

———————————

PART II

SUBWAY SERIES

Rival managers Casey Stengel of the New York Yankees and Chuck Dressen of the Brooklyn Dodgers share a friendly handshake at the New York dugout before opening game of the 1953 World Series. Casey was seeking a fifth straight title.

CHAPTER ELEVEN

Trains on Television— Metro's Subway Series

The term "Subway Series" has different meanings to different people.

Baseball fans immediately link the term with the grand battles of yesteryear between the New York Giants and the Brooklyn Dodgers; not to mention the encounters between the New York Yankees and the Dodgers or Giants, in assorted World Series.

More recently the Yankees and the New York Mets have infused the Subway Series with a new life.

But the Subway Series that most interests this writer refers to a number of telecasts orchestrated in Manhattan by Metro Channel.

Produced by Matthew Kells, "Subway Series" ran for over a year, and included a number of interesting segments—from an analysis of the best subway films, to a visit to the vast Coney Island repair yard.

Among the most amusing features involved an interview with a former Miss Subways, Ellen Hart-Sturum.

To give you a feel for what the Subway Series was like, the original scripts follow.

THE SUBWAY AND HOLLYWOOD

Ever since Hollywood began making motion pictures, the New York City subway has been a favorite among movie-makers. Some of the big names like Bruce Willis, Walter Matthau, and even Alfred Hitchcock have been linked to movies that featured the subway.

One of the first and best to be made about the subway was *Subway Express,* starring Eva Flint and Martha Madison. But the most widely known film ever made— the original 1933 version of *King Kong*— featured the Sixth Avenue elevated being ripped down by the great ape, and an el car being flipped like a toy and then tied in knots.

Alfred Hitchcock joined the act in 1957 by hiring an IND train for *The Wrong Man* starring Henry Fonda. A scene where Fonda sits in an R-1 car, reading a newspaper as the train rattles through a tunnel was actually filmed while the train was idling perfectly still at the IND's 5th Avenue station.

THEY'VE CAPTURED A TRAIN AND BROUGHT THE WORLD'S LARGEST CITY TO ITS KNEES.

"You're trapped like rats in an underground tunnel. Your every exit is covered by sharpshooters. You've got a million dollars but you'll never live to spend it."

HOW DID THEY GET AWAY WITH IT?

THE TAKING OF PELHAM ONE TWO THREE

THE TAKING OF PELHAM ONE TWO THREE
WALTER MATTHAU · ROBERT SHAW · MARTIN BALSAM
HECTOR ELIZONDO · Produced by GABRIEL KATZKA and EDGAR J. SCHERICK · Screenplay by PETER STONE
Based on the novel by JOHN GODEY · Music by DAVID SHIRE · Directed by JOSEPH SARGENT · United Artists

The busiest period of subway filmmaking occurred from 1970 through 1975 when a total of 36 movies were made using the subway in one form or another. *The French Connection* (1971) and *The Taking of Pelham One Two Three* (1974) were at the top of the list during this time.

The Taking of Pelham One Two Three was the most publicized of all the movies made. The Transit Authority was not at all eager to rent a subway car to United Artists, because it was not pleased with the story-line which involved the hijacking of an IRT local. The concern was that it might spark a similar situation in real life and the movie would bring negative publicity to the TA and the subway itself.

Producers were adamant about using a real-life car, and to continue with the movie plans they agreed to pay the TA $275,000 for the subway car rental, and another

$75,000 for anti-hijacking insurance. The film was shot at the Court Street station using a Number 6 car. Walter Matthau, Martin Balsam, Robert Shaw and Jerry Stiller starred in the film, which received many good reviews.

In films such as *Ghostbusters II* and *The Flamingo Kid,* the subway only appears in a cameo role, but in other movies like *The Warriors,* and *The Money Train,* it is an integral part of the entire script. In *The Money Train* thieves try to commandeer a money train for their own financial purposes. The practice of using money cars stopped long ago, so to have a realistic-looking money car the TA had to build one by converting an old R-21 type car at the Coney Island overhaul yard.

For sheer subway realism, *The Incident,* filmed in 1967, was among the best, containing dozens of scenes with real-life subway footage such as the 3rd Avenue elevated in the Bronx, and the 1939 World's Fair Low-V cars. The movie featured Beau Bridges, Jack Gilford, and was the film debut of Martin Sheen. The movie also starred a very young-looking Ed McMahon.

There have been dozens of other subway movies like *Die Hard with a Vengeance, Denouement, A Short Walk To Daylight, Extreme Measures, Girl 6, Conspiracy Theory, The Bachelor Party, Blade, Coming to America, The Cowboy Way, Devils Advocate, Fame, Fort Apache the Bronx, Ghost, Godzilla (1998), Hackers, The House on Carrol Street, Jacob's Ladder, Bananas, The Little Fugitive, Lost Weekend, The Lost World Jurassic Park, Mimic, Moscow on the Hudson, My Dinner with Andie, Naked City, Nighthawks, The Pawnbroker, Pi, The Pope of Greenwich Village, Saturday Night Fever, Teenage Mutant Ninja*

Turtles, Turk 182, and *Where Were You When The Lights Went Out.*

The Subway also made an appearance on the HBO film *Subway Stories.*

As the demand for subway filmmaking increased, the TA obliged by renting the abandoned Court Street Shuttle line to movie producers. The station was one of the blunders made when building the subway system, and was closed in June of 1946. Dennis Wendling, a TA public affairs man who had been the liaison with filmmakers and television producers, was called upon to be the system's official safety adviser:

"The closing of the Court Street line became a blessing for movie-making purposes," said Wendling. "The line has many features that film directors look for in a subway—a curve, curtain wall, and switches."

Movie buffs have the chance to visit some of the cars used in the movies. The money car used in *The Money Train,* and the R-1 Standard car that Henry Fonda sat in are in happy retirement at Coney Island, By the Sea and at the Transit Museum in Brooklyn. Chances are, there will be more movies in the near future with scenes, and maybe even scripts, based on the subway system. Until then, there are plenty already available However it is doubtful that they will match the thrill of enjoying an actual subway ride itself.

"MISS SUBWAYS" CONTEST BRINGS FAME AND FORTUNE

During World War II, pin-ups were very fashionable. Advertisements began adding attractive girls to promote and sell products. Magazines and the motion picture industry began using these beauties as well.

Esquire Magazine had the Varga girl, and 20th Century Fox had Betty Grable, and even the Subway system decided to get into the act. All you had to do was look up at the car-card. That's where Miss Subways hung out.

To trace the roots of the Miss Subways contest, sometimes referred to as Miss Turnstiles, we have to step back in time to the year 1941. The New York City Subway Company teamed up with the J. Walter Thompson Agency and wanted something that would be eye-catching to the rider during the everyday, dull commute.

The decision was to start a beauty pageant underground. Realizing that beautiful girls attract attention, and males were a major part of the subway ridership, Miss Subways was born.

Any young, pretty lady from the area could join the contest as long as she had no affiliation with any stage or camera work. One lucky winner was chosen, and her picture along with a short bio, adorned hundreds of subway cars, and platforms.

Miss Subway eventually made it to Broadway—literally. In 1944, the composer Leonard Bernstein teamed up with the lyricists Betty Comden and Adolph Green, and together they produced the musical "On The Town." It was a big hit and immediately turned into a movie starring Frank Sinatra and Gene Kelly.

Of the many perks Miss Subways brought, fame and fortune was among them. In 1941, Mona Freeman, the first Miss Subways, was rewarded with a career in Hollywood, proving the exposure the contest could bring. Several years later, Ruth Ericsson, a Waldorf-Astoria manicurist, received 258 marriage proposals from fellow riders.

Although Miss Subways was   phased

out for good in 1976, the memory lingers on at Ellen's Stardust Diner. Ellen Hart-Sturum, a Queens girl who in 1959 beat out 400 contestants to win the Miss Subway title, opened a 50's retro-style diner on Broadway in Times Square that features a singing wait-staff along with subway memorabilia.

"I started to have reunions to try to find all the old girls and get them together again," Ellen explained. "I remembered my placard, and I started to collect the posters because it's part of New York history. Nothing is more important than the city's subway system."

Today many ads run length-wide across subway cars, and in the stations, some featuring pretty women, most peddling some product. But one thing is certain though, they don't compare to the Subway girls of years ago.

HOW THE SUBWAY IS REPAIRED AT CONEY ISLAND

The New York City Subway system has the largest subway car fleet in the world, operating 24 hours, seven days a week. Roughly four million people ride the subway on an average weekday, adding up to 7,400 trips a day over 25 different routes throughout the Metropolitan area.

All combined, the trains travel nearly a million miles a day. Repair, rest, and refurbishing become a necessity. When it is time for a "checkup," the cars are sent to the Coney Island repair yard.

Everybody knows that Coney Island is the amusement capital of the world, but what they don't know is that Coney Island is also the home to the largest subway repair facility worldwide.

Opened in 1926, the Brooklyn-based repair yard spans over 75 acres. Three main buildings are located on the facility. The main overhaul area, motor repair shop and the pneumatic shop all focus on different aspects of the car, and specialize in its repair.

The main overhaul shop is where a majority of the work is done. The wheel and axle department, duct shop, and car repair area are all located off a main thoroughfare, which the repairmen labeled "Broadway." The areas are mostly adjacent to each other to make it easier for repair work to be done on the car in need.

Work on the cars is done on both the inside and the outside, but the main focus is on the trucks. The trucks are the guts of the subway car. Each subway car has two trucks, and they are what make the cars go. Frank Silecchia, a general superintendent for the Coney Island yard, explained how the trucks work:

"The trucks contain the wheels, the gearbox, and the motors," he said. *"Six hundred volts come in from the contact shoe, which runs along the third rail, then the volts go through the wires into the motor, which then turns the coupler. The coupler then turns the full gear, which then turns the wheels, making the car run. The bottom line is, without the trucks, the train doesn't run."*

Another frequent process that is done at the repair yard is the rehabilitation of wheels. Every six months, wheels are removed, and undergo a maintenance program to ensure their performance and safety.

"To begin the process, first the bearings are removed, and the wheel and axle sets are washed," said Silecchia. *"The wheels are then disassembled, the gear box is rebuilt, and then put back together. When*

this is done, the car is put back in service where it will begin another six-month tour until its next checkup."

The on-car repair section is where the work inside the car is done. The rider doesn't get to see what goes on beneath the car's exterior. The wiring, and mechanics of the car need maintenance, too. The doors, lights, ventilating system, sound system, all need attention. During this time approximately 200 men, working two tours, five days a week work to repair and restore the car's interior.

The paint shop is another part of the yard that is also busy. Unlike the cars years ago, the new cars are painted with a graffiti-resistant polyurethane so they maintain their shininess and new look.

To a subway buff, a Coney Island yard trip is like an anthropologist visiting the Museum of Natural History. The yard has guided tours, but whether or not you come, rest assured the 5,800 car fleet is in good hands at Coney Island.

TIMES SQUARE: HOW IT GOT ITS NAME; WHY THE THEATRE DISTRICT RELOCATED

They call it the crossroads of the world, otherwise known as the "Great White Way," but no matter what you call Times Square, it's also the crossroads of the subway world.

Every single day, a half million people use its subway station, and in a year 40 million pass through the portals making it the busiest subway complex in the entire universe.

A mere 400 years ago Times Square was the crossroads of a different world. A Native-American tribe called the *Recawawawancs* used to hang out on the site col-

lecting timber for their bows and arrows. The word Manhattan comes from the word *Manhattanak*, which means "a place of general inebriation." (Things haven't changed in four centuries.)

The crossroads of Broadway and Seventh Avenue wasn't always known as Times Square. In the 19th century it was called Long Acre Square. Along came a publisher named Alfred Ochs, who took a failing daily called the *New York Times* and turned it into a winner.

He decided to move his papers along the subway, which was a faster mode than his competition who were using horses and wagons. When he discovered that the subway was coming up to 43rd Street., Ochs decided to build his new headquarters up here, and exploit "upper" Manhattan.

The Times Square Tower was completed in 1900, and that's when Long Acre Square became Times Square forever.

When August Belmont finished his first subway in 1904, the Times Square station was nothing more than a miniscule stop. The platform could only handle five car trains, but it is now still in business as part of the Times Square Shuttle.

Two months after the subway opened, Adolf Ochs opened his second New York Times skyscraper, on New Years Eve 1904, with a tremendous celebration. He had fireworks topped off with a big white globe coming down a pole. That was the first great crowd celebration in Times Square, and many more have followed since.

Before the subway was built, New York's theater district was located at Herald Square. The reason for that was that there was an elevated stop at 34th Street and Sixth Avenue. When the subway opened in 1904, with a stop at 42nd Street, the theaters began to move uptown, and the new theater district was located around Times Square.

Composer George M. Cohan signaled this change with a hit tune that opened with the lines, "*Give my regards to Broadway, Remember me to Herald Square, Tell all the gang at 42nd Street, That I will soon be there.*"[24]

The Times Square station is as it should be—the biggest and liveliest in the world. Why, even the Recawawawancs, who lived here 400 years ago, would be proud to go through it today.

ARTISTRY GRACES THE UNDERGROUND

Many of the world's great art treasures are right here in New York, but what many don't know is that some of them are underground.

When the city's first subway, the IRT line, from Broadway to upper Manhattan, was planned, financial backer August Belmont ordered $500,000 to be allocated to decorate the new stations. Decorative panels made of brick, tile, ceramics and plaster adorned at least sixteen stations.

There are no official records pertaining to the mosaics that grace both the IRT and BMT stations, but an IRT brochure issued when the subway opened listed the wall-art as "instructive and decorative, as well as practical, and will have their effect on public taste just the same as anything else that tends to uplift and refine."

According to subway historian and map expert John Tauranac in *Historic Preservation* magazine (1973), some outstanding examples of subway art include: Canal Street, IRT Seventh Avenue line, Fulton Street, IRT Lexington Avenue line, Grand Central Station, IRT Lexington Avenue line, Columbus Circle, IRT Broadway West Side line, 116th Street, IRT Broadway West Side line, Borough Hall, Brooklyn, IRT Seventh Avenue Broadway line, Chambers Street, IRT Seventh Avenue Broadway line, Brooklyn Bridge, BMT Chambers Street, Astor Place, IRT Lexington Avenue line, Clark Street, Brooklyn, IRT Broadway Seventh Avenue line.

One of the neatest things about subway art is that it is so New York-centric. A perfect example is the Christopher Street station where there is an old mosaic that dates back to 1915 which depicts the penitentiary that stood above the station years ago. Another mosaic was done more recently by a local artist along with students from P.S. 41. It depicts the many Greenwich Village characters who have come and gone throughout the years.

The use of mosaics was abandoned when the third and last major subway, the Independent system (IND), was constructed in the thirties. Instead, a system of colored tiles for passengers who could not read was put in play. All stations on a particular line have a certain color so passengers can reach their destinations more efficiently.

There are many different types of subway art underground, just as there are many different personal tastes to art. Next time you are waiting on the platform take a look around. Chances are, you will see artistry in the subway, and maybe even for the first time.

———————

CHAPTER TWELVE

New York's Subway Series— Baseball Style— From 1921 to the Present

The Subway Series—baseball style—is as unique to New York as Times Square and the Statue of liberty.

Because the city once was home to three major league teams—Brooklyn Dodgers, New York Yankees and New York Giants—the opportunity occasionally presented itself for a championship tournament between one of the two (Giants, Dodgers) National League teams and the Yankees of the American League.

And since either a subway or an elevated train station adjoined the respective ball parks, most fans went to the matches via rapid transit.

However, it was not until the start of the Roarin' Twenties before Big Apple rooters were treated to this unique event.

The Subway Series originally took hold in 1921 when the Interborough Rapid transit (IRT) operated elevated trains to the Polo Grounds at 8th Avenue and 155th Street in Harlem.

In that season, both the Giants and Yankees shared the Polo Grounds as a home ball park although the Yankees were the tenants and the Giants the landlords.

In that year, the two teams met for the first time in the World Series and, thus, what became known as the Subway Series was launched.

The first Subway Series would set the stage for some of the most exciting major league baseball ever played right up to the 21st century when the Yankees defeated the Mets.

But when the teams first met in 1921 the Series hardly drew the attention that it would in later years.

Here's what happened in the World Premiere Subway Series.

SUBWAY SERIES I, OCTOBER 1921, NEW YORK GIANTS VS. NEW YORK YANKEES: The Yankees jumped out with the quick in the series, with Carl Mays and Waite Hoyt shutting out the Giants, 3-0 each. However, in the third game at the Polo grounds the Giants' bats awakened with an eight-run seventh inning to beat the Yankees, 13-5. The following two games would stay competitive, with the Giants and Yankees splitting the wins, 4-2 and 3-1, respectively. The final game of the series, Game Eight, was a low-scoring affair, but Hoyt allowed one run in the first, which is all the run support Art Nehf would need to win Game Eight. The Giants beat the Yankees in the best of nine set, five games to three.

SUBWAY SERIES II, OCTOBER 1922, NEW YORK GIANTS VS. NEW YORK YANKEES: Like the first of its kind, the second version also was played at the Polo Grounds although blueprints for a new Yankee home in the Bronx already had been drawn with a 1923 target date for completion. For Subway Series II, the Yankees had baseball's most prominent, all-time performer, Babe Ruth, reaching the apex of his glittering career. Unlike the 1921 World Series, this was a best-out-of-seven affair. All the 1922 games were played at the Polo Grounds from October 4–8, consecutively. The Giants won the first game 3-2, and were on their way to winning Game Two, with a three-run home run by Meusel off Yankee's starter Sharkey in the first inning. However, the Yankees battled back, scoring a run in each of the first, fourth, and eighth innings. The game would never come to a resolution because it would unexpectedly be called on account of darkness. From there on, the Giants would be on cruise control, topping the Yankees in their next three meetings, 3-0; 4-3; and 5-3 and would win their title by sweeping the Yankees in four games.

SUBWAY SERIES III, OCTOBER 1923, NEW YORK GIANTS VS. NEW YORK YANKEES: Many historians believe that the true Subway Series, as we know it today, actually began in 1923, the first year of Yankee Stadium's storied existence. Once again, the Giants and Yankees went head to head. Fans could take the el to Giants home games at the Polo Grounds or the subway—which actually became an el just before it reached the ball park—to the Stadium for the Bronx Bombers' home contests. The first contest would set the stage for all the others. The score was tied 4-4 going into the ninth inning and the player the Yankees feared most was at the plate: Casey Stengel. He hit an inside-the-park home run off Ross Ryan to give the Giants a victory. However, the Yankees returned to the Polo Grounds and evened the series. The match was punctuated by Babe Ruth's two home runs; one over the right-field roof. In Game Three, the Giants won 1-0, on yet another Stengel home run. But in subsequent games, the Yankees would outscore the Giants with a combined total of 22-9, thus winning the World Series four games to two, beating the Giants for the first time in their Subway Series competition.

SUBWAY SERIES IV, SEPTEMBER-OCTOBER 1936, NEW YORK GIANTS VS. NEW YORK YANKEES: After the 1923 Subway classic, thirteen years would pass before another one captured the attention of New Yorkers. By this time Babe Ruth was gone as a player, but interest remained keen thanks to several memorable performances. Again it was the Giants vs. Yankees. Game One remained tight until the bottom of the eighth inning when the Giants scored four runs for the 6-1 win. The Bombers retaliated at the Polo Grounds with a 17-hit, 18-run game capped by a seven run third inning. Bill Dickey and Tony Lazzeri each had five

Leo Durocher (left), manager of 1941 Dodgers, with ace pitcher, Fred (Fat Freddy) Fitzsimmons (right).

Grounds. Carl Hubbell finally gave the Giants some respect with a six-hit, 7-3 victory in Game Four but the Yanks sealed the series in five games with a 4-2 win behind Gomez.

SUBWAY SERIES VI, OCTOBER 1941, BROOKLYN DODGERS VS. NEW YORK YANKEES: One significant difference since the early championships was the fact that another web of underground subway lines serviced the ball parks. In Manhattan, the Independent (IND) city-owned subway placed its 155th Street entrance adjacent to the Polo Grounds' clubhouse. Meanwhile, the Bronx branch of the IND had an underground terminal adjacent to the Stadium. In Brooklyn both the IRT and BMT lines had stations close to Ebbets Field. Thus, fans had the opportunity to get to any ball park by subway. Unique about the 1941 classic was the fact that Brooklyn and the Yankees were meeting for the first time. The Bombers, who opened with the first two games at home, were led by Joe DiMaggio who, during the regular season had set a record by hitting safely in 56 straight games. The Yankees grabbed an opening game victory, 3-2, at the Stadium behind Red Ruffing, who pitched the nine innings, beating sidearmer, Curt Davis.

Game Two would be the same score, but with a different ending. The Dodgers won behind Whitlow Wyatt's complete game nine-hitter. The Series shifted to Brooklyn for Game Three. With the Brooks'

runs batted in for the night. However, Game Three would feature a home run by Lou Gehrig in the bottom of the first and Jimmy Ripple in the top of the fifth. The story of this game was that despite the Giants' 11 hits, they lost 2-1. The Yanks continued their winning ways in Game Four, extending their series lead to 3-1. The Bombers would finish their hunt, victorious, 13-5. This would be the Yankee's first World Series without Babe Ruth and also their first with Joe DiMaggio in the lineup.

SUBWAY SERIES V, OCTOBER 1937, NEW YORK GIANTS VS. NEW YORK YANKEES: The Bronx bombers dominance over their cross-town rivals was on the verge of becoming boring. Airtight pitching by Lefty Gomez (Game One, Yanks win 8-1) and Red Ruffing (Game Two, Yanks win, again 8-1) was followed by a 5-1 win after the Series moved to the Polo

Hitting stars of the 1941 World Series opener: Left to right: Pee Wee Reese of the Brooklyn Dodgers who got three of his team's six hits, Joe Gordon of the New York Yankees, who had a perfect day, 2 for 2, his homer and single batting in two runs, and teammate Bill Dickey who went 2 for 4, a double batting in the other Yankees' run.

Freddie Fitzsimmons facing Marius Russo, the game remained scoreless until the eighth inning when Joe DiMaggio and Charlie Keller both drove in a run, putting the Yankees ahead, 2-0. The Dodgers replied with a run and no more. The game ended, 2-1 for New York.

Game Four remains a classic of Promethian proportions, still discussed to this day. It seemed as if the Dodgers had won the game. Leading 4-3, the Dodgers' ace reliever, Hugh Casey, had two outs and none on against New York with Tommy Henrich at the plate. The next pitch was a strike and the game should have been over with a Brooklyn win and the series tied at two apiece. But Lady Luck was not on the Dodgers side. The pitch by Casey got away from catcher Mickey Owen and by the time he had retrieved it, Henrich was safe at first. Instead of winning the game, the Brooks fell apart after that. The Yanks scored four runs and won the game, 7-4. Thoroughly demoralized, the Dodgers dropped Game Five, 3-1, and Yankees fans enjoyed their long subway ride back to the Bronx.

As thrilling as all Yankee and Giants match ups had been, nothing could quite match the riveting series between the Dodgers and Yankees. The 1941 edition was merely the prelude for what became the greatest rivalry in sports history. The next one, which went seven games, proves the point.

After seething through World War II years awaiting revenge, Dodgers fans believed they finally would get their wish when the Brooks met the Bombers a second time for a baseball title. However, the second Brooklyn-Bronx collision once again devastated the Bums, setting the precedent that would remain well into the next decade.

SUBWAY SERIES VII, BROOKLYN DODGERS VS. NEW YORK YANKEES, SEPTEMBER-OCTOBER 1947: Once again, the Brooks came close—but no cigar. After the Bombers took a two game lead, (6-3, 10-3). The Dodgers tied the tournament (9-8, 3-2) with Game Five in Brooklyn. In a pitchers' battle between Spec Shea of the Yanks and Rex Barney, the Yankees, with Joe DiMaggio's home run, edged the Bums, 2-1. Undaunted, the Dodgers returned to the Bronx for Game Six and, in a comeback performance, beat the Bombers, 8-6. In the decisive Game Seven, Brooklyn jumped into a 2-0 lead at the top of the second but it was their last gasp. The Yankees, behind Joe Page, triumphed, 5-2.

Joe DiMaggio, Yankees' center-fielder, is greeted at home plate by teammates Gene Woodling and Yogi Berra as he scores in fourth 1951 World Series game at the Polo Grounds.

gave the Yanks a 3-1 second-game win—both games were at Yankee Stadium—but Jim Hearn tossed his own five-hitter in Game Three, won by the Giants at the Polo Grounds. Indomitable as always, the Yanks came back, behind Allie Reynolds' eight-hitter and Joe DiMaggio's home run, 6-2. From there, the Bombers never were headed. They won the the next pair, 13-1 at the Polo Grounds behind Ed Lopat's five-hitter, and 4-3 at home behind Vic Raschi. This would mark the last time the New York Giants and Yankees would meet in the World Series before the Jints moved from Manhattan to San Francisco.

SUBWAY SERIES VIII, BROOKLYN DODGERS VS. NEW YORK YANKEES, OCTOBER 1949: After exchanging 1-0 wins—Yanks behind Allie Reynolds in Game One and Dodgers behind Preacher Roe in Game Two—the Bombers withstood home runs from Peewee Reese, Luis Olmo and Roy Campanella in Game three to edge Brooklyn, 4-3. That essentially did it. Ed Lopat defeated the Bums, 6-4 in Game Four and Vic Raschi finished off the Dodgers in Game Five, 10-4.

SUBWAY SERIES IX, NEW YORK YANKEES VS. NEW YORK GIANTS, OCTOBER 1951: After Leo Durocher's Giants had defeated Brooklyn in the Bobby Thomson-led "Miracle of Coogan's Bluff" playoff series to determine the National League pennant-winner, the 1951 World Series was anti-climactic. With momentum on their side, the Jints took the opener, 5-1, behind Dave Koslo. Ed Lopat's five-hitter

SUBWAY SERIES X, NEW YORK YANKEES VS. BROOKLYN DODGERS, OCTOBER 1952: With one of the greatest Brooklyn teams ever, the Dodgers came ever so close to winning their first World Series one year after the Bobby Thomson disaster. They opened at home with a 4-2 decision with Joe Black beating Allie Reynolds, each with a six-hitter. Jackie Robinson, Duke Snider, Peewee Reese and Gil McDougald all homered. Still in Brooklyn, the Yanks tied the count with a 7-1 rout on Vic Raschi's three-hitter. Now in the Bronx, Preacher Roe limited New York to six hits to give Brooklyn a 5-3 triumph in Game Three. This was followed by a pitchers' battle between Allie Reynolds and Joe Black, each of whom tossed a four-hitter. Johnny Mize homered for the Yanks, who won, 2-0. Fitting for a series tied at two games apiece, Game Five went into extra innings, tied at 5-5. Still at the Stadium, the Dodgers got a run in the top of the eleventh to win, 6-5. Duke Snider and Johnny Mize each homered. Brooklyn was all prepared for a celebration following Game Six at Ebbets Field. The Brooks went ahead, 1-0 in the bottom of the sixth but the Yanks got two in the seventh and one in the eighth. Final score, 3-2, Yankees. The finale at Ebbets Field was almost predictable, based on past performances. A 2-2 tie was broken in the top of the sixth with a Yankees run. They got another in the seventh, winning going away, 4-2.

Amoros saves '55 World Series.

SUBWAY SERIES XI, NEW YORK YANKEES VS. BROOKLYN DODGERS, SEPTEMBER-OCTOBER 1953: "Wait 'til next year" had already become the Brooklyn mantra for good reason—and yet another reason was provided in 1953. The Yanks, at home, won the first pair, 9-5, 4-2, but Brooklyn rebounded, 3-2 and 7-3. Four Bombers home runs (Gene Woodling, Mickey Mantle, Billy Martin, Gil McDougald) proved the difference in Game Five, 11-7. In Game Six, at the Stadium , the Dodgers rallied at the top of the ninth with two runs—after being down 1-3—to knot the count. But the Bombers got a run in the bottom of the ninth. *Wait 'til next year?*

SUBWAY SERIES XII, NEW YORK YANKEES VS. BROOKLYN DODGERS, SEPTEMBER-OCTOBER 1955: The 1955 series could be called "The year that next year finally came," although it didn't look much like it after the Yanks raced to a two-game (6-5, 4-2) lead at the Stadium. But when the Dodgers returned to Brooklyn, the Bums' bats exploded for 8-3 and 8-5 tri-

umphs. The third straight game at Ebbets Field also belonged to the Dodgers, 5-3, but the Bombers stopped the bleeding in Game Six with a 5-1 decision at the Stadium. Game Seven, also in the Bronx, belonged to Johnny Podres, pitching for Brooklyn. His five-hitter was enough for the two Dodgers runs and bedlam in Brooklyn. Waiting 'til next year no longer was necessary!

SUBWAY SERIES XIII, NEW YORK YANKEES VS. BROOKLYN DODGERS, OCTOBER 1956: Brooklyn's quest for two-straight Series was defined by the borough's famed chant, "Almost doesn't count." Opening at Ebbets Field, the Bums triumphed, 6-3 and 13-8 and seemed hellbent for another championship until the teams moved on to the Bronx where the Bombers returned the favor, 5-3 and 6-2, followed by *the* Perfect Game, Don Larsen's 2-0 no-hitter. Game Six, back in Brooklyn, was scoreless going into the last of the tenth inning when the Brooks got the run, sending the series to a seventh game, also at Ebbets

The 1951 National League pennant race was unique. Brooklyn's Dodgers appeared to be running away from their arch rival, the New York Giants. On August 11, first place Brooklyn led New York by 13 games, but then the Giants launched one of the most amazing comebacks in sports history.

While the Dodgers played .500 ball the rest of the way, the Giants won 37 and lost 7. The teams finished in a tie for first place, leading to a best-of-three playoff for the pennant.

In the opening game, Bobby Thomson and Monte Irvin hit home runs while the Giants defeated Dodgers pitcher Ralph Branca, 3-1, at Ebbets Field.

Brooklyn rebounded the next day with a 10-0 romp behind rookie right-hander Clem Labine.

In the decisive game on October 3rd at the Polo Grounds, Brooklyn led 4-1 entering the last of the ninth inning.

Don Newcombe, pitching for the Dodgers, allowed a run, to make it 4-2. With one out, the Giants had runners at second and third, when manager Charlie Dressen replaced Newcombe with Branca.

With one strike on the batter, Branca threw a fastball, high and tight. Thomson took a good cut, driving the ball deep into the left field seats, 320 feet from home plate.

The Giants had won the pennant. Thomson's drive became known as "The Shot Heard 'Round the World."

Field. On a cloudy, bitter cold afternoon, the October 10, 1956 match would be the last Subway Series involving Brooklyn and the Bronx. From the top of the first, it was no contest. New York got two runs off Don Newcombe, *en route* to a 9-0 drubbing. Yogi Berra hit a pair of home runs for the Yanks while Elston Howard and Bill Skowron hit one apiece.

SUBWAY SERIES XIV, NEW YORK YANKEES VS. NEW YORK METS, OCTOBER 2000: Amid more media hoopla than any previous interborough baseball classic, the Mets-Yankees encounter involved use of the IRT's Flushing Line for the first time in a Subway Series. The Number Seven train, which connects Times Square with Main Street in Flushing, has a stop (Willets Point) servicing Shea Stadium. Fans could take the IRT either to Flushing or to the Yankee Stadium. Unfortunately for the Mets, the tone of the series cast them in a hard-luck

Brooklyn Dodgers' mold. Leading 3-2 going into the last of the ninth at Yankee Stadium, the Mets allowed a run and lost when the Bombers scored another run in the bottom of the twelfth inning. The game consumed four hours and fifty-one minutes, longest in World Series history in terms of minutes. The Yanks won 6-5 in Game Two—down 6-0, the Mets got five in the ninth—and finally the Shea boys took Game Three, at Flushing, 4-2 behind John Franco. That was it for Bobby Valentine's nine. The Bombers closed the Series on the road with 3-2 and 4-2 decisions.

**THE BEST SUBWAY SERIES
OF THE 1950'S
(BILL JAMES SAYS SO)**

Baseball historian Bill James is one of the most respected archivists in the business.

His book, *The Bill James Historical*

THE BROOKLYN DODGER NICKNAMED "SUBWAY."

Only one baseball player ever carried the nickname "Subway." He was a Brooklynite named Samuel (Sam) Nahem who had become a heroic figure on Kings County sandlots in the early 1930s. Ostensibly because he traveled to and from various Metropolitan Area ballfields such as the Parade Grounds and Dexter Park on the BMT, IRT and IND lines, Nahem was dubbed "Subway Sam."

In his one game with the Dodgers during the 1938 season, the Jewish hurler appeared promising. Not only did the righty pitch a complete game, but he went two-for-five at bat.

Despite the solid start, Brooklyn inexplicably released him. Writing Nahem's obituary in the May 4, 2004 edition of the New York Sun, Stephen Miller observed, "Family legend has it that Nahem caught manager Leo Durocher in flagrante with a woman not his wife, sparking Durocher's disfavor."

Subway Sam returned to the Dodgers' training camp in 1940, but Durocher was not inclined to do him any favors. According to one story, the manager let Nahem pitch to 19 batters in one inning.

At least Nahem had a sense of humor. Following that episode, Subway Sam chortled, "I'm now pitching batting practice to the batting practice pitchers!"

On another earlier occasion, Subway Sam was invited to pitch batting practice for the Dodgers.

Facing Brooklyn's zany pitcher Van Lingle Mungo, Nahem tossed a curve that hit Mungo in the derriere.

Then manager Casey Stengel walked out to the mound and told his pitcher, "Subway, if you can hurt that big sonofabitch, you must have something on the ball!"

Subway Sam died on April 26, 2004 at the age of 88.

Baseball Abstract, is filled with pungent commentary.

One such subject is called "The Best World Series of the 1950's."

"The 1952 Series is probably the least remembered World Series of the fifties—just another in a series of Yankee victories—but nonetheless it was one hell of a duel," says James.

One year after they had their hearts broken by the Giants and Bobby Thomson's "Shot Heard 'Round the World," the Dodgers made it back to the Series and met their neighbors from the Bronx, the Yankees.

The baseball world was introduced to Mickey Mantle in the 1952 Series and the Dodgers were the first in a long line of teams victimized by Mickey's might. Brooklyn was one victory away from the championship after an 11-inning, com-plete-game win by Carl Erskine in Game Five, but homers by Mantle in both Games Six and Seven powered the Yanks to their fourth-straight Series win.

"It was a Monday morning quarter-back's dream, abounding in crucial managerial decisions on both sides," says James.

Stan Baumgartner of *The Sporting News Guide* said the 1952 fall classic was "one of the most thrill-packed Series in history."

Dodger fans probably could have done without some of the thrills, however. Mantle's blasts in Games Six and Seven silenced an Ebbets Field crowd that saw its Dodgers let the hated Yanks off the ropes and fail to bring home its first championship.

PART III

SUBWAY PEOPLE SPEAK

The subways of New York were built for people.

They have, in fact, become the prime people-movers of the world.

Without question, the Big Apple's rapid transit system is the best and most comprehensive in the world.

It also carries the most varied cross-section of straphangers in the universe.

White-collar workers, blue-collar workers, Wall Street executives, professors and students are among those who comprise this fascinating ridership mosaic.

In addition there is a special cadre of commuters who not only ride New York's underground railroad for fun and study. They are the subway buffs who consider every single ride they take an adventure in transit.

The aim here is to present a cross-section of such straphangers who, in their own words, describe precisely what the subway means to them.

Matthew Kells
SUBWAY TV PRODUCER

David Perlmutter

One of the most accomplished independent television producers in New York, Matthew Kells has covered virtually every imaginable subject, from documentaries about the Catskill Mountains Borscht Belt hotels to the history of Atlantic City as a resort.

His affection for the subways comes natural, both as a New Yorker and as an orchestrator of television programming.

While working at Manhattan's Metro Channel, Kells produced "Subway Series," a collection of features about the system. These included Subway Movies and Art in the Underground, among others.

An award-winning show, "Subway Series," was followed at Metro by another prize-winning show, "Subway Q&A." Under Kells' direction, it too was a hit.

An advocate of mass transit, Kells rides the subways on a regular basis and regards "Subway Series" as one of his all-time favorite projects.

After all the years that I have been riding the subway system, what fascinates me most is the fact that it all still works a full century after the first line was built.

That, to me, is amazing when you consider the wear and tear it undergoes every single day, twenty-four hours in a row without a breather.

I've been to cities throughout the world that have subways but they can't be as favorably compared to New York's because ours never sleeps; never takes a rest. In other places, the subway shuts down at a certain point in the night to be cleaned and repaired but here in the Big Apple, it keeps on going.

Ours is the best—the most efficient and the biggest. A person can travel from all the way up at the northern tip

(Washington Heights) of Manhattan down to Rockaway Beach at the southern tip by the Atlantic Ocean for only two bucks. That's amazing!

I realize that New Yorkers like to complain about their subway; that there are delays and whatnot, but the fact remains that most of the time, it takes people where they want to go and does so pretty darn quickly.

Another aspect of it that never fails to intrigue me is the diversity of people who ride the various lines—especially during the rush-hour. Our subway symbolizes what New York is all about; a veritable melting pot. It gives you a good sense of who is living here; which is *everybody.*

Having grown up in the city, I can tell you that I'm just like other New Yorkers in the sense that we take the subway for granted. We go down the steps, swipe our *MetroCard,* get on the train and arrive at where we want to go. It seems so simple to us, and yet it is a very complicated process.

Think of it this way: I'll get on at 86th Street on the Upper East Side and ride the IRT downtown to Union Square station, and I'll be there in seven minutes!

That's terrific although, if there is a delay for whatever reason, then the complaints will be heard.

Being a New Yorker, I invariably have a love-hate relationship with the trains. As much as I like them—and use them—there's also a down side to commuting whether it's on the IRT, BMT or IND.

What bothers me is that the very thing that I like about the subway also happens to be what I also hate about it; and that's the people; specifically, a large number of people crammed into a relatively small amount of space.

Some days, when I'm in a good mood, I can handle it. On other days, when I'm not in a good mood—and someone bumps me in the head—I consider the subway ride a pain-in-the-ass.

Let's face it, the subway—more than anything else in the city—personifies the people who live here. I often tell people, if you want to know about New Yorkers, take a ride on the subway. You certainly won't learn as much by riding a cab or visiting a certain city block or even a neighborhood.

Another positive about the system is the sheer immensity of it all and that, after a century of use, much of the original track and infrastructure still is in use. I mean all you have to do is ride the Broadway IRT line between Times Square and 96th Street and you'll see all kinds of examples—old-style pillars, art work, original construction—of the very first line—and the beauty part is that it's still running.

I find it intriguing when I think that my great-grandmother rode this same IRT and now, years later, I'm riding the same line that she did.

In a sense the subway is a New York contradiction. Look at it this way: the word *new* is in New York. There's always a new building being built—stores opening and closing—but the subway is still the same and has held up for a hundred years. That can't be said for much else in New York.

When I was producing *Subway Series* for Metro the part that I wanted to emphasize was the subway's diversity; its history, art, Hollywood films shot underground. I wanted to show all the things about it that we take for granted.

Take the movies as an example. You would be amazed at how many films over the years—from *King Kong* to *The French Connection*—have links to the subway.

Myself, I ride the trains for business and

pleasure. Whatever lines go to Coney Island are my favorite lines. Also the IRT's Number Seven (Flushing) Line because it goes to Shea Stadium, and I *love* to go there and watch the Mets.

I get a kick out of being in the front car of the Flushing Line after it emerges from the tunnel in Long Island City and it first hits daylight. There are some wonderful views, especially when the train hits that big curve before Queens Plaza, and from the front car you actually can see the last car of the train.

That line has especially fond memories for me because my grandmother lived in Queens and I used to ride the IRT to visit her. Even as a kid, I was intrigued by those sharp elevated line curves in Long Island City, where I could see the rear car even as I was sitting in the front.

If I could do anything I wanted to make the system better I first would build the Second Avenue subway. That's a *must.* Anybody who has been on the overcrowded IRT East Side trains will tell you that. Also, I would see to it that more expresses are put on the Flushing Line to handle the Shea Stadium crowds after Mets games.

On the way to Shea in the late afternoon, there is local and express service. I can take the Flushing express and get to the ball park in fifteen minutes. But after the game—when there sometimes is a crowd of more than 25,000 fans trying to get home by subway—why the heck do I have to take a local, and make so many stops in Queens, to get home when we're all heading back to Manhattan?

Not that I want to sound like a *kvetch* talking about the subway; it's been a great part of my life, especially producing the train shows for television, both *Subway Series* and *Subway Q&A.*

We did some neat things including a Long Island Rail Road piece that began at the IRT's old Atlantic Avenue station near where the original LIRR started.

Unlike *Subway Series,* the *Subway Q&A* was shot completely underground. We had a host who would go up to random people in the subway and say something like, "Let's go back to your house and cook dinner."

Some of the folks we encountered would say "Yes," and they were very cool about it. Once we cracked their shell, they would give us a smile. And the ironic thing was that the meaner the people looked, the nicer they turned out to be. That was amazing.

Then, there were others we'd approach who would put on what I call their "Subway Face"—and look straight ahead and not want to talk to anybody.

Still, you'd be surprised at how many people we approached—who minutes earlier were on their way to work—would suddenly agree to do whatever we could come up with including off-the-wall stuff like paint-balling and going fishing!

We even had a guy cook us dinner, and once, we grabbed a couple down at City Hall who had just gotten married and we gave them a wedding reception—right there, down in the subway. Another time we dressed some people up as giant stuffed Teddy Bears and had them dance around on the subway platform.

Whenever someone would say okay to one of our crazy requests, I would be reminded of my mother's continuous advice to me as a kid: "Matthew, don't talk to anybody on the subway!"

Fortunately for *Subway Q&A,* most of them wouldn't *take* my mom's advice!

David Perlmutter
SUBWAY PHOTOGRAPHER

A professional photographer whose works have appeared at galleries both in New York and Paris, David Perlmutter focuses on subjects running the gamut from Parisian dogs to the Greenwich Village Gay Pride Parade.

The Greenwich Village resident—and lifetime straphanger—only recently took his camera underground. Fascinated by the subway's photographic possibilities, Perlmutter shot everything from the desolate tracks of the Transit Authority's Rockaway Line to the tumult of Times Square station.

With each day on the system, Perlmutter became more enamoured of subway people; their personalities, faces and mannerisms.

After four months of traveling as far north on the subway system as Van Cortlandt Park station and as far south as Coney Island, Perlmutter reveals what delights him about the underground and what arrests his attention about subway photography.

When I was a kid, I grew up in Long Beach, Long Island, which is not exactly subway country. But we did have the Long Island Rail Road, so when it was time for me to pay one of my periodic visits to my grandmother—she lived in Brooklyn—my mother and I would hop on the LIRR and ride it to Flatbush Avenue station, last stop on the railroad's Brooklyn Division.

I always got a kick out of riding the Long Island, but it was nothing—I mean *nothing*—compared with what followed—the subway ride through Brooklyn to Grandma's house near the Atlantic Ocean in Sheepshead Bay.

After we got out at the corner of Flatbush and Atlantic Avenues, Mom and I would walk a few blocks to the BMT Brighton Line station at Atlantic Avenue. That's where we'd get the train that came over the Manhattan Bridge heading for Coney Island.

It was the place where I got my first—and one of the lasting—impressions of New York's subway.

As an impressionable four-year-old, I looked all around me as we headed through the turnstiles—Mom didn't have to pay for me in those days so I ducked underneath—and down the stairs to the platform.

Before it arrived at Atlantic Avenue station, the Brighton Express stopped at nearby DeKalb Avenue. Which meant that it wasn't traveling all that fast when the train arrived at Atlantic.

Of course, you couldn't convince *me* of that.

When the train barreled toward the platform, it scared the hell out of me. It started with the exceptionally loud noise generated by the wheels over the tracks. Plus, there was the screech of brake shoes, hugging the outside of the wheels, forcing them to slow down—and eventually stop. Finally, I was mesmerized by the hubbub of people dashing in and out of the cars. It was a much more frantic scene than I was accustomed to on the LIRR.

The trip from Atlantic Avenue to Sheepshead Bay was a long ride—distance-wise—but it always went too fast for me. The express ride was especially neat; after Atlantic Avenue, the train stopped at Prospect Park (Ebbets Field), then ran express past a local stop (Parkside Avenue) to Church Avenue station in Flatbush.

By this time, the subway was out of its tunnel and running in daylight through what they call an "open cut" past more local stations (Beverley Road, Cortelyou Road) with terrific speed and wild side-to-side bounces. Sometimes I had the feeling the train would bounce right *off* the tracks but, fortunately, it never did.

After the stop at Newkirk Avenue, our trip *really* took off; as the train climbed up a long hill from the open cut and on to a high embankment at the Avenue H local stop. Standing on a little jump seat in the first car, I could see out the front window as the express hurtled through the middle of Flatbush before braking as it approached Kings Highway station. One more stop and we were at Grandma's house.

In less than a half-hour, the express has sped to Sheepshead Bay and, in that manner—over the years—I got my basic training in subway riding and straphanger-watching.

I absorbed that background knowledge and utilized it a half-century later when I launched my career as a New York City underground railway photographer.

Nowadays, when I go into the subway, I'm mostly fascinated by the people, although I would rather that my subjects not know that I'm shooting them.

Not all my favorite subjects are people. I love taking pictures of the stations and odd aspects such as the old-fashioned *kiosk* at City Hall and the various architectural features and how the riders relate to those surroundings.

What I try to do—among many things—is get viewers to appreciate how wonderful the subway experience—the *ambience*—really can be, and by that I mean the fascination as well as the convenience.

I'll give you an example: My nephew, David, travels every work day all the way from the northern end of the Bronx to the lower end of Manhattan. It takes him a little more than a half-hour and costs two bucks. If he took a cab it would cost him about twenty dollars—not counting the tip—and if he came by car, it would be a fortune for the parking fee because there would be no way he could legally park downtown.

If I had a friend who lived in New York and who never rode in the subway, he wouldn't be a friend. I wouldn't even talk to him. To me, he would be a total jerk for not riding in the subway.

As a photographer, I find that the best subjects of all are subway people; from the train operators to the people who have just finished shopping at Macy's and have climbed down to the 34th Street station.

What I learned in the past few years is that photographing underground is different from what I had been accustomed to doing in my earlier career with a camera.

It all started with a trip to France where I came upon a subject that interested me; Parisians and their pet dogs. It's a very special relationship with them and once I noticed that, I began snapping shots of the French and their pet pups. I did it for a decade and amassed a collection that was substantial enough to be shown at galleries.

After that, I became fascinated with the Gay Pride Parade which took place not far from my Greenwich Village apartment. I did a series of Parade shoots and each year the subjects became more interesting as I went along.

Friends have asked me about the type of camera that I've used on the various projects and I tell them that the model is totally unimportant. What matters most—in my humble estimation—is my vision of the shot; that is, how *I* see the subject, not so much the camera. To put it in tennis terms, the Williams sisters, Serena and Venus, could play tennis with a broom and still win!

Compared to other subjects, I found the subway most fascinating because of the variety of available topics and the huge mixture of people. I discovered riders from the lowest economic strata—barely hanging on to make a living—as well as the super-rich East Siders heading down to Wall Street on the Lexington Avenue (IRT) Express.

Plus, I saw everything in between, and that includes young, beautiful women and old ladies who also were beautiful in their own way. I saw good guys and bad guys; all races, all ethnic types—Hasidic, Black, White, Hispanic, Asian. I opened my eyes and my lens, looked and found wonderful things at every station.

My best photos were taken when riders were unaware that I had pointed the camera at them. As a rule, I place the camera up against my chest, shooting with a wide-angle lens which gives a broader appeal. There's an automatic focusing device which makes it easier for me, and when I snap the shutter, generally, the subjects have no idea that I'm taking pictures of them.

Occasionally, the Law of Averages catches up to me and a straphanger will catch on to what I'm doing. Most people don't care but some will move out of the way or voice a mild objection. I've never encountered anyone who objected violently to what I'm doing and that explains why I'm still able to tell the tale!

For me, the most difficult subway photos are those lacking the personal, human touch. Architectural shots such as the pictures of the arched viaduct at 125th Street and Broadway were challenging because I found it difficult to get what I considered a good angle from below.

When I photograph inanimate objects, such as the subway mosaics which were created in the 1904-era stations, I want to make them special shots, but I find that the photos are not terribly unusual, even though they may be suitable to match the subject in the book.

I prefer shooting people in the subway environment, or people juxtaposed against some form of art in the subway, or even merely on the station platform with the natural steel pillars as props.

From the very start, my favorite places for shooting have been those—like Grand Central station on the IRT East Side Line—that are the busiest. They provide the most interest and are the easiest for me. The more frantic the location, the more opportunities for varied pictures. Ironically, in those places, the commuters seem most at ease. Go figure!

My theory is that they're so busy, they

are least self-aware in contrast to a lone woman standing on a platform waiting for a train, who happens to notice me with a camera in my hand. No way that she'd be at ease. It was the same on some of the elevated lines—Van Cortlandt Park, Dyre Avenue—at off-hours; they were the least interesting.

On any given shoot, I work by an unwritten set of rules. I don't like to take pictures of what I call "victims of society"—the homeless people sleeping on a platform bench or on a train seat. I consider it unfair to take a photo that is in any way demeaning to the subject. I believe that there *is* a time to take a picture and, without question, a time *not* to push the button.

How many pictures would I take on an average shoot? The average would be about one hundred, give or take a dozen. I never establish a specific number in advance, or try to limit myself.

A more difficult question, artistically, is whether to take subway pictures in black-and-white or in color. I wish I could provide a definitive answer, but I don't have one. Sometimes I'll take a picture in color and yet develop it in black-and-white and it will actually look better that way than in the form I originally meant to use.

Black-and-white or color, the bottom line is that the subway *is* New York and that's why it makes such a wonderful, adventurous subject. Whenever I descend the steps, I know I'll encounter a human menagerie of the most arresting kind, especially on my favorite run, the IRT Number One Local, otherwise known as The Broadway Line.

I like it for several reasons, not the least of which is the fact that from Times Square north to Van Cortlandt Park, its essentially the same subway that it was a hundred years ago when the Interborough opened for business in 1904. Many of the mosaics and bas reliefs that were crafted back then are still looking very good today; and that's really saying something.

At Columbus Circle station the artwork of the explorer's ship, the *Santa Maria* is as clear and handsome as it was a century ago. The 168th Street and 181st Street stops on the same line have a *retro* look that gives you the feeling that the calendar was back in the pre-World War I days; bricks, beautiful architecture, globular lights; that wonderfully nostalgic, old look.

By the way, I also favor the Number One line because my daughter, Jane, lives a stone's throw from the 103rd Street-Broadway station.

Friends who knew I was working on this project would ask me from time to time whether I had a love-hate relationship with the subway. My answer always has been that there's nothing to hate about it. The system runs well and does so 24 hours a day; which is more than I can say for Paris and its Métro.

I consider the New York subway the *only* way to travel in the city. The subway *is* New York.

On second thought, there *is* one thing I do hate about it and that's when a young woman sees me standing and gets up to offer me her seat.

At age seventy-one, I can do without such humiliation!

Ray Nader
THE BROOKLYN SUBWAY BUFF

While his smiling presence has been linked with New York sporting events for decades as a premier television broadcast

technician, Ray Nader, 49, has been equally ubiquitous in the underground realm.

A Brooklyn native, Nader has traveled—and loved—the subways as long as he can remember.

And like many train buffs from his borough, the BMT Brighton Line—running from Coney Island through the borough's spine and into Manhattan—remains his favorite, dating back to childhood days when he would take it to school.

Nader's special Brighton feeling is evident by his photo collection, which includes Flatbush scenes from the days when steam locomotives carried trains from the populated northern portion of Kings County into Flatbush and through the southern Brooklyn countryside—and it was country then—to the Atlantic Ocean beaches.

He delights in showing, by means of chronologically progressing photos, how the Brighton Line evolved from a two-track local run at ground level to a four-track express-local main line powered by an electrified third rail.

Still living in his native borough, Nader remains as passionate about the subway as he did the first time he ever rode a BMT Standard north to DeKalb Avenue junction. Here he explains how his love affair with the Brighton Line began and—like the BMT—just keeps rolling along.

If you ask me what fascinates me most about the subway system, I have to say that it's the vastness of it all. I began to experience that feeling in earnest when I was a six-year-old riding the Brighton Local to and from school—from Avenue U station to Kings Highway. I rode the big trains and played with the little model trains my family used to set up in our living room.

As I grew older, I would take longer and longer rides; each time marveling at the railroad around me; what it was like and what it could do and how it got that way, from primitive beginnings in the 19th Century.

The more I rode the Brighton Line, the more I wanted to know all about it. So, I would read up on the history and how it originated with Corbin's Long Island Rail Road cutting through the woods of Flatbush and how it reached the ritzy hotels of Manhattan Beach along the Atlantic.

Other lines fascinated me as well, especially the Culver run—the first to touch Coney Island—at Shell Road where it makes that wonderful turn. It wasn't just the subways that turned me on, but the elevated lines as well.

The utter physicality of it all—from the Bronx up north to Brooklyn in the South of New York City—overwhelmed me; first as a youngster and right up to this day.

One way to understand this is to take

the BMT Culver Line to Coney Island. Just before it reaches the last stop at Stillwell Avenue, the trains roll along the elevated tracks over the Transit Authority's Coney Island train yards.

The tracks in the yards go on and on and on; plus there literally are hundreds of trains parked there, and they give you an idea of the magnitude of it all.

As a kid, I was awed by how the system worked. For me, it was a source of wonderment, studying the switches and the signals; trying to imagine how the tunnels were built and how they stayed up without falling into the abyss. Seeing trains on different levels—as it is at Herald Square in Manhattan where you have the Sixth Avenue line, the Broadway line *and* PATH—knocked me out. I'm astounded every time I contemplate how they ever were able to build so many layers of different subways and make them work without one collapsing on top of the other. It's all about mechanics; the stuff I love.

Apart from that, what I have admired is the incredible rate of speed the trains attained and the convenience of it all. And because I've always loved the subways so much, there also was a down side because I hate the filth, which at times seems to be everywhere.

But that dirty aspect is relatively insignificant to the beauty part, which includes the history and engineering wonders that were realized when tunnels were dug under the river and viaducts constructed over vast acres of land, especially in Brooklyn where we still have miles and miles of elevated lines from the Sea Beach to the West End, Culver and Brighton.

There's nothing like our system. Chicago has lots of els but not much of a subway. I've been up to Montreal and they have a neat rubber-tired *Métro* that's quaint—more of a tourist thing than a real, meaty transportation complex.

It's the same in San Francisco and Los Angeles. They try to mimick New York but none of them come close because our subway is the mother of them all.

The only feature those out-of-town subways have over New York's is the looks; the cleanliness. That's why, if I could do anything I wanted to improve our system it would be to pretty it up and make it the most gorgeous and elegant thing so that *everyone* would be delighted to ride it just for the beauty alone.

This *has* happened in New York from time to time. They made the subway cars pretty for the 1939-40 World's Fair and did it again in 1964 when the Fair returned to Flushing Meadow. The subway looked like something right out of a *Flash Gordon* comic book.

In New York, we natives tend to take our subway for granted. That's why I get a kick out of the reaction of out-of-towners when they go underground. They're invariably amazed that we have this means of transportation both below ground and high above ground that gets people from Point A to Point B without interfering with whatever else is going on in life on the surface.

That, to me, is the really unique thing about the subway. It actually succeeds in accomplishing all these tasks without ever interfering with all the other stuff going on upstairs.

Another interesting aspect is the mix of people who ride and how New Yorkers react to one another on the trains, whether it's during a hectic rush hour or on a holiday weekend.

I'm reminded of the time, many years

ago, when a couple of friends and myself went to a Saint Patrick's Day Parade in Manhattan. Believe it or not—and you'd *better* believe it!—the three of us got on at Kings Highway (Brighton Line) station with a keg of beer and rode the train all the way to Times Square.

The most crazy—and amazing—part was that nobody said "Boo!" to us. The other riders just figured we were normal New Yorkers and nobody even thought about stopping us. They figured we were just a bunch of Brooklyn guys having a blast. Why, we even offered some of the passengers free beer out of our keg!

So when all is said and done, you can say that I love the subway and its people, no matter what the line. It's been that way all my life and it will stay that way forever!

Robert Presbrey
SUBWAY ARCHIVIST-HISTORIAN

Robert Presbrey's home in Valley Stream, Long Island easily could pass for a mini-Smithsonian of rapid transit archives.

His photo collection touches every aspect of subway history, from the original Interborough Rapid Transit to the Independent System; not to mention the elevated and trolley lines that preceded them.

In his basement, the Brooklyn native meticulously has amassed file after file of extraordinary scenes from a New York when the subway was young and still growing. His collection numbers more than 32,000 photos, of which about 20,000 he personally photographed.

But it's more than just a massive collection of first-rate photography. Presbrey not

only has the ultimate collection, he also owns an exquisite knowledge of the subject, born of first-hand experience, study and the insights of family members who, themselves, were members of the city's transit family.

Bob, himself, worked for the Long Island Rail Road for twenty-two years, never missing a day of work. He was awarded a plaque for that as well as another for having a perfect safety record. A member of the LIRR planning and development bureau, he was instrumental in creating timetables for the entire Long Island system.

Over the years, I had encountered samples of Presbrey's work in several histories of New York transit but it wasn't until 1993 that I actually met Bob and learned what a remarkable individual he was; not only as a rail buff, but one whose interest in and knowledge of classic pop music of the 1920s, 1930s and 1940s was nonpareil.

It was then that Presbrey had graciously agreed to open his archives, supplying innumerable photos for my street-

car opus, "Confessions of a Trolley Dodger From Brooklyn."

I spent many delightful evenings in his Valley Stream basement, poring over pictures of PCC Cars and their ilk. Meaanwhile, my ears were graced by the crooning of Bing Crosby records. Bob would regale me with transit history as we went from photo to photo well into the night.

An avid record collector, Presbrey has a collection of more than 1,000 78 RPM disks, mostly tunes from the 1920s, 1930s and 1940s. .

When John Henderson and I decided to pool our interests with this celebration of the IRT's one-hundreth birthday, there was one—and only one—prime source of photography, the Presbrey collection.

Exactly a decade after we had collaborated on "Confessions of a Trolley Dodger From Brooklyn," Henderson enlisted Bob's help once more. As his fabulous photos throughout the book indicate, Presbrey came through as nobly as he had before.

For Bob, in a way, delving into the city's transit past is a labor of love, rooted in his childhood fascination with Brooklyn's trolleys. The following taped interview with Presbrey helps explain why:

As a youngster, I lived in the Flatlands section of Brooklyn, not far from where the IRT's Nostrand Avenue Line terminates at Flatbush Avenue. Our house was off Flatbush Avenue, between Avenue J and Avenue K.

When I was growing up, in the days before World War II, I became very interested in trolleys and subways. By the time I

was seven years old, I would be out on Flatbush Avenue at Avenue K taking photos of the old, four-wheeled Birney-type streetcar—the last of that venerable type—which ran on the Holy Cross Cemetery Shuttle. I returned to take my first pictures of old wooden cars at age twelve.

Note-taking was a part of my routine even when I was quite young. I would use my bicycle a lot and keep my briefcase with film and camera in the bike basket along with my notebook.

My interest in transit was enhanced by the fact that my father had once worked for the Brooklyn Rapid Transit in its East New York shops and he knew a number of people there.

My dad was a professional engineer who invented the electric chassis dynamometer that road tests automobiles, trucks and buses. That gave him a natural interest in the transit business, and he passed a lot of his knowledge on to me.

In fact, while my father still was in college in Virginia, studying engineering, he worked for the Washington and Old Dominion Railway, a small trolley company. Dad actually operated some of the old Brooklyn el cars that had been sold to the Old Dominion.

It was easy for me to take trolley photos when I was young because all I had to do was get on my bike and pedal over to the Flatbush Depot, which was at Avenue N where the Utica Avenue (trolley) line ended. When I had the time, I'd ride over to the 58th Street-Ninth Avenue Depot which was farther from my house but had some very interesting cars that were great subjects for photography.

The way I worked it was that after I took the pictures and had them developed, I would bring them back to the trolley people and show them that I was on the level and truly interested in the subject. They respected my enthusiasm and opened the doors for me to shoot more and more trolleys.

I obtained still more transit information from an uncle who had been a tower operator for the New York Central, which had been one of the country's largest railroads. For him, it was a natural progression, going from the Central to the Independent Subway in 1932 when the IND began hiring railway people with seasoned experience to help run the new subway.

Once, I actually visited him at the 168th Street station on the Washington Heights (A) Line when he still worked for the IND.

In 1941, my father and I set out to find some of the oldest trains on the system. We rode on the open-platform gate cars which were popular on the Myrtle Avenue and Lexington Avenue elevated lines in Brooklyn. A conductor would open and close the iron gates by pulling on a handle. When the gates were closed, he'd tug on a cord that pulled a bell notifying the conductor ahead that he could then close his gates, and eventually the motorman got the bell signal indicating that all gates were closed. Then, he could start the train. Such was the age-old procedure, as we rode the very last el train over the Brooklyn Bridge!

Among my top underground lines was the BMT 14th Street-Canarsie Line which ran from the West Side of 14th Street in Manhattan, all the way to the Southern tip of Brooklyn at Canarsie. The interesting operation on this two-track line was running local and express service on the same tracks. Locals utilized multi section cars which had rapid accelerations, and expresses ran with BMT Standards, which slowly drifted along between the Multi's. It

was quite a neat operation. Near the end of the run at East 105th Street there actually was an old railroad-type crossing gate because the train ran at grade in that area.

As a boy, my passion for trains was such that I would make diagrams of the more interesting things I had seen, especially the switching systems and their signal—or marker—lights. I was very careful, once I began taking photos, to enter information about every single picture that I took.

My favorite moment was an evening rush hour ride on the Third Avenue elevateds through express, starting at the City Hall station. I would wait for the arrival of one of those great 7-car open platform gate trains. Standing inside the front door of the leading car awarded me an open air tour of Manhattan. Upcoming would be that long, non-stop run from 42nd Street to 106th Street, as this wooden train would glide across hills and valleys of Third Avenue on smooth steel rails. In 1955, I rode the very last Third Avenue el train.

Between my interest in the trolleys and the subways, I was kept on the go. In fact by the age of fifteen, I had ridden the entire New York subway system and also had covered the entire Third Avenue Railway System in Manhattan and the Bronx, not to mention virtually every Brooklyn trolley line.

The relative who most helped me in terms of my interest in subway photography was yet another uncle who originally had worked with the Public Service Commission and, after 1918, the Transit Commission. Then, when the City's Board of Transportation came into being, he served with it after 1924.

He had access to many of the old photographs and helped familiarize me with the history of the city's subway and el system through the photos. My uncle also was privy to plenty of inside information and it was he who told me that the Board had planned to eliminate all the trolleys after World War II was over.

Knowing that the streetcars would soon be extinct in my borough, I made a point of getting out, shooting pictures and keeping a careful account of each and every car of which I had a negative, the location and time of day as well as the signage displayed.

I also found friends who shared my transit interests. One of them was Al Hirsch, whom I originally had met during the World War II years when I was fourteen-years-old. Al and I accidentally met—but rather appropriately—on an Erie Basin-Park Row trolley. We instantly realized that we had the same transit interests and became good friends for over 50 years, although he was four years older than me and soon got drafted into the Army.

After World War II we resumed our friendship and began restoring old streetcars at the Branford (Connecticut) trolley museum. We saved four—a PCC 1001, the first of its kind, an 8111 Peter Witt-type that ran all over Brooklyn in its heyday, a work car, 1792, that we restored to passenger car status, and convertible trolley 4573 with open platforms.

By the time I was eighteen, I enlisted in the Army under the GI Bill and eventually was sent to post-war Japan where they were restoring the destroyed subway and streetcar systems. Because I was a soldier—and at that time, the Japanese were a little afraid of Americans like me who were in the Army of Occupation—I was able to run the trolleys while in uniform. Usually, it would be a car that stopped near the movie theater the GIs frequented. The the-

ater was at the last stop so I would be able to get on the car and help out as it was being reversed and then take the trolley home.

I returned to the States in February 1948, just after the famed post-Christmas blizzard, and continued my interest in subways and trolleys. In those post-war years, the trolleys were, sadly, being phased out of existence, so I felt a certain urgency in photographing them and actually buying a couple through the car-saving committee of a local fan group.

In addition to Al Hirsch, I was working closely with another transit buff, Don Harold, who also was very interested in preserving as many of the old cars as possible.

We liked 8111 because it represented a significant era in Brooklyn's transit history and it was one of the types of trolleys that we had known all our lives. In 1951—the year that the Flatbush Avenue, Utica-Reid and Nostrand Avenue lines, among others, were terminated—we ran three fund-raising fan trips on 8111 and also had another car, 6180, which had run on the Flatbush line before that trolley line had quit only to see 6180 put on the scrap track at the close of that fan trip day.

I did whatever I could to keep the streetcars rolling; even so far as to attend a New York City Council meeting and questioning the decision to eliminate trolleys from a wide street such as Ocean Avenue in Brooklyn. My position was that trolleys should not be replaced by buses, but the Council did not want to hear any of that, nor concerns about air pollution.

Fortunately, we did save a few trolleys, but all the rest were burned, and I felt terrible about it because I was aware of the consequences of not having trolleys anymore.

I couldn't sleep. I was so used to the lull of an "Owl" car going back to the depot; it was music to my ears, until the "music" stopped.

After all the trolleys had gone, I maintained my interest in transit. Friends and I ran four Long Island Rail Road steam train trips, connections from the Brooklyn depot at Atlantic Avenue to Eastern Long Island. We were raising money to build carbarns at Branford for the Third Avenue Railway and Brooklyn trolleys that we preserved.

In addition, I continued to build my collection of rapid transit and trolley photos.

Even at the age of 75, I'm still as enthused about the subject of els, subways and trolleys as I was as a youngster taking pictures at Flatbush Avenue and Avenue K.

Tom Sarro
THE SUBWAY SERIES BUFF

If ever there was a subway fan who could be called an "Existential Man," it would be Tom Sarro of Dyker Heights, Brooklyn.

An author, historian, teacher, former goaltender and Civil War archivist, Sarro is unique as a collector of ice cream memorabilia.

In addition, his massive home adjoining Bay Ridge—which he shares with his wife, Angie—also is a veritable hockey museum as well as repository of baseball mementos including many photos of various Subway Series involving the New York Yankees, Brooklyn Dodgers and New York Giants.

Tom and Angie also have participated in Civil War battle reenactments, and, in his spare time, Sarro lectures on a variety of Civil War subjects.

Born June 25, 1941 in Bay Ridge Hospital, Tom was a student at St. Ephrem's (elementary) School and then Power Memorial Academy in Manhattan.

A graduate of Brooklyn College, Tom has been a lifelong New York Rangers fan, having attended games at the "old" Madison Square Garden on Eighth Avenue and 49th Street beginning in the 1950s.

His home subway is the BMT Fourth Avenue Line as well as the Sea Beach route.

His love for hockey has remained through his adult years, and in the Autumn of 2003 he emphasized the point by taking on a coaching stint with a Metropolitan Area high school team.

Like most Brooklynites, Sarro grew up with the subway, and in his adult years added rapid transit photos to his vast collection of historical material.

Although Tom has regularly taken the train to various New York venues, he readily admits that his favorite underground jaunts involved the round-trips to Madison Square Garden—first, the one on 49th Street and more recently, the one on 33rd Street—to watch his Rangers in action.

In the following taped interview, Sarro explains what the subway means to him:

Without question, the aspect of the subway that impresses me most is the fact that—in the simplest of terms—it gets you from one place to another and usually does it speedily and well. And riding the subway from borough to borough is much better than trying to get around the city by car. It's always seemed unbelievable to me that an operation as colossal as it is in size could be so large and yet work so well.

I started riding the trains when I was three-years-old. From that time until I was around seven or eight-years-old, I was enthralled by the subways. I found each and every ride a phenomenal experience for a lot of reasons.

One simply was the act of going on a trip, no matter how short or how long. I use the word *exploring* because that's what those train rides were like when I started riding underground. I'd get on a train and—wherever it went—it was an adventure. It was as if I was exploring a new area of the city; which, when you think about it, I *was.*

Growing up when I did, I had an opportunity to ride what was a classic of New York rapid transit, the Third Avenue el. This was in the early 1950s, before the Manhattan part of the line was torn down.

Riding that particular line was extra special for a Brooklynite like me because we had many elevated lines in our borough but the Third Avenue run was the last of its kind in Manhattan. Looking out of its windows, I could see buildings on either side of the street that were sixty, seventy, eighty and ninety-years-old, some of which had advertisements on their walls for products that didn't even exist any more.

Riding in an automobile, you don't meet any interesting people, but you sure do in the subway, although I'll grant you that the atmosphere underground was a little friendlier back in the 1940s and 1950s when I started riding.

In those days, people would talk to each other more than they do now. Also, courtesy from men toward women was more prevalent. It was not uncommon then for a man to get up and give a lady a seat. I saw a lot more chivalry on the BMT in the 1950s than I see today.

One of the differences between then and now, I find, is that straphangers seem to be more wary of one another. I remember not long ago, riding the IRT to Yankee Stadium, noticing that people were staring at one another, seeming to wonder what the other person was going to do; if he—or she—was going to do anything at all.

It gave me an uneasy feeling.

On the other hand, as a historian, I marvel at remnants of the original 1904 Interborough system and some of the other older lines. To me it's amazing to see stations which were built seventy, eighty, ninety and one hundred years ago.

And they're still intact, functioning and, in many cases, looking remarkably good.

The art work has always caught my attention. I'm talking about the tiles, the *bas reliefs,* the ornamental moldings, the name tablets.

I love the idea that they used a beaver emblem at the IRT Astor Place station and the good ship *Santa Maria* at Columbus Circle.

Over the years, when I have been a subway rider, I would find myself thinking as a historian; wondering about all the people who lived in the subway during the era when it originally opened in 1904, and the years that followed right through the 1920s and 1930s. I would try to imagine what life—and the people—were like down there compared to how it is today.

It was a different world—a *totally* different world—than today and that's a part of the subway that continually fascinates me about them.

My earliest rides on a regular basis took place in the 1950s after I enrolled at Power Memorial Academy, which was a Catholic high school located at 61st Street on the west side of Manhattan.

Since I was living in the Bay Ridge section of Brooklyn in 1955 when I was a freshman at Power, it meant that the only way I could get to school—in a fairly quick, cheap and efficient way—was by train.

I was lucky. The BMT Fourth Avenue Local was a short walk from my house. I'd ride the Fourth and then switch to the BMT Sea Beach Line and eventually hook up—with a free transfer—to the IRT that went up Manhattan's West Side.

The trip took me an hour each way, and most of the time I was riding during the morning or evening rush hours; which wasn't exactly a joy because I was standing nearly all the way.

It was a practical way to travel but certainly not a lot of fun. What really annoyed me was when, say, I was on an express and it pulled into a station and my local would be sitting across the platform. Before I could get out of my train, the doors of the local would be closing and I'd wind up stuck on the platform, having to wait for the next train.

Of course, since it happened often enough, I got used to such annoyances. The most important thing was that the subway usually worked and—since I didn't have a car—it was *the* way to go. I had to take the train whether I was going to school or heading up to Madison Square Garden (on Eighth Avenue and 49th Street) for a hockey game.

During my youthful days, I had no basis of comparison in terms of how other subway systems worked because I didn't travel out-of-town that much. But in later years, I visited cities such as Toronto and Montreal—each one has a relatively clean and quiet subway of its own—and came to appreciate the New York trains even more; even though the other systems are much newer than ours.

The difference is that New York's subway is just so big—and *so* long!

It's often difficult for out-of-towners to comprehend the enormity of our underground system. I'm reminded of a scene from the pre-World War II movie, "Sergeant York," starring Gary Cooper.

One of the soldiers in the movie happens to be a New York subway conductor and is trying to explain to Alvin York—who is from the backwoods of Tennessee—what a subway is all about, but Sergeant York simply couldn't comprehend it. Finally, exasperated, York says, "Does it run this way? Or does it run this way?"

As it happened, one of the first things the real-life Alvin York did after the war, when he came to New York, was ride our subway to find what it was all about. Actually, it's an experience that every out-of-towner should have.

If I wanted to take a long excursion by train through the four boroughs, I could be on the subway for hours and hours and hours.

For the fun of it, I would ride the Sea Beach Line, heading south, where it comes out of the tunnel in Brooklyn and goes outdoors to Coney Island. Then, I would ride what once was called the West End Line—unfortunately, in recent years, they have changed a lot of the names of lines to numbers—which is elevated and overlooks a very interesting part of Borough Park and Bensonhurst, Brooklyn. Or, I'd ride the Brighton Line which, like some of the other BMT trains, crosses the Manhattan Bridge. That's always good for a nifty—and historic—view of Manhattan and the old buildings.

Most of my subway trips were taken not for historic—but practical—purposes. If I wasn't taking it to school, I was riding uptown to see the Rangers play hockey at the old Madison Square Garden.

When I was young and single, my favorite subway to ride was the BMT Sea Beach line, because it not only could carry me to school but also to the Garden. Back in the 1950s—before they got the new rolling stock—the Sea Beach trains were throwbacks to a pre-World War II era when the BMT was a private operation disconnected from the city's Board of Transportation.

During those days, the BMT had two basic car designs. One was the old-time 67-footers (Standards) and the other was the one I was accustomed to riding on the Sea Beach. These trains were called the Triplex because three cars were linked together as one whole unit. Between the first car and the second car—as well as between the second and third car—there was a connection like they have on regular railroads. In other words, I could walk through the cars without having to open a door, because there were no doors at those connections. Even when the train was making a sharp turn, I could walk from car to car because the openings would turn with the train and it was impossible to fall out.

I remember on those Sea Beach trains there often was a guy playing an accordion—or a harmonica—and he would go through the three cars singing. I'd drop a nickel or a penny in his cup.

Another favorite of mine was the old Culver Line, which originated in Brooklyn and went to the City Hall station, adjacent to the Municipal Building—near Brooklyn Bridge—and the Superior Courthouse.

Riding the Culver Line, I made a point of standing by the front window and studying each station as we traveled to the city. What fascinated me the most were remnants of tunnels and abandoned stations. They always caught my attention because they looked so different. I would imagine myself alone on the abandoned platform with nobody else around.

Another line I liked—but for a different reason—was the Fourth Avenue local. It made so many stops that I would either study all the people on it or just doze off; or do both.

Over the years, I've had some off-beat experiences riding the trains, but the craziest of all took place back in the late 1950s when myself and two friends were coming back from a Saturday afternoon Rangers game at the old Garden.

We were on the Fourth Avenue local and feeling a lot of hockey in us on the way back. This was a normal reaction because of the excitement of the game we had just seen. In those days, at the Garden, we would crush a paper cup, drop it to the ground and kick it around the corridor, pretending it was a hockey puck. This was commonplace at the Garden.

On this day, we took the game a step further and smashed some cups on the floor of the subway car. The three of us were playing Cup Hockey in the empty car until two policemen got on board and hauled us into the precinct station house.

Fortunately for us, my father happened to be a fireman and my two other friends' fathers were cops, so nothing more came of it. Apparently, to some transit policemen, Cup Hockey was a bad thing!

Looking back to the days when I began riding the subway, and comparing them to the contemporary scene, I notice dramatic changes; many for the better. The trains are brighter—even quieter—and the air conditioning is good.

What I miss are some of the items that pleased me from the olden times. They took away lots of the newspaper and candy stands, not to mention the chewing gum and candy machines which adorned the stations. As a kid, I loved buying a tiny piece of chocolate for a penny. I would like to see the present Metropolitan Transit Authority bring back some of those wonderful, old-time features.

I don't like the idea that the MTA is trying to phase out token booth clerks. Whenever a real person is on duty, he—or she—provides a personal touch that can't be duplicated by a machine. I always felt that I could converse with our home station change-maker. In those days, everyone knew one another. I liked the subway better that way.

———————————

PART IV

100 YEARS
OF THE BEST

Predecessor to the subway—Broadway's horsecar.

100 Years of Rolling Stock

A Look At the Cars
That Carried the Straphangers

ABOVE: Early, experimental electric-powered set, with only one motor pulling five trailers.

BELOW: A typical seating arrangement on an old elevated car. Note the leather straps hanging from the ceiling.

Interior and exterior of Manhattan elevated rolling stock. The original gate cars were later supplied with sliding doors and reclassified MUDC, which stands for "multiple unit door control." The seating arrangement was exclusive to cars that operated in Manhattan and was therefore referred to as "Manhattan seating."

Early steam hauled coaches that were later electrified.

ABOVE AND BELOW: Earliest type of steam engine and Shadbelly coach used on the Ninth Avenue el.

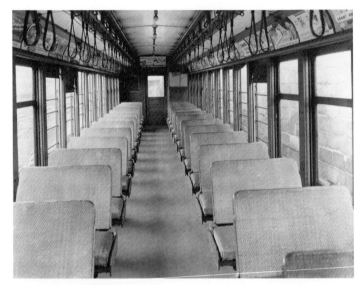

These coaches had railroad type seating with wicker "walkover" seats that were reversible.

The Interborough Rapid Transit Lines

Before actually opening what would become the greatest subway in the world, its founders had to produce a passenger car that would be exceptionally strong, attractive and sufficiently large enough to carry enough riders to be profitable.

Employing the foresight that characterized the original Interborough Rapid Transit administration, financier August Belmont and the IRT's Chief Engineer William Barclay Parsons oversaw development of the city's first subway coach and its immediate successors in what became a long line of rolling stock.

Belmont and Parsons designated respected railway expert George Gibbs, who headed the engineering firm, Gibbs and Hill, to orchestrate the project.

Gibbs immediately sent shock waves through the car-building industry when he deviated from traditional turn-of-the-century practices and suggested that rather than the abundant use of wood, an *all-steel* car be built.

Railroad coach companies were not prepared for such a radical change and, at first, balked at Gibbs' proposal. Faced with stiff opposion from train-builders, Gibbs delivered a compromise plan that would incorporate his ideas yet placate his foes.

On the drawing board, Gibbs produced what evolved into the "Composite" car, which featured a steel frame—revolutionary compared with elevated cars running throughout New York City—surrounded by the traditional wood.

Once car-builders accepted Gibbs' blueprint, a pair of experimental vehicles were built. The very first—appropriately named *August Belmont*—featured an ele-

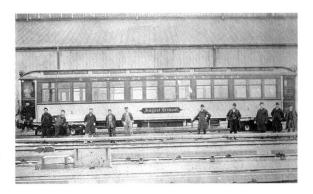

gance that would be too rich for the masses, but impressive nonetheless. At the time consideration was being given by Belmont to offer *First Class* service on his IRT at extra cost; a thought which was abandoned before the subway ever opened.

The second experimental car was named after the man heading the vast subway-building project, John B. MacDonald.

His outfit was the Rapid Transit Subway Construction Company.

Following the Gibbs' plan, the city's second subway car, *John B. McDonald*, took on the more traditional, less gaudy appearance which later would characterize most rolling stock on the system. Each of the experimental cars was built in Springfield, Massachussets by the Wason Company, a major car-builder of that era.

Despite the use of wood, safety in every aspect—from electrical wiring to collision protection—had a top priority. The result was a car that won industry acclaim for its practicality with very few exceptions.

Ironically, the most severe critic of the IRT's maiden coach was the man who conceived it himself, Gibbs. He steadfastly maintained that a system that would be so heavily-used and speedy—trains would run as fast as 40 miles per hour—as the IRT required an even stronger car than the Composite. Gibbs demanded that the all-steel version was the only way to go in the future and, eventually, he won his case.

With the significant help of Pennsylvania Railroad boss Alexander Cassatt, Gibbs was able to have an experimental steel coach built in 1903—before the IRT opened for business—at the PRR's base in Altoona, Pennsylvania.

The Interborough received the vehicle as a Christmas present in December 1903. Although it was flawed in some ways—it did not measure up to weight constraints—the steel car displayed so many advantages it was only a matter of time before Gibbs won his case.

Unlike many of its industry cohorts, the American Car and Foundry Company endorsed Gibbs' idea and offered to construct a fleet of steel cars for the IRT. Early in 1904, five months before the subway's debut, construction of 300 steel cars was underway at the American Car and Foundry plant.

Gibbs' revolutionary concept immediately proved a hit and the Composite car became obsolete the moment it hit the rails despite the fact that a fleet already had been delivered between 1903 and 1904.

The lesson delivered by Gibbs was repeated over and over through the subway century as innovation followed innovation in the changing of the fleet.

Although the author was not around to ride the Composites, he has travelled on virtually every other form of rolling stock that has graced the city's rails. The following are capsule comments on rolling stock which followed the original IRT cars with the author's personal reaction to each of the designs right up to the newest trains:

* THE COMPOSITES: All things considered, the original wood-steel compromise design was an admirable vehicle with which to launch the first subway. Despite the fact that George Gibbs failed to win critics over to his all-steel-car concept, the Composite proved to be state-of-the-art

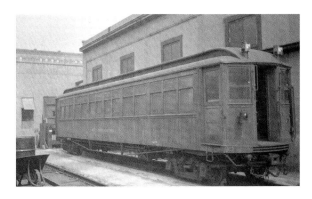

for its time. More importantly, it paved the way for steel-only construction immediately thereafter. In terms of appearance, the composites had more the look of a railroad car than subway rolling stock as we know it today. That was primarily due to the fact that doors were located at each end of the car but, conspicuously, there were none in the middle of the body. The single, sliding doors—manually-operated by a *guard* who was stationed between the adjoining vestibules—soon proved to be inadequate for the crowds and, in time, a center door was added. At first, leather straps—as in *straphangers*—hung from upper piping, similar to those used on elevated cars. However, they eventually were replaced by porcelain-coated metal handholds, the likes of which became rudimentary equipment on many later lines. Unfortunately, the car size was set at nine-feet wide and fifty-one-feet long. The width was designed to accommodate the smallish IRT tunnels which should not have been so constricted in the first place. While the 9-by-51 dimensions may have been adequate for 1904, they certainly are inadequate by today's demands, especially since they could seat no more than 44 passengers. Yet the IRT lines in the 21st Century continue to use cars with the century-old sizes simply because of tunnel-size dictates.

* THE FIRST (GIBBS) ALL-STEEL MODELS: Well before the original IRT began operation, Gibbs had triumphed in his campaign to make total-steel rolling stock *de rigueur* on the subway. Apart from the inner design alterations to accommodate steel side girders, "The Gibbs Fleet," as it

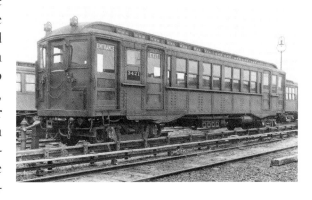

was known in the trade, looked very much like the original Composites. Like its predecessor, the steel car boasted an attractive coating of Tuscan Red paint with Burnt Orange around the windows. As an added fillip, the designers provided pinstripes and gold leaf lettering. The early steel models had leather straps for standee passengers and lacked center doors. However, the IRT realized that more doors would be required and, after experimentation with a couple of concepts, added center doors. Easily, the most advanced modification, for its time, was the addition of large, windmill-type fans, four of which hung from the ceiling of each car. While it wasn't air conditioning as we know it, the fans created quite a breeze and proved a welcome addition for the early subway era.

* THE DECK-ROOFED CARS: Since the Composites and All-Steel cars arrived almost simultaneously, each could be considered part of the original rolling stock. What emerged as the first, true successor in the IRT fleet was a vehicle with a "new look."

Arriving in 1908—coinciding with the Interborough's big push into Brooklyn—the cars were manufactured by American Car and Foundry. Their distinguishing feature was on top. Instead of the traditional style displayed by the Composites and Gibbs models, the new trains had a roof clerestory which squared off behind the motorman's area. To some observers, it looked like a flat deck; hence the term "Deck-Roofed Cars." With the center door now standard equipment, the "Deck Roof Motors," as they were designated among transit professionals, looked more like the subway cars we came to know and love. One esthetic drawback was the IRT's decision to eschew its Tuscan Red-Burnt Orange colors in favor of a darker, less fetching paint job.

* THE MINEOLA: While it is commonplace for multi-millionaire executives to own at least one limousine-automobile, none in our time can claim to have a limousine-subway car. In fact the only person *ever* to boast such a distinction was the IRT's founder and Sugar Daddy, August Belmont. Although the subway *was* for the public, it didn't mean that a patrician such as financier Belmont couldn't enjoy the Interborough as his own private electric train set. With that in mind, he assigned his staff to design a private subway car which would resemble, in some ways, the types of vehicles used by railroad barons on their long-distance lines. After blueprints were dispatched to Springfield, Massachussets, the Wason Car Company assembled a once-in-a-lifetime subway car. Belmont dubbed it *Mineola* and proudly displayed it to his blue-blooded cronies after delivery to the IRT tracks adjacent to its Grand Central subway station. Adorned with the finest woods as well as stained glass windows, a curved plate glass front window and other

sophisticated amenities, the Mineola featured everything a subway founder could want. Among the *de luxe* items were a galley with (then) high-tech electric equipment, a refrigerator, wine shelf, pantry, coffee-maker, lavatory, as well as an office section replete with roll-top desk. And if that wasn't enough, the Mineola softened everyone's heels with a broadloom carpet. Imagine a subway car which included a butler available for any dining order. The IRT boss opened a hotel in his name at 42nd Street and Park Avenue. In the basement he had a circular bar along contours of the curved subway track from where Belmont and friends could reach the Mineola via a bar-to-tracks passageway.

The Mineola rolled over the IRT line at Belmont's whim and—thanks to a connection at Atlantic Avenue station in Brooklyn—linked with Long Island Rail Road tracks. From there, Belmont, et. al. could reach Elmont, New York to watch the races at—you guessed it!—Belmont Park. After Belmont's death, Mineola was put to pasture in the IRT yards and later sold to a scrap dealer who — after mounting it on a foundation — used it as a "retreat" on his New Jersey farm. When the scrapdealer passed away, Mineola was passed on to a Pennsylvania collector. After flood damaged the car, it was transferred to the Shoreline Trolley Museum in Branford, Connecticut where efforts have been underway to restore it to something resembling its original condition.

* HEDLEY HIGH-VOLTAGE CARS: In addition to August Belmont, John B. McDonald and George Gibbs, an early titan of the IRT operation was Frank Hedley, the company's General Superintendent and who eventually would become the Inter-

borough's President. Among Hedley's innovations was a collision protective device called the *anti-climber* located at the end sills of cars and created to prevent one car from telescoping into another at impact. When the IRT added 325 new cars between 1910 and 1911, the re-designed vehicles were called "Hedley Motors" by some and "Battleships" by others. The later term, suggesting indomitability, referred to its steel plate fuselage. So practical was the new design that it would become "official IRT" for over a decade and a half, including no less than 1,600 new cars. The Hedley Hi-V Cars were the first of the IRT fleet that I recall riding as a youth. Apart from the awful whine of the motors, the one feature that arrested my attention was the slow-opening and equally slow-closing doors, each with a large rubber bumper along its edge. Like its successors, the Hi-V offered a large front window out of which to explore the tunnels as well as a smaller—yet useful for a train-buff—window to the left. All in all, the Hi-V was an interesting car if for no other reason than that it was a throwback to pre-World War I subway riding.

* THE STEINWAY CARS: With precious few exceptions, right-of-way on the New

York City subways followed a pre-ordained design. There were, however, precious few exceptions where a previous route—not originally planned for the city subway—later was annexed and integrated into the overall system. The IRT's Dyre Avenue Line, once part of the New York, Westchester and Boston Railroad, is one example. Another is the Steinway Route. The tunnel—from

William Brennan

William Brennan

Manhattan's East 42nd Street to Queens' Long Island City neighborhood—originally was blueprinted for a trolley car line.

Piano magnate William Steinway envisioned service from the community around his Long Island City plant to the streets near Grand Central Terminal. Although the trolley tunnels under the East River were finished in 1907 and fifty streetcars were built for the Steinway Tunnels, the project only got as far as a test run for the vehicles. Despite the immense accomplishment of the underwater construction, actual revenue service never began because of franchise hassles.

Remarkably, the spanking new tunnel—fully equipped with overhead trolley wires, signaling and stations—remained unused for six years. By that time the original IRT Subway had become so popular it was decided, via the Dual Contracts, to expand the system to the Bronx, Brooklyn and Queens. The ready-made Steinway

Tunnels were too good to overlook, so they were re-designed for use by the Interborough Line as part of the IRT's Times Square-to-Flushing route.

Beginning in 1913, when the Dual Contracts went into effect, the Steinway Tunnels were renovated for subway use. However, there was sufficient concern that the steep grades might prove too great a challenge for traditional IRT rolling stock. To cope with this dilemma, the IRT ordered a dozen cars in 1915 from the Pressed Steel Car Company.

Known as the Steinway Cars, the equipment had power in each vehicle—as opposed to unpowered trailer cars on other lines—and a better gear ratio to handle the tunnel gradients in a manner superior to the regular rolling stock. The Steinways became the first IRT Low Voltage (Low V) cars as opposed to the High Voltage (High V) trains which comprised the Gibbs, Standard (Hedley, Battleship) and Deck Roof models.

The Low V Steinways made their debut on June 22, 1915 and tunnel service to Queens—still in use today on the IRT's Number Seven run—proved as successful as the new technology cars.

The Steinways, which also were manufactured by the Pullman Company, continued gracing the IRT well after World War II and proved one of the most popular cars on the system. Prior to the 1939 World's Fair in Flushing Meadow, Steinways were given a new paint job to impress Fair-goers.

In addition to operating on the Flushing Line, Steinways also could be found on Bronx IRT runs as well as the Polo Grounds Shuttle.

* THE LOW-VOLTAGE CARS: Although modernization of the IRT fleet was never that obvious to the naked eye of average straphangers—exterior designs essentially

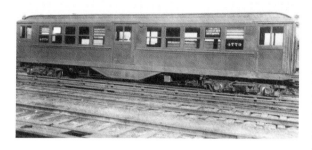

were the same from 1910 through 1939—significant changes were taking place in the cars themselves. Put in use during the middle of World War I, the Low-V cars were renowned for the use of automatic acceleration, battery-controlled circuits and improved braking. Success of the Low Voltage fleet can be measured by the fact that re-orders of essentially the same car were made in large quantities in 1920, 1922, 1924 and 1925. I remember the Low-Vs best of all the IRT rolling stock. I rode them on the New Lots Avenue Line, the Broadway (Manhattan) Line and the Nostrand Avenue route, among many others. Virtually identical—at least to my eyes—to the High-Vs, the Low Voltage cars had an "old" feel about

them. For example, while the IND and BMT had well-lit rolling, fabric route signs, the Low Vs had old, metal plates placed on racks at each end of the car; not to mention, old-fashioned kerosene lamps at the front and rear ends. The Low-Vs seemed more like large, toy trains than any I ever had the pleasure to ride.

* 1939 WORLD'S FAIR CARS: To service the New York World's Fair at Flushing Meadow, Queens, the IRT purchased fifty new cars for use on its Flushing Line. Although the Interborough had gone bankrupt by this time, it was able to cut design and construction costs while still producing a reasonably modern vehicle. How modern? Well, it looked a trifle more streamlined than its IND (R-1 through R-9) counterparts which still were being delivered. Perhaps the one aspect that set the IRT's World's Fair Cars apart from the Independent's was the roof. Discarding the clerestory design, the Interborough opted for a lyrically curved roof dotted with ventilators. In another departure from standard IRT procedure, route signs were clearly placed atop the front windows although metal signage still would be used inside the cars. It may not have seemed like much but those few innovations were so radically different from what I had become accustomed to seeing on the IRT (High-V, Low-

William Brennan

V), I thought that it was truly nifty. As it happened, the World's Fair Cars proved to be the last model to operate on the system before the Interborough merged with the IND and BMT to become part of the city's subway system.

Brooklyn Rapid Transit and Brooklyn, Manhattan Transit

* THE STANDARDS: When in 1913 the Brooklyn Rapid Transit was recognized as an operator—alongside the Interborough—of new subway routes, BRT executives had to choose a prototype car to carry its passengers. In preparation for such an eventuality the BRT had examined many possible car designs including the 51-foot IRT model which had been in use for almost a decade. After careful consideration, the BRT hired a man already acclaimed for car planning. His name was Lewis B. Stillwell and, among many accomplishments, he had helped George Gibbs in creating the IRT's innovative steel car. Stillwell also designed similarly unusual coaches for the Erie Railroad as well as the Hudson Tubes. The most dramatic departure from IRT practice was in car size. What become known as the BRT Standard would be ten-feet wide and sixty-seven-feet long.

A huge advantage over the IRT model was door-placement. The Standard utilized three sets of pneumatic doors that comprised almost one-quarter of the car's sides. Another arresting improvement was in seating design. Stillwell employed triple and double cross seats which gave the Standard an aura of first-class travel never really duplicated on any other city subway vehicle. The BRT's first car had many other innovations such as advanced braking and

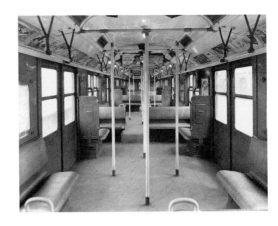

William Brennan

coupling systems as well as electric marker light systems. The competition continued using kerosene lamps. Whereas later versions of the Standard would use a deck roof, the originals had the arch variety, dotted with streamlined ventilators. James Clifford Greller, historian and author of *Subway Cars of the BMT*, said it best when he observed that the Standard, "was a large but very graceful and light-looking piece of equipment."[25] From the first time I rode a Standard in the mid-1930s to my very last ride on the rolling stock three decades later, I always felt that this was as good as subway design could get. Of course, my favorite thing was the front window which opened from the top, allowing a subway buff like myself clear access to the train world around me. Nothing could beat that!

* THE TRIPLEX—D-TYPE CAR: From its very start in the subway business, the BRT high command displayed a passion for

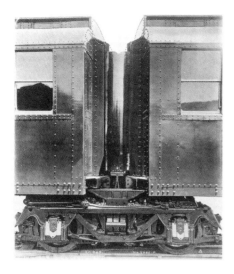

William Brennan

innovation and excellence. Early leaders such as Chief BRT Engineer William Menden and Superintendent of Equipment William Gove simply would not settle for the ordinary in rapid transit design and this philosophy would permeate BRT thinking even after the traumatic Malbone Street Disaster in 1918.

Aftereffects of the crash caused bankruptcy of the BRT and its re-organization as the Brooklyn Manhattan Transit Company (BMT) with Menden at the top as president and Gove in his same position. They were accompanied by Gerhard Dahl, Chairman of the Executive Committee of the Board of Directors.

This brain-trust was unwilling to sit on the success of its highly-acclaimed Stan-

dard, and a decade after the classic BRT car made its debut, the BMT general staff decided that the time had come for an even better piece of rolling stock. After careful study the high command decided it would produce a car featuring articulation which—improving on the Standard—would haul more riders while cutting back on the number of moving parts.

Although it was difficult to imagine production of a car more comfortable and attractive than the 67-footers, the soon-to-be Triplex (or D-type) would—in the estimation of many BMT critics—be just that.

And it was.

To begin with, the fact that passengers could walk between cars unimpeded and without having to open doors was an immense leap forward in terms of straphangers' mobility and, even more importantly, safety.

Attractive but in a style distinctly different from the smooth-silhouetted Standards, the Triplex looked bolder in a positive, *macho* manner that led James Clifford Greller to label it a "heavy, menacing look."

Like its predecessor, the Triplex also featured a front window which opened and was considerably larger—two kids' heads could comfortably fit through it—than the Standard's. All in all, the D-type lived up to its hype and remained a BMT staple long after the once-private line became a part of the city's Board of Transportation.

* THE Q CARS: Shortly after the turn of the (20th) Century, the Brooklyn Union Elevated Railroad Company purchased a number of open-ended elevated cars from an assortment of manufacturers. They were

nicknamed BU cars because of the Brooklyn Union order and all were built of wood except for the necessary steel trucks, gates, etc.

For example, among the 1200 series BU cars obtained in 1903, Osgood Bradley, a well-known firm, was the builder. Likewise the Cincinnati Car Company delivered a number of 1300 series cars in 1905, among them convertibles (1327 is an example) for summer use. When I rode the Myrtle Avenue el, I often would find myself on a 1400 series car build by the Jewett Company in 1907.

Although to the casual eye, the BU cars appeared the same—they all had open platforms with gates for alighting and departing—some had center doors and others boasted curved back roofs instead of the monitor variety.

In 1938, the Brooklyn, Manhattan Transit (BMT) which long ago had annexed the Brooklyn elevated lines, decided to upgrade many of the BU cars.

As part of the process, the manually-operated iron gates were removed along with the open platforms at each end. The refurbished cars had enclosed vestibules and automatic sliding doors rather than the old-fashioned manual type that required a conductor between each car.

The "new" BU cars were re-christened Q (as in Queens) cars and numbered from 1600 to 1629.

As part of the BMT's World's Fair service, the Q cars began service in January 1939 and were dolled-up in orange and blue-grey fair colors.

While the refurbished Qs couldn't compare with the IRT's brand-new World's Fair cars, they did have a curiously-attractive look.

Ironically, the Myrtle Avenue Line—my home el—was the last route to operate the open-gated BU cars. They continued operating on that run until 1958 when they were replaced by once-again-upgraded Q cars.

The Myrtle Avenue el remained the last home to the Qs until 1969 when the western part of the line—from Broadway-Myrtle station to Sands Street—was razed. At that point the last batch of wooden el cars were retired.

* THE C CARS: Following the November, 1918 Malbone Street Disaster, the Brooklyn Rapid Transit (BRT) went into receivership and eventually emerged by 1925 as the Brooklyn Manhattan Transit (BMT). Under new BMT management, many improvements in rolling stock were planned, including modern designs for

new cars as well as the upgrading of older, elevated cars. The New York State Public Service Commission—maintaining an Argus eye on the subway-el operation—had mandated replacement of the wooden cars such as those involved in the Malbone crash.

A group of 75 of the open-gated el cars, which had been part of the BRT fleet, were overhauled and upgraded. They were dubbed C-types and represented the first BMT attempt at re-claiming and renovating some of its venerable—yet sturdy—cars.

Manufactured by such noteworthy com-panies as Stephenson, Laconia, Brill, Wason and Osgood Bradley, some of the cars dated back to the steam engine era. At that time, the wooden cars had been trailers attached to the steam-powered locomotive. When the steam era gave way to electrification, the wooden cars were outfitted with elec-tric motors and successfully operated on such lines as the Myrtle, Lexington and Fulton Street els.

The rebuilding included replacement of the open platforms with an enclosed vestibule. At a time when the BMT was designing its D-type Triplex car, it also chose to unite sets of three C cars as per-manent triplets

Superficially, the cars appeared distinct-ly different from the open-platform ver-sions but they certainly were not pretty; and I can vouch for that.

From time to time, I would ride the Fulton Street el—on which the C units were placed—and marveled at the strange-looking cars. By far the most striking ele-ments were the replacement doors.

Instead of gates, which opened and closed manually on the original el cars, the C cars were equipped with sliding doors which open and closed in response to a huge "arm," located on the *outside* of the cars.

Attached to the door, the arm—upon activation by the conductor—would pull the door open and closed accordingly. To my eyes, it appeared to be as bizarre a con-traption as I had ever seen on a subway or el train.

Despite its oddball appearance, the C units adequately functioned on Brooklyn's Fulton Street el through the World War II years and thereafter. At the start of the 1950s, they still were alive and well, but soon to be heading for the scrapheap.

Experimental Cars, Pre-World War II

Despite the Great Depression and obvious success of the Triplex, BMT planners—unlike their bankrupt IRT counterparts—continued to seek ways and means to develop the "perfect" subway car.

Designers knew that there remained several potential areas of improvement including acceleration, air conditioning, seating and overall streamlining. With that in mind, the fertile minds at BMT produced three remarkable designs, the first of which was targeted for use on elevated lines.

* THE GREEN HORNET: Exploiting the virtues of lightweight materials such as aluminum and rubber, BMT experts conceived a streamlined, updated version of the Triplex. However, the ressemblance ended there. Five cars were linked together rather than three. In a modernistic departure from previous cars, seats employed soft cushioning rather than *rattan*. The attractive green paint job inspired BMTites to name it after a popular radio, mystery hero, The Green Hornet. Built by Pullman, it was completed in 1934 and went on display at the Brooklyn Bridge terminal across from City Hall amid considerable press atten-

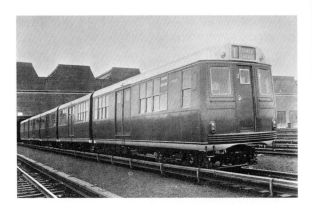

tion. The most innovative subway car in the world at the time, Green Hornet was placed in service on several BMT el lines including the Fulton Street route as well as the Franklin Avenue Shuttle. The one-of-a-kind train remained a hit until World War II when it was deemed more useful for the war effort. The Federal government requisitioned it for scrap and the Board of Transportation obliged.

* THE BMT ZEPHYR: The Philadelphia-based Budd Company—relatively new to the transit industry—scored a *coup* of sorts when it produced a stainless steel articulated train called *The Zephyr* for The Burlington Route (Chicago Burlington and Quincy Railroad). So successful was the use of stainless steel—with abundant rubber to reduce noise—that Budd was able to sell BMT moguls on the possibilities of a city-version of the concept. Also a five-car articulated unit, the Budd product received as much hype as the *Green Hornet*. A Budd pamphlet touted the new subway *Zephyr* as a stainless steel car having "great capaci-

ty with comfort." This was not an overstatement. Completed in 1934, *The Zephyr* fulfilled its notices, and, to that point, I speak firsthand. I rode the train many times while it was in revenue service on the BMT's

Franklin Avenue Shuttle. As the world's first stainless steel subway train, *The Zephyr* immediately captured my—and thousands of other riders'—attention with its unique silvery look. The interior was just as fetching, what with soft, red cushioned seats, state of the art lighting and plenty of window space. Best of all, it accelerated unlike any other subway car. (The brochure claimed that it could "pick up speed at a rate of five miles an hour each second.") Unfortunately, a second *Zephyr* never was built, and by the end of World War II, the silvery beauty no longer was a featured star on the BMT any more.

*   THE BLUEBIRD: The BMT's pioneering with streamliners did not end with the *Zephyr* as the company's think-tankers continued to experiment with even better designs. Only a year before the BMT and IRT merged with the IND to become a city-owned entity, yet another BMT subway beauty was created with help from the Clark Equipment Company. This piece of rolling stock, which was called *Bluebird,* was produced by a relative unknown in the subway industry. Based in Battle Creek, Michigan, Clark had produced the first aluminum streamline (PCC) trolley for the BMT's surface affiliate, the Brooklyn and Queens Transit. As a sequel—and with the encouragement of the Aluminum Company of America—Clark tried its luck with an

articulated train divided into three parts, much in the Triplex manner. In 1938 the first model made its debut amid rave revues. The BMT's promotional pamphlet boasted that the Bluebird was "Pleasing to Eye and Ear," and so it was, both inside and out. Its blue-hued exterior combined with a blue-green interior motif was uniquely appealing as were a number of engineering improvements from air filtration to rubber bumpers at each end of the train. Unfortunately, a dispute with Mayor Fiorello LaGuardia shortly before the IRT-BMT-IND merger limited production to just a handful which usually ran on the 14th Street-Canarsie line. In 1956 the Bluebirds became extinct.

*   THE LAST FULL-PRODUCTION BMT CARS: Experimentation on the Brooklyn Manhattan Transit lines bore fruit over and over again. The Triplex demonstrated that a multi-section car not only was practical but attractive to passengers. The *Zephyr* and *Green Hornet* underlined the point. In 1935 the BMT took the process yet another step forward when it introduced yet another articulated design with five connected units rather than three. The *Quintet*—or *Multi-Sections*—were produced by both Pullman and the St. Louis Car Company and borrowed from past BMT designs. Arch front windows suggested the 67-foot Standards, bare interior bulbs had a Triplex look and the lacklustre exterior paint job—light brown with silver on top—offered none of the experimental cars' flair for superficial beauty. A five-section unit equalled approximately a pair of Standards. Although the *Quintet* failed to incorporate many of the advances incorporated into both the *Green Hornet* and *Zephyr,* it

had much to commend. What I liked most about them was the speedy starts and the *Multi-Sections'* ability to round curves faster than other BMT regular models. What I didn't like were the ineffective little ceiling fans which never could provide the emphatic air currents delivered by windmill fans used on the Standard and Triplex. To me the worst part of the *Multi-Sections* was the decision to design a full width motorman's cab at the front. This prevented train buffs from enjoying the scenery with ease as was the case on both the Standards and Triplex. I never forgave the BMT for allowing such a drastic anti-subway-fan layout. Otherwise—following the elimination of some early kinks—the *Quintet* proved to be as solid a product as previous BMT standbys. Tragically, the lightweight trains were eliminated in September 1961—and not a single unit was preserved for museum use!

The City's Own
Independent System

* THE IND'S FIRST MODELS—R-1 THROUGH R-9: Once the Board of Transportation began laying out New York City's first publicly-owned subway in 1924, its planning originally focused on routes and construction. When those challenges were met—and the decade of the

1930s had begun—it was time to design cars that would make their debut when the Independent System opened for business in 1932. Several possible models were considered, starting with the IRT's Low-V concept which was quickly rejected. A 51-foot-long car simply was not big enough for the expanded IND tunnels and stations. Both the BMT's 67-foot Standard as well as the articulated Triplex also commanded attention. In the end, however, the IND eschewed articulation as well as the concept of a truly long piece of rolling stock. Board of Transportation designers instead opted for what could be best described as a compromise car. It was long (60-feet, six inches) but not too long. In some ways—especially the frontal look—it resembled the Triplex but it wasn't artciulated and it boasted no less than four, two-door side openings per vehicle. If there was any similarity between the new IND car and the Low-V it was the fact that the R-1—as the IND designated its maiden design—had a large front window that could *not*, to the dismay of rail fans, be opened! From a utilitarian standpoint, the R-1 was an efficient, well-built car which essentially remained unchanged through several series culminating with the R-9. Originally built in Berwick,

Pennsylvania by the American Car and Foundry Company, the original IND car also had versions built by Pullman-Standard and the Pressed Steel Car Company. A foot wider than its IRT counterpart, the R-1 utilized the big, windmill fans seen on the Triplex and Standard. Triplex-like double seats made of *rattan* were used and they created a sense of spaciousness with plenty of standee room. The R-1 was my "home" train and, therefore, the one I used more than any other car. The only change I ever noticed from the original R-1 through the final R-9 set had to do with the front windows. The first four sets through R-4 utilized full panes without any obstruction. From R-5 through R-9, a metal plate separated the two halves of the window. This somewhat annoyed me but not enough to affect the joy of track-watching. R-9s continued operating through the post-World War II years and remained in service until the 1970s. One such car is on exhibit at the Transit Museum in Brooklyn.

POST-WORLD WAR II ROLLING STOCK—R-10 (IND), R-12 (IRT): Once the Second World War had ended, the time had come for the Board of Transportation to demonstrate that it could innovate in the manner of BMT designers. The city's train people came through with an updated version of R-9 but with distinctive improvements which included lightweight construction, flourescent lighting and more colorful *rattan* seats. Delivered in August 1948, the R-10s caused considerable excitement among the public and media because they were different enough in meaningful areas. For starters, the roof was streamlined so the first look was impressive. Secondly, the R-10 accel-

erated noticeably faster than its predecessor and could enter a station at much higher speeds thanks to a new (dynamic) braking system. Plus, there still was a front window out of which to peer, although it was somewhat smaller than those on the R-1-R-9 fleet. Since the R-10 was placed on the A Line, I had the good fortune to take many rides on it while the cars still were new. Without a doubt, the most attractive aspects included the design, speed and effective braking. The R-10 provided an exciting ride and a generally pleasant one—except in the summertime. The problem was choice of fans. Instead of using the effective windmill ceiling fans employed on the Standards, Triplex and R-1-R-9 series, small fans bracketed to the sides—rather than overhead—were used. In terms of cooling the car, the bracket-fans were an unmitigated disaster. Equally unpleasant was the discovery of a valve design problem that negatively affected

William Brennan

the braking. This was followed by another embarassment; discovery of cracks in the trucks. Modifications were necessary in both cases before the R-10s were granted a complete bill of good health. Similarly, a scaled-down version was built for the IRT (R-12 and R-14). Among the differences—to accommodate the smaller IRT tunnels—was in width and length. Instead of four door openings per car, three were provided.

NOTABLE ROLLING STOCK FOLLOWING R-10, R-12. While neither the Board of Transportation nor its successor, the Transit Authority ever came up with a design to compare either with the *Bluebird* or *Zephyr*, several noteworthy car series were developed with varying results. A sampling of them will be discussed here:

* R-11s—BMT: Although the private BMT management had long gone with amalgamation, its spirit lived on into the post-war years. Just four years after the end of hostilities, the Budd Company successfully pushed its plan for a stainless steel car which would become standard on both the BMT and IND. The R-11 was built in 1949 as a new technology test train. It was the first stainless steel train on the city system since the Budd *Zephyr* and included

such specialty items as sterilizing lamps, recirculating air through ceiling and under-seat diffusers and a nifty outer design that had an unusual circular front window. Interestingly, it ran on the same Franklin Avenue Shuttle as the *Zephyr*. And like its predecessor, it remained a one-of-a-kind curio.

* R-16s—BMT and IND: Standards and Triplex trains continued to roam the BMT lines well after unification and the end of World War II. BMT fans like myself wondered how they eventually would be

replaced and with what design cars. The answer came in 1953 when the Transit Authority began a program of not only replacing the vintage BMT units—some of which were nearly forty years old—but also adding new models to the IND inven-

William Brennan

tory. Dubbed R-16s, the cars were manufactured by that old standby, American Car and Foundry and placed on the BMT's elevated Broadway-Jamaica Line.

* R-17s THROUGH R-36s—IRT: When the Transit Authority turned its attention to the IRT, it did so in a big way, beginning with the R-17s and continuing through R-36. While the essential design remained the same, there were distinct variations. For example, the R-17 model included the first serious experimentation with air con-

ditioning on a New York subway train. While it received thumbs-down notices from the TA, it did show an acknowledgment of a problem that eventually would be solved on later fleets. The IRT's R-22s were a delight if only because they featured a front window which actually opened—similar to the ones on both Standards and Triplexes of yesteryear. The wonderful aspect of R-29 models when they left the St. Louis Car Company shops was the coloring—an invigorating deep red; hence The Redbirds which in no way shape or form had any link to the extinct Bluebirds of BMT fame. To service the 1964 World's Fair at Flushing Meadow, the TA introduced R-33/R-36 cars. Embellished

with a refreshing blue-and-white paint scheme, the rolling stock was breathtaking and featured on TA subway maps. A portion of the cars even had the names of states—as in STATE OF KANSAS—emblazoned on the car sides. World's Fair cars also had larger windows than were normal on this fleet.

* R-32 BMT-IND BRIGHTLINERS: After the World's Fair cars were introduced on the IRT in 1963, the BMT and IND—which

did not directly service the Fair—were graced with attractive new trains of their own a year later. The R-32s were made of stainless steel—the Budd Company was proven right!—and were otherwise noteworthy because of bright blue side and front end doors.

* R-38 IND (REPLACING R-1 THROUGH R-9s): Built by the St. Louis Car Company, the R-38s were delayed in delivery first by quality-control problems and then by a

strike at the plant. They were ordered early in 1965 but were not delivered until August 1966. The final ten cars of this large order were embellished with an air conditioning system that actually was successful after tests were made beginning in July 1967.

* R-40 IND/BMT—RAYMOND LOEWY CARS: Stunningly streamlined—and totally unlike any previous New York subway model—the R-40s could best be described as a build-up-to-a-letdown. Famed designer Raymond Loewy already had been hailed in the industry for his electric locomotive,

Pennsylvania GG-1 creation, not to mention innumerable other industrial designs. His contribution to the subways, R-40, also looked like a winner particularly with its sloped front end and long up-and-down front window. Sadly, the very attractive features also turned into safety nightmares, especially the sloped ends. When the protective devices—handrails, among them—were installed, the Loewy Cars lost much of their immediate visual appeal. Additional orders (R-42) corrected the problem, eliminating the slope. Also noteworthy was the fact that the R-40s became the initial major order with trains fitted with air conditioning. From that point on, air conditioned cars became *de rigueur* on the New York subways.

* R-44 IND/BMT—THE GIANTS: After the Metropolitan Transportation Authority took control of the the Transit Authority in March 1968, the MTA became involved with subway car purchase and design. The first such manifistation of this was production of a car by the St. Louis Car Company which was a full *eight* feet longer than the 67-foot Standards which had been considered huge at the time. Apart from being so big, the *Giants* featured semi-automatic controls and a newer interior color design. Operation began in April 1972 after the

All photos on page, Eric Oszustowicz

rolling stock got a thumbs-down on stress tests. A newer, improved version—built by Pullman—was called the R-46. Clearance problems prevented the *Giants* from operating on the BMT's L, M, J and Z lines. However, they were employed on the Staten Island Railway.

* R-62—STAINLESS STEEL ON THE IRT: It wasn't until 1983 before the IRT Division received its first batch of stainless steel cars. Because of the dramatic change in looks

All photos on page, Eric Oszustowicz

compared to earlier rolling stock, the IRT's Silverliners grabbed the attention of straphangers although the cars which had full-width cabs—not all did—greatly disappointed the subway buff fraternity of which I am a member. Fortunately, most of the silver cars on my Broadway Line featured the traditional old-time small cabs which permitted window-watching through the turn of the century when the fun ended with full-width usage. This was a *very* sad day for those of us—especially kids—who enjoyed pretending to be motormen while standing at the front window.

* R-68—IND/BMT: Improving the fleet continued to be a primary MTA goal in the latter part of the 20th Century and this group of stainless steel cars once again proved the agency's point that up-to-date, attractive cars would lure riders to the underground. Built by Westinghous-Amrail

and with full-width cabs, these models were absolutely no fun for me to ride. They were introduced to the New York rails between 1986 and 1989. The updated R68A was built by Kawasaki between 1988 and 1989.

* R-110A AND R-110B—PREPARING FOR THE NEW CENTURY: State of the Art became uppermost in the minds of MTA planners when it came to designing rolling stock that would fill all three divisions in

the 21st Century. Planning ahead, the MTA introduced prototype cars, built by Bombardier, in 1992. Never intended to be actual parts of the fleet, the cars merely were used for testing purposes. Computerization was part of this new technology as well as modern design that included linoleum floors and an emergency passenger intercom.

Eric Oszustowicz

* R-142 AND R-143—THE NEW FLEET: The result of the MTA's experimentation through the 1990s was an entirely new set of cars which made their debut in the new century on both the IRT, IND and BMT lines although, as we know, the latter two are indistinguishable when it comes to the rolling stock. R-143 was the IND-BMT designation while R-142 was the IRT's listing. Cars were built by Kawasaki and Bombardier and received a huge touting from the TA and MTA as one might expect. But apart from gimmickry such as programmed station announcements, comput-

than has been offered. While attempts were made to produce an attractive interior, the lighting is actually *too* bright for comfort. One of the strangest aspects occurs on the IRT fleet once the train is loaded and begins its initial movement. A most curious *whine* that closely resembles the first bar being played by a rehearsing string quartet invariably accompanies almost every set of trains. This is *not* what one expects from state of the art rolling stock in the 21st Century; especially not after all the experimentation which preceded full production!

_____

Eric Oszustowicz

erized station listings in each car and minute by minute notices of the time of day, the cars lacked the subtle refinery of such legendary vehicles as the *Zephyr* and *Bluebird.* Excuses aside, one expected a quieter car—noise from the air conditioning is close to deafening to passengers waiting on platforms—with much smoother braking

"Then..."

A Nostalgic Look at the Subways

The plaque that's worth 10,000 words, at City Hall Station.

Watch the birdie—and look out for the trains. An el scene in 1895.

ABOVE: The Union Pacific, it's not! The Sixth Avenue el's Iron Horse it is; with the original wooden grandstand of the Polo Grounds in the background, in this 1901 photo.
OPPOSITE PAGE: The old (horsecars) giving way to the new elevated trains of the Ninth Avenue el.

Designing the 1939 IRT World's Fair Car.

The pride—and workhorse—of the IRT.

ABOVE LEFT: Who needed air-conditioning in 1904?
ABOVE RIGHT: Rattan seats, windmill fans and plenty of holders for the straphangers—a 1920s IRT interior.

Where are they all going? To Yankee Stadium—by car and the Ninth Avenue elevated connection to the Jerome Avenue line.

Poetry in motion: The Flushing Line's rush-hour (IRT) express, clickety-clacking over Queens Boulevard.

Old into new—Borough Park, Brooklyn never will be the same once the el is completed at 49th Street and New Utrecht Avenue, 1915.

Take me out to the ball game. Endless rows of ticket-choppers at the IRT's Yankee Stadium (161st Street) Station, July 1924, three years before turnstiles.

An express worthy of Clark Kent—Its debut, March 1953.

Where the bridge meets the el —The Bowery and Canal Street, August 1914. The nearby Manhattan Bridge and the Third Avenue el intersect.

Sunlight and shadows—A Manhattan street scene under the Sixth Avenue el at West 53rd Street, May 1927.

Paris? No. New York City, 1912. The IRT meets Broadway.

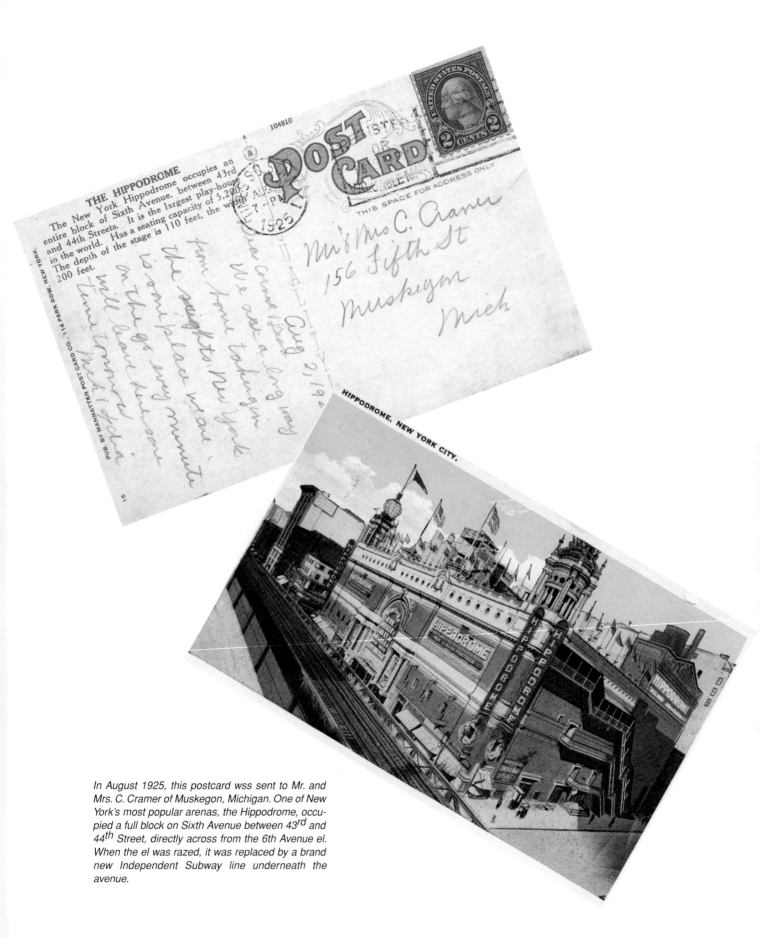

In August 1925, this postcard wss sent to Mr. and Mrs. C. Cramer of Muskegon, Michigan. One of New York's most popular arenas, the Hippodrome, occupied a full block on Sixth Avenue between 43rd and 44th Street, directly across from the 6th Avenue el. When the el was razed, it was replaced by a brand new Independent Subway line underneath the avenue.

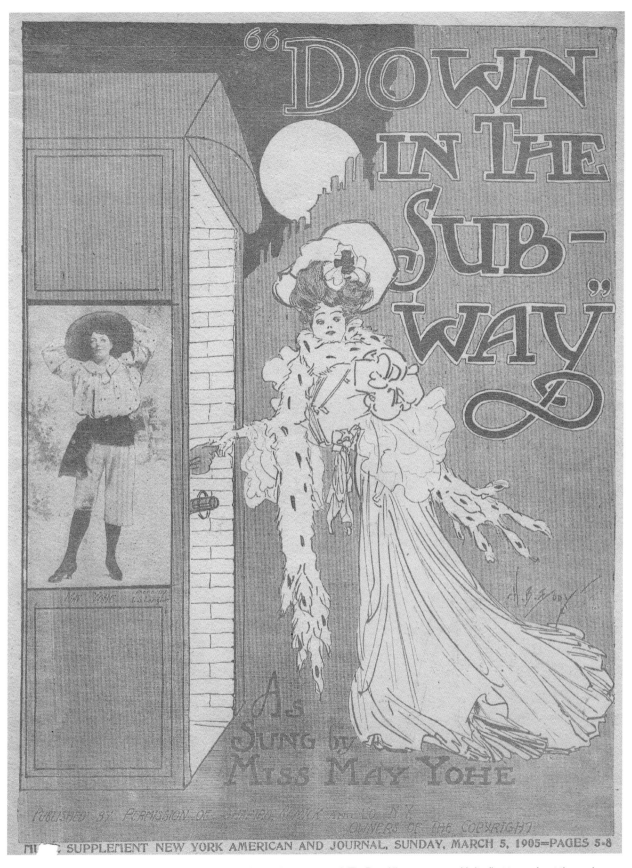

In March 1905, just five months after New York's first subway opened, Tin Pan Alley came up with its first tune about the underground railroad—"Down in the Subway." The sheet music was featured in Hearst's New York American and Journal newspapers.

The Brooklyn Rapid Transit System reached such heights of popularity that it even had its own hit song, "I Saw It in the BRT."

New York's straphangers were immortalized in song soon after the first IRT opened in 1904. "The Subway Glide" featured a vocal by Maude Raymond, a popular performer of the early 20th century.

"Now..."

Gallery of Contemporary Subway Photos
by David Perlmutter

The East River—through a subway car window's "scratchiti" and the Manhattan Bridge struts.

"Hold that door!" From express to local in four seconds.

ABOVE: Standing room only! Also some leering, dozing and meditating.
OPPOSITE PAGE: "Heads up, lady, you're gonna miss your train!"

"Hurry up, man, batting practice is almost over!"

The subway and the stadium—Yankees style.

From 1904 to the present, art has embellished the subway experience in one form or another at every station.

TOP LEFT: It is true, after all—subways are for sleeping!
BOTTOM LEFT: 100 years old but still ornate and artsy—the 181st Street-Broadway IRT stop.
ABOVE: You can't look too good on the Eighth Avenue line.

The chandelier station—IRT 168th Street-Broadway—minus its original 1904 chandeliers, but <u>with</u> stainless steel subway cars.

OPPOSITE PAGE: Mister Clean—subway style.
BELOW: How deep is the subway? Very! The only way out at 168th Street Station is by elevator.

ABOVE: Going to the Bronx Zoo in a brand new train.

Art and the underground.

As the (Peggy Lee) song goes—"Waitin' for the train to come in..."

The "other" New York subway—PATH, alias Hudson Tunnels, a.k.a. "The Hudson Tubes."

Signage on the original Independent System (IND) was simpler than those used on either the BMT or IRT.

Give my <u>hello</u> to Broadway! 49th Street—Times Square BMT station

The Queen Mother of kiosks—72nd Street Broadway, IRT station, opened in 1904!

490 THE SUBWAY AND THE CITY

As comedian Marty Allen would have said, "Hello dere!"

Contrasts in contemplation.

The "Subway to the Sea"—21st century model—en route to Rockaway.

As evidenced by commuters at the IRT's 68th Street station, the subway is for all people, zebra-imitators included.

From the plane to the train!

Twins and their parents on the IND.

George Gershwin wrote it; three straphangers act it—"I'm biding my time."

ABOVE: A subway moment can mean anything from reading to window-watching, to wondering whether a local will be waiting at the next stop. LEFT: The term "straphanger" was not meant to include this form of subway gymnastics!

OPPOSITE PAGE: A train's-eye view of lower Manhattan and the Brooklyn Bridge, taken from a subway crossing the Manhattan Bridge.

The entrance to the Transit Museum in Downtown Brooklyn.

PART V

OFF THE BEATEN TRACKS

Borough Hall, Brooklyn, 1932, the year Stan was born. Court Street, which will soon get its IND shuttle, is the avenue to the right of Borough Hall. The Fulton Street el eventually will be replaced by the IND subway. The Transit Museum will be to the left of Borough Hall.

Me and the Transit Museum (Alias Court Street Station)

To most patrons of the New York Transit Museum in Brooklyn, it is regarded as one of the city's unique institutions in a class with its counterparts across the river such as the Metropolitan Museum of Art on Fifth Avenue or the Museum of Natural History on Central Park West.

To me, the Transit Museum is much more than a mere collection of historic exhibits, but rather a part of my subway life.

Whenever I reach the corner of Boerum Place and Schermerhorn Street in Downtown Brooklyn—and begin descending the stairs—my primary thought is that I'm once again entering the old Court Street station of the Independent Subway as it was in pre-World War II years.

It's a reflexive response, of course, because long, long before anyone ever dreamed of putting a subway museum underground, I was using the Court Street station to take the HH local back home to Marcy Avenue.

I loved the Court Street station when it had real R-1 subway trains stopping there,

because it was such a quaint and neat little operation, so unlike anything on the vast system.

Where else in Brooklyn could you find a brand, new subway line that only ran a *few blocks*—actually *less* than a half-mile—in the borough's Downtown shopping district? Answer: Nowhere!

The HH local, otherwise known as the Court Street Shuttle, was the New York subway's version of the Fontaine Fox cartoon strip, *Toonerville Trolley That Meets All The Trains,* which regularly ran in the *New York Sun,* daily newspaper.

One end of the Court Street line was Hoyt-Schermerhorn station, which we always entered through the Frederic Loeser department store entrance on Fulton Street, across from the RKO Albee Theater.

Hoyt-Schermerhorn was one of those rare six-track IND stations that included rails carrying the famed A (Washington Heights) Eighth Avenue Express and the less-renowned GG Brooklyn-Queens

Crosstown local, which is most fondly remembered in our family for having the Myrtle-Willoughby station located directly under our house at 582 Marcy Avenue.

The GG operated over the center two tracks while the A used the pair on either side of the A line. That—rather appropriately—left the tracks on the farthest ends of Hoyt-Schermerhorn for the somewhat forlorn Court Street Shuttle.

It opened for business on April 9, 1936 to less than overwhelming crowds, because the fact remained that only a precious few commuters had any reason to ride our subway *Toonerville;* but I was among that select *clique.*

Not long after our very own GG line began operating in 1937, my Aunt Helen Friedman, who shared our Marcy Avenue house with my parents and grandparents, took a job with the Harry Bigeleisen goggles-making firm in a small factory on Bergen Street near Court.

Since Aunt Helen—nicknamed "Hale" by Yours Truly to her endless dismay—was like an older sister to me, she would take me on various trips, including treks with her New York Hiking Club.

From time to time, she would also invite me to go to the movies—or shopping—along Fulton Street after she finished her work at the Bigeleisen plant.

Granted, it would have been just as easy for me to get there by taking the GG local past Hoyt-Schermerhorn to the next station, Bergen Street.

But that wasn't as much fun, and I imagine that only a subway buff would understand that it was much *more* fun to get off at Hoyt and switch to the Court Street Shuttle.

Part of the fun was its *exclusivity.* So few people rode the brand-new cars that

the HH felt like my private train; a veritable limousine on rails that rolled from Hoyt Street, under eight city blocks, before concluding its abbreviated run at the corner of Boerum Place and Schermerhorn Street, alias Court Street depot.

Once there, it was a mere stone's throw to Aunt Helen's place. Usually, I'd walk over to Court Street because I loved window shopping at a Pyramid Auto Supply store which happened to have an excellent toy selection, most of which was easily viewed from the sidewalk.

From time to time, I would have lunch with Aunt Helen and take the HH Shuttle back from Court Street station to Hoyt-Schermerhorn, then switch to the GG for my five-stop ride to Myrtle-Willoughby.

Whenever I happened to be a passenger on the HH, I would wonder just why such a tiny stub of a line even existed apart from the genuine pleasure it afforded me.

It was much later in life that I learned that it was a part of the original IND plan to include a Second Avenue subway line which would extend from the Northeast end of the Bronx (Throgs Neck section), into Manhattan, along Second Avenue and then into Brooklyn.

Court Street—built as an "extra" stub by the contractor when the Fulton Street (A Train) Subway was built—was to be a station on a proposed South Brooklyn Subway which would finish its run under Fort Hamilton Parkway and terminate in Bay Ridge.

This was part of a grand IND expansion blueprint originally planned by the Board of Transportation in 1939. A year later, once the unification of the BMT, IRT and IND took place, another proposal was put forth linking a Second Avenue Subway with Court Street.

According to that plan, revealed on July 16, 1940, the Bronx terminus would be at Harding Avenue. The proposed subway would be dug under the East River and then head south down Second Avenue to Coenties Slip and then under the river again to the depot at Court Street.

To every straphanger's chagrin, the Second Avenue Subway—designed to replace the Third Avenue Elevated Line—to Court Street failed to materialize.

That left the Court Street Shuttle virtually abandoned and forlorn until the HH finally was declared a lost cause and permanently closed on June 1, 1946, which was rather timely in my case because that was about the time that Aunt Helen stopped working for Harry Beigeleisen's goggle company. Besides, I had been riding the HH more than eight years and at age fourteen (in 1946) it no longer was intriguing to me.

Once it had been officially shuttered, Court Street station became a forgotten spur to just about everyone but a tiny segment of transit buffs and Hollywood filmmakers who used it for subway scenes in some of their movies.

For example, "The Taking of Pelham One Two Three," starring Walter Matthau, included scenes that were filmed in Court Street station, as well as Charles Bronson's notorious flick, "Death Wish." Bronson's own dressing room was located in what is now the museum.

Court Street station might well have remained an empty relic, used only as a cinematic backdrop, were it not for a dedicated group of subway fans led by a former Transit Authority spokesman named Don Harold.

One of the most respected subway historians, Harold was described by former *New York Times* transit columnist Randy Kennedy as "the man acknowledged to be the father of the museum."

Harold—with the help of what Kennedy called "a tiny guerrilla army of like-minded transit employes"—rounded up a collection of vintage cars that previously appeared doomed to the scrapheap.

Working hand in hand with subway car dispatcher Frank Turdik, Harold was able to save cars, some of which eventually would comprise the magnificent fleet now on display in the museum.

"Turdik was often enlisted by Harold to take condemned cars and actually hide them on seldom-used tracks inside the system," wrote Kennedy in an article about Harold titled MILLIONS RIDE THE SUBWAY, ONLY A FEW DARE TO HIDE IT.

Speaking of his accomplice, Turdik, Harold recalled, "He was talented. He would do lots of little creative adjustments, let's say."

Those "adjustments"—and many others orchestrated by Harold—enabled the band of buffs to launch the Transit Museum in defiance of high odds against them.

I had heard bits and pieces of their story from my subway friends until—*Eureka!*—the museum actually opened in 1976. Needless to say, I hustled over there as soon as possible with my first son, Ben.

Whenever Ben and I would travel by subway—as we did on this day *en route* to the museum—we followed a traditional family routine.

Our standard move was to advance to the front of any platform so that we were well-positioned to easily enter the first car and annex control of the front window. When Ben was still too small to reach the window, I would carry him on my shoulders—same with younger son, Simon, years

ABOVE LEFT: *Predecessor to the nickel turnstile was the ticket chopper, here on display at the Transit Museum.*
ABOVE RIGHT: *More modern Perey turnstiles used stainless steel. This "Kompak" model is on view at the Transit Museum.*

An Independent System (IND) standard turnstile from the 1930s exhibited at the Transit Museum.

The Transit Museum features off-beat turnstiles including this Perey "Coinpassor."

ABOVE LEFT: The New York Transit Museum features everything from toy subways to station mosaics and even a model of a Brooklyn electric trolley bus (left).

ABOVE RIGHT: Wooden Brooklyn Rapid Transit (BRT) elevated gate cars on display at the Transit Museum. The semaphore signal once was used on the el.

A scale model of an early Brooklyn Trolley, at the Transit Museum.

ABOVE: A collection of Interborough Rapid Transit (IRT) signage on display at the Transit Museum.

At elevated station waiting rooms, the ticket chopper was usually side-by-side with a pot-bellied stove. Both are on view at the Transit Museum.

later—so that he could easily view the tracks ahead.

Ben and I would board the Number One Local at 110th Street (Broadway) station and ride it to 96th Street where we switched to either the Number Two or Three Express.

Those were the days *before* the June 5, 1995 Williamsburg Bridge rear-end (Broadway-Brooklyn Line) train crash that inspired the imposition of severe speed restrictions throughout the New York subway system.

During the pre-1995, non-restrictive speed years, trains would barrel down the tracks with what seemed to be reckless abandon. This made for wonderful subway-viewing from the front window and I never failed to impress this upon my son once we had boarded the express and roared past local stops such as 86, 79, 66, 59, 50, 28, 23, 18, Christopher, Houston, Canal and Franklin before reaching Chambers Street station and the more prosaic run to Brooklyn.

To reach the museum, we got off at Borough Hall Station and walked a few blocks south to the corner of Boerum Place and Schermerhorn Street.

It always was a sentimental journey for me because, as a youth, I had spent so many years in the area with family and friends. One day I might have been going to the Loew's Metropolitan Theater on Fulton Street with my grandmother, and another time it could have been heading to the Coward Shoe store for a pair of Boy Scout brogues with my mom.

As a dyed-in-the-wool Brooklynite, I savored everything about Downtown, from the stately Greek Revival-style Borough Hall, which opened in 1848 as (Kings County) City Hall because at the time

Brooklyn *was* an independent city, to the towering Williamsburg Savings Bank building.

I often pointed out to Ben where the magnificent Automat cafeteria was located on Fulton Street, a couple of blocks east of Borough Hall, where my father invariably took me for dinner after our Sunday afternoon Bushwicks baseball games at Dexter Park.

The Transit Museum entrance was as unobtrusive as one could imagine—and still is! It was nothing more than an IND kiosk, decorated just as it had been with the standard Independent metal work and station sign.

We headed down the steps and there, as it was when I once visited Aunt Helen, was the change booth and all the other IND trappings including the turnstiles—the wood looked as fresh as it had in 1937—and signs indicating which track handled the Hoyt-Schermerhorn trains.

Like many IND stations, Court Street had a mezzanine because it originally was to be part of a larger junction that never materialized. As it happened, the mezzanine proved a bonanza for the museum because it provided extra room for displays.

One of the very first exhibits we saw was a real-life model of a subway signal light—illuminated, of course—which caught Ben's eyes and, in its simplicity, entranced me as well. (Then again, I've always been easily entranced by just about *anything* that had to do with the subway because I still view it as a gigantic set of toy electric trains!)

We didn't stay on the mezzanine very long because the primary attractions were at the platform level below. So, down the steps we went and there, before our eyes, was the two-track station I had visited so often and so happily when Aunt Helen worked on nearby Bergen Street.

The difference, of course, was that the platform level now was the museum's main pavilion. Its chief exhibits featured rolling stock from an assortment of eras, including a gated, open-ended elevated line relic that once had been pulled by a steam engine.

With Ben on my shoulders, we stepped on to the car's platform where I instantly noticed the cord used by the conductors to signal when the gates were closed. Then, I lifted him down to the floor and showed him the iron handles which the conductor pulled and pushed to open and close the gates.

Walking through the car, I pointed out the ancient leather overhead straps—from which the term *straphanger* is derived—and Ben quickly got hold of one and began doing gymnastics with it until I discreetly pointed out that the museum's curator would take a dim view of such shenanigans.

Not only does the museum currently display the el cars but it features a BMT Standard, the Triplex, an R-1 just like the one I used to ride to Court Street, and a few other gems from yesteryear.

In addition, a real, live (train) *truck* sits in the middle of the platform, providing a close, up-front look at one of the most important elements on a subway car.

What impressed me as much as anything was the fact that the station's original look had been preserved so well that one had the feeling he was in a genuine railroad setting while surrounded by all manner of subway objects.

Through the years, I would visit and revisit Court Street station with both lads,

each of whom enjoyed the mock bus driver's seat—replete with wheel and other dashboard *accoutrements*—mostly because they could actually *play* bus driver by turning the wheel and beeping the horn; with no sound, of course!

After both kids had grown old enough to not require dad's accompaniment to the museum, I would reappear there from time to time leading subway tours for the 92nd Street Y.

The joy of viewing its collection never diminished, so it was with some dismay that I learned one day that the Court Street station had been closed in August 2001 for alterations. Like other *aficionados,* I wondered how anyone could improve on the exhibit without diminishing the natural *ambience* of the original.

When I finally did return to the revamped New York Transit Museum, which re-opened in September 2003, I was more than just pleasantly surprised; I was tickled pink with the manner in which the old station had been improved with intriguing exhibits.

Now it was being billed as "the largest museum of public transportation history in the United States and one of the premier institutions of its kind in the world."

I couldn't argue with that.

The 60,000-square-foot facility in Brooklyn Heights was not only renewed but expanded with exhibits—more than 6,000 objects and 250,000 archival materials—that included an interactive, hands-on experience tracing the 175-year history of aboveground transit in the city.

In one corner, I found one of the original IRT *ticket-choppers,* which was operated by a gate man before turnstiles were installed, and in another was an exhibit called "Steel, Stone and Backbone," telling the story about building the subways.

Historic photos were pleasantly ubiquitous as well as the 1940s chewing gum and penny-candy vending machines which adorned every underground platform. Signage dating back to the IRT's opening in 1904 arrested my attention as well as the working signal tower at the far end of the platform and, naturally, scale models of Brooklyn and Manhattan trolleys and elevated trains.

I enjoyed a pleasant chat with Charles Sachs, Senior Curator, as well as Roxanne Robertson, the Transit Museum's Director of Special Projects, and Gabrielle Shubert, Director of the Museum. Another who was extremely helpful in helping me understand the workings of this fine museum was Junnko Tozaki, Assistant Director, Development, New York Transit Museum.

Climbing up the stairs from the lower level to the mezzanine, I visited the excellent gift shop, featuring a wonderful assortment of subway books as well as posters, toys and other transit-related items.

The two-hour visit breezed by as if it was only two minutes long and, finally, it had come time to find my way home.

As I made my way to daylight—actually, it was dusk—the first thing I did was visualize Court Street, circa 1940, when at age eight, I walked hand-in-hand with Aunt Helen, as we gazed at the Pyramid Store's entrancing main window and its dazzling (at least to me!) Christmas display.

Then, I walked over to Borough Hall where, in many ways, the venerable IRT station looks just as it did a century ago.

I slowly—ever so slowly—walked down the steps, one by one, gazing at the ancient, but well-preserved, art and iron work.

I could hear the train noise in the distance and couldn't help but think to myself that I was going from one transit museum—a stationary one—to another; only the latter museum actually is a subway that runs just well as it did when it was brand-new in the early 1900s!

———————

Me and the Franklin Avenue Shuttle

The Franklin Avenue Shuttle, which runs from Fulton Street and Franklin Avenue in Brooklyn's Bedford-Stuyvesant section, to Prospect Park, made an impression on me very early in my life.

When I was of *kindergarten* age, a story circulated through family members that some relative had been on the Brighton Beach Express during the infamous Malbone Street disaster in 1918.

Details always had been sketchy as to how this cousin managed to survive the worst crash in subway history, when 97 commuters were killed at the ninety-degree curve leading into the tunnel at Prospect Park station.

But I didn't need many details; the whispers about Malbone Street were enough to pique my curiosity, and one day, during a visit to Prospect Park, my mother walked me east along the north side of Empire Boulevard (formerly Malbone Street), past the Botanic Gardens to an unusual overpass.

The sidewalk was adjoined by concrete fencing featuring a succession of rectangular openings which allowed a clear view of the open railroad cut below.

Two tracks dipped from an elevated structure north of Eastern Parkway along an open cut that carried the trains into the tunnel and the perilous *S* curve leading to Prospect Park station.

By peeking my head against one of the fence apertures, I could easily look at the tracks toward the Botanic Garden station, or I could peer directly down at the portal where, on November 1, 1918, during the waning days of World War I, the Brighton train—comprised of fragile wooden cars—plunged into the newly-completed concrete wall.

Actually seeing the precise point-of-disaster, after hearing so many sobering family stories about Malbone Street, left me with a queasy feeling that was reiterated every time I visited the overpass site; or actually rode the 1.7-mile route of the Franklin Shuttle.

As luck would have it, I would become

a regular shuttle rider starting in 1940—at the age of eight—immediately after the BMT and the IRT had been absorbed into the city's Board of Transportation.

A pleasant feature of the subway unification was launching of a free-transfer bonus system that enabled me to take the IND's A train from Hoyt-Schermerhorn subway station to Franklin Avenue and then climb a rickety wooden staircase up to the junction of the Fulton Street el and the Franklin Shuttle.

It was at that crossroads in 1918 that the ill-fated motorman, Edward Luciano, allowed his Brighton Express to move so fast, that towerman Peter Gorman refused to throw the switch into curve position—leading the train to a right (southbound) turn on to the Franklin tracks—fearing a derailment and potential calamity.

When I reached the top stair, I could visualize the outline of Luciano's route and the spot where Gorman allowed the Brighton train to back up and then, slowly, switch over to the tracks that would eventually enter the Malbone tunnel.

Although wooden cars still were commonplace along the Myrtle Avenue and Lexington Avenue els, the Franklin Shuttle now boasted the wonderful, sixty-seven-foot BMT Standard cars.

Better still, in summer months—which was when I regularly rode the line—the Franklin train was transformed from a Toonerville-type shuttle into a full-fledged, no-kidding-around, long-range express.

Instead of terminating at Prospect Park, the former Franklin Shuttle was transformed into the Franklin Avenue Express, destined for Coney Island.

As if to emphasize the point, the eight-car train had a big, white disk affixed to its front bumper, an emblem I had never seen in the subway before. The insignia specifically connoted "Express" rather than shuttle and gave the dark brown consist a look of distinction not evident on its logo-less sister trains.

The idea of being able to climb aboard an express at Franklin Avenue seemed like a fabulous "extra added attraction"—as the movie theaters billed short subjects in those days—to an eight-year-old kid like me.

Even better was the fact that the ride kept getting better as it progressed. Dean Street loomed just a couple of blocks from Franklin-Fulton. Park Place, the next stop, practically rubbed shoulders with Dean on the elevated portion.

Next came Eastern Parkway as the train began its descent. Brooklyn's Grand Boulevard was separated from the tracks by a modest tunnel which had been constructed four decades *before* the Malbone Street disaster.

The short, brick tube actually preceded the Brooklyn Rapid Transit, having been built when steam engines were operated by the Brooklyn, Flatbush and Coney Island Railroad.

Peering out the front window, I imagined what it might have been like careening down the incline in 1918 without any fail-safe devices such as automatic brake *trippers* to halt the train if it ran through a red light as motorman Luciano's did, approaching a six miles per hour warning sign at relatively high speed, variously estimated at between thirty and sixty miles per hour.

Needless to say, during my rides, the motorman always brought our train to an appropriate crawl before reaching the hairpin turn although on one occasion—riding, ironically, a high-tech stainless steel

Zephyr—I feared that the brakes never would be applied in time.

As we slowed for the tunnel, I also visualized how the train looked from the street above when I would peek through the rectangular openings.

Entering the tunnel, our Standard lurched hard to the left, its wheel flanges screeching as the momentum forced them against the rails. Just as quickly, the express pulled hard in the other direction, eventually straightening out. It finally stopped at the far (local) platform of the four-track Prospect Park station. The depot had been modernized and completed in 1920, virtually—but not quite—cutting off the Franklin Line from the BMT's Brooklyn-Manhattan spine.

Only after rolling south from Prospect Park station, did the Franklin train come into its own. A few hundred feet beyond the platform, the lead car reached a switch and *click-clacked* leftward over to the express track. A few hundred yards down the track, it burst up to top speed, galloping to Coney Island, the old gray mare of the BMT turning into a majestic thoroughbred.

The return trip to Franklin Avenue was no less exciting, although in a more relaxed sort of way.

Once the train switched from express to local at Prospect Park, there was no anxiety about a Malbone-type wreck. Unlike the southbound tracks, the northbound rails ran straight through the tunnel and continued that way up the grade, bouncing along the elevated tracks until the bulls-eyed Franklin Express slowed to a stop ten feet before the terminating bumper.

Since my early riding days on the Franklin Line, it has undergone a metamorphosis of sorts. Rides that I once took—and took for granted—no longer were available.

For example, from time to time, I would take the Franklin Shuttle to Prospect Park station and then walk a few blocks along Empire Boulevard to catch a Brooklyn Dodgers baseball game at nearby Ebbets Field.

After 1957, it was no longer necessary to take the BMT for a ball game, because the Dodgers had emigrated to Los Angeles. No subway went *that* far!

As the neighborhood adjoining the Franklin route deteriorated in the 1970s and 1980s, patronage between Fulton Street and Prospect Park diminished.

By the beginning of the 1990s, talk about closing the shuttle was heard among Transit Authority officials, but community activists persuaded the MTA that the Toonerville line was worth saving.

The miniscule railroad—and its stations—was refurbished and up-to-date rolling stock graced the rails.

New York Times transit columnist Randy Kennedy described the Franklin Shuttle as "The Little Train That Refused to Die."

Or, as one passenger once told Kennedy, "I guess it doesn't really go anywhere all that exciting."

Perhaps not now, but I can assure you that there were few events more exciting to me than a ride on the white-disked BMT Franklin Avenue *Express;* the one that leisurely bounced its way through rustic parts of Bedford-Stuyvesant, through the (Malbone) *S*-curve tunnel and, finally, sped all the way to the joys of Coney Island!

———————————

Me and the Two Most Important Subways That Never Were Built to Our Two Most Important Airports

The Independent (IND) System did a wonderful thing in the late 1930s when the World's Fair in Flushing Meadow was being built. It constructed a brand-new subway, linking the IND's four-track Queens Boulevard main line with the fairgrounds.

As mentioned earlier, I often rode in those R-1 through R-9 IND cars from the Forest Hills (Continental Avenue) station at 71st Avenue, then to 75th Avenue stop before the World's Fair Special turned left (northward) under Queens Boulevard, emerging to daylight on a trestle over Grand Central Parkway.

It then accelerated past the just-completed Jamaica subway yard, proceeding toward what we all considered the pageant-of-all-pageants.

Meandering through what then were unused sections of Queens borough, the Independent's World's Fair subway—as opposed to its IRT and BMT counterparts—was the only one to have its own spanking new ground level station *right on* the fairgrounds.

Handsome in its modern design, the terminal featured wide ramps that delivered fairgoers to and from the myriad exhibits spread around it.

Without question, the depot could have been a permanent Flushing Meadow station, servicing the vast park which was created in the fair's aftermath. Flushing Meadow remains heavily-used. The New York City Building—including its popular ice skating rink—is one of the few permanent remnants of the 1939-40 pageant.

Shea Stadium—serviced by the IRT Flushing el—would have greatly benefited from an IND connection as would the Arthur Ashe Tennis Center nearby.

Most of all, the IND Train to the Fair also could have been a Train to the Planes.

LaGuardia Airport, opened on December 2, 1939, was located a relatively short distance northwest of the IND's World's Fair terminal. Extending the tracks through the northern portion of Flushing Meadow Park, then past Northern Boulevard to Flushing Bay and on to the nearby airfield certainly was a do-able project, particularly in view of highway projects completed in the immediate area at that time and thereafter.

Unfortunately, rapid transit foresight was not the order of the day when it came to making a subway connection to the municipal airport. Instead, the subway to Flushing Meadow was destroyed, starting on January 15, 1941.

To this day, planners talk about a subway link to LaGuardia, and have been for half a century.

Even if such a link never had been built, imagine how useful the 1.83-mile spur from Forest Hills to Flushing Meadow Park would have been today had the IND route to the Fair not been destroyed.

LaGuardia's sister airport to the South, Idlewild—later renamed Kennedy—also cried for a direct subway connection when it opened in 1948. Unfortunately, most of the cries were stifled from the start by New York's prime power broker, Robert Moses, who constantly—and mistakenly, in my opinion—favored automobiles over rapid transit.

As Idlewild International Airport gained in popularity during the 1950s, demands for a rail connection continued, and I become a part of that clamor as a transit reporter for the New York *Journal-American* daily newspaper during the late 1950s and 1960s.

Spearheaded by my editor, John W. Newton and one of his close associates, Bill Sexton, we wrote several stories about the realistic possibility of a subway connection between the Queens IND line—the same one as mentioned above—and what then had become Kennedy International Airport.

In our *Journal-American* newsroom,

we referred to our train-to-the-plane story as the "Whitepot piece."

Over the course of four years, I must have written at least eight different stories which were *slugged* WHITEPOT JUNCTION.

Why Whitepot? What is Whitepot?

According to respected Queens historian Vincent Seyfried, the name is of unknown origin. It was applied—until 1910—to Rego Park and Forest Hills Gardens. Seyfried noted that a Whitepot School House was located at Woodhaven Boulevard and 66th Avenue for many years.

In terms of the transit reference, Whitepot goes back to the IND's expansion into Queens during the early 1930s.

At the time, Long Island Rail Road officials offered to sell its Rockaway Beach line to the city (Independent) system. If the plans had jelled, IND trains would have switched off in Rego Park and run along LIRR right-of-way—similar to the current A train—to the beach.

Although the deal fell through, it is believed that IND long-range planners had hoped that negotiations would be revived. This point is proven by the fact that a connection between the Queens Boulevard line (E and F expresses and GG local) and the Long Island Rail Road Rockaway Beach route was designated at a point in the Rego Park section of Queens called White Pot.

According to transit historians, a flying junction and interlocking tower would be included for a LIRR link east of the IND's 63rd Drive station.

"A short tunnel under Rego Park," said transit historian Bernard Ente, "would have connected the IND subway to the Rockaway Line with a one-seat ride to the airport. All that was needed was a short connection at Howard Beach east to Kennedy Airport."

The Whitepot story heated up at the *Journal-American* after the LIRR abandoned its Rockaway Line in 1962, but no amount of journalistic pressure could be mounted to persuade city fathers that an IND train-plane connection was feasible.

Decades later—after the IND finally had annexed the Rockaway Line—hearings were held in Rego Park over the feasibility of a subway connection from Queens Boulevard to the Rockaway Line and on to Kennedy.

A native of Rego Park, Bernie Ente, who was aware of the junction on the IND between 63rd Drive station and the 67th Avenue station, attended the community meeting in the hopes of promoting the idea of the subway-airport link

"I wanted to convince the people in Rego Park of the sensible option of using the ex-LIRR Rockaway Line," Ente recalled. "However, I never got the chance to make my points. I blame those people for the AirTrain to Kennedy we now have."

The AirTrain, built by the Port Authority, became the compromise train-monorail Kennedy Airport-Manhattan connection.

More than three decades after the *Journal-American* closed its doors, construction of the AirTrain began.

It consists of a computer-operated elevated light-rail system connecting Kennedy Airport's nine terminals with the IND subway terminal (A train) at Howard Beach and the LIRR Jamaica junction.

The AirTrain alone costs five dollars per ride. It's a total of seven dollars if one connects with the IND. If the commuter takes the LIRR, the total cost is $11.75.

AirTrain proponents assert that the preferred LIRR connection is a better deal than a taxi ride. A cab costs at least thirty-five dollars—not counting tolls—and is subject to traffic delays that could extend the Manhattan-Kennedy trip to as much as two hours.

Opponents charge that the train-to-the-plane automatically is flawed because it requires transferring either to the subway or LIRR. In either case, travelers—particularly those with luggage—would be disinclined to switch from the AirTrain to the fixed-rail LIRR or IND simply because of the inconvenience.

Other AirTrain foes note that cities such as Cleveland, Washington and Chicago have direct airport-center city train connections without the hassle of any changes from one mode of rapid transit to another.

The 8.1-mile AirTrain cost $1.9 billion to build.

"It is," Ente concluded, "a tremendous waste of money!"

―――――――――――

PART VI

ABOUT NICKELS, TOKENS, TICKETS, CARDS AND MAPS

A series of New York subway tokens—gone forever.

Early turnstiles, such as these on the IRT, had wooden turning devices and large metal recepticles for nickels.

From the Nickel
to the Metrocard

When the first Interborough Rapid Transit subway got the green light from city fathers to move ahead, it was with the understanding that the fare would be five cents.

For a nickel the prospective straphanger received a ticket which, among other things, proclaimed "Valid For One Fare."

The rider-to-be then presented his ducat to a station attendant who dropped it into a receptacle. A blade chopped the ticket, thus enabling the straphanger to move on to the platform and await arrival of the train.

Eventually, the ticket-chopper gave way to a rather cumbersome—yet efficient—turnstile made of both metal and wood. August Belmont, the IRT's patron saint, introduced the turnstile after his company bought out the elevated lines.

The turnstile worked simply enough. Once the nickel was inserted into a slot, the propeller-looking turnstile could be moved enough for the patron to advance.

The coin was swallowed and digested by the wonderful machine that did not need the help of any attendant.

Thus, great savings were made by simply removing the ticket-chopper from the IRT's employment lists and that pleased Belmont no end.

The nickel fare remained on the IRT, Brooklyn Rapid Transit—later the BMT—as well as the Independent System when the IND was completed in the early 1930s.

Turnstiles were modernized—perhaps *simplified* would be the more appropriate term—but the essential propeller device remained in use as did the coin-receiving slot.

Once turnstiles had become permanent fixtures on the system, the next significant change involved the price of admission. In 1948, it doubled from a nickel to a dime, which meant that the turnstiles had to be altered to suit the smaller ten-cent piece.

Just five years later another fare

increase—this time to fifteen-cents—was approved. That complicated matters, since the turnstiles could only handle one coin and there was no such item as a fifteen-cent piece.

However, the transit geniuses invented one and called it a *token*.

On July 2, 1953, the first of 48,000,000 fifteen-cent tokens—conveniently designed to be nearly the size of a dime—began plunging into the slots.

Unlike the traditional dime, a fifteen-cent token featured a "Y" shape hole that gave it an inimitable look. The golden original token remained in use even after the fare was hiked to twenty cents in 1966.

A good seventeen years went by before a new token appeared; a bigger version of the original but still with the "Y" in the middle. Some 50,000,000 were minted, beginning January 4, 1970 when the fare again jumped, this time to thirty cents.

Increases to thirty-five cents in 1972 and a half-dollar three years later did not affect the token size, but on October 12, 1979 a significantly better-looking token had its world premiere to hail the subway's seventy-fifth birthday.

Appropriately, the Diamond Jubilee token featured a small diamond-shaped hole near the top and the message, "People Moving People." The outline of an original IRT kiosk also adorned the special coin. It was used side by side with its predecessor and only 5,800,000 were issued.

When the next fare hike raised the cost of a ride to sixty cents in 1980, a new token—minus the hole—made its debut. A total of 60,000,000 of the solid brass tokens were minted beginning on June 28, 1980. The same token was used when the fare moved up to seventy-five cents in 1981 as well as when it climbed to ninety-

cents in 1984, before reaching one dollar in 1986.

The dollar token differed from its counterparts by virtue of a steel centerpiece, otherwise known in the trade as a *Bullseye*.

The *Bullseye* survived two more increases—one dollar and fifteen cents in 1990 and one dollar and a quarter in 1992—and reached a total mintage of 90,000,000.

A second commemorative token entered the transit world on December 11, 1988, hailing completion of the Archer Avenue, Parsons and Jamaica Center stations. Only 100,000 were minted to honor the Queens event because the *Bullseye* still was in regular use.

The last token minted in New York was issued on November 12, 1995 and remained in use through the turn of the century and beyond. Dubbed the "Five-Borough," this coin was easily distinguishable from its predecessors thanks to a relatively large pentagonal hole in the middle. Its appearance coincided with the highest-ever price for a subway ride—to that point in time—one dollar and fifty cents!

On January 6, 1994 the handwriting was on the wall for subway tokens. On that date the Metropolitan Transit Authority issued its first batch of MetroCards which could be swiped through the turnstile instead of a coin-dropping through a slot.

At first the MetroCards were greeted with skepticism by rank-and-file straphangers who had become accustomed to using a coin all their riding lives.

Subway buffs originally rebelled against the cards simply on the grounds that they were un-train-like whereas the tokens represented the *real* thing.

But soon even the most traditional train fans began to realize that the cards were faster and more efficient, especially since riders could electronically charge up their MetroCard so that many rides could be obtained before a renewal was necessary.

Senior citizens favored them as well because special MetroCards were issued to them along with a regular discount.

In time the MetroCard became so universally accepted that the MTA finally phased out the token in May 2003, one year short of the subway's 100th Anniversary.

The decision to do so was made when the fare jumped from one dollar and fifty cents to two dollars. "The token," said Transit Authority president Lawrence Reuter, "has outlived its usefulness."

However, the fifty-year-old symbol of the city remained in use on New York buses until December 31, 2003, when the metal discs were declared null and void. In addition the Roosevelt Island Operating Corporation—operators of the Roosevelt Island tram—bought seven thousand tokens for its 200 daily tram riders.

"Since tokens were going the way of the woolly mammoth, we had to make sure we had a supply for a few years," said corporation spokesman John Melia.

Some riders waxed nostalgic over the beloved slugs.

"It was easy to just go to the turnstile and drop one in," said Tony Nisbet, a Manhattan ticket broker.

But the majority opinion was echoed by Bronx resident Francine Curtis who opined, "The MetroCards are more convenient. I used to lose the tokens in my bag."

For those who simply could not part with their beloved tokens, the *Daily News* had this to say in its December 30, 2003 edition: DON'T THROW OUT THOSE TOKENS—RECYCLE!

The News offered several possibilities for the overnight antique. These included: A. Rearview-mirror décor; B. Hair clips; C. Earrings; D. Cuff links; E. Nose rings; F. Fishing lures; and, finally, if you can believe this, Elton John glasses!

———————

John Tauranac—
Mapmaker Extraordinaire

Producing a readable, understandable and—most of all—practical subway map has been a challenge for cartographers ever since the first IRT line opened in 1904.

As the system grew—and after 1940, when consolidation of the IRT, BMT and IND took place—the challenge became even greater.

Decade after decade, subway maps were flawed in one way or another—and then John Tauranac came along.

Tauranac is to subway maps what Michelangelo is to ceilings or—if you will—Woody Allen is to comedy.

Some acquaintances suggest that Tauranac bears a certain physical resemblance to Allen but if the comedian and the cartographer have anything in common it *is* a passionate love affair with Manhattan.

An adjunct associate professor at NYU's School of Professional and Continuing Studies, where he teaches New York history and architecture, Tauranac is the author of several books on New York City as well as countless articles. He, literally, knows every single street on Manhattan island, having walked them while researching his definitive street atlas, *Manhattan Block by Block*.

And if there is anything John likes better than mapmaking, it is strolling the city's boulevards, avenues and alleys.

His passion for mapping the subway, like his affection for the city, is all consuming. In his latest labor of love, *Manhattan Line By Line: A Subway & Bus Atlas*, he creates both geographic, subway and bus maps as well as "strip maps," non-geographic descriptions of each line.

In his Introduction to *Manhattan Line By Line*, Tauranac explains that "strip maps," which are featured in his guide, are rooted in a venerable tradition dating back to the 13th century.

"The monk Matthew Paris created what for all intents and purposes are the first strip maps," says Tauranac. "They show pilgrimage routes in England. The Automobile Association and Map Quest do essentially the same thing today when you request a road map that shows how to get from city A to town B. As Sergeant Joe Friday might have said, "Just the facts, ma'am."

Those who know Tauranac best are hardly surprised that *Manhattan Line By Line* received critical acclaim. His re-design of the Metropolitan Transportation Authority's subway map in 1979 was regarded at the time as the finest ever crafted.

The result prompted John—an Upper West Sider—to observe that his tombstone should read, "He Designed The Subway Map That Works."

Critics have supported his assertion. The *New York Times* noted, "AT LAST A USABLE SUBWAY MAP." The acclaim hardly satisfied its creator, and after the MTA declared him redundant, Tauranac started his own small map company and designed his own subway map that was published under the Tauranac imprint. It is a distinct improvement on what already was *the* best.

Although his interests are as far-ranging and detailed as his maps, Tauranac is a subway fan. He rides the IRT Broadway-Seventh Avenue (Number One) line and he cares about the system. In an interview

with Victoria Kohl of *Promenade* magazine, he pointed out that he would appreciate New York's underground a lot more if it could duplicate a feature of London's Circle Line.

That would include, "a designated loop train traveling downtown from 125th Street along the Lexington line to 42nd Street, shuttling across to the West Side Broadway/Seventh Avenue line and then uptown to 125th Street, requiring new track only across 125th."

Typically, it is an insightful, useful idea and underscores why the *Columbia Spectator* newspaper ranked him among the university's 250 greatest undergraduate alumni.

In an interview with David Perlmutter, Tauranac offered his thoughts on the subways.

———————————

Maps have fascinated me ever since I was a youngster growing up in Manhattan. I used to collect *National Geographic* maps and pin them up on my bedroom wall.

My love affair with the city began at an early age, and I can thank my father for that. My mother died when I was a kid, and when people would ask my father how he could think of raising my sister and me in Manhattan he would answer that he couldn't think of a better place to raise two kids.

He helped me develop an affection for Manhattan that I have obviously never shaken.

Dad had been an assistant manager of the Biltmore Hotel on Madison Avenue. When he got finished with work, dad would take me on walks around Manhattan, filling me with information that had intrigued him.

I originally developed an interest in subways while seeking out a route to Ebbets Field in Brooklyn, which then was the home of the baseball Dodgers.

From that point on, I became more and more familiar with the various lines in Manhattan, the Bronx, Brooklyn and Queens.

To answer the question at its most rudimentary level about why I like the subway, public transportation has a basic advantage over private—you don't have to drive.

You're always a passenger, which means you have the luxury of time that you can spend reading. I've discovered that the subway is an ideal place to proofread papers and other things. I can somehow drive out all distractions on the subway and zero in on what I have to deal with.

When proofreading a map, I frequently turn it upside down, since the different perspective shows different relationships. I'll mark up the proof to indicate that I should push something there and pull another here.

When people look over my shoulder and see that I am reading upside down, I get the strangest looks. I ignore them, of course. Although my neighbors might not know what I'm doing, I like to believe at least I know what I'm doing.

Thanks to my father, I was able to enhance my knowledge of Manhattan's streets and eventually learned to move around the borough *underground*. I discovered corridors beneath buildings that enabled me to traverse long distances underground without having to surface.

My first maps, in fact, were published by *New York Magazine* and appropriately called "Undercover maps." Essentially, they showed how to find and use the passageways under the major buildings in the Wall Street area as well as Midtown Manhattan.

I had to use public transportation to get to school—for a while my family lived on 79th Street and I had to get to and from grammar school at 11th Street. I began riding subways and buses at a tender age. I have never stopped using subways and buses. When I tell people from anywhere but Manhattan that I never owned a car until I was 47, they think I'm nuts.

Once I began working for the J. Walter Thompson advertising agency, I would take the subway to the job. My interest continued and then multiplied when I was hired by the Metropolitan Transportation Authority, where I was asked to re-design what then was the existing subway map.

Curiously, I was not hired by the MTA in 1974 to design maps, but to finish writing the guidebooks for the Culture Bus Loops. They had been started as a Municipal Art Society project. I was asked to write and edit a tourist guide to the city similar to London Transport's *Visitor's London*. What developed was *Seeing New York: The Official MTA Travel Guide*.

The MTA map at the time was a schematic one that was aesthetically pleasing but geographically inaccurate and not terribly didactic. Those are not such very good credentials for a map. Since everything for the guidebook project had to be done on the double, we took a City Planning Commission map and placed the routes of the subway atop the streets. It proved the first step in the right direction.

The schematic map had been created in 1972 by the designer Massimo Vignelli who was clearly influenced by the Bauhaus philosophy that less is more. I'm probably influenced by the Beaux Arts school, which held that more was not enough. If I have a chance, I stick in all kinds of "useless" but intriguing information. For example, on the maps in *Manhattan Block by Block*, I noted where the first Oreo cookies were made. The abstract nature of schematic maps fail one of my primary principles of a subway map—to get you not just from point A to point B by subway, but to get you from your starting point (A) to the closest convenient subway station (B) to the most convenient subway station (C) that will get you to your ultimate destination (D).

Schematic subway maps just don't work that way—not the London Underground map, not the DC map, and certainly not the Vignelli map. I guess that's why, when the schematic map was published by the TA in 1972, I started designing a subway map for myself.

During my world travels, I've ridden on several subway systems in other cities. In 1975 I was in Paris and purchased what the Parisians called a *Carte Orange*. It was a monthly pass for the Paris *Métro*.

The *Carte Orange* seemed to me like an idea that would work well on the New York Subway system. In fact, I was so excited by the prospect that I took my *Carte Orange* to the first departmental meeting upon my return from the trip, took it out of my pocket and, with a great sense of drama, produced it, saying that this was what we should do. I was told "not in your lifetime" by the MTA's then-executive director.

I've been described as a terrier. Once I have my teeth in that ankle I won't let go. I wound up co-chairing what was called the "Automatic Fare Collection" committee when I was reporting to a future MTA chairman, Peter Stangl. I called the card a *CityPass*, and, like the *Carte Orange*, I advocated a permanent piece of ID *cum* photo, and a monthly color-coded pass. (The TA was very concerned about people passing around their unlimited pass, and a photo ID seemed a good way to nip that problem in the bud.) I am delighted that the TA has caught up with other transportation systems in fare collection, but you can imagine my response when the MTA ran an ad recently for the MetroCard asking if you had ever thought that you could charge a monthly pass. "Well, yes," I said to myself when I saw that ad, "I had."

It is satisfying for me to think that the guys on Madison Avenue and over at Jay Street are all excited about the success of *MetroCard*, which basically is the same thing I had proposed to them more than two decades ago.

Fortunately, the MTA did give me the opportunity to redesign its subway map, although I had been working on a design for years before they asked me to do it.

I think that one of the most important contributions to the 1979 map was the introduction of a color-coding system based on trunk lines. In the 1970s the color-coding system ascribed a color to each of the subsets of a trunk line, so there were three colors for the Broadway-Seventh Avenue line, for instance—orange for the number 1, red for the 2, and pale blue for the 3 (there was no 9 in those days, but it would have been a fourth color). You couldn't say, "It's easy. Look, take the red line here from the 103rd Street and Broadway and transfer to the yellow line at 42nd Street-Times Square to get to 14th Street-Union Square."

Compounding the problem, it was recognized that the human eye can only distinguish so many colors easily, so the same color was frequently used for several different lines. There were four orange lines—the 1, 7, D, and EE—which meant that you really could not tell anyone to take the Orange Line without being specific about which one.

I was confronted with the reality of 18 colors operating on the uptown-downtown routes in Midtown, which made creating a map that appeared, at least, geographically accurate to be an impossibility. You can understand why I said we had to develop a new color coding system.

When the MTA and I parted in 1987, I continued to write—*The Empire State Building: The Making of a Landmark* was published by Scribner in 1995—and I continued to make maps. I have designed maps for the Grand Central Partnership, for the Lincoln Square and Madison Avenue Business Improvement districts, for the Port Authority of New York and New Jersey, and under the Tauranac imprint, the most recent being *Manhattan Line By Line.*

I like to think that *Manhattan Line By Line* is a clear and simple presentation, revealing what I call "The Mysteries of Manhattan's subway and bus lines."

To help solve these "mysteries," I show the street system, places of interest, and subways and buses on their own geographic maps. Each subway and bus line is shown on its own non-geographic strip map as well. In short, all the essential information is at the reader's fingertips.

In designing these maps, I am sometimes called a "cartographer," a term which I reject. Actually, I call myself a "mapmaker." I make that distinction because a cartographer follows a certain scientific approach and puts everything to exact scale whereas I believe that this is impossible and impractical when doing a map of the subway system.

Whatever the case, I find myself enjoying the best of all worlds. I live in Manhattan and love it. What I had started as a map-making avocation has become my vocation. What could be more enjoyable than writing about New York and making maps about it?

AUTHOR'S NOTE:

Over the years, many New Yorkers have made significant contributions to subway map-making.

Two such individuals deserving of recognition—and high commendation—are Michael Hertz and Dr. Arline L. Bronzaft.

Dr. Bronzaft's map research led to the 1979 re-design which was carried out by Hertz.

Involved in map-making since 1969, Hertz helped design the 1996 pilot edition map as well as "The Map" which followed in 1998 and which remained in use through the 100th anniversary of the subway system.

When one questions who is *most* responsible for the official subway map, perhaps *Newsday* columnist Ray Sanchez has the best answer. "In fact, people all over the map deserve some credit for its creation."

PART VII

THE WORLD'S ONLY
NEW YORK SUBWAY JOKE,
COURTESY OF
HENNY YOUNGMAN

The King of One-Liners, Brooklynite Henny Youngman, produced the only known joke about the New York City subway system.

It goes this way:

A couple from Boston checked into the St. George Hotel in Downtown Brooklyn.

The St. George had been built atop the Clark Street Station on the IRT subway.

From time to time when trains would rumble underneath, the hotel would vibrate.

After the husband and wife had unpacked in their second floor hotel room, the man decided to take a walk down Fulton Street, while the wife chose to nap.

Once her hubby walked out, the woman got into bed and was about to fall asleep, when an IRT express rumbled into Clark Street Station.

The hotel room vibrated and the woman fell out of bed onto the floor.

Within ten minutes, five subway trains had pulled in, and five times the lady fell out of bed.

Finally, she phoned the manager and said, "Every time a train comes in, I fall out of bed."

To which the manager replied, "That's impossible, lady."

"Well," she demanded, "you come up and see for yourself."

A half hour later, the manager knocked on the door, and the woman ushered him in.

"Come to bed with me," she said, "and I'll show you what I mean."

The manager obliged and climbed into bed with the female guest.

At that precise moment, the husband walked in and, seeing the manager in bed with his wife, demanded, "What the hell are you doing there?"

To that, the manager shot back, "You won't believe this – but I'm waiting for a train to come in!"

GUIDED SUBWAY TOURS

Personalized three-hour subway tours are conducted by the author for limited groups.
The original 1904 route is followed to the Van Cortlandt Park station.
Several stops are made along the way to analyze historic sites and art work.
For further information, write the author
or contact him at fischlersp@aol.com.

Related Books of Interest

My view of the subways from the beginning always has been that of a passionate fan and historian rather than one deeply interested in the statistical, engineering aspects of the system.

As an emotional devotee of our underground masterpiece, I nevertheless, deeply appreciate the interest, research, and scholarly approach taken by others.

What that in mind, a tip of the hat to the many and worthy subway authors and their fine works:

Cudahy, Brian. *The Malbone Street Wreck.* New York: Fordham University Press, 1999.

Cudahy, Brian J. *Under the Sidewalks of New York.* New York: The Stephen Greene Press, 1979.

Cunningham, Joseph, and Leonard De Hart. *A History of the New York City Subway System (Part I, II, III).* New York: 1977.

Greller, James C., and Edward B. Watson. *Brooklyn Trolleys.* New York: N.J. International Inc., 1986.

Greller, James Clifford. *New York City Subway Cars.* Beleville: Xplorer Press, 1999.

Kramer, Frederick A. *Building the Independent Subway.* New York: Quadrant Press, Inc., 1990.

McCullough, David. *Brooklyn…And How It Got That Way.* New York: The Dial Press, 1983.

Merlis, Brian. *Brooklyn the Way It Was.* New York: Israelowitz Publishing, 1995.

Reisler, Jim. *Babe Ruth Slept Here.* South Bend: Diamond Communications, 1999.

Salwen, Peter. *Upper West Side Story.* New York: Abbeville Press, 1989.

Seyfried, Vincent F. *The New York and Queens County Railroad and the Steinway Lines.* New York: 1950.

Willensky, Elliot. *When Brooklyn Was the World, 1920-1957.* New York: Crown Publishers, 1986.

Other Books by the Author

Moving Millions, A History of Mass Transit

Uptown, Downtown: A Trip Through Time on New York's Subway

Confessions of a Trolley Dodger from Brooklyn

Subways of the World

The Subway

Who's Who of Hockey (with Shirley Fischler)

Metro Ice

Gordie Howe

Hockey! The Story of the World's Fastest Sport

Bobby Orr and the Big, Bad Bruins

I've Got to be Me, Derek Sanderson's Autobiography

Strange But True Hockey Stories

Play the Man, Brad Park's Autobiography

Fire on Ice

Power Play, An Affectionate History of the Toronto Maple Leafs

Slapshot

Bobby Clarke and the Ferocious Flyers

The Great Book of Hockey

Gordie Howe

Goal! My Life on Ice: Rod Gilbert's Story

Stan Mikita: The Turbulent Career of a Hockey Superstar

Hockey Stars of 1969-1976

The Flying Frenchmen: Hockey's Greatest Dynasty

Up From the Minor Leagues of Hockey

Heroes of Hockey

The Burly Bruins

The Conquering Canadiens

The Roaring Rangers

Go, Leafs, Go!

The Fast Flying Wings

The Blazing North Stars

Saga of the St. Louis Blues

Chicago's Black Hawks

The Battling Bruins: Stanley Cup Champions

Phil Esposito

Ranger Fever

Hockey's Greatest Teams

Sports Stumpers

Hockey Action

The Philadelphia Flyers, Supermen of the Ice

The Buffalo Sabres, Swashbucklers of the Ice

New York Rangers, The Icemen Cometh

Hockey's Toughest Ten

Hockey's Great Rivalries

Slashing!

Fischler's Hockey Encyclopedia (with Shirley Fischler)

This is Hockey

Scoring Punch: Gilbert, Mahovlich, Apps, Dionne

Make Way for the Leafs: Toronto's Comeback

Speed and Style: The Montreal Canadiens

Those Were the Days

The Triumphant Islanders—Hockey's Newest Dynasty

Garry Unger and the Battling Blues

Power on Ice: Denis Potvin's Autobiography

The Comeback Yankees

Showdown! Baseball's Ultimate Confrontations

The Hammer: Confessions of a Hockey Enforcer

Boston Bruins, Greatest Moments and Players

The Greatest Players and Moments of the Philadelphia Flyers

Detroit Red Wings Greatest Moments and Players

The Amazin' Bill Mazer's Baseball Trivia Book

Stan Fischler's All-Time Hockey Trivia Book

Bibliography

Abramovitch, Ilana, and Seán Galvin.
Jews of Brooklyn. Hannover: Brandeis
University Press, 2002.

Arno Press. I.R.T. *The New York Subway
Its Construction and Equipment*.
New York: Arno Press, 1904.

Asinof, Eliot. *Eight Men Out*. Canada:
Holt, Rinehart & Wilson, 1963.

Bobrick, Benson. *Labyrinths of Iron*.
New York: Newsweek Books, 1982.

Branford Electric Association. *Ride
Down Memory Lane*. Branford:
Branford Electric Association, 1991.

Bunyan, Patrick. *All Around the Town*.
New York: Fordham University Press,
1999.

Cheape, Charles W. *Moving the Masses*.
Cambridge: Harvard University
Press, 1980.

Collier, James Lincoln. *Benny Goodman
and the Swing Era*. New York: Oxford
University Press, 1989.

Conklin, Groff. *All About Subways*. New
York: Julian Messner Inc., 1938.

Cudahy, Brian. *The Malbone Street
Wreck*. New York: Fordham
University Press, 1999.

Cudahy, Brian J. *Under the Sidewalks of
New York*. New York: The Stephen
Greene Press, 1979.

Cunningham, Joseph. *Interborough Fleet*.
Beleville: Xplorer Press, 1997.

Cunningham, Joseph, and Leonard
De Hart. *A History of the New York
City Subway System (Part I, II, III)*.
New York: 1977.

Fischler, Stan. *Uptown, Downtown*. New
York: Hawthorn Books Inc., 1976.

Fischler, Stan. *Moving Millions*. New
York: Harper & Row Publishers,
1979.

Fischler, Stan. *Next Stop Grand Central*.
Ontario: Boston Mills Press, 1986.

Fischler, Stan. *Subways of the World*.
MBI Publishing Company, 1988.

Fischler, Stan. *Confessions of a Trolley
Dodger from Brooklyn*. New York:
H&M Productions II Inc., 1995.

Fischler, Stan. *The Subway, A Trip
Through Time on New York's
Rapid Transit*. New York: H&M
Productions II Inc., 1997.

Fordham University Press. *The New York
Subway Its Construction and
Equipment, I.R.T.* New York:
Fordham University Press, 1991.

Frattini, Dave. *The Underground Guide
to New York City Subways*. New York:
St. Martin's Griffin, 2000.

Frommer, Myrna Katz, and Harvey

Frommer. *It Happened in the Catskills.* Orlando: Harcourt Brace Jovanovich Publishers, 1991.

Frommer, Myrna Katz, and Harvey Frommer. *It Happened in Brooklyn.* Orlando: Harcourt Brace Jovanovich Publishers, 1993.

Garbut, P.E. *How the Underground Works.* London: London Transport, 1968.

Garrett, Charles. *The La Guardia Years.* New Brunswick: Rutgers University Press, 1967.

Gelernter, David. *1939 The Lost World of the Fair.* New York: The Free Press, 1995.

Glueck, Grace, and Paul Gardner. *Brooklyn, People and Places, Past and Present.* New York: Abradale Press, 1997.

Greller, James C., and Edward B. Watson. *Brooklyn Trolleys.* New York: N.J. International Inc., 1986.

Greller, James Clifford. *New York City Subway Cars.* Beleville: Xplorer Press, 1999.

Greller, James Clifford. *Subway Cars of the BMT.* Beleville: Xplorer Press. 1996.

H&M Productions. *Twelve Historical New York City Street and Transit Maps, Volume II, from 1847-1939.* New York: H&M Productions II, Inc., 2000.

Henderson, John. *Gotham Turnstiles.* New York: H&M Productions, 1992.

Hood, Clifton. *722 Miles—The Building of the Subways and How They Transformed New York.* New York: Simon & Schuster, 1993.

Interborough Rapid Transit. *The New York City Subway—Its Construction and Equipment.* New York: Arno Press-Crown Publishers, 1904.

Israelowitz, Oscar. *New York City Subway Guide.* New York: Israelowitz Publishing, 1989.

Jackson, Kenneth T. *The Encyclopedia of New York City.* New Haven & London: Yale University Press, 1995.

James, Bill. The Bill James *Historical Baseball Abstract.* New York: Villard Books, 1985.

Kahn, Alan Paul, and Jack May. *The Tracks of New York, Number II, III. Brooklyn Elevated Railroads—1910.* New York: Electric Railroaders Association, 1975.

Kramer, Frederick A. *Building the Independent Subway.* New York: Quadrant Press, Inc., 1990.

Kramer, Frederick A. *Subway to the World's Fair.* Westfield: Bells & Whistles, 1991.

Lavis, Fred. *Building the New Rapid Transit System of New York City Circa 1915.* Beleville: Xplorer Press, 1996.

Lee Younger, William. *Old Brooklyn in Early Photographs 1865-1929.* New York: Dover Publications, 1978.

Lincoln Collier, James. *Benny Goodman and the Swing Era.* New York: Oxford University Press, 1989.

Mattfield, Julius. *Variety Music Cavalcade, 1620-1961.* New Jersey: Prentice Hall, 1952.

McCullough, David. *Brooklyn…And How it Got that Way.* New York: The Dial Press, 1983.

Merlis, Brian. *Brooklyn The Way It Was.* New York: Israelowitz Publishing, 1995.

Metropolitan Transportation Authority. *NYC Subway. A Brief History.* Ronkonkoma: NY Minute Enterprises Ltd., 2003.

Railrodians of America. *Book Number 2.* New York: Railroadians of America, 1940.

Reed, Henry Hope, and Sophia Duckworth. *Central Park, A History and A Guide.* New York: Clarkson N. Potter, Inc., 1967.

Reed, Robert C. *New York Elevated.*

Cranbury: A.S. Barnes and Co. Inc.,
   1978.
Reisler, Jim. *Babe Ruth Slept Here*.
   South Bend: Diamond Communi-
   cations, 1999.
Ritter, Lawrence S. *East Side, West Side—*
   Tales of New York Sporting Life,
   1910-1960. New York: Total Sports,
   1998.
Salwen, Peter. *Upper West Side Story*.
   New York: Abbeville Press, 1989.
Seyfried, Vincent F. *The New York and*
   Queens County Railroad and the
   Steinway Lines. New York: 1950.
Snyder, Robert W. *The Voice of the City*.
   New York: Oxford University Press,
   1989.
Snyder, Robert W. *Transit Talk*. New
   Brunswick: Rutgers University Press,
   1997.
Stookey, Lee. *Subway Ceramics—*
   A History and Iconography.
   Connecticut: The William J. Jack Co.,
   1992.
Willensky, Elliot. *When Brooklyn Was*
   the World, 1920-1957. New York:
   Crown Publishers, 1986.

WEBSITES:
   http://thejoekorner.quuxuum.org
   www.delaneybooks.com
   www.forgotton-ny.com
   www.frankmerriwell.com
   www.mta.nyc
   www.newyorkcitytransit.com
   www.nycsubway.org
   www.nyctrackbook.com
   www.passbooks.com

Footnotes

CHAPTER ONE

1. Eliot Willensky, *When Brooklyn Was the World, 1920-1957* (New York: Crown Publishers, 1986).
2. Kenneth T. Jackson, *The Encyclopedia of New York City* (New Haven & London: Yale University Press, 1995).
3. "After You've Gone," words and music Henry Creamer and Turner Layton (Broadway Music Corp., © 1918).
4. "The World Is Waiting for the Sunrise," words Eugene Lockhart, music Ernest Seitz (Chappell & Co., Ltd., © 1919).

CHAPTER THREE

5. Kenneth T. Jackson, *The Encyclopedia of New York City* (New Haven & London: Yale University Press, 1995).
6. Lawrence Ritter, *East Side, West Side, Tales of New York Sporting Life, 1910-1960* (New York: Total Sports, 1998).

CHAPTER FOUR

7. Joseph Cunningham, Leonard De Hart, *A History of the New York City Subway System (Part I, II, III)* (New York: 1977).

CHAPTER FIVE

8. David Gelernter, *1939 The Lost World of the Fair* (New York: The Free Press, 1995).
9. Frederick A. Kramer, *Subway to the World's Fair* (Westfield: Bells & Whistles, 1991).

CHAPTER SIX

10. Brian J. Cudahy, *Under the Sidewalks of New York* (New York: The Stephen Greene Press, 1979).

CHAPTER SEVEN

11. Peter Salwen, *Upper West Side Story* (New York: Abbeville Press, 1989).
12. Jim Reisler, *Babe Ruth Slept Here* (South Bend: Diamond Communications, 1999).
13. Eliot Asinof, *Eight Men Out* (Canada: Holt, Rinehart and Winston, 1963).
14. Peter Salwen, *Upper West Side Story* (New York: Abbeville Press, 1989).

CHAPTER EIGHT

15. Kenneth T. Jackson, *The Encyclopedia of New York City* (New Haven & London: Yale University Press, 1995).
16. Henry Hope Reed, Sophia Duckworth, *Central Park, A History and a Guide* (New York: Clarkson N. Potter, Inc., 1967).
17. Peter Salwen, *Upper West Side Story* (New York: Abbeville Press, 1989).
18. Joseph Cunningham, Leonard De Hart, *A History of the New York City Subway System (Part I, II, III)* (New York: 1977).
19. "Sing, Sing, Sing," words and music Louis Prima (Smithsonian, RCA label of BMG Entertainment: 1931).
20. Grace Glueck, Paul Gardiner, *Brooklyn— People and Places, Past and Present* (New York: Abradale Press, 1997).
21. Ibid.

CHAPTER NINE

22. William D. Middleton, *Grand Central: The World's Greatest Railway Station* (California: Golden West Books, 1977).

CHAPTER TEN

23. Kenneth T. Jackson, Elliot S. Meadows, *The Encyclopedia of New York City* (New Haven & London: Yale University Press, 1995).

CHAPTER ELEVEN

24. "Give My Regards to Broadway (Little Johnny Jones)," words and music George [Michael] Cohan (F.A. Mills, © 1904).

100 YEARS OF ROLLING STOCK

25. James Clifford Greller, *Subway Cars of the BMT* (Beleville: Xplorer Press, 1996).

Index

Frank Merriwell® Is Back!

The Original Frank Merriwell Stories Which Thrilled Untold Millions in Previous Generations, Including Your Parents, Are Now Back in Hardbound and Paperback Form.

by
BURT L. STANDISH

FRANK MERRIWELL INC.
212 Michael Drive, Syosset, New York 11791
Tel: 800-632-8888 • Fax: 516-921-8743
www.frankmerriwell.com

Frank Merriwell® Is Back!

THE SERIES OF BOOKS THAT ENTHRALLED MILLIONS of young men some generations ago, literally outselling the Bible (with a total of 500 million copies between 1896 and 1918), is being revived, and the ideals, life, and society of the first quarter of the century are recaptured in stories of the greatest adventure and sport ever written.

It is a nostalgic trip back to when heroes were humble, fearless, and unbeatable. But most of all, they believed in fair play. The never-say-die spirit of this hero and the ideals of personal honor guide Frank Merriwell in thousands of moments of adversity.

Frank Merriwell's career led him from Fardale Academy to the playing fields of Yale College, with incredible journeys abroad. Greatly athletic, he broke tackles with winning touchdowns and was at his best against Harvard in upholding the "old democratic spirit" of Yale. He played virtually every position in baseball, and his doubleshoot—a pitch which curved two ways—could not be hit. He boasted a .1000 batting average in clutch situations, and his reflexes were sharp.

His real stature lay in his moral strength, however. He never harbored grudges. He rose above all injury or odds, and he faced down innumerable villains whom he not only defeated, but also reformed. Frank Merriwell is the democratic ethic in action. He epitomizes the roots of America. He spurned the idea of using money or influence in making his way. He fought his own battles. He believed in deeds, not words, and he confronts danger—doesn't avoid it. He is all-American—honest, courageous, law-abiding, and never shirking his duties.

Now is the opportunity for you to relive stories of a hero who loves the game. Again, it is the ninth inning, there are two out, the bases are full, Yale is behind 3 to 0, and Frank Merriwell is at bat. The count is three and two, and---. Rich in fun in all branches of sports and athletics, the Merriwell novels are exciting, and the hero is inspirational. So relive a time when hard work was a prerequisite for success. Read and be thrilled by the most exciting adventures of modern times.

Book List

Cat. #	Book Title	Paperback $9.95	Hardbound $29.95
FM-001	Frank Merriwell's Schooldays	0-8373-9001-X	0-8373-9301-9
FM-002	Frank Merriwell's Chums	0-8373-9002-8	0-8373-9302-7
FM-003	Frank Merriwell's Foes	0-8373-9003-6	0-8373-9303-5
FM-004	Frank Merriwell's Trip West	0-8373-9004-4	0-8373-9304-3
FM-005	Frank Merriwell Down South	0-8373-9005-2	0-8373-9305-1
FM-006	Frank Merriwell's Bravery	0-8373-9006-0	0-8373-9306-X
FM-007	Frank Merriwell's Hunting Tour	0-8373-9007-9	0-8373-9307-8
FM-008	Frank Merriwell in Europe	0-8373-9008-7	0-8373-9308-6
FM-009	Frank Merriwell at Yale	0-8373-9009-5	0-8373-9309-4
FM-010	Frank Merriwell's Sports Afield	0-8373-9010-9	0-8373-9310-8
FM-011	Frank Merriwell's Races	0-8373-9011-7	0-8373-9311-6
FM-012	Frank Merriwell's Party	0-8373-9012-5	0-8373-9312-4
FM-013	Frank Merriwell's Bicycle Tour	0-8373-9013-3	0-8373-9313-2
FM-014	Frank Merriwell's Courage	0-8373-9014-1	0-8373-9314-0
FM-015	Frank Merriwell's Daring	0-8373-9015-X	0-8373-9315-9
FM-016	Frank Merriwell's Alarm	0-8373-9016-8	0-8373-9316-7
FM-017	Frank Merriwell's Athletes	0-8373-9017-6	0-8373-9317-5
FM-018	Frank Merriwell's Skill	0-8373-9018-4	0-8373-9318-3
FM-019	Frank Merriwell's Champions	0-8373-9019-2	0-8373-9319-1
FM-020	Frank Merriwell's Return to Yale	0-8373-9020-6	0-8373-9320-5
FM-021	Frank Merriwell's Secret	0-8373-9021-4	0-8373-9321-3
FM-022	Frank Merriwell's Danger	0-8373-9022-2	0-8373-9322-1
FM-023	Frank Merriwell's Loyalty	0-8373-9023-0	0-8373-9323-X
FM-024	Frank Merriwell in Camp	0-8373-9024-9	0-8373-9324-8
FM-025	Frank Merriwell's Vacation	0-8373-9025-7	0-8373-9325-6
FM-026	Frank Merriwell's Cruise	0-8373-9026-5	0-8373-9326-4
FM-027	Frank Merriwell's Chase	0-8373-9027-3	0-8373-9327-2
FM-028	Frank Merriwell in Maine	0-8373-9028-1	0-8373-9328-0

Cat. #	Book Title	Paperback $9.95	Hardbound $29.95
FM-029	Frank Merriwell's Struggle	0-8373-9029-X	0-8373-9329-9
FM-030	Frank Merriwell's First Job	0-8373-9030-3	0-8373-9330-2
FM-031	Frank Merriwell's Opportunity	0-8373-9031-1	0-8373-9331-0
FM-032	Frank Merriwell's Hard Luck	0-8373-9032-X	0-8373-9332-9
FM-033	Frank Merriwell's Protege	0-8373-9033-8	0-8373-9333-7
FM-034	Frank Merriwell on the Road	0-8373-9034-6	0-8373-9334-5
FM-035	Frank Merriwell's Own Company	0-8373-9035-4	0-8373-9335-3
FM-036	Frank Merriwell's Fame	0-8373-9036-2	0-8373-9336-1
FM-037	Frank Merriwell's College Chums	0-8373-9037-0	0-8373-9337-X
FM-038	Frank Merriwell's Problem	0-8373-9038-9	0-8373-9338-8
FM-039	Frank Merriwell's Fortune	0-8373-9039-7	0-8373-9339-6
FM-040	Frank Merriwell's New Comedian	0-8373-9040-0	0-8373-9340-X
FM-041	Frank Merriwell's Prosperity	0-8373-9041-9	0-8373-9341-8
FM-042	Frank Merriwell's Stage Hit	0-8373-9042-7	0-8373-9342-6
FM-043	Frank Merriwell's Great Scheme	0-8373-9043-5	0-8373-9343-4
FM-044	Frank Merriwell in England	0-8373-9044-3	0-8373-9344-2
FM-045	Frank Merriwell on the Boulevards	0-8373-9045-1	0-8373-9345-0
FM-046	Frank Merriwell's Duel	0-8373-9046-X	0-8373-9346-9
FM-047	Frank Merriwell's Double Shot	0-8373-9047-8	0-8373-9347-7
FM-048	Frank Merriwell's Baseball Victories	0-8373-9048-6	0-8373-9348-5
FM-049	Frank Merriwell's Confidence	0-8373-9049-4	0-8373-9349-3
FM-050	Frank Merriwell's Auto	0-8373-9050-8	0-8373-9350-7
FM-051	Frank Merriwell's Fun	0-8373-9051-6	0-8373-9351-5
FM-052	Frank Merriwell's Generosity	0-8373-9052-4	0-8373-9352-3
FM-053	Frank Merriwell's Tricks	0-8373-9053-2	0-8373-9353-1
FM-054	Frank Merriwell's Temptation	0-8373-9054-0	0-8373-9354-X
FM-055	Frank Merriwell on Top	0-8373-9055-9	0-8373-9355-8
FM-056	Frank Merriwell's Luck	0-8373-9056-7	0-8373-9356-6
FM-057	Frank Merriwell's Mascot	0-8373-9057-5	0-8373-9357-4
FM-058	Frank Merriwell's Reward	0-8373-9058-3	0-8373-9358-2
FM-059	Frank Merriwell's Phantom	0-8373-9059-1	0-8373-9359-0
FM-060	Frank Merriwell's Faith	0-8373-9060-5	0-8373-9360-4
FM-061	Frank Merriwell's Victories	0-8373-9061-3	0-8373-9361-2
FM-062	Frank Merriwell's Iron Nerve	0-8373-9062-1	0-8373-9362-0
FM-063	Frank Merriwell in Kentucky	0-8373-9063-X	0-8373-9363-9
FM-064	Frank Merriwell's Power	0-8373-9064-8	0-8373-9364-7
FM-065	Frank Merriwell's Shrewdness	0-8373-9065-6	0-8373-9365-5
FM-066	Frank Merriwell's Setback	0-8373-9066-4	0-8373-9366-3
FM-067	Frank Merriwell's Search	0-8373-9067-2	0-8373-9367-1
FM-068	Frank Merriwell's Club	0-8373-9068-0	0-8373-9368-X
FM-069	Frank Merriwell's Trust	0-8373-9069-9	0-8373-9369-8
FM-070	Frank Merriwell's False Friend	0-8373-9070-2	0-8373-9370-1
FM-071	Frank Merriwell's Strong Arm	0-8373-9071-0	0-8373-9371-X
FM-072	Frank Merriwell as Coach	0-8373-9072-9	0-8373-9372-8
FM-073	Frank Merriwell's Brother	0-8373-9073-7	0-8373-9373-6
FM-074	Frank Merriwell's Marvel	0-8373-9074-5	0-8373-9374-4
FM-075	Frank Merriwell's Support	0-8373-9075-3	0-8373-9375-2
FM-076	Dick Merriwell at Fardale	0-8373-9076-1	0-8373-9376-0
FM-077	Dick Merriwell's Glory	0-8373-9077-X	0-8373-9377-9
FM-078	Dick Merriwell's Promise	0-8373-9078-8	0-8373-9378-7
FM-079	Dick Merriwell's Rescue	0-8373-9079-6	0-8373-9379-5
FM-080	Dick Merriwell's Narrow Escape	0-8373-9080-X	0-8373-9380-9
FM-081	Dick Merriwell's Racket	0-8373-9081-8	0-8373-9381-7
FM-082	Dick Merriwell's Revenge	0-8373-9082-6	0-8373-9382-5
FM-083	Dick Merriwell's Ruse	0-8373-9083-4	0-8373-9383-3
FM-084	Dick Merriwell's Delivery	0-8373-9084-2	0-8373-9384-1
FM-085	Dick Merriwell's Wonders	0-8373-9085-0	0-8373-9385-X
FM-086	Frank Merriwell's Honor	0-8373-9086-9	0-8373-9386-8
FM-087	Dick Merriwell's Diamond	0-8373-9087-7	0-8373-9387-6
FM-088	Frank Merriwell's Winners	0-8373-9088-5	0-8373-9388-4
FM-089	Dick Merriwell's Dash	0-8373-9089-3	0-8373-9389-2
FM-090	Dick Merriwell's Ability	0-8373-9090-7	0-8373-9390-6
FM-091	Dick Merriwell's Trap	0-8373-9091-5	0-8373-9391-4

CALL TO ORDER TODAY! (800) 632-8888

Cat. #	Book Title	Paperback $9.95	Hardbound $29.95	Cat. #	Book Title	Paperback $9.95	Hardbound $29.95
FM-092	Dick Merriwell's Defense	0-8373-9092-3	0-8373-9392-2	FM-155	Frank Merriwell's Worst Boy	0-8373-9155-5	0-8373-9455-4
FM-093	Dick Merriwell's Model	0-8373-9093-1	0-8373-9393-0	FM-156	Dick Merriwell's Close Call	0-8373-9156-3	0-8373-9456-2
FM-094	Dick Merriwell's Mystery	0-8373-9094-X	0-8373-9394-9	FM-157	Frank Merriwell's Air Voyage	0-8373-9157-1	0-8373-9457-0
FM-095	Frank Merriwell's Backers	0-8373-9095-8	0-8373-9395-7	FM-158	Dick Merriwell's Black Star	0-8373-9158-X	0-8373-9458-9
FM-096	Dick Merriwell's Backstop	0-8373-9096-6	0-8373-9396-5	FM-159	Frank Merriwell in Wall Street	0-8373-9159-8	0-8373-9459-7
FM-097	Dick Merriwell's Western Mission	0-8373-9097-4	0-8373-9397-3	FM-160	Frank Merriwell Facing his Foes	0-8373-9160-1	0-8373-9460-0
FM-098	Frank Merriwell's Rescue	0-8373-9098-2	0-8373-9398-1	FM-161	Dick Merriwell's Stanchness	0-8373-9161-X	0-8373-9461-9
FM-099	Frank Merriwell's Encounter	0-8373-9099-0	0-8373-9399-X	FM-162	Frank Merriwell's Hard Case	0-8373-9162-8	0-8373-9462-7
FM-100	Dick Merriwell's Marked Money	0-8373-9100-8	0-8373-9400-7	FM-163	Dick Merriwell's Stand	0-8373-9163-6	0-8373-9463-5
FM-101	Frank Merriwell's Nomads	0-8373-9101-6	0-8373-9401-5	FM-164	Dick Merriwell Doubted	0-8373-9164-4	0-8373-9464-3
FM-102	Dick Merriwell on the Gridiron	0-8373-9102-4	0-8373-9402-3	FM-165	Frank Merriwell's Steadying Hand	0-8373-9165-2	0-8373-9465-1
FM-103	Dick Merriwell's Disguise	0-8373-9103-2	0-8373-9403-1	FM-166	Dick Merriwell's Example	0-8373-9166-0	0-8373-9466-X
FM-104	Dick Merriwell's Test	0-8373-9104-0	0-8373-9404-X	FM-167	Dick Merriwell in the Wilds	0-8373-9167-9	0-8373-9467-8
FM-105	Frank Merriwell's Trump Card	0-8373-9105-9	0-8373-9405-8	FM-168	Frank Merriwell's Ranch	0-8373-9168-7	0-8373-9468-6
FM-106	Frank Merriwell's Strategy	0-8373-9106-7	0-8373-9406-6	FM-169	Dick Merriwell's Way	0-8373-9169-5	0-8373-9469-4
FM-107	Frank Merriwell's Triumph	0-8373-9107-5	0-8373-9407-4	FM-170	Frank Merriwell's Lesson	0-8373-9170-9	0-8373-9470-8
FM-108	Dick Merriwell's Grit	0-8373-9108-3	0-8373-9408-2	FM-171	Dick Merriwell's Reputation	0-8373-9171-7	0-8373-9471-6
FM-109	Dick Merriwell's Assurance	0-8373-9109-1	0-8373-9409-0	FM-172	Frank Merriwell's Encouragement	0-8373-9172-5	0-8373-9472-4
FM-110	Dick Merriwell's Long Slide	0-8373-9110-5	0-8373-9410-4	FM-173	Dick Merriwell's Honors	0-8373-9173-3	0-8373-9473-2
FM-111	Frank Merriwell's Rough Deal	0-8373-9111-3	0-8373-9411-2	FM-174	Frank Merriwell's Wizard	0-8373-9174-1	0-8373-9474-0
FM-112	Dick Merriwell's Threat	0-8373-9112-1	0-8373-9412-0	FM-175	Dick Merriwell's Race	0-8373-9175-X	0-8373-9475-9
FM-113	Dick Merriwell's Persistence	0-8373-9113-X	0-8373-9413-9	FM-176	Dick Merriwell's Star Play	0-8373-9176-8	0-8373-9476-7
FM-114	Dick Merriwell's Day	0-8373-9114-8	0-8373-9414-7	FM-177	Frank Merriwell at Phantom Lake	0-8373-9177-6	0-8373-9477-5
FM-115	Frank Merriwell's Peril	0-8373-9115-6	0-8373-9415-5	FM-178	Dick Merriwell a Winner	0-8373-9178-4	0-8373-9478-3
FM-116	Dick Merriwell's Downfall	0-8373-9116-4	0-8373-9416-3	FM-179	Dick Merriwell At the County Fair	0-8373-9179-2	0-8373-9479-1
FM-117	Frank Merriwell's Pursuit	0-8373-9117-2	0-8373-9417-1	FM-180	Frank Merriwell's Grit	0-8373-9180-6	0-8373-9480-5
FM-118	Dick Merriwell Abroad	0-8373-9118-0	0-8373-9418-X	FM-181	Dick Merriwell's Power	0-8373-9181-4	0-8373-9481-3
FM-119	Frank Merriwell in the Rockies	0-8373-9119-9	0-8373-9419-8	FM-182	Frank Merriwell in Peru	0-8373-9182-2	0-8373-9482-1
FM-120	Dick Merriwell's Pranks	0-8373-9120-2	0-8373-9420-1	FM-183	Frank Merriwell's Long Chance	0-8373-9183-0	0-8373-9483-X
FM-121	Frank Merriwell's Pride	0-8373-9121-0	0-8373-9421-X	FM-184	Frank Merriwell's Old Form	0-8373-9184-9	0-8373-9484-8
FM-122	Frank Merriwell's Challengers	0-8373-9122-9	0-8373-9422-8	FM-185	Frank Merriwell's Treasure Hunt	0-8373-9185-7	0-8373-9485-6
FM-123	Frank Merriwell's Endurance	0-8373-9123-7	0-8373-9423-6	FM-186	Dick Merriwell, Game to the Last	0-8373-9186-5	0-8373-9486-4
FM-124	Dick Merriwell's Cleverness	0-8373-9124-5	0-8373-9424-4	FM-187	Dick Merriwell, Motor King	0-8373-9187-3	0-8373-9487-2
FM-125	Frank Merriwell's Marriage	0-8373-9125-3	0-8373-9425-2	FM-188	Dick Merriwell's Tussle	0-8373-9188-1	0-8373-9488-0
FM-126	Dick Merriwell, The Wizard	0-8373-9126-1	0-8373-9426-0	FM-189	Dick Merriwell's Aero Dash	0-8373-9189-X	0-8373-9489-9
FM-127	Dick Merriwell's Stroke	0-8373-9127-X	0-8373-9427-9	FM-190	Dick Merriwell's Intuition	0-8373-9190-3	0-8373-9490-2
FM-128	Dick Merriwell's Return	0-8373-9128-8	0-8373-9428-7	FM-191	Dick Merriwell's Placer Find	0-8373-9191-1	0-8373-9491-0
FM-129	Dick Merriwell's Resource	0-8373-9129-6	0-8373-9429-5	FM-192	Dick Merriwell's Fighting Chance	0-8373-9192-X	0-8373-9492-9
FM-130	Dick Merriwell's Five	0-8373-9130-X	0-8373-9430-9	FM-193	Frank Merriwell's Tact	0-8373-9193-8	0-8373-9493-7
FM-131	Frank Merriwell's Tigers	0-8373-9131-8	0-8373-9431-7	FM-194	Frank Merriwell's Puzzle	0-8373-9194-6	0-8373-9494-5
FM-132	Dick Merriwell's Polo Team	0-8373-9132-6	0-8373-9432-5	FM-195	Frank Merriwell's Mystery	0-8373-9195-4	0-8373-9495-3
FM-133	Frank Merriwell's Pupils	0-8373-9133-4	0-8373-9433-3	FM-196	Frank Merriwell, The Lionhearted	0-8373-9196-2	0-8373-9496-1
FM-134	Frank Merriwell's New Boy	0-8373-9134-2	0-8373-9434-1	FM-197	Frank Merriwell's Tenacity	0-8373-9197-0	0-8373-9497-X
FM-135	Dick Merriwell's Home Run	0-8373-9135-0	0-8373-9435-X	FM-198	Dick Merriwell's Perception	0-8373-9198-9	0-8373-9498-8
FM-136	Dick Merriwell's Dare	0-8373-9136-9	0-8373-9436-8	FM-199	Dick Merriwell's Detective Work	0-8373-9199-7	0-8373-9499-6
FM-137	Frank Merriwell's Son	0-8373-9137-7	0-8373-9437-6	FM-200	Dick Merriwell's Commencement	0-8373-9200-4	0-8373-9500-3
FM-138	Dick Merriwell's Team Mate	0-8373-9138-5	0-8373-9438-4	FM-201	Dick Merriwell's Decision	0-8373-9201-2	0-8373-9501-1
FM-139	Frank Merriwell's Leaguers	0-8373-9139-3	0-8373-9439-2	FM-202	Dick Merriwell's Coolness	0-8373-9202-0	0-8373-9502-X
FM-140	Frank Merriwell's Happy Camp	0-8373-9140-7	0-8373-9440-6	FM-203	Dick Merriwell's Reliance	0-8373-9203-9	0-8373-9503-8
FM-141	Dick Merriwell's Influence	0-8373-9141-5	0-8373-9441-4	FM-204	Frank Merriwell's Young Warriors	0-8373-9204-7	0-8373-9504-6
FM-142	Dick Merriwell, Freshman	0-8373-9142-3	0-8373-9442-2				
FM-143	Dick Merriwell's Staying Power	0-8373-9143-1	0-8373-9443-0				
FM-144	Dick Merriwell's Joke	0-8373-9144-X	0-8373-9444-9				
FM-145	Frank Merriwell's Talisman	0-8373-9145-8	0-8373-9445-7				
FM-146	Frank Merriwell's Horse	0-8373-9146-6	0-8373-9446-5				
FM-147	Dick Merriwell's Regret	0-8373-9147-4	0-8373-9447-3				
FM-148	Dick Merriwell's Magnetism	0-8373-9148-2	0-8373-9448-1				
FM-149	Dick Merriwell's Backers	0-8373-9149-0	0-8373-9449-X				
FM-150	Dick Merriwell's Best Work	0-8373-9150-4	0-8373-9450-3				
FM-151	Dick Merriwell's Distrust	0-8373-9151-2	0-8373-9451-1				
FM-152	Dick Merriwell's Debt	0-8373-9152-0	0-8373-9452-X				
FM-153	Dick Merriwell's Mastery	0-8373-9153-9	0-8373-9453-8				
FM-154	Dick Merriwell Adrift	0-8373-9154-7	0-8373-9454-6				

MERRIWELL SERIES No.2
Frank Merriwell's Chums
by
BURT L. STANDISH

MERRIWELL SERIES No.3
Frank Merriwell's Foes
by
BURT L. STANDISH

MERRIWELL SERIES No.1
Frank Merriwell's Schooldays
by
BURT L. STANDISH

CALL TO ORDER TODAY! (800) 632-8888

Cat. #	Book Title	Paperback $9.95	Hardbound $29.95	Cat. #	Book Title	Paperback $9.95	Hardbound $29.95
FM-205	Frank Merriwell's Lads	0-8373-9205-5	0-8373-9505-4	FM-228	Frank Merriwell Jr. at the Old School	0-8373-9228-4	0-8373-9528-3
FM-206	Dick Merriwell in Panama	0-8373-9206-3	0-8373-9506-2	FM-229	Frank Merriwell Jr.'s Repentant Enemy	0-8373-9229-2	0-8373-9529-1
FM-207	Dick Merriwell in South America	0-8373-9207-1	0-8373-9507-0	FM-230	Frank Merriwell Jr.'s Gridiron Honors	0-8373-9230-6	0-8373-9530-5
FM-208	Dick Merriwell's Counsel	0-8373-9208-X	0-8373-9508-9	FM-231	Frank Merriwell Jr. on the Border	0-8373-9231-4	0-8373-9531-3
FM-209	Dick Merriwell, Universal Coach	0-8373-9209-8	0-8373-9509-7	FM-232	Frank Merriwell's Diamond Foes	0-8373-9232-2	0-8373-9532-1
FM-210	Dick Merriwell's Varsity Nine	0-8373-9210-1	0-8373-9510-0	FM-233	The Merriwell Company	0-8373-9233-0	0-8373-9533-X
FM-211	Dick Merriwell's Heroic Players	0-8373-9211-X	0-8373-9511-9	FM-234	Dick Merriwell and June Arlington	0-8373-9234-9	0-8373-9534-8
FM-212	Dick Merriwell At the Olympics	0-8373-9212-8	0-8373-9512-7	FM-235	Merriwell vs. Merriwell	0-8373-9235-7	0-8373-9535-6
FM-213	Frank Merriwell Jr. Tested	0-8373-9213-6	0-8373-9513-5	FM-236	Dick Merriwell and the Burglar	0-8373-9236-5	0-8373-9536-4
FM-214	Frank Merriwell Jr.'s Conquests	0-8373-9214-4	0-8373-9514-3	FM-237	Frank Merriwell at the Cowboy Carnival	0-8373-9237-3	0-8373-9537-2
FM-215	Frank Merriwell Jr.'s Rivals	0-8373-9215-2	0-8373-9515-1	FM-238	Frank Merriwell Jr.'s Cross-Country Run	0-8373-9238-1	0-8373-9538-0
FM-216	Frank Merriwell Jr.'s Helping Hand	0-8373-9216-0	0-8373-9516-X	FM-239	Frank Merriwell Jr.'s Indian Entanglement	0-8373-9239-X	0-8373-9539-9
FM-217	Frank Merriwell Jr. In Arizona	0-8373-9217-9	0-8373-9517-8	FM-240	Frank Merriwell Wins an Enemy	0-8373-9240-3	0-8373-9540-2
FM-218	Frank Merriwell Jr.'s Mission	0-8373-9218-7	0-8373-9518-6	FM-241	Dick Merriwell's Charm	0-8373-9241-1	0-8373-9541-0
FM-219	Frank Merriwell Jr.'s Ice Boat Adventure	0-8373-9219-5	0-8373-9519-4	FM-242	Frank Merriwell Jr.'s Fardale Visit	0-8373-9242-X	0-8373-9542-9
FM-220	Frank Merriwell Jr.'s Timely Aid	0-8373-9220-9	0-8373-9520-8	FM-243	Frank Merriwell in The Yellowstone	0-8373-9243-8	0-8373-9543-7
FM-221	Frank Merriwell Jr. In the Desert	0-8373-9221-7	0-8373-9521-6	FM-244	Frank Merriwell Jr.'s Yacht Victory	0-8373-9244-6	0-8373-9544-5
FM-222	Frank Merriwell Jr.'s Fight for Right	0-8373-9222-5	0-8373-9522-4	FM-245	Frank Merriwell Jr. and the Talking Head	0-8373-9245-4	0-8373-9545-3
FM-223	Frank Merriwell Jr.'s Team Work	0-8373-9223-3	0-8373-9523-2				
FM-224	Frank Merriwell Jr.'s Athletic Team	0-8373-9224-1	0-8373-9524-0	Frank Merriwell Series Paperbound		0-8373-9000-1	$2,437.75
FM-225	Frank Merriwell Jr.'s Peck of Trouble	0-8373-9225-X	0-8373-9525-9	Frank Merriwell Series Hardbound		0-8373-9300-8	$7,337.75
FM-226	Frank Merriwell Jr.'s Ordeal	0-8373-9226-8	0-8373-9526-7	F-251 The Subway and the City Paperbound (when avail.)	$34.95	0-8373-9251-9	
FM-227	Frank Merriwell Jr., Birdman	0-8373-9227-6	0-8373-9527-5	F-551 The Subway and the City Hardbound	$39.95	0-8373-9551-8	

FRANK MERRIWELL
ORDER FORM

Gentlemen: Please send me the book(s) listed by number and title below:

☐ I am enclosing a Money Order

or ☐ Please charge my Credit Card

Name _____

Address _____

City _____ State _____ Zip _____

Card Number _____

Expiration Date _____ Phone Number _____

● Signature _____ (Must Be Signed)

Catalog Number	Title	Paper/Hard	$ Price	Quantity	Total

SHIPPING: Frank Merriwell Series $7.50 first book; $2.50 each additional
The Subway and the City $10.00 first book; $5.00 each additional

Prices subject to change without notice.

MAIL ORDER TO: FRANK MERRIWELL INC.
212 Michael Drive, Syosset, New York 11791
Tel: 800-632-8888 • Fax: 516-921-8743
www.frankmerriwell.com

New York Residents Sales Tax: _____

TOTAL: _____